After Auschwitz

After Auschwitz
The Difficult Legacies of the GDR

Edited by
Enrico Heitzer, Martin Jander,
Anetta Kahane, and Patrice G. Poutrus

Published in 2021 by
Berghahn Books
www.berghahnbooks.com

English-language edition
© 2021, 2024 Berghahn Books
First paperback edition published in 2024

German-language edition
© 2018 Wochenschau Verlag, Frankfurt am Main

Originally published in German as *Nach Auschwitz: Schwieriges Erbe DDR*

Translation published on behalf of the Amadeu Antonio Foundation and the Sachsenhausen Memorial and Museum (Stiftung Brandenburgische Gedenkstätten). Publication supported by generous grants from the Amadeu Antonio Foundation.

All rights reserved. Except for the quotation of short passages for the purposes of criticism and review, no part of this book may be reproduced in any form or by any means, electronic or mechanical, including photocopying, recording, or any information storage and retrieval system now known or to be invented, without written permission of the publisher.

Library of Congress Cataloging-in-Publication Data

Names: Heitzer, Enrico, 1977– editor. | Jander, Martin, editor. | Kahane, Anetta, 1954– editor. | Poutrus, Patrice G., editor.
Title: After Auschwitz: The Difficult Legacies of the GDR / edited by Enrico Heitzer, Martin Jander, Anetta Kahane, Patrice G. Poutrus.
Other titles: Nach Auschwitz: Schwieriges Erbe DDR. English | Difficult legacies of the GDR
Description: English language edition. | New York: Berghahn, 2021. | Originally published in German as Nach Auschwitz: Schwieriges Erbe DDR, © 2018 Wochenschau Verlag, Frankfurt am Main.—Title page verso. | Includes bibliographical references and index.
Identifiers: LCCN 2020048770 (print) | LCCN 2020048771 (ebook) | ISBN 9781789208528 (hardback) | ISBN 9781789208535 (ebook)
Subjects: LCSH: Germany (East)—History. | Holocaust, Jewish (1939–1945)—Germany (East)—Influence. | Oświęcim (Poland)—History. | Germany (East)—Ethnic relations. | Holocaust, Jewish (1939–1945)—Germany (East)—Historiography.
Classification: LCC DD282 .N3313 2021 (print) | LCC DD282 (ebook) | DDC 943/.1087—dc23
LC record available at https://lccn.loc.gov/2020048770
LC ebook record available at https://lccn.loc.gov/2020048771

British Library Cataloguing in Publication Data
A catalogue record for this book is available from the British Library

ISBN 978-1-78920-852-8 hardback
ISBN 978-1-80539-321-4 paperback
ISBN 978-1-80539-434-1 epub
ISBN 978-1-78920-853-5 web pdf

https://doi.org/10.3167/9781789208528

Contents

List of Illustrations — viii

Introduction. New Perspectives on the GDR: A Plea for a Paradigm Shift — 1
  Enrico Heitzer, Martin Jander, Anetta Kahane, and Patrice G. Poutrus

PART I. German Democratic Republic

Chapter 1. The Loyalty Trap: Wolfgang Steinitz and the Generation of GDR-Founding Fathers and Mothers — 19
  Annette Leo

Chapter 2. The Effects of a Taboo: Jews and Antisemitism in the GDR — 32
  Anetta Kahane

Chapter 3. Divided City—Shared Memory? Dealing with the Nazi Past in East and West Berlin from 1948 to 1961 — 41
  Gerd Kühling

Chapter 4. The GDR and Opposition from the Right: A Plea for Broader Perspectives — 57
  Enrico Heitzer

Chapter 5. The GDR's Judgment against Hans Globke: On the Conviction of the Nazi Lawyer and Head of the Federal Chancellery under Konrad Adenauer by the Supreme Court of the GDR in the Summer of 1963 — 74
  Klaus Bästlein

Chapter 6. Might through Morality? Some Comments on Antifascism in the GDR — 88
  Christoph Classen

Chapter 7. Toward a Sociology of Intelligence Agents: The GDR
	Foreign Intelligence Service as an Example	100
	Helmut Müller-Enbergs

Chapter 8. At War with Israel: Anti-Zionism in East Germany
	from the 1960s to the 1980s	115
	Jeffrey Herf

Chapter 9. Holocaust Lite? Fiction in Works by Christa Wolf
	and Fred Wander	138
	Agnes C. Mueller

Chapter 10. The Stigma of "Asociality" in the GDR:
	Reconstructing the Language of Marginalization	150
	Katharina Lenski

Chapter 11. Lesbians and Gays in the GDR: Self-Organizing,
	Politics of Remembrance, Discrimination, and Public
	Silencing	163
	Christiane Leidinger and Heike Radvan

Chapter 12. Have We Learned the "Right" Lessons from
	History? Antigypsyism and the GDR's Dealings with Sinti
	and Roma	175
	Ingrid Bettwieser and Tobias von Borcke

Chapter 13. The GDR People's Chamber Declaration of 12 April
	1990: Ending the "Universalization" of the Holocaust	191
	Martin Jander

PART II. Federal Republic of Germany

Chapter 14. Understanding Silence: An Ongoing Search for
	People, Things, and Connections Not Really Unknown	209
	Regina Scheer

Chapter 15. "A Reassessment of European History?"
	Developments, Trends, and Problems of a Culture of
	Remembrance in Europe	216
	Günter Morsch

Chapter 16. Analogies and Imbalances: The Effects of Memorial
	Site Policies on Dealing with Places from the GDR Past on
	NS Reappraisal	233
	Carola S. Rudnick

Chapter 17. From the Ideological Repudiation of Culpability to
  Ethnocentric Propaganda   247
  Anetta Kahane

Chapter 18. The Book and the Audience: Comments on the
  Reception of *Undeclared Wars with Israel* in Germany   259
  Jeffrey Herf

Chapter 19. Another Past That Lives On: My Trying Journey
  from Contemporary Witness to Contemporary Historian   266
  Patrice G. Poutrus

Chapter 20. Nonconformity in a German Postwar Society:
  Questions for GDR and Transformation Studies   281
  Raiko Hannemann

Chapter 21. Monumental Problems: Freedom and Unity Come
  to Berlin   299
  Daniela Blei

Index   311

Illustrations

Figures

3.1. International press conference of the Committee for German Unity, at which Albert Norden (2nd from left) presents a "brown book" on Theodor Oberländer Berlin (East), 2 February 1960.   45

3.2. View into the exhibition *15 Years of Liberation* in the Museum of German History in the Zeughaus, Berlin (East), 26 April 1960.   47

3.3. Blackened exhibition board at the opening of the exhibition *Die Vergangenheit mahnt* in the Berlin Congress Hall, Berlin (West), 8 April 1960.   50

3.4. Representatives of the GDR-Reichsbahn at a commemoration ceremony at Grunewald station, Berlin (West), 13 September 1970.   52

4.1. Call of the Fighting Group against Inhumanity for "Rat Control." Stickers distributed in the GDR 1951/52.   58

4.2. Front page of a leaflet of the "Fighting Group against Inhumanity," which was distributed in large numbers in the GDR in the late 1940s.   60

Tables

7.1. Professions of West German IM/KP of the HV A (as of December 1988).   108

7.2. Economic capital of West German IM/KP der HV A (as of December 1988).   111

Introduction

New Perspectives on the GDR

A Plea for a Paradigm Shift

Enrico Heitzer, Martin Jander, Anetta Kahane, and Patrice G. Poutrus

It took some time in the (pre-unification) Federal Republic of Germany for not only researchers but also educators, museums, and memorial policymakers to begin asking critical questions. But there have been debates about National Socialism and its aftereffects since 1945. What started hesitatingly and then assumed increasing clarity and importance were questions about how many people were involved in criminal acts; the successes or failures of denazification; the comprehensiveness of compensation for Nazi wrongdoing; whether every victim group had been recognized; and whether the state and its citizens were meeting their material and moral obligations to Israel, among other issues. At first tentatively and then with increasing urgency, historians and other researchers—through their investigations and the ensuing public debate—completed the work initiated by the Allies at the Nuremberg Trials and the twelve tribunals that followed.

Critical inquiry on the aftereffects of National Socialism but also earlier periods in German history, including colonialism, continue. Whether football, the secret service, antisemitism, medicine, or immigration policy, no institution, phenomenon, subject, or concept should be excluded from critical scrutiny. The destruction of law and civilization and the establishment of megalomaniacal nationalism, racism, antisemitism, and other movements opposed to minorities and modernity as such demand that the Federal Republic of Germany repeatedly address these legacies as long as it wishes to remain a democracy. Its democratic culture is nurtured in significant ways by the ability to pose questions of this nature.

The GDR: Soviet-Style Dictatorship and Post–National Socialist Society

The impetus for this book comes from our belief that critical questions about the aftereffects of National Socialism and other chapters in Germany's past, such as colonialism, are most definitely relevant beyond the rupture of 1945, not least with regard to the German Democratic Republic (GDR), its political system, foreign policy, society, culture, and everyday life. Researchers and publishers have addressed these issues, but not in the depth and breadth presented in this book.

In various ways, the contributors here wrestle with precisely how denazification was addressed, in what manner Nazis were excluded from or integrated into the GDR, how antisemitism cultivated by National Socialism was eradicated or persisted, and how surviving Nazi victims were compensated or not. It asks how communists deployed their history as victims of Nazi persecution to legitimize a new dictatorship, whether antifascism was underpinned by antisemitism, and whether antifascism and denazification can lay claim to a lasting contribution to the democratization of the Federal Republic of Germany. These questions have not yet received systematic analytical attention.

Today, journalists, schools, museums, and memorials have some catching up to do, given that the GDR and other "Soviet-style dictatorships" (Mlynar 1982–1989) did not adequately address National Socialism and its aftereffects. The extermination of European Jews, the mass murder of Sinti and Roma, and the war of pillage and extermination against the Soviet Union were only mentioned in the context of preserving the power of ruling elites and their ideological alliances in the GDR and other societies of the former Soviet Bloc. The often heroic communist and noncommunist resistance to Nazi Germany's policies and allies, the Warsaw ghetto insurrection of 1943, and the uprising led by the Polish Home Army in 1944 were equally neglected.

Indeed, the aftereffects of National Socialism and its historical antecedents were clearly observable in the satellite states of the Soviet Union until its dissolution. Large numbers of Nazi victims were never recognized, received no compensation, and faced persecution once again, while Nazi perpetrators were never held to account. The persistence of antisemitism, racism, homophobia, and antiziganism was conspicuous. Engaging with origins and causes was possible only within strictly enforced limits. As closed societies, the communist SED state and other Soviet-style dictatorships that defined themselves as socialist were unwilling and unable to confront these problems and to allow public discussion and, with it, potential controversy (Amadeu Antonio Foundation 2010).

The GDR: Demonization, Limits of Discourse, and Germany's History of Suffering

This book makes a plea for a more intensive, systematic focus on the SED state as one of three successor societies to National Socialism (Bergmann, Erb, and Lichtblau 1995). It is also—but by no means exclusively—a plea for the rediscovery of history as a method of ideological critique. The SED (Socialist Unity Party of Germany) legitimized the existence of the GDR by adopting a highly idiosyncratic view of German history. Its narratives revolved around terms such as "capitalism," "fascism," "antifascism," "imperialism," and "Zionism." Used in highly disparate ways, these terms had functions detached from their analytical meaning. Since free, controversial discourse was impossible, the terms of analytical critique that citizens were required to adopt, and that appeared in official prescriptions that limited permissible debate, were adversarial, even demonizing. The critical deconstruction and analysis of their propagandistic functions are tasks that are indispensable to our proposed shift toward examining the GDR as a post–National Socialist society.

Engaging in an ideological critique of terms like "fascism" and "antifascism" and their functions goes beyond engagement with the GDR. Neither the analytical concept of "fascism" nor the political concept of "antifascism" disappeared with the fall of the GDR. Their salient features, the "left-wing" relativization of Nazi crimes, and the demonization of Western democracies, particularly the United States and Israel, have persisted, though now under the conditions of social pluralism and the possibility of free and open debate.

Recovering contemporary historical research as a method of ideological critique proves indispensable in another context. In the eyes of many opponents of the German Soviet-style dictatorship, the origins and development of the SED state constitute a narrative of suffering for the German people.

Instead of critical reflection on the continuities of German history and ties to transnational contexts, or examining links to present-day society, criticism of the SED dictatorship was sometimes imbued with a more conservative, anti-communist national revisionism and, not infrequently, with forms of anti-Americanism and antisemitism.

This is why opponents of the SED in the (pre-unification) Federal Republic of Germany often called for a "reversal in commemorative policy" and a shift toward a historiography that was designed less to empower responsible citizens to form their own critical judgments and more to underpin a form of German nationalism. The ideological critique of this historiography should not only focus on the past; it must remain a work in progress.

Role Models and Productive Input

Our plea for a new perspective on the GDR draws on diverse influences. The first deserving mention is historian Helmut Eschwege. His research and writing focused on the GDR, the history of the Holocaust, and the history of the Jews in the GDR (Berg 2003: 442–447). Examining Jewish resistance to National Socialism, he criticized the antifascist tradition enshrined in the GDR's historiography. His work, like other research on the history of the Jews in the GDR, could be published only in the Federal Republic of Germany. Some of his works have never been published at all.

We drew additional inspiration from the Crises in Soviet-Style Systems series, published in the 1980s (Mlynar 1982–1989). It advanced critical discourse on the Soviet Union and its satellite states, and the authors involved in this project came from across Eastern Europe. Their publications described the societies of Eastern Europe as examples of the shared category "Soviet-style dictatorship" on the one hand, but emphasized their disparate histories and crisis elements on the other.

Another important influence is *Schwieriges Erbe* (Difficult heritage), an anthology published by Werner Bergmann, Rainer Erb, and Albert Lichtblau in 1995. Six years after the fall of the Berlin Wall, authors from Austria and the (new) Federal Republic of Germany outlined and compared portraits of three societies in the post-Nazi era: the GDR, Austria, and the FRG. Seldom has a more accurate treatment of the history and structure of the GDR as a post–National Socialist society been achieved.[1]

Historian Jeffrey Herf's *Divided Memory* (1997), in which he compares the treatment of the Shoah in the FRG and the GDR, also informs this book. Although Herf has continued to publish on National Socialism and the Cold War, and has received international recognition for his research on National Socialism and antisemitism, among his books, only *Divided Memory* has been translated into German.

We also looked to the anthology *Fremde und Fremd-Sein in der DDR* (Foreigners and misfits in the GDR; Behrends, Kuck, and Poutrus 2003). Following racist riots after the demise of the GDR and in the 1990s, the anthology's editors asked "whether the racist, nationalist and anti-Bolshevist stereotypes of Nazi propaganda, which were undoubtedly widespread among the population, had in fact been expunged simply because of the mantra-like repetition of the GDR's anti-fascist foundation myth" (Behrends, Kuck, and Poutrus 2003: 327).

Another reference point for this project was Salomon Korn's warning against the rise of an "equivalence mindset."[2] In 2004, Korn, pointing to the state of Saxony's memorial policy, cautioned against the general equating of National Socialism and the GDR in the commemorative culture of the new Federal Republic. Such an equation was analytically senseless, he argued, and showed a persistent need to avoid culpability. The goal was not a critical reflection on the past but its termination.

While these interventions have not yet triggered a paradigm shift in GDR studies, the rise of the popular movement PEGIDA (Patriotic Europeans Against the Islamization of the Occident) and the ascendant right-wing AfD party make clear that, as was true more than twenty years ago, the GDR and its political system and society cannot be detached from the history of National Socialism and present-day right-wing radicalism any more than the old and new Federal Republic can be.

New Inputs

The contributions collected here do not claim to fully fill the blind spots in existing research on Soviet-style dictatorships, the GDR, or its legacies. They are merely elements in a debate in the humanities about the GDR and a plea for a different perspective. The starting point for this volume is not the end of the Cold War and the reunification of the two German states, but the Third Reich, including its unprecedented crimes.

Since 1989, the history, structure, and ideology of the SED dictatorship have belonged to a shared postwar history. The heritage of the GDR as a post–National Socialist society has played an ambiguous role in a reunited Germany in quotidian contexts, historical research, and debates on commemorative policy. This book represents an effort to situate the GDR within the "major flows" of twentieth-century history and can be understood simply as a starting point for further research.

The book's first half features essays that engage with events, people, or social structures in the GDR. Historian Anette Leo opens with an empathetic portrait of the Jewish communist, folklorist, and Finno-Ugrian Wolfgang Steinitz. She describes his return to the GDR after his time in exile with friends and colleagues. In discomfiting detail, Leo illustrates the "trap of loyalty" that ensnared Steinitz and many of his companions.

Their journey, following the campaign against "cosmopolitans" and emigrants to the West in the early 1950s, ended in disillusionment and self-abnegation. Leo writes, "In constant danger of being caught between the millstones of the Cold War, pursued by the demons of the past, and clinging to messages of salvation for the future, there seemed to be no place for [Steinitz and his friends] in this Germany in which they could simply have lived in the present without abandoning their principles."

Chairperson of the Amadeu Antonio Foundation Anetta Kahane reports on "the taboo of antisemitism," picking up on Anette Leo's story. Kahane recounts her parents' return from the resistance in France and her own never entirely successful attempt, following the anti-Zionist/antisemitic purges of the 1950s, to embrace her Jewish identity and at the same time conceal it. Writing about the hidden history of Jewish communists in the GDR, Kahane says,

> According to the logic of class struggle in the GDR, anyone who believed in God was a Jew. And anyone who did this voluntarily renounced the enlightened spirit of historical materialism. This meant that this person was regarded as reactionary, since religions were presumed to always suppress and manipulate the masses. The reduction of Jewish identity to religious faith not only demonstrated catastrophic ignorance but also served above all to exonerate the German working class, which had acclaimed the Nazis, thus becoming complicit in their crimes. The communists explained the seduction by Hitler almost exclusively in terms of economic and social factors, like mass unemployment. This explanatory model has served as a justification for right-wing extremist or right-wing populist movements up until the present.

Historian Gerd Kühling, a staff member at the Wannsee Conference Memorial, examines the beginnings of the GDR from yet another vantage point. He analyzes the rise of divergent commemorative cultures in East and West Germany, exemplified by new divisions in the city of Berlin. The instrumentalization of National Socialism for the reciprocal delegitimation of the two German states began early on. The discourse on the victims of National Socialism and forms of memorialization was crushed between the fronts of the Cold War.

Historian and political scientist Enrico Heitzer, a staff member at the Sachsenhausen Memorial and Museum, adopts a different perspective. He describes "systemic opposition from the right," not only in the initial phase of the Soviet Occupation Zone/GDR but also up until the GDR's demise. Until now, this phenomenon has been poorly documented. Researchers have hardly pursued the traces of this systemic opposition, which existed from the beginning to the end of the GDR, presumably not least because the SED attempted to discredit its opponents as Nazis. Against the backdrop of this defamatory propaganda, researchers have largely overlooked opposition to the system from the right.

Historian and lawyer Klaus Bästlein, for many years an assistant to Berlin's commissioner for reappraisal of the SED dictatorship, examines the GDR's most infamous political trial: the proceedings against Hans Globke, Konrad Adenauer's senior advisor and the former author of the Nazi race laws. Bästlein shows that despite its utility for SED propaganda, the verdict against Globke (in contrast to other trials against prominent National Socialists) reflected knowledge that was available at the time concerning the extermination of the Jews, and Globke's role in it. He writes, "In contrast to the propagandistic exploitation of the proceedings, no objection can be raised to the verdict reached by the Supreme Court of the GDR. The only problematic aspect is the depiction of the GDR as the 'better' ('antifascist') German state."

Christoph Classen, a long-serving staff member at the Center for Contemporary Historical Research, investigates the origins of the GDR's antifascist foundation myth and its significance for engaging with the GDR in the reunited Federal Republic. After 1989, alongside criticism and support for antifascism, controversy emerged regarding the political meanings of the reunited Federal Republic. Classen writes,

> One of the issues addressed here is the recent controversy between conservatives and left-wing liberals in the so-called *Historikerstreit* about how the anti-totalitarian foundation consensus of the old Federal Republic should be viewed. After the collapse of the communist bloc and amid fears of a resurgent Germany in the center of Europe, the political controversy over whether anti-communist or anti-National Socialist identity should constitute the main reference point for Germany entered a second phase under changed conditions.

Political scientist Helmut Müller-Enbergs, an expert on East German secret police documents, presents "empirical social research on a highly invisible group" in his contribution. Employing empirical evidence, Müller-Enbergs shows that the Ministry of State Security (MfS), in contrast to the secret services of the FRG, did not have ex–National Socialists on its permanent staff, though some of its informers were in fact former Nazis. Contrary to expectations, says Müller-Enbergs, professional spies tended to come from the upper echelons of the GDR's social hierarchy rather than from the purportedly preeminent working class.

Historian Jeffrey Herf, professor of modern European history at the University of Maryland, shares an essay that offers an overview of his book, *Undeclared Wars with Israel*, which was published in English. Drawing on archival documents from the GDR, he follows a path from the expulsion of Jews from the GDR in the early 1950s to support for Arab countries and the PLO in the war to destroy Israel. Citing recently deceased Robert Wistrich, Herf analyzes the ideology of the SED as "Holocaust Inversion." Former comrades in the war against the Nazis were declared enemies of socialism, and in the case of Israel, warred upon.

Agnes C. Mueller, professor of German and comparative studies at the University of South Carolina, examines the relationship between literature in the GDR and popular engagement with the Holocaust as exemplified by Christa Wolf and Fred Wander. Mueller explains her essay:

> Holocaust trauma, Jewish identity, and the guilt of the perpetrators are allegedly spotlighted in Wolf's fictional and essayistic work, but in fact are glossed over in terms of their relevance for future generations. The emotionalizing strategies displayed in Wolf's texts, some of which utilize the literary theories of socialist realism, are then contrasted with those featured in the work of Fred Wander. He provides explicit descriptions of camp experiences, unmediated in their directness and affective impact, whereas in Wolf's works, the figures, themes, and motifs concerned are more profoundly encoded.

Historian Katharina Lenski directs the Thuringian Matthias Domaschk Archives for Contemporary History, which she established in 1991. Today, she is a research associate at Jena University. Her contribution examines the stigmatization of political dissidents and young people searching for new lifestyles in the GDR. Her text focuses on a hitherto almost unknown public hair-cutting initiative in the Thuringian town of Pössneck in October 1969. Lenski writes,

> The practice displays elements reminiscent of the Nazi era. Though the context of exclusion had changed, certain elements survived the 1945 "zero hour." Compulsory haircutting was one of several disciplinary elements designed to punish nonconforming lifestyles. Labeling someone as "anti-social" was a simple (though spurious) solution. Using existing laws and their subordinate institutions, an exclusionary force was established in the GDR.

The contribution by sociologist Christiane Leidinger and education scholar Heike Radvan investigates the rarely addressed issue of lesbians and gays in the GDR. Focusing on self-organizing activities, which began in the 1970s, and on attempts to memorialize lesbian and gay victims of National Socialism, Leidinger and Radvan show how these initiatives contradicted the one-sided official commemoration of the communist resistance. Lesbians and gays were placed under surveillance and encountered numerous obstacles. As shown by these initiatives, the authors examine how self-organizing activity had a democratizing effect. This contribution concludes by asking why lesbian and gay commemorative activities have gone largely unmentioned in public discourse, even until the present.

Ingrid Bettwieser, a staff member of the Ravensbrück Memorial, and Tobias von Borcke, a project executive in the Berlin office of the Documentation and Cultural Center for German Sinti and Roma, address another important and neglected subject. Turning to Sinti and Roma, their contribution draws on empirical research that examines perceptions of minorities in *Neues Deutschland*, the leading SED daily. Given the scarcity of available publications, the authors use the newspaper to analyze the history of Sinti and Roma in the GDR. Their verdict:

> Disparate as the GDR and the FRG were, in terms of societal dealings with the Nazi genocide of Sinti and Roma and the continuation of antiziganism, the parallels are significant. In neither of these two states were these issues appropriately addressed, while survivors were subjected to renewed reprisals. Whereas in the GDR there was exigent pressure to conform, in the FRG, Sinti and Roma were in many cases socially marginalized.

Historian Martin Jander, a participant on the SED State Research Team at Berlin's Free University for many years and now a lecturer in various programs at American universities in Berlin, grapples with the relationship of left-wing and Christian GDR opposition to the "universalization" of German culpability during the collapse of the GDR in his essay. He shows that only small segments of the GDR's opposition—mostly around Helmut Eschwege and Lothar Kreyssig—were able to criticize the SED's antifascism, which was frequently imbued with antisemitism. Most looked to role models who reproduced an antifascism that relativized German culpability. Yet there were some courageous individuals on the fringes of the GDR's left-wing and Christian groups, particularly from circles around the Reconciliation Initiative and the Jewish Cultural Association, which in 1989/90 were able to break with the GDR's position: an "antifascism without Jews" that "universalized" German culpability.

The second half of this book contains essays that offer a critical assessment of the reappraisal of the GDR in the reunited Federal Republic. This part of the anthology opens with the award-winning author Regina Scheer. In her essay, she reflects on the experience of interviewing diverse individuals from the GDR and gathering life stories from the five new federal states of reunited Germany. Her verdict: "It almost seems to be a law of human society that some things can only be expressed once the grandchildren have arrived. But the grandchildren, too, will become mothers and fathers. I believe we should be asking ourselves about guilt and responsibility, not those who preceded us. And to understand our own history, we need to listen to those who came before us. Not least to the silences between the words."

Günter Morsch has been the head of the Sachsenhausen Memorial and Museum and director of the Brandenburg Memorials Foundation. His contribution wrestles with the return of the totalitarianism paradigm in analyses of National Socialism and communism in Europe. In "many European countries, a stronger impulse has emerged ... to unite disparate commemorative cultures with a new policy based on a shared European master narrative, and thus to instrumentalize the past for present-day political goals much more emphatically and unambiguously than before." With the end of the Cold War, a "commemoration boom" took place in Europe. Alongside it, an "interpretation battle" was triggered. "The old adversarial images are wheeled out, . . . victimhood competitions are unleashed, parties and governments transmute resurging resentments into 'policies for remembrance and reappraisal of the past.'" History is weaponized, and in extreme cases, such as the disintegration of Yugoslavia and the Soviet Union, the weapons have been lethal.

Carola Rudnick, who leads the redesign of the Euthanasia Memorial in Lüneburg, elucidates the effects of memorial policy in her essay on the GDR's historical sites in the context of the reunited Federal Republic's reappraisals of the Nazi era. Her findings come as a positive surprise. Only with the reappraisal of the Soviet Occupation Zone and the GDR in two Commissions of Inquiry set up by the Bundestag, and associated government subsidies for reappraisal initiatives—and with the former central commemorative monuments of the GDR—did support for concentration camp memorials as a whole become possible. Only then did Nazi memorials from the old FRG come to enjoy support from the federal government. The political crisis of legitimation for memorials in Germany, she writes, has been largely resolved, even if conflicts persist.

The causes and origins of ethnically based racist movements, which have shown renewed vigor everywhere, but especially in the five states of eastern Germany, is a particular source of controversy in the reunited Federal Republic. In her essay, Anetta Kahane, founder and chairperson of the Amadeu Antonio Foundation, shows that while the strength of these movements in the five new states of reunited Germany is by no means a mystery, scholars have yet to analyze conditions in the GDR with sufficient precision. As she explains,

> In almost every reference cited nowadays in debates on the GDR, one thing above all is missing: the fact that it was itself a product of the war,

the Shoah, and postwar history. That the GDR would not have existed without Auschwitz and that without the war of extermination unleashed by Germans, Europe would have looked different and sixty million lives could have been saved seem to have lost their perceived relevance. As a reference point, the crimes committed by Germans have disappeared, just as the ethnic dimension gradually assumes the mantle of normalcy.

Historian Jeffrey Herf from the University of Maryland describes in a short essay how his books *Divided Memory* (1997) and *Undeclared Wars with Israel* (2016) were received in Germany. As a consequence of the Holocaust, research on Jewish issues in Germany is often written by authors who do not live in Germany. However, since the declaration of the GDR's first freely elected parliament on 12 April 1990, the subject of antisemitic domestic and foreign policy in the GDR has reached ever wider circles. It has not remained a topic only for academic researchers.

In a personal retrospective, Patrice G. Poutrus, a historian and research fellow of the University of Erfurt, deals with his own attempts and those of some of his colleagues to create a solid academic foundation for public debate on migration and xenophobia in the GDR. Poutrus also illuminates the early history of the Soviet Occupation Zone/GDR. Antifascists returning from exile were stigmatized as "misfits," as were "contract workers" who were subsequently recruited to the GDR from many socialist countries.

A somewhat different perspective on this issue emerges in the contribution from political scientist Raiko Hannemann. His research project at Berlin's Alice Salomon University of Applied Sciences is titled Undemocratic Mindsets in Common: The Example of Marzahn-Hellersdorf. It examines opposition and resistance in the GDR and its role in the development of democracy in the reunited Federal Republic. In his essay here, Hannemann first emphasizes the dearth of research on opposition to the system from the right. Second, he calls attention to shortcomings in the research on the origins of the GDR's pro-democracy movement. He attributes both failures to the totalitarianism paradigm that has guided much of the research on opposition. Questions regarding resistance activities within the framework of an industrial society, which emerged as part of GDR-related research in the pre-unification Federal Republic, he writes, have been taboo since the upheaval of 1989/90.

The book concludes with an essay by Daniela Blei, a historian, editor, and writer based in San Francisco, California. She visited Berlin for the first time as an undergraduate in the 1990s and has observed the city's commemorative culture ever since. Her essay explores the origins and evolution of the Freedom and Unification Monument. Blei establishes that the monument in no way originated from a broad societal discussion, like the *Stolpersteine* (Stumbling Stones) and other memorials in Berlin. Instead, four men conceived the memorial, and, rather than seeking public support, they sought to persuade influential politicians and parliament. This was presumably why the public failed to perceive that parliament's crucial decision to greenlight the monument was by no means just about honoring the peaceful revolutionaries of 1989, says Blei. Instead, the monument offers a metaphysical view of history based on the notion that anti-democratic German traditions were "canceled out" by the upheaval of 1989. Blei's verdict: the initiators of the Freedom and Unification Monument "can be accused of advancing the old endeavors of conservatives to relativize the Nazi past." At the same time, she strikes a positive note. More impressive than the monument is the "silence that surrounds it." The monument will likely "fade into irrelevance" and unintentionally "serve as a lasting reminder that German history is a long way from being over and that unification can never be perfect."

Acknowledgments

Much of the research in this book was discussed during a workshop in Berlin in January 2017. Enrico Heitzer, Martin Jander, and Anetta Kahane shared additional research as part of the Annual Conference of the German Studies Association in Atlanta in the autumn of 2017, while Patrice G. Poutrus presented his findings in October 2014 at a forum of the Catholic University of America in Washington, DC. Jeffrey Herf presented work related to both of his essays during workshops of the Amadeu Antonio Foundation in Berlin—the first one in January 2017, the second one in January 2020. Some of the authors represented in this book were approached by the editors. All authors were requested to present a contribution of their choice that focused on how the GDR addressed National Socialism and how the reunited Federal Republic has wrestled with the GDR and its legacies. We thank all of the authors involved in this project, and hope that they find the book as successful as we do. Our special "thank you" for this publication goes to Daniela Blei, who edited all the articles for this publication. Without the help of Miriamne Fields, Alan Johnson, Martina Jones, Anthony Hood, Marian Koebner, and Daniela Blei, who translated some of the articles from German into English, this edition of our book would not have been possible. We are delighted that this book is published by Berghahn Books. The German version, *Nach Auschwitz: Schwieriges Erbe DDR*, was published in 2018 by Wochenschau Verlag.

Introduction

Enrico Heitzer, born in 1977 in Altenburg in Thuringia, was with the Bundeswehr from 1996 to 1998. Beginning in 1998, he studied history and political science in Potsdam and Halle. From 2005 to 2007, he held a scholarship from the Graduate Program of the State of Saxony-Anhalt. In 2007, he received a doctoral scholarship from the German Historical Institute in Washington, DC. In 2007/8 he worked as a research assistant for the Chair of Modern History at the Martin Luther University Halle-Wittenberg. Since 2005, he has been an associate doctoral student at the Center for Contemporary Historical Research in Potsdam (ZZF) and, since 2010–12, has worked as a research assistant at the Berlin Wall Foundation. Today he is a research assistant at the Sachsenhausen Memorial and the Museum Sachsenhausen/Stiftung Brandenburgische Gedenkstätten. In addition to his exhibition activities, his research interests include the end of the World War II and the early Cold War, denazification, the history of opposition and resistance in the SBZ/GDR, and the politics and culture of remembrance. His publications include *Die Kampfgruppe gegen Unmenschlichkeit (KgU): Widerstand und Spionage im Kalten Krieg 1948–1959* (volume 53 in the series Zeithistorische Studien by Böhlau-Verlag, 2015); and with Günter Morsch, Robert Traba, and Katarzyna Woniak, *Im Schatten von Nürnberg: Transnationale Ahndung von NS-Verbrechen* (In the shadow of Nuremberg: Transnational persecution of Nazi crimes, volume 25 in the series Forschungsbeiträge und Materialien der Stiftung Brandenburgische Gedenkstätten by Metropol Verlag, 2019).

Martin Jander, born in 1955 in Freiburg, is a historian, lecturer, and journalist and teaches German and European history at Stanford University (Berlin), New York University (Berlin), and in the Freie Universität Berlin European Studies Program. He completed his dissertation in 1995 on "Formation and Crisis of the GDR Opposition" at the Otto Suhr Institute of the Freie Universität Berlin. Until 2017, he chronicled left-wing terrorism, a project sponsored by the Hamburg Foundation for the Advancement of Science and Culture, some of which has been published. In addition to his teaching and research, Jander works as an adult educator in the trade unions, produces teaching materials for school curricula, and offers guided tours of Berlin and Potsdam (www.unwrapping-history.de). His most recent publication, with Enrico Heitzer, Martin Jander, Anetta Kahane, and Patrice G. Poutrus (eds.), is *Nach Auschwitz: Schwieriges Erbe DDR* (Frankfurt, 2018).

Anetta Kahane, born in 1954 in East Berlin, is a German journalist and author. She holds a degree in Latin American Studies and has worked as a translator. In 1990, she was the first commissioner for foreigners of the East Berlin Magistrate, and after reunification she helped establish the Regional Office for Foreigners (RAA) in Berlin and advocated intercultural education at schools in the new federal states. In late 1998, she cofounded the Amadeu Antonio Foundation, where she has been full-time chairperson since 2003. From 1974 to 1982, she was forced to work as an unofficial collaborator with GDR State Security. She ended this forced cooperation in 1982 because she no longer wanted to support racist practices of GDR functionaries. Since this collaboration became publicly known in 2002, right-wing extremists and right-wing populists have targeted her in campaigns against her and the foundation. In 1991, she was awarded the Theodor Heuss Medal, alongside Joachim Gauck, Christian Führer, David Gill, Ulrike Poppe, and Jens Reich. In 2002, she was awarded the Moses Mendelssohn Prize of the State of Berlin. For several years, she has worked as a columnist for *Berliner Zeitung* and has written for *Zeit, Tageszeitung, Stern, Tagesspiegel*, and other publications. She is the author of the book *Ich sehe was, was du nicht siehst* (I see what you don't see) (Berlin 2004).

Patrice G. Poutrus, born in 1961 in East Berlin, is a historian and migration researcher. He is currently a research assistant at the University of Erfurt. He received his doctorate in 2001 from the European University Viadrina, Frankfurt/Oder, and subsequently conducted research at the German Historical Institute in Washington, DC, the Center for Contemporary Historical Research in Potsdam, the Simon Wiesenthal Institute for Holocaust Studies in Vienna, and the Institute for Contemporary History at the University of Vienna. He is a member of the DFG research network Grundlagen der Flüchtlingsforschung. His book *Umkämpftes Asyl. Vom Nachkriegsdeutschland bis in die Gegenwart* was published in spring 2019.

Notes

1. See one work that adopts a similar approach: Herz 1997.
2. See the term in "Press Release from the Central Council of Jews in Germany," 21 January 2004 (Bibliothek der Jüdischen Gemeinde zu Berlin, Berlin).

References

Amadeu Antonio Foundation, ed. 2010. *"Das hat es bei uns nicht gegeben" – Antisemitismus in der DDR*. Berlin.
Behrends, Jan C., Dennis Kuck, and Patrice G. Poutrus. 2003. "Historische Ursachen der Fremdenfeindlichkeit in den Neuen Bundesländern." In *Fremde und Fremd-Sein in der DDR*, edited by Jan C. Behrends, 301–307. Berlin.

Introduction

Berg, Nikolaus. 2003. *Der Holocaust und die westdeutschen Historiker. Erforschung und Erinnerung*. Göttingen.
Bergmann, Werner, Rainer Erb, and Albert Lichtblau, eds. 1995. *Schwieriges Erbe. Der Umgang mit Nationalsozialismus und Antisemitismus in Österreich, der DDR und der Bundesrepublik Deutschland*. Frankfurt.
Herf, Jeffrey. 1997. *Divided Memory*. Cambridge.
Herz, Thomas A. 1997. "NS-Vergangenheit contra SED-Vergangenheit." In *Umkämpfte Vergangenheit: Diskurse über den Nationalsozialismus seit 1945*, edited by Michael Schwab-Trapp and Thomas A. Herz, 264–286. Opladen.
Mlynar, Zdenek, eds. 1982–1989. *Krisen in den Systemen sowjetischen Typs*. Vienna.

Part I

German Democratic Republic

Chapter 1

The Loyalty Trap

Wolfgang Steinitz and the Generation of GDR-Founding Fathers and Mothers

Annette Leo

"I sit by the roadside. / The driver changes the wheel." So begins a poem by Bertolt Brecht, written in the early 1950s after his return from exile.

> I don't like where I came from.
> I don't like where I'm going.
> Why am I impatient
> as I watch him change the wheel? (Brecht 1969: 85)

"I'm sitting in Trelleborg by the ferry.... Four hours to Saßnitz—but they're not going to make our return that easy," wrote Wolfgang Steinitz, more prosaically, to his brother in Palestine. The situation was similar, but the date was January 1946. "The ferry goes to Danzig," he continued, "and from there, on an even less familiar but less dependable not-express route to Berlin."[1] The author was waiting for the ship's departure in the company of other German communist emigrants from Stockholm.

Steinitz, a Finno-Ugric specialist and folklorist, was eager to leave his country of exile. By no account did he want to miss Germany's long-awaited new beginning. At last, he'd be able to carry out academic work and take on responsibility. "Of course life in Berlin won't be easy," he wrote, "but it will be interesting and productive, and I can and must develop and apply my capabilities." Responding to the opportunity presented by a new contact after a four-year interruption, Steinitz, the ever-loyal Stalinist, began to engage in political discourse. True progress today, he lectured his brother Hans, was not to be found in communist settlements in Palestine, but rather in Yugoslavia, Bulgaria, Romania, and Poland, where "life's crucial problems were solved."

By comparison, Brecht's words seem more doubtful, more tentative. They capture the dichotomy between departure and arrival, the fear of never again feeling at home in today's Germany, and possibly not anywhere. In 1947, in the Stockholm phase of his exile, Brecht ran the Schutzverband deutscher Schriftsteller (League of German Writers) with Wolfgang Steinitz, who had just returned to Europe from the United States following his interrogation by the House Committee on Un-American Activities. In late October 1948, after an interlude of eleven months in Switzerland, he arrived in the Soviet occupation zone and wrote in his diary: "Berlin, an etching by Churchill following an idea of Hitler's. Berlin, the rubbish tip near Potsdam" (Brecht 1983: 457).

The optimistic Wolfgang Steinitz also felt apprehensive on arrival. As the train finally crossed the Oder—vanquished Germany's new border— he and his traveling companions realized they had arrived. "We're singing the Internationale," Steinitz wrote to his wife who had stayed behind in Stockholm. "But the atmosphere wasn't exactly celebratory."[2] Perhaps, this was the moment when he understood how inappropriate the song was for the situation: "So comrades rally," it goes. The travelers were returning to a country whose inhabitants could not possibly share their vision of the future. Would they otherwise have defended the Nazi regime to the bitter end? "We will not be welcomed with jubilation," read Alfred Kantorowicz's diary entry on 7 December 1946 as he crossed the border. "Defeated we fled, and defeated we return home to the land of the defeated; they who know nothing about us and who probably have no wish to" (Kantorowicz 1961a: 201).

Remigration

After leaving in the 1930s, exiles returned at the war's end with few belongings, mainly books, diaries, and manuscripts. They came from England and France, Sweden, the United States, and Mexico. Alfred Kantorowicz had served as an information officer with the International Brigade in Spain before fleeing to the United States via France. Anna Seghers, together with her husband and children, found refuge first in France and then Mexico, where, together with other comrades in exile, she published the periodical *Freies Deutschland*. Wolfgang Steinitz reached Stockholm via Moscow, where he lectured at the university but sometimes earned his keep as a lumberjack. The economic historian Jürgen Kuczynski arrived in Germany wearing a U.S. Army uniform. They were intellectuals, academics, or artists and came mainly from middle-class Jewish families. Before Hitler's seizure of power, they had joined the Communist Party as youth members. They and their families had been persecuted and driven out by the Nazis. Yet they regarded themselves as communist warriors.

Braving difficult journeys, the remigrants reached and traversed a shattered Europe, finally arriving in Berlin, where the Soviet occupation army had established its headquarters. Also in Berlin was the headquarters of the Communist Party, at whose disposal they wished to be in order to rebuild a new Germany just as they had dreamed of doing during their persecution, flight, and privation.

In January 1947, the writer Anna Seghers arrived in Gothenburg from New York on board a Swedish ship. In Stockholm, she spent a few days with Ruth Steinitz, Wolfgang Steinitz's sister, before continuing to Paris, where her son and daughter were studying. Traveling on her Mexican passport, Seghers boarded a French military train in Paris and was thus able to reach Berlin, passing with ease through every occupied zone. Kurt and Jeanne Stern, a Franco-German couple, both writers, who had also traveled through Mexico, collected her from the station on 22 April and brought her to the part of the Adlon Hotel that survived the war. Anna Seghers was already a well-known writer, especially since the worldwide success of her book *Das Siebte Kreuz*.

The first port of call for less prominent remigrants was the German Communist Party headquarters near the Maerkisches Museum underground station on Wallstrasse. Wolfgang Steinitz and his Stockholm traveling companions arrived at the Stettiner railway station on 18 January 1946. New arrivals were given lodging for the first few nights and then were to complete a lengthy questionnaire and compose a CV. Precise information was required, particularly about the period after 1933. Asked about his future plans, Steinitz wrote, "University" and "Teaching Russian." With a Russian teaching manual in his suitcase, which he edited in exile in Sweden, he was convinced that the Germans would now have to learn Russian.

When, a year later, Alfred Kantorowicz came from New York via Bremen and applied for an opening in the house on Wallstrasse, his American references were useless. He was admitted only when his fellow exile Albert Norden vouched for him. Norden took him to the Klub des Kulturbundes on Jägerstrasse where, to his great delight, he met Peter Huchel in the dining room; they had both lived in the artists' block on Breitenbach Platz. Kantorowicz arrived with big plans. He wanted to establish an independent political-literary journal in Berlin that would bridge the divide between East and West. Socialist Unity Party (SED) officials showed little appreciation for his idea, but Soviet and American occupation officials gave the writer-publicist the licenses he requested. He wrote in his *Deutsches Tagebuch*, "With a naivete which, after all, is not even to be sneered at but rather, with hindsight, seems humiliating, I transferred the East-West ideal into my private life as well. My flat should have been in the American sector, my workplace, editing the journal, in the Soviet sector" (Kantorowicz 1961a: 287).

Kantorowicz found a small flat for himself and his wife, Friedel, on the Argentinisches Allee. Anna Seghers moved to a small hotel on the same street soon after moving from the Adlon. Wolfgang Steinitz and his brother-in-law Jürgen Peters moved from Wallstrasse to a room on Zehlendorfer Onkel-Tom-Strasse before renting a house with his remigrant family in Ithweg. Kurt and Jeanne Stern, later parents-in-law of Steinitz's son, lived nearby, as did Jürgen Kuczynski, who left his duties with the American army to lecture on Marxism in the unheated halls of Berlin University.

And so they settled into life in the relatively undamaged part of the shattered city, suffering, like all Berliners, from adverse postwar conditions that included chaos, coal scarcity, and power cuts. They were privileged both as remigrants from exile and as victims of Nazi persecution. The Klub des Kulturbundes on Jägerstrasse, where they sometimes met, offered dinner without food coupons. Thanks to *Pajok* (the Soviet occupier's special allocations for officials), they were able to improve their meager food rations. They stuck very closely together, perhaps so as not to feel too estranged in this city where almost all of them had lived until they fled, but whose dismal history they followed from afar.

Compared to the local population, which viewed the end of the war in terms of disintegration, they were atypical in seeing an opportunity for a hopeful new beginning. But party functionaries returning from Moscow seemed equally strange to them; they spoke another language and were constantly on the lookout for something. "It seems customary," Kantorowicz (1961a: 368) observed, irritably, "to describe absentees as agents, traitors, bribable. Honestly, I feel as if I've got a millwheel going round inside my head."

From London, Jürgen Kuczynski had written to Anna Seghers that he believed "a people is not lost, not even the German people, not even after everything that has happened, as long as there are men and women who know the right path" (Seghers 2000: 56). In a letter to his wife, Wolfgang Steinitz swore that this was to be "the beginning of a new chapter in our lives which once and for all brings us the fulfillment of all our thoughts and hopes (despite being hard fought and constantly needing to be worked on)" (Peters 1989: 128). Beyond a doubt, they believed they knew "the right way," that they had a place in postwar Germany and a task to fulfill. But this outward single-mindedness also hid the fear and the pain of remembering family members murdered by the Nazis. "How beautiful is the rim of Europe and how unpleasant is its center" wrote Anna Seghers in December 1947, expressing her alienation in a letter to the exiled Egon Erwin Kisch and his wife in Prague. Although people were kind to her, she wrote to Georg Lukacs around the same time that she sometimes felt her blood run cold. "I've landed in the ice age, that's how cold everything seems to me" (Romero 1993: 17).

It had been their decision to return to cold, gray postwar Germany. Their loyalty was to the Soviet occupying power and the Communist Party. But they brought with them memories of cafés in Paris, pizza in Marseille, Picasso's paintings, the rhythms of the boogie-woogie, the warm Mexican sunshine, and BBC radio programs. As long as they lived in one of Berlin's Western zones, they could keep one foot in this world in the hope that the division of the city would last. At the outset, they could have had no idea how quickly this city and country would be split into East and West.

"The End of the Honeymoon"

The "remigrants' honeymoon," as Alfred Kantowicz called it, ended with the creation of the Federal Republic and the German Democratic Republic (GDR). In 1950, Anna Seghers caved to pressure from the SED and moved to Weissensee, to the Brecht family home, before renting a flat in East Berlin's Adlershof. Kantorowicz bid farewell to his East-West life. The journal *Ost-West*, which should have been a bridge, ceased to exist in 1949 due to lack of trust and interest on both sides. Jürgen Kuczynski, Wolfgang Steinitz, the Sterns, and many other communists accommodated the demands of the SED leadership, and in 1950 moved from West to East Berlin. First, they had to repudiate their experiences in exile, their urban nature, and friendships with those from other countries whose fate they shared.

Stalinist purges of the party had just started in 1949/1950. In the feverish search for Trotskyist or Titoist agents, "cosmopolitans," or however these evils were described, remigrants from Western exile came under scrutiny. Today, the obvious question is why they eagerly embraced their controllers in the East. The agony of finding an answer lies, above all, with the next generation, which no longer believed in devout, unconditional loyalty to the founding fathers and mothers of the GDR.

Anna Seghers personally knew László Rajk, president of the Hungarian Communist Party; in 1950, he was sentenced to death and hanged in Budapest because of his relationship with the alleged agent Noel Field. According to the logic of *Kontaktschuld* (guilt by association), she was equally obligated to justify her close friendship with her companion in Mexican exile, Paul Merker, who in the same year and for the same reason as Rajk, was excluded from the SED and arrested two years later. Seghers got off lightly after making her case to the SED Control Commission. There is no doubt that her international fame protected her from any further hardship. But her fear of ostracism must have loomed large. Instead of keeping the regime at arm's length, she felt compelled to prove how reliable she was by exchanging her Mexican passport for a GDR identity card.

In late 1949, the Soviet occupation engineered Wolfgang Steinitz's dismissal from the chairmanship of the German-Soviet Friendship Association. A few months later, Jürgen Kuczynski, president of the association, experienced the same treatment. Thirty-five years later, writing in his book *Dialogue with My Great-Grandson*, Kuczynski assumed a conversational tone, explaining that his dismissal was a consequence of antisemitic tendencies in Soviet politics at the time. "I'm sure you know," he wrote, "that under Stalin, antisemitic attitudes developed in the Soviet Union from time to time, attitudes which, by the way, our party leadership never adopted, not even in the smallest degree" (Kuczynski 1985: 51).

Kuczynski's great-grandson, whose role is only symbolic, would have been too young at the time of the *Dialogue*'s publication to pose questions about the SED campaign in 1952/1953 against "Zionist agents," or about allegations that Paul Merker wanted to smuggle "German national property abroad" because he had expressed the view that Jewish property stolen by the Nazis should be returned.[3] His great-grandfather had long since forgotten or suppressed all that, elegantly sweeping it under the carpet.

Like Wolfgang Steinitz and many others, Kuczynski had acquiesced to antisemitic tropes only a few years after the Holocaust. Perhaps they were relieved that nothing worse had befallen them, and probably turned a blind eye to even tougher reprisals meted out to their comrades in exile. But in public, they continued to assert that socialism was the only secure protection against the barbarity of fascism.

Neither fell far from official favor. Jürgen Kuczynski and Wolfgang Steinitz retained their full professorships at Humboldt University and remained indispensable to officials. In 1954, Steinitz was even elected to the SED Central Committee. In the following years, both academics became deeply involved in the development of the Academy of Sciences. They authorized special contracts with dizzyingly high salaries (for those days), lived in comfortable mansions, and had access to company cars with or without a chauffeur. With these attractive enticements came threats and pressure.

Anna Seghers had been president of the GDR Writers' Association since 1952. She was a member of the Praesidium of the Council for World Peace, founding member of the Academy of Fine Arts, and had the distinction of being awarded the National Prize and the Stalin Peace Prize. Even Alfred Kantorowicz, who kept the greatest distance from the structures of power, at least among those mentioned here, was appointed professor of German at the Humboldt University of Berlin after the collapse of his *Ost-West* journal. It is unlikely that either communist or Jewish-communist intellectuals were offered such opportunities for advancement anywhere else in the world. They belonged to the elite of the East German state without actually gaining access to the levers of power. Their lives amounted to a daily balancing act between the unreasonable demands of party bureaucrats and their own artistic or scientific aspirations. Only the farsighted Bertolt Brecht, forever battling suspicions and prohibitions targeting his Berlin ensemble, had at least given his copyrights to Suhrkamp in Frankfurt/Main.

Doubts, Splits, Injuries

In the insular world of the GDR, remigrants from exile added some color and luster. Their creativity and rhetorical talents created an aura of liberality and urbanity, but they effectively practiced fraudulent labeling. They represented a country even though it differed from their representations of it (and wishes for it). Often contrary to their better judgment, they gave us, the subsequent generation, a sugarcoated view of the GDR. The doubts, disparities, and injuries they sustained, their futile battles and sad gestures of subservience—all of these were kept secret. They had not wanted to mislead us, they later said, and in any case, they felt that every criticism or warning would only help the much detested "class enemy."

The year 1956 became the waterloo for the founding fathers and mothers of the GDR. Incidentally, Bertolt Brecht died far too early, in August 1956, of a heart condition; perhaps his death was connected to the emotional rollercoaster of hope and failure that characterized that year. In February, Soviet Party leader Nikita Khrushchev spoke publicly for the first time about Stalin's war crimes at the Twentieth Congress of the Communist Party. Reading Jürgen Kuczynski's postwar memoir, published only after reunification, one searches in vain for a reaction to these disclosures. Yet not a word appears about the shattering effect of the persecution and killing of so many innocent people, no questioning of their own religious blindness. Kuczynski wrote that, "regardless," he immediately started "to take advantage of the new freedom." In a few articles, he called into question the rigid tenets of Marxist-Leninist theory and argued for "impartial thinking" (Kuczynski 1992: 101).

In 1956, Wolfgang Steinitz demanded in a speech to the SED Central Committee that the writings of Kuczynski and other critics should finally be published. Somewhat acerbically, he declared himself in favor of a genuine academic controversy which, as he noted, the party theoretically required but in practice constantly prevented. In addition, he defended students in Humboldt University's German faculty who, encouraged by their professor, Alfred Kantorowicz, had called for debate on Stalin's war crimes and a discussion of the reforms. Steinitz had just returned from a study tour in Hungary where matters were considerably more advanced than in the GDR. He read and understood Hungarian well enough to follow the debate in the press and among his colleagues. Zealous informants later reported to State Security that the professor visited events hosted by the Petőfi Club. There is, however, no reference to these events in Steinitz's diary. He certainly had no ambitions to distance himself from the party but may have been hoping that conditions in the GDR would be liberalized following the examples of the Soviet Union, Hungary, and Poland, and wanted to make his contribution. These hopes collapsed with the Hungarian Uprising in October 1956.

Many years after Wolfgang Steinitz's death, his wife, Inge, described, in an interview with Hans Bunge, how on the evening of 27 October 1956 her husband returned from an SED Central Committee meeting and alighted from the car, looking pale and not saying a word. He retched throughout the night. "He was utterly exhausted," she said. "Something inside him had collapsed."[4] Inge Steinitz believed, and this is what she told Bunge, that her husband was reacting to Khrushchev's disclosures of Stalin's war crimes. From that moment on, he became a "very critical person." She remembered the date, 27 October, because it was her birthday. While the date was likely correct, she must have transposed the cause of her husband's collapse. It was not Khrushchev's speech but events in Hungary that had so deeply shattered Steinitz—and not him alone.

On 27 October, Wolfgang Steinitz returned from China via Moscow as a member of an Academy of Sciences delegation, where news of the Hungarian Uprising had reached him. GDR media talked of counterrevolution, plundering, and mob law. The borders were closed, and railway and telephone connections were interrupted. The director of the academy, Walter Freund, later informed State Security that Steinitz had suddenly become very ill in Moscow. He had considerable pain and could hardly walk but desperately wanted to meet Greta Kuckhoff, who was booked at the same hotel. Freund guessed that Steinitz wanted to discuss "the news from Hungary."[5] To his great regret, he was unable to tell State Security anything about the discussion because his boss left him standing at the door.

Preserving Socialism?

While the "thaw" (cautious liberalization "from above") awakened hopes of a new Spring of Dreams among the GDR's communist intellectuals, forced destalinization caused great anxiety in the streets of Hungarian cities, as had been the case with earlier unrest in June 1953.

Now the only issue at stake was preserving socialism, a secure island in a hostile sea. All criticism of party politics was to cease. Anna Seghers gave expression to her uncertain fears when she appealed to the head of the Aufbau publishing company, Walter Janka, to get her friend, the internationally renowned cultural scientist Georg Lukács, out of Hungary and save him. She had already discussed the details with the minister for culture, Becher. Accordingly, Janka was to try and reach Hungary via Austria and use US dollars "to buy Lukács from the Counterrevolutionaries" (this was how it was described at the time). In an essay written in 1989, Walter Janka (1989: 32) likened it "to being in a second-rate criminal film."

The plan failed because Walter Ulbricht vetoed it, so Janka did not even set off from Hungary. How could Anna Seghers have imagined that her Hungarian friend wished to be rescued? Lukács became minister of culture in Imre Nagy's reform government. His life was only really in danger when Soviet troops marched into Hungary and deported him and other ministers to Romania. But that is another story.

Nine months later in July 1957, Walter Janka was sentenced to five years' imprisonment by the Supreme Court in the GDR. The indictment stated that he had wanted to bring Georg Lukács to Berlin to import "counterrevolution" into the GDR. As Janka later bitterly recalled, Anna Seghers sat in the courtroom's front row, together with other writers, and looked down in silence while listening to the absurd allegations. It was said that her presence at the hearing was arranged at a higher level—a calculated form of intimidation and humiliation that she accepted without protest.

Jürgen Kuczynski called the period after the suppression of the Hungarian Uprising the "frost after the thaw." The 2 December 1956 entry in Alfred Kantorowicz's (1961b: 691) journal reads, "The terrorization of beliefs takes on ever more unbearable forms. When Soviet troops marched into Hungary it was the signal for our Gauleiter to hit out at all those who dared to voice criticism in the previous months."

Wolfgang Steinitz "fled" to the hospital, where for months he suffered from jaundice and severe scoliosis. At the Thirty-Fifth Convention of the SED Central Committee in February 1958, a triumphant Walter Ulbricht, once again firmly in the saddle, exposed Schirdewan-Wollweber, a faction antagonistic to the party. He also attacked Wolfgang Steinitz, alleging that by promoting the publication of the article by Kuczynski and Behrens in June 1956, Steinitz had "posed the question about the representation of revisionist opinions."[6] This accusation seemed all the more threatening since now ostracized SED officials Karl Schirdewan and Ernst Wollweber had been comrades to Steinitz in Breslau since the 1920s.

On 23 June 1958, after his discharge from the hospital and a few days after Imre Nagy had been hanged in Hungary, Wolfgang Steinitz wrote a letter to the SED leadership distancing himself from earlier statements. On no account, he wrote, had he intended to defend the position taken by Kuczynski and Behrens, nor did he support "the freedom to express revisionist opinions." He maintained that he had never read Kuczynski's contentious article titled "Controversy, Dogmatism and Liberal Critique." He accused himself of "formal and undialectical" behavior and assured that "in the future he would toe the party line as he had done until now."[7] His prostration could not have been lower. Steinitz surrendered every position he had adopted between the Twentieth Communist Party Congress and the Hungarian Uprising. Jürgen Kuczynski, against his better judgment, also practiced the requisite self-criticism after months of agitation and threats against him. Only Alfred Kantorowicz, one of the few to refuse to lend support to the SED leadership's "Hungary resolution," left the GDR for the FRG in August 1957. As recently as October 1949, he had viewed such a step as unacceptable: "In West Germany, where Nazism as an attitude in life is still, and is again, virulent," he wrote in his diary, "I would be discriminated against as a Spanish civil war fighter, an emigrant and even a writer" (Kantorowicz 1961a: 649). Despite that approach, he still found himself fallen between two stools, as he predicted.

The Everyday Routine of Repression

Others paid a high price for staying. The Spring of Dreams was over, only to be followed by the everyday routine of repression. There is no doubt that those who stayed had retreated not only in the face of Soviet panzers and pressure from party bureaucrats. It is in fact likely that the exiled remigrants of Jewish extraction were not even conscious of the extent to which their thinking and feeling were influenced by the experiences of Nazi persecution and the murder of close family members. The people eulogized in poems and festive speeches seemed to change before their very eyes into the screaming masses of the Third Reich, brandishing torches and screaming "Heil." Fears of the unforeseeable consequences of an uprising that they—silently of course—saw as a pogrom drove them into the arms of the authorities. They were caught in the trap of their own loyalty.

Disillusioned, Wolfgang Steinitz withdrew from political engagement. In March 1959, he was once again elected vice president of the Academy of Sciences for another four years, even though his eligibility for office had long since expired; this was apparently because the SED regarded him as a key figure in academic relations with the Federal Republic and Austria, and as irreplaceable for the Eastern European academies. At the same time, Steinitz was the subject of surveillance by State Security, something that could not be kept from him, as his wife and secretary later explained. His health in tatters, he died in 1967 at the age of sixty-two.

Disillusion and self-denunciation left their mark on the work of Anna Seghers. Her socialist contemporary novels did not achieve the intensity and clarity of her earlier work. "It doesn't stick as it used to," she wrote in 1958 to her Brazilian writer colleague Jorge Amado and his wife Celia. "It is colder than it used to be whether someone condones it or not." She referred to her unfairly persecuted comrades in poetic code as "my brother ravens" who had scattered and whom she had to find again. In another letter, she conjured the image of the raven and added, "If I see them again they won't have any feathers. I will permit myself the illusion that my presence might occasionally have prevented the loss of a feather" (Romero 1993: 178).

Apparently, only Jürgen Kuczynski remained unscathed for another three decades, having maintained his balancing act between autonomy and repression and between spirit and power. He was also the only member of the generation of GDR founding fathers who, after peaceful revolution and German reunification, publicly came to terms with the failure of his own strategy. The aged academic castigated himself for the "political stupidity" that caused him to join with the SED leadership in making mistakes that he kept justifying. He had criticized only specific phenomena of the system, he wrote, instead of perceiving its "basic errors"—for example, the lack of democracy (Kuczynski 1998: 18).

The virtuous tactician conceded all this only to perform a rhetorical somersault, presenting his blindness and compromises as a success. How should he have behaved, he asked in his book *Der treue Rebell* (The loyal rebel), had he recognized the system's weakness in 1958:

Had I publicized my realization, I would have been "finished" . . . . It would have been out of the question for me to abscond to the FRG because I took the view that their system was even worse than ours. But if I had said nothing, would I not have always felt a coward? No matter the result, the paradox is that only by committing the worst political mistake, namely, to affirm the GDR system, could I be useful to thousands, nay tens of thousands of people. (Kuczynski 1998: 22)

Presumably unintentionally, Kuczynski sketched the dilemma from which, one way or another, neither he nor anyone in his cohort could escape. In constant danger of being caught between the millstones of the Cold War, pursued by the demons of the past, clinging to the gospel of the future, there was obviously nowhere in Germany where they could simply live in the present without distortion.

Annette Leo was born in 1948 in Düsseldorf. In 1952, Leo moved with her parents to Berlin. Her father was the journalist Gerhard Leo. She graduated from high school in 1966, completed a traineeship at the *Berliner Zeitung* in 1968, studied history and romance studies at the Humboldt-Universität zu Berlin in East Berlin from 1968 to 1973, and worked as a journalist for the magazine *Horizont*. From 1982 to 1986, she worked as an editor for *Neue Berliner Illustrierte*, and from 1986 to 1989 as a freelance historian and journalist. In 1991, Annette Leo published a biography of her grandfather Dagobert Lubinski, a communist journalist and resistance fighter who was murdered as a Jew at Auschwitz (*Briefe zwischen Kommen und Gehen* [Letters between coming and going]). From 1991 to 1993, she worked as a research assistant at the Prenzlauer Berg Museum, and from 1993 to 1996 at the Research Institute for Worker Education in Recklinghausen. From 2001 to 2005, she worked at the Center for Research on Antisemitism at the Technical University of Berlin, where she published a biography of Wolfgang Steinitz in 2004. She then moved to the Historical Institute of the Friedrich Schiller University of Jena as a research assistant. Her biography of GDR author Erwin Strittmatter was published in 2012.

Notes

This essay first appeared in German in a volume published by the Wallstein Verlag Göttingen (von der Lühe, Schildt, and Schüler-Springorum 2008). The editors are grateful to be able to offer a second imprint.

1. From a letter from Wolfgang Steinitz to Hans Steinitz dated 1 November 1946 (from author's private archive).
2. From a letter from Wolfgang Steinitz to Inge Steinitz dated January/February1946 (Peters 1989, 110–111).

3. See "Lessons from the Trial against the Slansky Conspiracy Center: Resolution of the Central Committee of the SED of 20 December 1952" (Keßler 1995, 153–155).

4. Cited from an unpublished interview by Hans Bunge with Inge Steinitz during 1979 (from author's private archive).

5. Cited in Notifications from Gen. Walter Freund, 17 January 1958, Bundesbeauftragter für die Stasi Unterlagen (BStU), APO 5532/64, Vol. 2, Sheet 85.

6. Walter Ulbricht, Closing Speech at the 35th Convention of the SED Central Committee. Archive of the Berlin-Brandenburg Academy of Sciences, Steinitz Estate, no. 81.

7. Wolfgang Steinitz to the political office of the SED Central Committee, 23 June 1958, Archive of Berlin-Brandenburg, Academy of Sciences, Steinitz Estate, no. 81.

References

Brecht, Bertolt. 1969. "Radwechsel." In *Buckower Elegien,* vol. 7, 85. Berlin.
———. 1983. *Arbeitsjournal, 1938–1955.* Berlin.
Janka, Walter. 1989. *Schwierigkeiten mit der Wahrheit.* Reinbek.
Kantorowicz, Alfred. 1961a. *Deutsches Tagebuch,* vol. 1. Munich.
———. 1961b. *Deutsches Tagebuch,* vol. 2. Munich.
Keßler, Mario. 1995. *Die SED und die Juden: Zwischen Repression und Toleranz.* Berlin.
Kuczynski, Jürgen. 1985. *Dialog mit meinem Urenkel: Neunzehn Briefe und ein Tagebuch. . . .* Berlin.
———. 1992. *Ein linientreuer Dissident: Erinnerungen 1945–1989.* Berlin.
———. 1998. *Ein treuer Rebell: Erinnerungen 1994–1997.* Berlin.
Peters, Jan, ed. 1989. *Zweimal Stockholm-Berlin 1946.* Berlin.
Romero, Christiane Zehl. 1993. *Anna Seghers.* Reinbek.
Berger, Christel, ed. 2000. *Anna Seghers. Hier im Volk der kalten Herzen: Briefwechsel 1947.* Berlin.
Von der Lühe, Irmela, Axel Schildt, and Stefanie Schüler-Springorum, eds. 2008. *Auch in Deutschland waren wir nicht wirklich zu Hause.* Göttingen.

Chapter 2

The Effects of a Taboo

Jews and Antisemitism in the GDR

Anetta Kahane

My brief essay addresses a topic that has not received much critical attention in Germany: antisemitism in the German Democratic Republic (GDR) and its consequences. I begin by explaining this taboo and how it functioned, and then draw on my parents' story, which was fairly typical for Jews in the GDR, to explain how this taboo affected them. I will outline six different phases that I have identified.

A taboo is a ban whose content is perceived as so disturbing to the social or personal circumstances of those involved that it is made to disappear. It is not quite the same as a proscription—the outright prohibition of a behavior. With a taboo, those who do not avoid the behavior in question are punished, and in this way behavior is controlled.

In the narrative of the GDR, the mass murder of the Jews simply because they were Jews was largely ignored. What was known: among the numerous crimes committed by the "fascists," some Jews also met their deaths. But the main perceived victims of National Socialism were the German people, in particular the working class.

Accordingly, antisemitism or racism appeared merely as ancillary contradictions staged by capitalists to divert attention from the class struggle. The fate of the Jews, insofar as it was mentioned at all, was regarded as a minor incident. The subject was fascism—i.e., not National

Socialism—and a plot by capitalist financiers that involved particularly aggressive exploitation. The concentration camps, sources of slave labor for German companies, held inmates from all over Europe, including Poland, the Netherlands, and beyond. The victims of persecution and extermination were primarily resistance fighters, communists, socialists, and trade unionists. And, somehow, Jews as well. Jewish living and Jewish dying were rendered invisible in the GDR. The perpetrator's motives for exterminating the Jews remained unmentioned.

Following the logic of class struggle in the GDR, anyone who believed in God was a Jew. Anyone who held this belief did so voluntarily, renouncing the enlightened spirit of historical materialism. This person was regarded as reactionary, since religions were presumed to serve the suppression and manipulation of the masses.

The reduction of Jewish identity to religious faith not only demonstrated disastrous ignorance but it also served above all to exonerate the German working class, which had supported the Nazis and was thus complicit in their crimes. Communists explained the seduction by Hitler almost exclusively in terms of economic and social factors such as mass unemployment. Incidentally, this explanatory model has endured until the present day as a justification for right-wing extremist or right-wing populist movements.

According to this interpretation, antisemitism did not really exist in the GDR. It was merely a capitalist diversionary tactic. For socialists, the problem had been overcome. If there is no capitalism, then there's no antisemitism either. It had been, according to Erich Honecker, extirpated root and branch.

From the narrative of antisemitism, the taboo lost its function and the Jews as its object. Gradually, even the word "Jew" disappeared in the GDR. And with it, the memory of, and—much more important—an engagement with, Jewish history and antisemitism. The result: antisemitism prevailed. And its effects were all the more potent. How did the taboo affect the GDR's Jews? In my family, I have identified six different phases in this process.

The Return

Why did Jews return to Germany? Here, I do not mean displaced persons emerging from the camps who were stranded in Germany and ultimately remained there. Rather, I'm talking about German Jews. As a rule, following a successful emigration, they did not return to Germany.

There were exceptions, however. Returnees were often those who did not regard their Jewishness, and thus the narrative of persecution, as identity-forming. Instead, they shared a commitment to opposing social inequity and political and ideological convictions. They subordinated their experiences as individuals to a larger interest in political change. This required a great deal of repression but also a great deal of courage. In a way, their social conscience tapped into a Jewish tradition called *Zedaka*, which Gershon Sholem described as secular messianism. Moreover, many communist Jews who were active in the labor movement not only believed in the idea of socialism but also belonged, in their view, to the only group that was authentic and rigorous in its antifascism. This is why they felt protected and, at the same time, subject to potent peer pressure. Under threats of rejection, isolation, or worse, they were well advised to conform. The stronger and longer lasting their ties to the Communist Party, the more the Jews feared losing these bonds.

Among those returning, many had been active in the resistance to fascism. Armed or as spies, they fought against the Nazis. Returning home to a defeated Germany brought the satisfaction of having contributed, as Jews, to liberation. In the Communist Party, many had had their first experiences of being treated as equals.

Yet Jews in the movement remained well aware that these experiences were not without contradictions. If they could not endure these contradictions, their inviolable loyalty to the party would end. This happened frequently during the resistance and then subsequently during the establishment of socialism. The consequences were invariably dramatic. Those who endured developed a marked ability to cope with cognitive dissonance, which they retained until the very end.

Fear

Choosing between fears—this was the phrase used in my parents' circles. In 1945, they arrived in bombed-out Berlin's Soviet Occupation Zone (SBZ). They were, said the party, urgently needed for building the new society. Following terror, war, and camps, this was an alluring prospect. My father, a child from the ghetto, saw the possibility of doing something meaningful as an equal among equals. His confidence in the idea, his struggle, and his will to survive had carried him this far. My mother's case was similar. Both happily seized the opportunity to attend the Nuremberg trials as reporters for the Soviet News Bureau (Sowjetisches Nachrichtenbüro / SNB). This was a welcome curative to the trauma of the preceding twelve years. Sitting face to face with the murderers and reporting on the guilty verdicts was some sort of recompense for the suffering they had endured.

In those initial years after 1945, the party and government were reconstituted in the SBZ. For the first time, German communists were tasked with forming a government, setting up an economy, and putting institutions in place. It cannot be doubted that this was a major motivating factor behind efforts to begin rebuilding. The high hopes invested in this process are easy to imagine. As a child and teenager, my father, who grew up in the Berlin ghetto, endured endless discriminatory and humiliating experiences as a "Jewish brat," even before the Nazis came to power.

My parents were sent to Prague by the party in 1949 but left the city even before a year had passed. Alongside the communist rise to power, the political atmosphere was becoming suffused with Stalinist-style antisemitism. In the power struggles of those years, Jews in the party, subjected to conspiracy theories, fell into disfavor. It wasn't long until the Slánský trials began, which ended in multiple executions.

My parents, too, had reasons to be afraid. They fit the pattern by which alleged enemies of the revolution were identified. A wave of persecution began in the newly founded German Democratic Republic (GDR). Jewish communists and, above all, those who were emigrants to the West during the war were treated with suspicion and persecuted.

Those unable to recover from the humiliation or cover it with the taboo left the country. Persecutions reached a climax in 1953, when the first trials had already begun. The victims included some of my parents' closest friends, and my parents were placed under surveillance. The secret police had a comprehensive file on the General German News Service (Allgemeiner Deutscher Nachrichtendienst / ADN), the GDR's news agency, which was cofounded by my father. He and his Jewish colleagues were accused of Zionism and cosmopolitanism, both antisemitic code words.

What remained after the persecutions, which gradually ended after Stalin's death, was loyalty to the taboo and to the party, and the realization that being a Jew under socialism entailed a high level of risk.

Flight

Following my parents' departure from Prague and waiting out the wave of persecution against wartime emigrants to the West came a period of relative tranquility. Provided their loyalty to the party was assured, Jews were still permitted to assist in establishing socialism. But most were relegated to second- or third-tier positions. Many promising careers ended before they properly began, and my father was no exception. He was a journalist, not a diplomat, and not even the editor of a newspaper. He never made it to a top-ranking post, which was both painful and liberating. He was freed from responsibility and dangerous pressure. At all costs, he was determined to avoid becoming a target of antisemitic accusations once more.

But the fear sat too deep, and the humiliation that stemmed from his exclusion from the upper echelons upset him profoundly. For this reason, he asked an old influential comrade to post him abroad as a foreign correspondent as soon as possible. He wanted to observe the GDR from a distance, and report from other countries rather than engaging too closely at home. His friend understood his request, and offered him a choice between two locations: Cairo and New Delhi. My father opted for New Delhi, of course. As a Jew, Cairo would not have been a good choice.

Thus began Max Kahane's existence outside Germany and the GDR. The family followed him to India from 1957 to 1960. All his working life, he was traveling and thus escaping fear and reality in the GDR. Like many Jewish remigrants who opted for the GDR, fear and escaping reality were interlinked.

The party sent him and two other Jews to the Eichmann trial in 1961. At this point, it must be noted unequivocally that Jews who remained in Germany feared Nazi officials and dignitaries in the FRG even more than antisemitic persecution by their own comrades. For them, these were more than just class enemies; they were the murderers of their families. While the ideological narrative of the class character of these Nazis had enabled them to return to the new Germany, these Jews shared with all victims rage and fear of the perpetrators.

The journey to Israel was a huge challenge for my father. First, he loved Israel and admired the pioneering spirit and freedom of young Jews there. But as a citizen of the GDR, he was absolutely prohibited from being a "Zionist." He was required to not perceive himself as a Jew. And if he perceived himself as a Jew, then he was required to identify as an anti-Zionist Jew, which he wasn't.

Second, while tasked with reporting on the trial, he was not allowed to invoke the perspectives of Jewish victims. Not only because, in the narrative of the GDR, the victims of fascism were mostly resistance fighters, but also because Jews were peripheral figures in this story. He was also instructed by the party to focus on the perpetrators. His editorial for the *Neues Deutschland* was tailored to this mission statement: "In the person of Eichmann, Bonn is on trial." Former Nazis in the federal government, particularly Hans Globke, were to be linked to Eichmann. What was at stake here was nothing less than the moral heritage of the GDR, which was to be portrayed as diametrically opposed to the FRG, a hotbed of unrepentant Nazis.

The taboo shaped these contradictions: not recognizing Jewish victims meant suppressing his own life story, while focusing on Globke meant ignoring his own experiences following the antisemitic trials and projecting onto the West his feelings of fear and rage. This should in no way be taken to signify that accusations against the FRG were unjustified. But the ability to transfer conflicts and doubts onto one's opponent was a defining characteristic of socialism, consummately perfected by Jewish communists.

Tensions and Detente

The 1970s ushered in a phase of relative tranquility; the eras of Walter Ulbricht and Stalin were over. The GDR was admitted to the UN, and my father traveled around the world. The GDR attempted to project an appealing image abroad. Under Erich Honecker, there was also an economic upturn. Fear vanished, but the taboo remained. The schizophrenia of a Jewish existence in socialist Germany persisted but was held at bay by hope and consolidation.

My mother was an artist who died in the mid-1970s. She was the daughter of an assimilated Jewish engineer and a Polish-born shoe shop assistant. Her father was a nephew of Victor Klemperer. Since the emancipation of the Jews, the Klemperers carefully obliterated any possible traces of their Jewish identity. When the Nazis came to power, my grandmother, who was already divorced, immediately emigrated to Spain. Her Jewish ex-husband remained, and together with his new family, was murdered in Auschwitz. So there were few traces of Jewish identity in my mother's social life. Still, she felt particularly alienated in Germany after the war. This was because she, much more than my father, was a true cosmopolitan.

Yet the taboo seemed to affect her not as severely as my father. My mother lost her unloved father and stepsiblings in Auschwitz, and her brother died shortly after the two of them were liberated from the concentration camp. Victor Klemperer was her only remaining family. Following his experiences in Dresden from 1933 to 1945, Klemperer learned to reluctantly identify as a Jew. He was an intellectual with charm, a sense of humor, and a sophisticated awareness of his environment. He noticed early on that the GDR also employed totalitarian language patterns, something he repeatedly expressed in his conversations with my mother.

My mother lived as a painter in the GDR. She received orders, had exhibitions, and obeyed the rules of socialist realism. She enjoyed her best times abroad, where she didn't have to conceal her polyglot talents or suppress her personal warmth. Her childhood and adolescence were difficult: she struggled to survive outside the law in France and was denounced, managed to escape Vichy police, and was denounced once again. She was sent to the camp where trains left for Auschwitz and every day witnessed trains filled with children destined for death. This experience had a profound and lasting effect on her. She didn't need an explicitly Jewish upbringing to fall under the taboo; it was reflected in my mother's reluctance to engage at all with the vagaries of her life story and her emotions. She died at the age of 56.

Doubts

In the 1980s, doubts set in. Erich Honecker had not delivered on hopes for deregulation, and the GDR's economy was in crisis. Popular dissatisfaction with the regime was growing. Due to labor shortages, workers arrived from "friendly" nations. Racism in society became evident, directed at many Vietnamese and Africans who came to study but ended up working on a production line. The most striking symptom of the crisis, however, was the growing neo-Nazi scene in the GDR. In addition to hooligans and racist skinheads, some milieus—unrepentantly right-wing and openly racist—had links to government. These racist tendencies were also apparent in the police and the People's Army. Thus the taboo proved ineffective.

Watching these developments, my father closed his eyes. A right-wing extremist mindset was being disseminated subcutaneously, so to speak. But my father, long retired, refused to allow old fears to regain their power over him. Despite criticism of real socialism, which even he expressed, he was not prepared to consider the imminent failure of antifascism, the paramount motive for his return.

Finally realizing that the GDR no longer served its purpose as a protective instrument against Nazis, I applied for emigration. This offended my father so deeply that he stopped talking to me. For me, as a child of the second generation of Shoah survivors, this was impossible to endure. My father was prepared to see his daughter depart without a word, instead of discussing whether his decision to return to Germany might have been wrong. We spoke about Jewish identity and knew that we partially embraced it in our own lives. But preferring to sacrifice your own child to the god of cognitive dissonance rather than questioning ideology was a human disaster. However circuitous, it was the effect of the taboo.

The End

For an enlightened intellectual socialist, my father accepted the fall of the Berlin Wall with relative equanimity. When the GDR then collapsed, he became gloomy for quite some time. He was undoubtedly asking himself all the salient political questions: What did we do wrong? How could we have prevented this? Was it wrong to return to Germany? He avoided speaking openly on these matters.

When the taboo vanished, together with the GDR, he rejoined the Jewish congregation and even sometimes attended synagogue. He was happy that his life looked Jewish once again. And he began to tell stories from his Hassidic childhood.

With concern, my father observed my own efforts to oppose Nazis in the five new eastern states of reunified Germany. Gradually, he came to share my analysis: the problem was inherent to the GDR, and antisemitism was still intact after a period of hibernation.

On 21 August 2004, my father died at the age of ninety-four. In his will, he left instructions to bury him in the Jewish cemetery in Berlin-Weissensee, next to the grave of his parents, which like 103 others, had been destroyed by neo-Nazis five years earlier. He forbade his old comrades from attending the funeral. The only exception was Nathan Steinberger, his childhood friend from the Scheunenviertel district, who spent twenty-two years in a gulag in Kazakhstan under Stalin.

Anetta Kahane, born in 1954 in East Berlin, is a German journalist and author. She holds a degree in Latin American Studies and has worked as a translator. In 1990, she was the first commissioner for foreigners of the East Berlin Magistrate, and after reunification she helped establish the Regional Office for Foreigners (RAA) in Berlin and advocated intercultural education at schools in the new federal states. In late 1998, she co-founded the Amadeu Antonio Foundation, where she has been full-time chairperson since 2003. From 1974 to 1982, she was forced to work as an unofficial collaborator with GDR State Security. She ended this forced cooperation in 1982 because she no longer wanted to support racist practices of GDR functionaries. Since this collaboration became publicly known in 2002, right-wing extremists and right-wing populists have targeted her in campaigns against her and the foundation. In 1991, she was awarded the Theodor Heuss Medal, alongside Joachim Gauck, Christian Führer, David Gill, Ulrike Poppe, and Jens Reich. In 2002, she was awarded the Moses Mendelssohn Prize of the State of Berlin. For several years, she has worked as a columnist for *Berliner Zeitung* and has written for *Zeit, Tageszeitung,*

Stern, *Tagesspiegel*, and other publications. She is the author of the book *Ich sehe was, was du nicht siehst* (I see what you don't see) (Berlin 2004).

References

Kahane, Anetta. 1992. "Fremdheit mit Folgen: Geschichte einer Ausländerbeauftragten." In *Fremd in einem kalten Land: Ausländer in Deutschland*, edited by Namo Aziz and Thea Bauriedl, 137–146. Freiburg.

———. 1993. "Ich durfte, die anderen mußten . . . ." In *Zwischen Thora und Trabant. Juden in der DDR*, edited by Vincent von Wroblewsky, 124–144. Berlin.

———. 2000. "Manche Dinge brauchen eben Zeit." In *Wir sind da! Die Geschichte der Juden in Deutschland von 1945 bis heute*, edited by Richard Chaim Schneider, 324–340. Berlin.

———. 2003. "Ich habe die Möglichkeit, etwas zu tun." In *Augenblicke. Portraits von Juden in Deutschland*, edited by Elma Balster, 45–46. Berlin.

———. 2004. *Ich sehe was, was du nicht siehst: Meine deutschen Geschichten*. Berlin.

———. 2005. "Jeckes in der DDR." In *Die Jeckes*, edited by Gisela Dachs, 95–106. Frankfurt a. M.

Chapter 3

Divided City—Shared Memory?

Dealing with the Nazi Past in
East and West Berlin from 1948 to 1961

Gerd Kühling

Amid Cold War tensions between the Federal Republic of Germany (FRG) and the German Democratic Republic (GDR), the ways in which the two states addressed National Socialism emerged as one of the most contentious issues. Historical and political controversies were particularly pronounced in divided Berlin, where divergent approaches to dealing with the past became more evident than anywhere else. This phenomenon has been the subject of historical research. Just a few years after reunification, scholars examined how the Nazi past was addressed in East and West Germany. The literature includes Jeffrey Herf's (German translation 1997) *Divided Memory: The Nazi Past in the Two Germanys* and Jürgen Danyel's (1995) *Die geteilte Vergangenheit*. Yet only recently has critical attention turned to the politics of memory in the "Cold War capital" (Endlich 2014). The emergence of a memorial landscape in Berlin was shaped by the East-West conflict and by decisive events in German-German postwar history, including the Berlin blockade and airlift, the founding of the FRG and the GDR, and the construction of the Berlin Wall. Another important factor for the shaping of memory politics was that it was possible to cross the border between 1948 and 1961, which allowed for joint forms of "coming to terms with the past" (Kühling 2016a).

There are a few studies of divided Berlin's open border and its "relative permeability of (political) systems" (Lemke 2011: 11–12). Most research only marginally addresses the commemoration of Nazi crimes (Lemke 2011) or looks at border traffic as a general phenomenon (Roggenbuch 2008). While these studies consider particular themes and actors within the process of "coming to terms with the past," the border's permeability is not examined in detail. In West Berlin, for example, Reinhard Strecker initiated the late 1950s exhibition *Unpunished Nazi Judiciary*, which called attention to the many former Nazi lawyers who continued to play a role in the legal system of the Federal Republic (Glienke 2008a). Turning to East Berlin, essays have covered history exhibitions, for example, at the Museum of German History (MfDG) (Brait 2013), and the GDR's attacks on the FRG concerning policies that dealt with the past. The latter includes the so-called "blood judges" campaign established by the Committee for German Unity (Ausschuß für Deutsche Einheit, ADE). Between 1957 and 1959, more than a thousand former Nazi lawyers in the West German judiciary were "exposed" (Bästlein 1994). The open border between the two political systems, however, has not figured in this analysis.

In the 1990s, historians of contemporary history began using the phrase "asymmetric interwoven parallel history" (Kleßmann 1999) to call for an all-German "integrated history" (Brunner 2013). Berlin from 1948 to 1961 offers "almost ideal-typical" conditions (Hochmuth 2013), but this approach remains unusual. In 2015, when Reinhard Strecker was awarded the Federal Cross of Merit, reports and speeches noted that his exhibition *Unpunished Nazi Judiciary* was unfairly criticized as communist propaganda, and that Strecker was personally defamed as an "agitator on behalf of the Soviets."[1] There was no mention, however, of the taboos Strecker had breached. In late 1958, for example, after he was denied access to the archives in the Federal Republic, he ventured across the open sector border to research files at the ADE in East Berlin (Glienke 2008a: 69–71).

The following essay will elucidate the development of the landscape of commemoration and memorials in Berlin after the city was divided and while connections continued between the two German states from 1948 to 1961. Special attention is given to the actions of private individuals involved in commemorative efforts, such as Gerhard Schoenberner, an initiator of the exhibition *The Past Admonishes*. Schoenberner later became the first chairman of the association Aktives Museum and founding director of the House of the Wannsee Conference Memorial.[2] The approach adopted here makes it possible to address the confrontation with the Nazi past as an all-German experience since it was easier for nongovernmental actors to defy the borders of the Cold War. This essay also investigates where traces of early commemorations of Nazi crimes can be found in Berlin's present-day memorial landscape.

Commemoration in Berlin Following the City's Division

At first glance, it appears that before 1948/49, the city's partition into four sectors had little impact on the commemoration of Nazi crimes. Beginning in the summer of 1945, remembrance policies in the entire city were organized by the Victims of Fascism Main Committee, a department of the Office for Social Services that planned a memorial day for the "victims of fascism," among other events. Official East-West commemorative efforts parted ways in September 1948. As a result of the Soviet blockade of Berlin and SED-directed attacks on the city council, that year's memorial day for the victims of fascism took place as separate events on both sides of the city. On the west side of Berlin, a small event was held at the former execution site in Plötzensee. On the city's east side, the SED orchestrated a mass rally in the Lustgarten (Kühling 2016a: 118–130). The SED's central newspaper *Neues Deutschland* stressed the "mass participation" of residents of Berlin's Western sectors.[3]

Berlin's commemorative efforts were completely divided even before Berlin's administration was split and the two German states were founded in 1949. From that point on, commemoration in East and West remained strictly separate, although in East Berlin, the capital of the GDR, negative references to the opponent's side were pronounced. Despite this asymmetry in memorial rituals, each side appealed unequivocally to their role in the resistance against Hitler as a means of legitimizing their claim to rule. While West Berlin and the Federal Republic highlighted the military resistance of 20 July 1944, in the GDR, official commemoration was narrowly focused on communist resistance. On both sides of the border, the integration of the majority population into its respective political system was emphasized. This had a direct impact on remembrance initiatives: The state deferred from establishing monuments dedicated to the Jewish victims of the Nazis, since this would have raised the implicit question of the role played by the perpetrators and their accomplices in the genocide. Commemoration remained vague. A search for the names of crime sites or the number of victims was futile. Organizations representing former Nazi victims and the Jewish community were alone in their efforts to counter these trends (Kühling 2016b: 35–36).

Gerd Kühling

Coming to Terms with the Past in East Berlin and Its References to the West

As Germany's division solidified in the mid-1950s, the GDR's rhetorical attacks on the Federal Republic grew increasingly vehement (Lemke 1999: 76–78). Those in charge of politics and propaganda in East Berlin kept close watch over what was happening on the west side of the city. The book *Das Dritte Reich und die Juden* (The Third Reich and the Jews), published by Arani in 1955, illustrates this point. This collection of documents, compiled by Joseph Wulf and Léon Poliakov, was one of the first publications on the Nazi genocide of Jews to appear in German in the Federal Republic.

The GDR promptly exploited this book to orchestrate an attack on a political opponent (Seydewitz 1956: 43). The point of contention was the book's references to Otto Bräutigam, an employee of the West German Foreign Office, and his involvement in Nazi crimes. The "Bräutigam Affair" dominated German newspapers at the time (Conze et al. 2010: 587–589). The ADE described a "second Nazi takeover in Bonn."[4] The GDR newspaper *Neues Deutschland* asserted, "No matter where one looks in West Germany, one finds the Hitler fascists and Nazi military in prominent positions. There is Bräutigam and Globke, Kraft and Oberländer."[5] These attacks revealed a dominant feature of the GDR's dealings with the Nazi past. When the genocide of the Jews was addressed by GDR politicians, it was almost always in reference to the Federal Republic—to assign all criminal responsibility to the West German elite.

The GDR aimed to destabilize the West German state and expose it internationally. Additionally, it hoped to appeal to critical groups in the Federal Republic and West Berlin and legitimize its own system of rule. Although the borders of the Federal Republic and crossings between Berlin's western sectors and their surrounding areas had been closed since 1952, it was still possible, within Berlin, to cross sector boundaries in both directions. The GDR made constant reference to this situation, pointing out that people on both sides of the city were participating in events against people who murdered Jews "and pogrom heroes of the Bonn government."[6] In fact, the locations of these protests and commemorative events were often chosen for their attractiveness and accessibility to West Berlin residents. In 1956, on the anniversary of the November pogrom (*Kristallnacht*), for example, a rally was held in the Friedrichstadt-Palast,[7] a variety theater that was popular among West Berliners (Lemke 2011: 631). For press conferences on the "blood judges" campaign, the ADE invited guests to the House of the National Council,[8] located at Thälmannplatz (formerly Wilhelmplatz), south of the Brandenburg Gate and right at the

Figure 3.1. International press conference of the Committee for German Unity, at which Albert Norden (2nd from left) presents a "brown book" on Theodor Oberländer Berlin (East), 2 February 1960. Bundesarchiv, Photo 183-70560-006, photographer: Heinz Junge.

sector boundary. In 1960, an elaborately orchestrated show trial was held (in absentia) against Theodor Oberländer—who was serving as Federal Minister for Displaced Persons, Refugees, and Victims of War in Bonn—at the Supreme Court of the GDR on Invalidenstrasse. The courthouse was located just a "stone's throw . . . from the sector boundary," reported the trial observer of the West Berlin *Telegraf*.[9] It was equally convenient to reach the ADE's exhibition on people who murdered Jews and Hans Globke, which was held in the BZ Pavilion on Friedrichstrasse in the late summer of 1960. According to a report in *Neues Deutschland*, the exhibition was especially well attended by "West Berliners, West Germans, and foreigners."[10] The East Berlin *Berliner Zeitung* even quoted one visitor from Bonn, who asked, "Why don't we see something like this in West Germany?"[11]

Another site that illustrates the competition over remembrance in divided Berlin was the Museum of German History, which opened in 1952 in the Zeughaus building on Unter den Linden. This central history museum of the GDR attracted large numbers of visitors from the West, a fact that the GDR, in its constant need for recognition, frequently noted. In this context, a West Berlin working-class family was ostentatiously celebrated as the museum's "one millionth visitor" in 1958.[12] The temporary exhibition *Ten Years of the GDR* that opened that year demonstrated how the GDR incorporated the museum into its efforts to undermine the West. Museum staff were instructed on how to respond to certain questions from West Berliners, and an entire section of the exhibition focused exclusively on the Federal Republic (Andrews 2015: 45). The press stated that "photos and documents prove that West Germany is governed by monopoly, militarism, and revanchism; that the spoilers of the past have once again become the powerful of today."[13] To underscore this point, the words of a West German visitor were cited; he conceded that "the former fascists among us have been given too much freedom."[14] Shortly after the opening, the *Berliner Zeitung* reported from the east side of the city that "hundreds of West Berliners" had already visited the exhibition.[15]

The GDR's eagerness to build on the expectations and viewing habits of Western visitors was illustrated in the April 1960 exhibition *Fifteen Years of Liberation*. Resistance against National Socialism was one theme addressed in the exhibition,[16] and, as expected, attention was overwhelmingly focused on communist resistance. Keeping Western visitors in mind, the exhibition honored Social Democrat Rudolf Breitscheid, trade unionist Wilhelm Leuschner, the resistance group Uncle Emil, the Scholl siblings, and the 20 July 1944 assassin Count Schenk von Stauffenberg. When it came to the genocide of European Jewry, the exhibition also took into account its Western viewers. One photograph presented the well-known image of a young boy with his arms raised following the defeat of the Warsaw Ghetto uprising.[17] This photograph had become familiar to the public in the Federal Republic through the film *Night and Fog*, and through copies printed in school textbooks and magazines (Knoch 2001: 529, 571).

Needless to say, the exhibition harshly attacked the Federal Republic. *Neues Deutschland* reported, "This was the spirit that was supposed to 'heal the world,' according to the views of Hitler, Himmler, Göring, and their compliant henchmen Oberländer, Globke, Schröder, Speidel, Heusinger, who we find in the second part of the exhibition, once again in exalted positions in the Bonn state."[18] A few days later, the SED newspaper

Figure 3.2. View into the exhibition *15 Years of Liberation* in the Museum of German History in the Zeughaus, Berlin (East), 26 April 1960. Bundesarchiv, Picture 183-72629-000, photographer: not specified.

Die Wahrheit, which was printed for Berlin's western sectors, published a letter to the editor from a West Berlin Social Democrat on the "liberation exhibition." He recommended "bringing a great many West Berliners to this exhibition."[19] Quite a few residents of the western sectors did in fact find their way to the Zeughaus, according to the Eastern press, which later stated that ninety-nine West German school classes had visited in a single month.[20] The exhibition *The Past Admonishes*, presented in Convention Hall from April to May 1960, was attended by thousands of visitors, confirming that there was indeed interest in presentations of Nazi history on the west side of the city.

Confronting Nazi Crimes on the Island of West Berlin

The GDR's efforts to influence West Berlin's population were supported in several ways. For one, the Eastern press was available at kiosks on the west side of the city (much to the displeasure of the West Berlin Senate).[21] The distribution of publications by the Committee for German Unity was also possible in West Berlin, since sector boundaries were open and not everyone crossing the border could be checked (Sälter, Dietrich, and Kuhn 2016: 67). The S-Bahn, the commuter rail under the administration of East Berlin, also did its part to make GDR publications available. Since 1955, the West Berlin SED newspaper *Die Wahrheit* was publicly displayed in all Berlin S-Bahn stations (Roggenbuch 2008: 65). As a result of Berlin's special status, it was not difficult for protagonists of the ADE to make appearances in the western sectors. After West Germany banned the German Communist Party (KPD) in 1956, the committee had to suspend its activities; its agitators, as members of an "anti-constitutional" organization, risked criminal prosecution. Because of Allied regulations, a ban of this kind did not exist in West Berlin. GDR propaganda chief Albert Norden even made a personal appearance in the West Berlin Sportpalast in 1958 during an SED event in the run-up to the Berlin Parliament elections.[22]

The permeability of the border in West Berlin also shaped German society's confrontation with the Nazi past. GDR campaigns and publications sparked animated discussions in West Berlin, especially among students, which is not to say that they were met with unreserved approval. One outspoken critic, publicist Gerhard Schoenberner, whose 1960 photographic collection *The Yellow Star: The Persecution of the Jews in Europe, 1933–1945* repeatedly defied the political borders of the Cold War by criticizing the ban on the German Communist Party, conducting research in archives on the other side of the Iron Curtain, and incorporating work by East German publishers into his own (Schoenberner 1962: 426–427). Schoenberner, who had friends and distant relatives on the east side of Berlin, frequently crossed the border, sometimes to attend theater performances. He also exchanged material in East Berlin with others who, like him, were preoccupied with the Nazi past.[23] In 1957, Schoenberner and a few fellow students visited the former Auschwitz-Birkenau concentration camp memorial. Afterward, they planned an exhibition that was presented in West Berlin in the spring of 1960, called *The Past Admonishes* (Glienke 2008b: 160). In preparation for this exhibit, Schoenberner benefited from assistance and contacts from Rudolf Wunderlich,[24] who belonged to the Committee of Anti-Fascist Resistance Fighters in the GDR. Schoenberner maintained a close friendship with the young publicist and former inmate of the Sachsenhausen concentration camp for more than three decades (Hohmann 1997: 99).

Looking back at the anticommunist climate in the Federal Republic in the 1950s, Schoenberner (1999: 133) noted, "Anyone who wanted to speak about the Nazi past . . . was labeled, if not a communist agent, then an objective accessory to Eastern powers and interests." This assessment applied all the more to West Berlin, where the creators of *The Past Admonishes* felt similar effects. Although the focus of their exhibition, which received state funding, was Nazi extermination policies against European Jews, it aimed to draw attention to the Nazi past of certain figures who served in an official capacity in the Federal Republic. The Senate thwarted these plans, threatening to revoke the funds it had granted if references to the current situation were not removed (Glienke 2008b: 163–170). Exhibition organizers were also prevented from carrying out their plan to erect a panel at the entrance featuring a collage of headlines from the West German press. The panel included reports on high-level functionaries of the Nazi state who currently held positions in Bonn, including Hans Globke and Theodor Oberländer. The panel had to be covered in black during the presentation in Convention Hall.[25] Evidently, it was Berlin's special status as a "frontline city" that influenced the Senate's actions; the exhibition was shown with the collage of news clippings in other cities in West Germany in 1961 without raising any concerns.[26]

The Senate's censorship policies were not concealed from the public. The incident was promptly reported in the GDR press and elsewhere (Schmid 2012: 337 and Glienke 2008b: 165). The East German *Berliner Zeitung* harshly criticized the Senate for not granting exhibition organizers the right to "condemn the servants of the Nazi Reich . . . who are residing in Bonn and West Berlin today."[27] The paper also pointed to the exemplary situation in the capital of the GDR, where the Museum for German History showed how the Nazi past had been "overcome" in the GDR in the exhibition *Fifteen Years of Liberation*. "Go and see for yourselves," wrote the newspaper. "More than 40,000 have already been there."[28] It was a sanctimonious call for freedom of speech, a right that was far from guaranteed in the GDR.

The East Berlin press reported on *The Past Admonishes* when it offered an opportunity to attack the West Berlin Senate. It cited passages from the exhibition's guestbook, where West Berliners complained that "the murderers are among us," some of whom receive "high pensions."[29] It kept quiet about the fact that East Berliners and other GDR citizens could also visit the exhibit. But evidently some did. An entry in the exhibition guestbook states, "I left the Soviet zone on 6.4.1960 because of the tyranny and repression of defenseless farmers, workers, and artisans. I am deeply dis-

Figure 3.3. Blackened exhibition board at the opening of the exhibition *Die Vergangenheit mahnt* in the Berlin Congress Hall, Berlin (West), 8 April 1960. Federal Archive, Picture 183-72243-002, photographer: Zehe.

turbed by this exhibition. What was employed as improbable propaganda over there takes place here without concern."[30] In August 1961, when the Berlin Wall went up, the possibility of directly comparing how the two sides were "coming to terms with the past" ended abruptly.

Contested Terrain: The Former Deportation Station in Berlin-Grunewald

When sector boundaries were still open, several memorial sites in Berlin offered opportunities for people from East and West to exchange ideas and engage in commemorations together. A prime example of this was the former deportation station in Berlin-Grunewald. Since the 1950s, a simple memorial plaque hung at the station in the West Berlin district of Wilmersdorf, drawing attention to the fate of the Jews who had been deported from there. The plaque's inscription was the most explicit public acknowledgment of Nazi crimes in all of Berlin.[31] When the Association of Victims of the Nazi Regime tried to mount the plaque in November 1953, West Berlin police obstructed the dedication ceremony because the association was viewed as a communist front organization. That the group was able to mount the memorial plaque at all had to do with the site's special political status. Like other S-Bahn stations in the four-sector city, the railway grounds remained under the control of the East German Deutsche Reichsbahn, and therefore under the jurisdiction of the GDR (Ciesla 2006). West Berlin police, therefore, could not ban the association from mounting the plaque, and could only try to prevent ceremony guests from entering the railway grounds. The plaque in Grunewald soon became a meeting place for Berliners from both sides of the city; members of the Jewish community from the eastern sector also attended the commemoration held in southwest Berlin in November 1953 (Kühling 2016d: 20–22.).

The cross-border commemoration at the Grunewald station came to an end with the construction of the Berlin Wall in 1961. Memorial ceremonies did, however, continue at the site. They were organized by the Federation of Political, Racial and Religious Victims, a victim organization that won official acceptance in West Berlin. In 1973, during a ceremony attended by Reichsbahn officials, the association installed a new memorial plaque with an almost identical inscription accompanied by a Hebrew translation. After this plaque was stolen in 1986, the West Berlin Senate announced its intention to have it replaced. But doing so required the approval of the Reichsbahn. At the time, employees in the Senate office regarded it as "inappropriate" to contact the Reichsbahn management regarding this matter, and instead sent Heinz Galinski, chairman of the Jewish Community of West Berlin, as its representative. The Reichsbahn did not stand in the way of the plans, and the new memorial plaque with its slightly altered inscription was finally mounted in April 1987 (Kühling 2014: 3, 8, and 12).

In 1994, after the Cold War and the division of Germany had come to an end, the West German railway company Deutsche Bundesbahn and the East German Deutsche Reichsbahn merged to become the Deutsche Bahn AG. Soon its board decided to establish a central deportation memorial at the Grunewald station. *Track 17 Memorial* was finally dedicated in January 1998. The signal house, where various memorial signs had commemorated the deportations since 1953, was torn down to make way for the new memorial. The memorial plaque that had been mounted in 1987, however,

Figure 3.4. Representatives of the GDR-Reichsbahn at a commemoration ceremony at Grunewald station, Berlin (West), 13 September 1970. Antifascist Press Archive and Education Centre Berlin e.V., photographer: Jürgen Henschel.

was integrated into the new presentation. Most visitors are probably not aware of the long history of this small plaque. It is a relic of the Cold War. This historical site is a prime example of the connections that existed between the East and West from 1948 to 1961, especially in Berlin.

Gerd Kühling studied history, politics, and sociology in Berlin and earned his doctorate at the Historical Institute of the Friedrich Schiller University in Jena. Since 2015, he has been a research assistant at the House of the Wannsee Conference Memorial and Educational Site, where he is currently part of the curatorial team working on a new permanent exhibition.

He is also an associate member on the board of the association Aktives Museum Faschismus und Widerstand in Berlin. He researches and publishes on dealing with National Socialism in the FRG and in the GDR, among other subjects

Notes

1. See praise by state secretary Timm Renner at the ceremony where Reinhard Strecker was awarded the Medal of Merit with Ribbon on 25 August 2015. Accessed 23 March 2017, https://ilmr.de/wp-content/uploads/2015/09/LaudatioTIM MaufReinhard-Strecker-1.pdf.

2. I would like to thank the Aktives Museum, Fascism and Resistance in Berlin and the House of the Wannsee Conference Memorial and Educational Site for providing support for the translation of this essay.

3. "Massenbeteiligung der Westsektoren," *Neues Deutschland*, 14 September 1948.

4. "Zweite Nazi-Machtergreifung in Bonn," *Berliner Zeitung*, 2 March 1956.

5. "Aggressionsspezialist an der Spitze des Bonner Generalstabs," *Neues Deutschland*, 1 March 1956.

6. "Nie wieder Beamte des Todes," *Neue Zeit*, 6 March 1956.

7. "Zum 18. Jahrestag der Kristallnacht," *Berliner Zeitung*, 10 November 1956.

8. "Der Freisler ist tot, die Freisler blieben," *Neue Zeit*, 22 October 1958.

9. Gottfried Vetter, "Der Hauptdarsteller fehlt," *Der Telegraf*, 24 April 1960.

10. "Sofortige Abberufung Globkes," *Neues Deutschland*, 20 September 1960.

11. "Ein Besuch lohnt," *Berliner Zeitung*, 6 September 1960.

12. "Der millionste Besucher," *Neues Deutschland*, 17 April 1958.

13. "3650 Tage und ihr Ergebnis," *Neue Zeit*, 22 September 1959.

14. "Die Voraussetzungen haben Sie schon heute," *Berliner Zeitung*, 26 September 1959.

15. "Über 5200 Besucher in den ersten vier Stunden," *Berliner Zeitung*, 22 September 1959.

16. Jan, "Nacht und Tag unseres Volkes," *Neue Zeit*, 24 April 1960.

17. Peter Jantzen, "Kampf um das bessere Deutschland," *Die Wahrheit*, 5 May 1960.

18. Werner Müller, "Geschichte—von uns erlebt und mitgestaltet," *Neues Deutschland*, 27 April 1960.

19. H. L., "Geschichtsunterricht—leicht und lehrreich," *Die Wahrheit*, 7 May 1960.

20. "Neun Jahre Museum für Deutsche Geschichte," *Berliner Zeitung*, 9 July 1961.

21. Noncommunist papers from West Berlin, however, were forbidden in the Eastern sector (Lemke 2011: 434).

22. "SED-Politik des totalen Friedens," *Neues Deutschland*, 14 November 1958.

23. My deep appreciation goes to Mira Schoenberner and Dr. Christine Fischer-Defoy for this information.

24. Interview with Gerhard Schoenberner on 14 February 2012.
25. Gerhard Schoenberner, "Schlagzeilen weg oder kein Geld," *Frankfurter Allgemeine Zeitung*, 12 February 2002. See also Schmid 2012: 337–338.
26. For example in Mannheim, see O. N., "Vergangenheit mahnt, weil sie lebt," *Rhein-Neckar-Zeitung*, 6/7 May 1961.
27. "Senats-Bumerang," *Berliner Zeitung*, 14 April 1960.
28. Valentin Lupescu, "Unbewältigte—bewältigte Vergangenheit." *Berliner Zeitung*, 2 June 1960.
29. "Die Schuldigen sind uns bekannt," *Berliner Zeitung*, 4 May 1960.
30. See a selection of entries from the exhibition guestbook *Archiv Internationale Liga für Menschenrechte, Ordner "Ausstellung Die Vergangenheit mahnt VII."*
31. The inscription reads, "Dedicated to the tens of thousands of Jewish citizens of Berlin who were deported to the death camps by the henchmen of the inhumane Hitler regime." See Kühling 2016c: 19.

References

Andrews, Mary-Elizabeth. 2015. "Das Zeughaus als Spiegel deutscher Geschichte." In *Gemeinsame und geteilte deutsche Geschichte 1945–1990*, edited by Stiftung Deutsches Historisches Museum, 44–45. Berlin.

Bästlein, Klaus. 1994. "Nazi-Blutrichter als Stützen des Adenauer-Regimes. Die DDR-Kampagnen gegen NS-Richter und Staatsanwälte, die Reaktionen der bundesdeutschen Justiz und ihre gescheiterte 'Selbstreinigung' 1957–1968." In *Die Normalität des Verbrechens. Bilanz und Perspektiven der Forschung zu den nationalsozialistischen Gewaltverbrechen*, edited by Helge Grabitz, Klaus Bästlein, and Johannes Tuchel, 408–443. Berlin.

Brait, Andrea. 2013. "Im Kampf um die Konstruktion des 'deutschen' Geschichtsbildes. Zur Entwicklung von historischen Nationalmuseen in Ost- und Westdeutschland." In *Asymmetrisch verflochten? Neue Forschungen zur gesamtdeutschen Nachkriegsgeschichte*, edited by Detlev Brunner, Udo Grashoff, and Andreas Kötzing, 21–36. Berlin.

Brunner, Detlev, Udo Grashoff, and Andreas Kötzing, eds. 2013. *Asymmetrisch verflochten?* Berlin.

Kleßmann, Christoph, ed. 1999. *Deutsche Vergangenheiten – eine gemeinsame Herausforderung. Der schwierige Umgang mit der doppelten Nachkriegsgeschichte.* Berlin.

Cielsa, Burghard. 2006. *Als der Osten durch den Westen fuhr. Die Geschichte der Deutschen Reichsbahn in Westberlin.* Cologne.

Conze, Eckart, Norbert Frei, Peter Hayes, and Moshe Zimmermann. 2010. *Das Amt und die Vergangenheit. Deutsche Diplomaten im Dritten Reich und der Bundesrepublik.* Munich.

Danyel, Jürgen, ed. 1995. *Die geteilte Vergangenheit. Zum Umgang mit Nationalsozialismus und Widerstand in beiden deutschen Staaten.* Berlin.

Endlich, Stefanie. 2014. "NS-Erinnerungsorte im geteilten Berlin." In *Stadtentwicklung im doppelten Berlin. Zeitgenossenschaften und Erinnerungsorte*, edited by Günter Schlusche, Verena Pfeiffer-Kloss, Gabi Dolff-Bonekämper, and Axel Klausmeier, 136–144. Berlin.

Glienke, Stephan Alexander. 2008a. "Die Ausstellung 'Ungesühnte Nazijustiz,' 1959–1962. Zur Geschichte der Aufarbeitung nationalsozialistischer Justizverbrechen." Baden-Baden.

———. 2008b. "Die Darstellung der Shoa im öffentlichen Raum. Die Ausstellung 'Die Vergangenheit mahnt,' 1960–1962." In *Erfolgsgeschichte Bundesrepublik? Die Nachkriegsgesellschaft im langen Schatten des Nationalsozialismus*, edited by Stefan Alexander Glienke, Volker Paulmann, and Joachim Perels, 147–184. Göttingen.

Herf, Jeffrey. 1998. *Zweierlei Erinnerung. Die NS-Vergangenheit im geteilten Deutschland*. Berlin.

Hochmuth, Hanno. 2013. "Eine Brücke zwischen Ost und West. Friedrichshain und Kreuzberg als Verflechtungsraum." In *Asymmetrisch verflochten?* edited by Detlev Brunner, Udo Grashoff, and Andreas Kötzing, 195–208. Berlin.

Hohmann, Joachim S., and Günther Wieland, eds. 1997. *Konzentrationslager Sachsenhausen bei Oranienburg 1939 bis 1944. Die Aufzeichnungen des KZ-Häftlings Rudolf Wunderlich*. Frankfurt a. M.

Knoch, Habbo. 2001. *Die Tat als Bild. Fotografien des Holocaust in der deutschen Erinnerungskultur*. Hamburg.

Kühling, Gerd. 2014. "Ein vergessener Streiter der frühen Holocaust-Erinnerung: Adolf Burg und der ehemalige Deportationsbahnhof Berlin-Grunewald." *Medaon—Magazin für jüdisches Leben in Kultur und Bildung* 8, no. 15: 1–15.

———. 2016a. *Erinnerung an nationalsozialistische Verbrechen in Berlin. Verfolgte des Dritten Reiches und geschichtspolitisches Engagement im Kalten Krieg 1945–1979*. Berlin.

———. 2016b. "Von der Verdrängung zur Konkretion. Der Umgang mit den Deportationen der Juden von 1945 bis in die Gegenwart." In *Die Deportationen der Juden aus Deutschland und ihre verdrängte Geschichte nach 1945*, edited by Akim Jah and Gerd Kühling, 30–48. Göttingen.

———. 2016c. "Frühes Gedenken am ehemaligen Deportationsbahnhof Berlin-Grunewald. Ein Fund aus dem Bildarchiv." *Aktives Museum Faschismus und Widerstand in Berlin e.V. Mitgliederrundbrief 74* (January): 18–22.

———. 2016d. "'Ich habe ja nur pressegezeichnet!' Das Leben und Wirken Erich Blochs vom Kaiserreich bis in den Kalten Krieg." *Aktives Museum Faschismus und Widerstand in Berlin e.V. Mitgliederrundbrief 75* (August): 20–24.

Lemke, Michael. 1999. "Der lange Weg zum 'geregelten Nebeneinander.' Die Deutschlandpolitik der DDR Mitte der fünfziger bis Mitte der siebziger Jahre." In *Deutsche Vergangenheiten—eine gemeinsame Herausforderung. Der schwierige Umgang mit der doppelten Nachkriegsgeschichte*, edited by Christoph Kleßmann, Hans Misselwitz, and Günter Wichert, 73–96. Berlin.

———. 2011. *Vor der Mauer. Berlin in der Ost-West-Konkurrenz 1948 bis 1961*. Cologne.

Roggenbuch, Frank. 2008. *Das Berliner Grenzgängerproblem. Verflechtung und Systemkonkurrenz vor dem Mauerbau*. Berlin.

Sälter, Gerhard, Johanna Dietrich, and Fabian Kuhn. 2016. *Die vergessenen Toten. Todesopfer des DDR-Grenzregimes in Berlin von der Teilung bis zum Mauerbau (1948–1961)*. Berlin.

Schmid, Harald. 2012. "'Die Vergangenheit mahnt': Genese und Rezeption einer Wanderausstellung zur nationalsozialistischen Judenverfolgung (1960–1962)." *Zeitschrift für Geschichtswissenschaft* 60, no. 4: 331–348.

Schoenberner, Gerhard. 1962. *"Wir haben es gesehen"—Augenzeugenberichte über die Judenverfolgung im Dritten Reich*. Gütersloh.

———. 1999. "Joseph Wulf. Die Dokumentation des Verbrechens." In *Engagierte Demokraten. Vergangenheitspolitik in kritischer Absicht*, edited by Claudia Fröhlich and Michael Kohlstruck, 132–142. Münster.

Seydewitz, Ruth, and Max Seydewitz. 1956. *Antisemitismus in der Bundesrepublik*, edited by Ausschuss für Deutsche Einheit. Berlin (East).

Chapter 4

The GDR and Opposition from the Right

A Plea for Broader Perspectives

Enrico Heitzer

In 2009, I gave a lecture on the topic of my dissertation titled "The Fighting Group against Inhumanity" (Kampfgruppe gegen Unmenschlichkeit / KgU) during an exhibition opening at the Memorial Site for Freedom Movements in German History at Rastatt Castle. During my presentation, I showed the audience a number of KgU leaflets, among them one that was distributed in large numbers in the German Democratic Republic (GDR) in 1951/1952. "Exterminating Rats" is a "national obligation" for all Germans, it declares, alongside an illustration of a red rat with a hammer and sickle embossed on its fur and a human face framed in black, red, and gold. Another leaflet expresses the following demands: "Give us the names of the victims!" "Give us the names of the henchmen!" In my lecture, I raised the question of the commensurability of arson attacks with other forms of sabotage used in "resistance" against the East German SED regime. While doing so, I remained intentionally vague about the political motives and ideological backgrounds of the KgU (Heitzer 2011).

In the discussion following the lecture, an interesting dispute took place between the Bavarian historian Rainer Elkar and the East German theologian and historian Erhart Neubert. Elkar was bewildered by a passage on the "Give us the names" leaflet. It postulated the need to "eradicate" communist snitches, using the German term *ausmerzen*, which has

Figure 4.1. Call of the Fighting Group against Inhumanity for "Rat Control." Stickers distributed in the GDR 1951/52. Private archive Enrico Heitzer.

National Socialist connotations. For Elkar, the flyer blatantly used Nazi language. Neubert countered this argument, explaining that such phrases had to be viewed in temporal context and that such language was not uncommon in the early Cold War era.

It is true that the political language of the 1940s and 1950s in both East and West Germany was harsh and often dehumanizing. Yet it cannot be overlooked that the KgU deliberately played with references to Nazi ideology. The organization, operating mainly from West Berlin, and with up to six hundred confidential human sources in the GDR, *also* wanted to address people who had not completely broken with Nazi ideology (Heitzer 2015a).

The phenomenon of right-wing opposition to the SED system since the period of the Soviet Occupation Zone (SBZ) has been overlooked.

Today, little is known about its relevance, and current scholarship on the topic has yet to provide an overview that covers the postwar period to the end of the GDR.

In this essay, I first present events that make clear the existence of right-wing opposition to the system, and not just in the early years of the SBZ/GDR. These events illustrate how this opposition was articulated. Next, I formulate a plea for current scholars to broaden their perspectives on right-wing actors, and to view them as part of diverse streams of opposition to the SED when considering resistance and opposition to the system in the GDR. It should not be said that right-wing opponents to the GDR system formed a dominant current within the amorphous and constantly changing "field" of opponents of the SED, since the development of "national opposition" was largely repressed (Botsch 2012: 557). Neither should every act of militancy against the regime simply be viewed as having right-wing motives. This also holds true for the actors discussed here, as well as other opponents of the SED system. There were several generations of resistance whose members were not necessarily acquainted with one another; as a rule, repression by the system caused breaks between them. This makes it important to keep track of both continuities and discontinuities between generations.

My essay seeks to clarify a perspective, not to present an empirical investigation. I discuss a few ideas in the hope that they will inspire further research and broaden the discourse in an area that has received too little attention.

"Better a Hitler from Berchtesgaden than a Pieck from Stalin's Mercy": Examples of Right-Wing Opposition in the Soviet Occupation Zone

A "zero hour" cannot be invoked to refer to the GDR, just as it cannot be used to refer to the old Federal Republic of Germany and Austria. In 1945, the break with anti-liberal as well as fascist traditions of thought affected only part of society. In my research, I found examples that clarify this hitherto poorly illuminated aspect of the transition from National Socialism to the SBZ/GDR that can push our critical analysis toward broader perspectives.[1]

In autumn 1945, an organization called "Blue S" threatened the KPD mayor of Fürstenwalde in a series of letters. The group was alleged to have planned the assassination of the city's Soviet commander and another—Jewish—member of the Kommandatura. At the beginning of January 1946, following the arrest of the group's alleged leader, H. Czechowski, and a

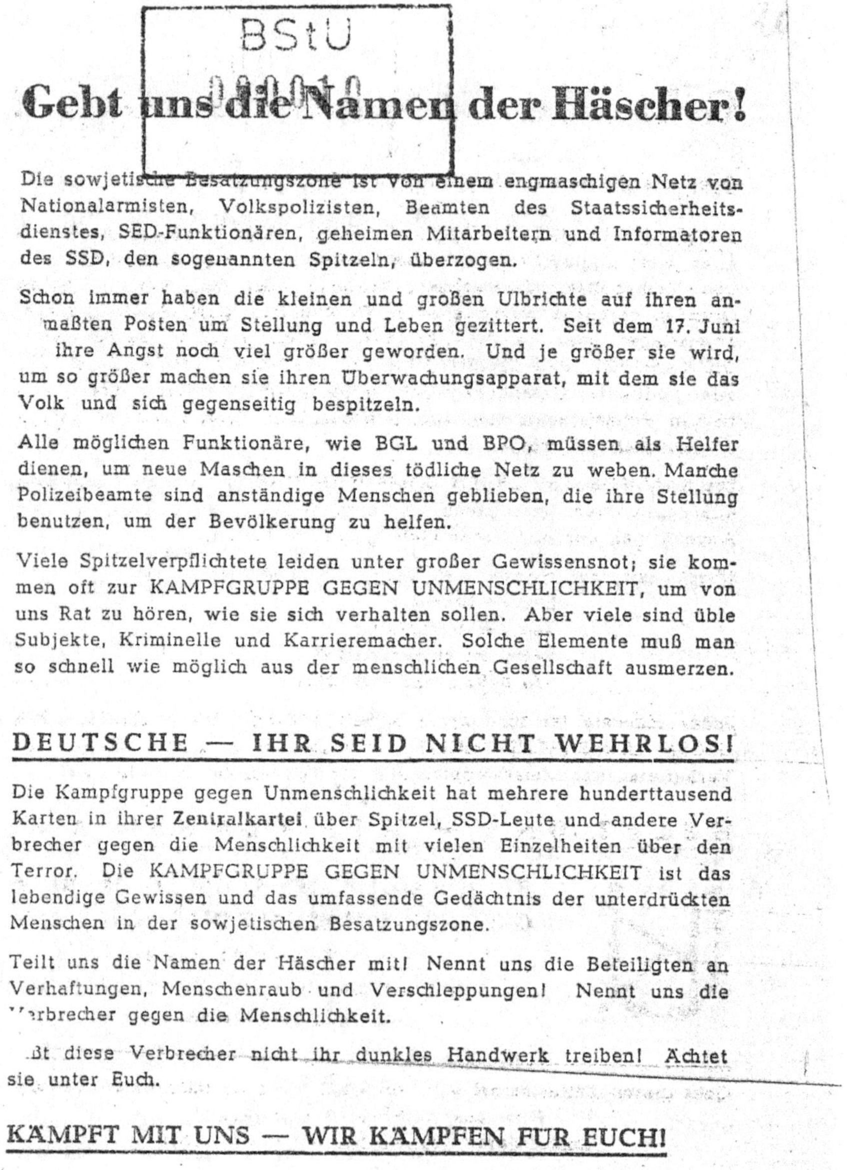

Gebt uns die Namen der Häscher!

Die sowjetische Besatzungszone ist von einem engmaschigen Netz von Nationalarmisten, Volkspolizisten, Beamten des Staatssicherheitsdienstes, SED-Funktionären, geheimen Mitarbeitern und Informatoren des SSD, den sogenannten Spitzeln, überzogen.

Schon immer haben die kleinen und großen Ulbrichte auf ihren anmaßten Posten um Stellung und Leben gezittert. Seit dem 17. Juni ihre Angst noch viel größer geworden. Und je größer sie wird, um so größer machen sie ihren Überwachungsapparat, mit dem sie das Volk und sich gegenseitig bespitzeln.

Alle möglichen Funktionäre, wie BGL und BPO, müssen als Helfer dienen, um neue Maschen in dieses tödliche Netz zu weben. Manche Polizeibeamte sind anständige Menschen geblieben, die ihre Stellung benutzen, um der Bevölkerung zu helfen.

Viele Spitzelverpflichtete leiden unter großer Gewissensnot; sie kommen oft zur KAMPFGRUPPE GEGEN UNMENSCHLICHKEIT, um von uns Rat zu hören, wie sie sich verhalten sollen. Aber viele sind üble Subjekte, Kriminelle und Karrieremacher. Solche Elemente muß man so schnell wie möglich aus der menschlichen Gesellschaft ausmerzen.

DEUTSCHE — IHR SEID NICHT WEHRLOS!

Die Kampfgruppe gegen Unmenschlichkeit hat mehrere hunderttausend Karten in ihrer Zentralkartei über Spitzel, SSD-Leute und andere Verbrecher gegen die Menschlichkeit mit vielen Einzelheiten über den Terror. Die KAMPFGRUPPE GEGEN UNMENSCHLICHKEIT ist das lebendige Gewissen und das umfassende Gedächtnis der unterdrückten Menschen in der sowjetischen Besatzungszone.

Teilt uns die Namen der Häscher mit! Nennt uns die Beteiligten an Verhaftungen, Menschenraub und Verschleppungen! Nennt uns die Verbrecher gegen die Menschlichkeit.

Laßt diese Verbrecher nicht ihr dunkles Handwerk treiben! Achtet sie unter Euch.

KÄMPFT MIT UNS — WIR KÄMPFEN FÜR EUCH!

Figure 4.2. Front page of a leaflet of the "Fighting Group against Inhumanity," which was distributed in large numbers in the GDR in the late 1940s. Archive: Federal Commissioner for the Records of the State Security Service of the former German Democratic Republic.

number of other members, a homemade explosive device failed to detonate at the local police station. This incident "was seen as an attempted assassination of the commander." Czechowski, who was sentenced to death and executed, wrote during his time in Soviet custody that "only former Hitler Youth leaders" were organized "in our organization, who were trustworthy and could be expected not to blab something" (Weigelt 2015: 368–370).

In 1947, several bomb attacks were carried out against the SED office in Bernburg, and it was only a matter of chance that no one was harmed. Another series of attacks occurred on the eve of the Memorial Day for the Victims of Fascism in September 1947. If the SED publication *Neues Deutschland* (20 March 1948) is to be believed, a hand grenade was thrown into the empty car of the city's Soviet commander. Additionally, a "bombing raid" was carried out against a denazification commission. The newspaper article assumed—externalizing right-wing phenomena—that the group had links to the West, despite a lack of evidence.[2] Six months after the third bomb attack on 6 December 1947,[3] twenty men and a woman, all born between 1927 and 1932, were arrested.[4] They were sentenced to long prison terms in Halle by a Soviet military tribunal (SMT) for "terror," sabotage, and "diversion."[5]

The British diplomatic service received information about the Bernburg incidents, indicating right-wing extremism. An informant provided documents from the SBZ, which read, "The window of the . . . GESCHÄFTSSTELLE . . . , of the VOLKSHAUS, of the Sanatorium, and of the crematorium were smashed. The photographs of HITLER, GÖRING, and GÖBBELS [sic] were put into them as well as the HAKENKREUZ-flag." Next the documents noted, "Sunday was commemoration day for the victims of fascism, Saturday night the windows of the SED office . . . were smashed and swastikas . . . and SS-runes . . . painted everywhere. Also in the . . . HEILANSTALT . . . where a survey of cremation-rooms was to take place." Unspecified SED sources are quoted in the British documents: "Last Sunday 'OPFER DES FASCHISMUS' [sic] day, they tore down the posters and spread a swastika flag inside. On the cremation oven in the hospital here, they showed us, they placed a scroll bearing the following inscription: 'The day of revenge will come. The communists will be thrown into these ovens, long live the FÜHRER! HEIL HITLER!' Things like these are an everyday occurrence." The informant downplayed the possible Nazi source of the attacks. He claimed that "such a thing" was more common in the SBZ. "In the whole of the East Zone similar things happened the same day. . . . This has extremely little to do with Fascism. Everyone is, quite rightly, dissatisfied; and as the S.E.D. has lied the most to the people, and only makes itself a tool for the Russians; hatred, for good reasons, is directed against that party."[6]

If on the night of the Memorial Day for the Victims of Fascism, however, a threat was left on the crematorium oven of the "sanatorium" previously used as an euthanasia facility, stating that Communists would soon be burned, this served as proof that the perpetrators not only knew the details of what happened there from 1940 to 1943, but also that they approved of the murder of political enemies or people they considered to be inferior.

In November and December 1947, leaflets were found in Ziltendorf (Guben district), mentioning several men, probably officials, by name. A threat followed: "The hour is not far off when we will lay the rope around the necks of these traitors. When the call comes to you, storm troopers of the SA and party comrades, then appear in the said place. Weapons and ammunition are already packed in the woods. . . . We remain faithful to Hitler, Heil!"[7]

Finally, such examples can be found in the monthly reports of the predecessors to the Ministry of State Security (MfS) in quite impressive numbers, at least until 1949. If one includes slogans that appeared on walls and other forms of expression, it is possible to call this an all-encompassing phenomenon. Even if the nascent secret police fabricated events, even with fatal consequences, in order to prove its "revolutionary vigilance," such as the case of the "Greußen boys," in which a communist invented a Werewolf terror group, and which led to the incarceration of several young men, the phenomenon holds true.

We will now examine an incident in Saxony, where the nature of opposition was disguised. In the spring and summer of 1949, pamphlets from a Democratic Resistance Movement of Germany appeared several times in Dresden and its environs. These pamphlets displayed a lictor bundle, the party badge of Italian fascists.[8] Between May 1947 and January 1948, a man in Bad Elster painted slogans that read, "Anyone who knows our Führer knows how we lived, and the goddamn Stalin makes us starve to death," and "Hang Wilhelm Pieck, that fat Russian pig."[9] The man was arrested and sentenced to ten years' imprisonment by an SMT for "anti-Soviet propaganda." He served six years, partly in the Soviet special camp in Sachsenhausen.[10]

Yet such activities were vigorously prevented, at times through extralegal means, and their public impact in the years following 1945 was marginalized. Still, these activities belong to the historical reality of the postwar years. As Gerd Kühling notes, the events of 17 June 1953 can also be interpreted as a nationalist-based uprising (in which the badge-wearers of the Union of Victims of National Socialism suffered attacks), and both the SED and opposition groups such as the KgU tried to win over this hidden potential. Kühling (2016: 227, 250–252) stresses that "with the Slánský trial and supporting campaigns" at the end of 1952 in Prague, East German communists "anticipated" accommodating "sections of the populations in which latent anti-Semitism was present." While a great deal is known about integration strategies and their "successes" in the East, further investigation is needed in cases where integration, in the SED's terms, met with no, or only partial, success, or where it turned into systemic antagonism within the system.

Statements from the actors in these events are missing.[11] Many researchers have become familiar with these actors from the perspective of their political opponents and persecutors, which seems to diminish the validity of the sources. This does not apply to every instance of right-wing opposition, however. In some cases, personal testimonies are available.

We can, for example, examine a larger group of predominantly young people who were active across the region, calling themselves the German Freedom Movement (Deutsche Freiheitsbewegung / DFG). A member of the organization, released from GDR custody, reported in 1954 after his flight to West Berlin during the "federal emergency procedure" (Bundesnotaufnahmeverfahren). In July 1945, several Hitler Youth leaders, pupils of the NAPOLA (Nationalpolitische Erziehungsanstalt, or Nazi Elite School) and former members of the Reich School Heinrich Himmler, founded a resistance group in Mecklenburg and called it the German Freedom Movement. In 1947, connections were established with like-minded people in Brandenburg and Saxony. Farther west, it allegedly had ties to the British military government. The group was purported to only print and distribute its own leaflets. In 1948, it was said to have been about 150 members strong.[12] In March 1949, several groups within the DFG were arrested in Brandenburg and Mecklenburg. Meanwhile, members of the group and above all, its leaders, fled to West Germany. Yet the DFG was by no means crushed. It continued to distribute thousands of leaflets in and around Leipzig between March and September 1949. But it was not long before there were five arrests, resulting in harsh sentences (Heitzer 2015b: 40–42).

Furthermore, a statement from the KgU's confidential source "Tröger" was recorded. "Tröger" was a Hitler Youth leader and later a member of the SS (Heitzer 2008: 78–80), for which he was sent to an internment camp from 1946 to early 1950. After his release, he contacted the KgU, which suggested that he establish a resistance group. He built up the active intelligence group Talleyrand, which, according to his statements in West Berlin, was "composed almost entirely of trustworthy old comrades of the Hitler Youth and SS."[13]

The "Elephant" in the "Ivory Tower of GDR Research"

In the SBZ/GDR, opposition to prevailing conditions, politics, and officially proclaimed visions of the future existed from the beginning to the end. The construction of the Berlin Wall was an important turning point. Links and support from the West became possible only with great danger. The motives for resistance were as diverse as the people who held them. In their goals and plans to reorganize political life after possible success, they agreed upon little or nothing. Their ideas ranged from various democratic forms of government to a communist society that would differ from what the SBZ/GDR imposed. There were, of course, also adherents to right-wing or even fascist political models among them, especially in the 1940s and 1950s, but probably also after. Many of these individuals could not be classified as adherents to parliamentary democracy, at least in today's sense of the term.

When dealing with systemic opposition in the GDR, scholars often disregard the fact that dedicated anti-Bolshevism, which was held by many of the system's opponents in the early years, was widespread among Nazis on the one hand, but could be combined with other political orientations on the other. Even the trivial point that the lives of contemporaries did not begin in 1945 has been ignored in almost all accounts of opposition and resistance, unless the affected people were victims of "double persecution" in Nazi and Communist periods, such as Heinz Brandt, among others (Pampel and Reiprich 2013).

It is possible to find a more general picture of systemic right-wing opposition in the GDR, but only if one examines the early GDR, like the old Federal Republic and Austria, as a society "after fascism," a perspective that is underdeveloped in almost every way (Wierling 2016).[14]

This dearth of research is also responsible for the treatment of political statements from the SED and its security organs. SED opponents were often defamed as "fascists." From these denunciations, some researchers have concluded that the outing of politically right-wing orientations have simply belonged to smear campaigns against opponents. My research, as well as the research of others, contradicts this view.

Mary Fulbrook (2016: 92–93) has referred to an "elephant" in the "ivory tower of GDR research," or the "fact that everyone is aware of and nobody addresses: the manner in which the Nazi past persisted in postwar Germany."[15] Most scholars of totalitarianism reject comparisons between the Nazi successor societies, even if the fruitfulness of this approach has been proven (Bergmann, Erb, and Lichtblau 1995; Hockerts 1998; Hammerstein 2017). As Dorothee Wierling (2016: 209) writes, "The 'detour' through the history of the GDR as a post-fascist history embedded in the entire 20th century, could give the postwar phenomena a deeper dimension" that could "also have a ripple effect on the historiography of the Federal Republic."

In the context of this essay, we must look to numerous arson and explosive attacks that occurred from 1946 to 1948 on buildings that were used for denazification, or by the occupying powers in the Stuttgart and Nuremberg areas, Munich, Schlüchtern, or Wesermünde-Geestemünde (Biddiscombe 2004: 196–198). These attacks make visible the "all-German dimension" of right-wing opposition to the system, which should be considered further in future research.

There are various indications that right-wing groups operated and formed networks that reached from the FRG into the GDR. Take, for example, the right-wing extremist Union of German Youth (Bund Deutscher Jugend / BDJ) (Buschke 2003: 210–212; Dudek and Jaschke 1984: 356–358). The BDJ was financed by the CIA and followed an agenda of small-scale guerilla warfare in the GDR, where it supposedly had four hundred followers. It was banned and dissolved in West Germany in 1952/1953 (Heitzer 2015a: 390–392).

Another example is the Investigation Committee of Free Lawyers (Untersuchungsausschuss freiheitlicher Juristen / UfJ), in the ranks of which were former Nazi cadres, including Dr. Walter Linse. Linse was the former *Arisierungsbeauftragte* (representative of Aryanization) in the Chemnitz Chamber of Industry and Commerce. During the Nazi era, alongside his involvement in the plunder of Jews before their mass murder, he organized forced laborers in his region. In the simple logic of a binary system of confrontation like the Cold War, people such as Linse were often depicted simply as freedom fighters (Bästlein 2008).

My own research as well as investigations by Ines Reich and Maria Schultz (2015), the Independent Commission of Historians for the History of the Federal Intelligence Service (Heidenreich, Münkel, and Stadelmann-Wenz 2016), and others (Breitman et al. 2005; Maddrell 2006: 131–133; Boghardt 2015; Müller et al. 2015) suggest that considerable, systemic right-wing opposition existed in the GDR, and could also be mobilized for activities against the East German system.

An overall view of this systemic opposition in the SBZ/GDR, which takes into account the particular constellations and logic of the Cold War, as well as the internal logic of a post-Nazi and dictatorial society like that of the SBZ/GDR, is still pending. While political publicists, such as Neubert (1998), interpret right-wing radicalism as a rather internal phenomenon that should not be seen as an oppositional movement, historian Harry Waibel (2011), in his important but unfortunately somewhat cluttered analysis, accuses the entire field of GDR research of having systematically disregarded the system of actors on the far right.

Until now, researchers have not clarified whether and to what extent opponents of the system were motivated to carry out extreme right-wing activities. Neubert (1998: 36) surmises that due to the burden of German guilt, the "connection of the national idea with the power state . . . failed and was deeply discredited." A critical questioning of such a generalizing thesis is appropriate, especially if one takes seriously the memories of former political prisoners such as Peter Eisenfeld or Gabriel Berger. The son of a Jewish communist, Berger reported that in GDR prisons in the 1970s, slogans such as "Germany, Wake Up" (Deutschland erwache!) but also "Heil Pinochet" (a persiflage of "Heil Hitler") were heard daily. Meanwhile, in a secret "Bundestag election" in Cottbus prisons in 1969, the West German neo-Nazi National Democratic Party (NPD) succeeded with 25 percent of the votes. According to Eisenfeld's own statements, this "election" made clear that there was "in the GDR obviously a considerable potential" that considered a "strong united Germany cleansed of communists, foreigners, and 'leftist slobs'" desirable (quoted in Alisch 2014: 148–150). Waibel (2017: 345–347) points to the active and open involvement of extreme right-wing actors at demonstrations and other public events since the summer and fall of 1989, which were usually seen as not an issue at all, or were not until the following year believed to be relevant (Kowalczuk 2009: 511).

According to "secret examinations of the mood at eastern and western agencies," conducted by the polling institute Infratest, about a quarter of GDR citizens were system opponents (Bösch and Gieseke 2015: 49) between 1975 and 1985. Since charging alleged or actual opponents of the system as fascists played a central role in GDR propaganda, it is unfortunate that debates among researchers have remained superficial, neglecting to uncover whether incidents of swastika graffiti, the desecration of Jewish cemeteries and monuments for victims of fascism (Schmidt 2007), or extreme right-wing statements against the SED system represented genuine political beliefs or forms of political provocation.

The historian Siegfried Suckut has pointed to gaps and blind spots in the research on system opposition from the right. Drawing on letters collected and evaluated by the MfS since 1964, he shows how GDR citizens turned to government figures, media, or other authorities. In his book, Suckut (2016) argues that "West Berlin-based organizations close to the government" of the FRG, such as the Eastern offices, the KgU, and the UfJ, "called the East Germans to resistance and outright protest," yet this "call . . . was apparently not the initial spark for a GDR-wide movement." Also, he assumes that demands for freedom in the streets with a highly visible "F" received "little attention in the fifties." He makes another observation: "Whoever wanted to show his protest with a simple symbol, it seems, preferred the swastika" (Suckut 2016).

Regrettably, Suckut, who provides only sparing comments on the edited letters, does not pursue possible implications. In a separate chapter, he presents impressive examples that offer a detailed picture of right-wing protest and systemic opposition. He quotes, for example, letters in which authors signed their statements, "Heinrich Himmler, Reichsführer SS" (1985) or "SS-Brigadeführer (Brigadier General of the SS) at the Gestapo-Leitstelle Drewitz" (1983),[16] yet does not adequately analyze right-wing system opposition.

Summary

In light of this research, one does not have to go as far as Charles S. Maier, who in the early 1980s described the "failure of the neofascist Right to emerge in greater strength" as the "major surprise of postwar European politics," and noted that there were no violent mergers comparable to the German Freikorps or the Italian Arditi formed after 1945 (Maier 1981: 330; Maier 1987: 157–158). Canadian historian Perry Biddiscombe (1999) and others have shown that there were attempts to develop Freikorps in German territories after 1945 (Weigelt 2015: 413–414). Thinking about postwar Germany, Biddiscombe (1999: 53) sees one of the challenges as "explain[ing] the apparent absence of a paramilitary effervescence accompanying the collapse of the Third Reich."

He offers four reasons why militant, often Nazi-inspired resistance to US occupation after 1945—a broad Freikorps movement deprived by the occupation—collapsed after 1948. In addition to economic and political stabilization, the most important factors were the rapid end of denazification and the reintegration of Nazi-incriminated groups, alongside the admission of right-wing parties, the Berlin blockade, and the visible break between the Allies of the Anti-Hitler Coalition (Biddiscombe 2004: 229–230).

For the SBZ/GDR, comparable factors also need to be investigated. For example, did the founding of the National Democratic Party of Germany (National-Demokratische Partei Deutschlands/NDPD) as a form of integration for former Nazis change the situation? Although violent activities by the system's opponents apparently lasted somewhat longer in the SBZ/GDR than in the western zones, they gradually collapsed in the first half of the 1950s under repression.

Despite public repression, write Bösch and Gieseke (2015: 75), "extreme right-wing extremist and racist stereotypes persisted among sections of the GDR population, and these expressed themselves in exclusion and physical violence against foreigners." Only casually do Bösch and

Gieseke comment on opposition from that end of the spectrum. This would be a fruitful subject of investigation. In the late 1980s alone, a working group from the GDR Interior Ministry counted a national neo-Nazi milieu consisting of more than fifteen thousand people. The Leipzig Central Institute for Youth Research found sympathy for right-wing activities in up to 30 percent of GDR adolescents (Reinhard 2012). In the 1980s, as a form of counterreaction, an independent Antifa in East Germany was formed, which likewise played a political role in the processes of upheaval (Weiß 2015; Jänicke/Paul-Siewert 2017). In addition, several studies point to roots in the GDR and the experiences of system transformation with regard to booming extreme right-wing and right-wing populist movements in East Germany after 1989/90.[17]

Aside from further empirical research, a comparative view of the Federal Republic and Austria is desirable. Alongside work with a sharper methodological and conceptual focus, future research can examine not only continuities and fractures but also transnational developments and interdependencies. For example, with the opening of US secret sources but also with partial access to the files of the Bundesnachrichtendienst, which one can read alongside the written traces of the MfS, it is possible to engage more closely with other Cold War organizations in the Federal Republic, for which no known files exist.

Consider the BDJ, but also right-wing Russian organizations such as NTS or ZOPE, which were active with the help of German informants in the SBZ/DDR. These groups included "white" emigrants from the Soviet Union, who not only partially sympathized with the Nazi regime but also collaborated with it, often sitting in crucial places (Stöver 2002: 283–285, 519–521). There is also the UfJ, which in 1958 published a document on former Nazis in the GDR (Herf 1997: 185–187), an incident that is by no means sufficiently researched. In 1958, for example, chairman Horst Erdmann had to resign because of his Nazi membership, which until then was misrepresented as a story about Nazi persecution (together with alleged Jewish descent), alongside other forms of "ironing out" his curriculum vita (Allen 2013: 161). The actors' possible Nazi involvement should be considered. We know nothing about the backgrounds of GDR agents who led the UfJ B-Division until 1955, and were intended to be used in the event of war in the rear of the opposing army (Heitzer 2015a: 393–394). Researchers have already shown that Western "stay-behind" structures bore the hallmarks of a particularly staunch anticommunism that often assumed a right-wing character (Kisatsky 2005).

"Repentance" and "recivilization" lasted for decades in East Germany, and differed from the process in the Federal Republic (Jarausch 2004). The power of those who supported the National Socialist regime did not dissipate in 1945. Further research is needed to address how the SED regime viewed this potential, how it was integrated, and how it was repressed and hidden from the public.

Enrico Heitzer, born in 1977 in Altenburg in Thuringia, was with the Bundeswehr from 1996 to 1998. Beginning in 1998, he studied history and political science in Potsdam and Halle. From 2005 to 2007, he held a scholarship from the Graduate Program of the State of Saxony-Anhalt. In 2007, he received a doctoral scholarship from the German Historical Institute in Washington, DC. In 2007/8 he worked as a research assistant for the Chair of Modern History at the Martin Luther University Halle-Wittenberg. Since 2005, he has been an associate doctoral student at the Center for Contemporary Historical Research in Potsdam (ZZF) and, since 2010–12, has worked as a research assistant at the Berlin Wall Foundation. Today he is a research assistant at the Sachsenhausen Memorial and the Museum Sachsenhausen/Stiftung Brandenburgische Gedenkstätten. In addition to his exhibition activities, his research interests include the end of World War II and the early Cold War, denazification, the history of opposition and resistance in the SBZ/DDR, and the politics and culture of remembrance. His publications include *Die Kampfgruppe gegen Unmenschlichkeit (KgU): Widerstand und Spionage im Kalten Krieg 1948–1959* (volume 53 in the series Zeithistorische Studien by Böhlau-Verlag, 2015); and with Günter Morsch, Robert Traba, and Katarzyna Woniak, *Im Schatten von Nürnberg: Transnationale Ahndung von NS-Verbrechen* (In the shadow of Nuremberg: Transnational persecution of Nazi crimes, volume 25 in the series Forschungsbeiträge und Materialien der Stiftung Brandenburgische Gedenkstätten by Metropol Verlag, 2019).

Notes

Translated by the author with help from Emma Mikuska-Tinman.

1. Regarding the heading of this section, "Lieber ein Hitler von Berchtesgaden, als ein Pieck von Stalingnaden": on 15 October 1949, this slogan was smeared on a wagon in a coal mine in the district of Altenburg. SED District Administration Altenburg, monthly report, 27 October 1949. Saxonian State Archive Leipzig, SED-Kreisleitung Altenburg, no. 91.

2. "Westliche Nazibande ausgehoben," *Neues Deutschland*, 20 March 1948, 2.

3. A second attack took place on 4 December 1947 (Petrow and Foitzik 2009: 326), and, while the premises were "heavily destroyed," people were not harmed. Commissariat K5 Working Group B3, Monthly Report December 1947, 5 January 1948, BStU, MfS AS 947/67, 6.

4. Report Commissariat K5 Saxony-Anhalt for April 1948, 11 May 1948; BStU, MfS AS 237/66, Bl. 288 f.

5. KgU report, Gerhard Finn, 29 August 1957, Bundesarchiv B 289 VA 63/20-7/106.

6. Censorship Intercepts 6 November 1947, the National Archives, Kew, Foreign Office FO 371/64310.

7. Monthly Report Commissariat K5, Working Group B3, December 1947, 5 January 1948, BStU MfS AS 947/67, 4f.

8. Monthly Reports Commissariat K5 Saxony, March, April and June 1949; BStU MfS AS 229/66, Vol. 3, 717, 747, and 764.

9. Monthly Report Landeskriminalamt Saxony, January 1948, Commissariat K5, 10 February 1948; BStU MfS AS 229/66 Vol. 3, 581.

10. Archive Sachsenhausen, GARF f. 9409, op. 1, d. 197, l. 9.

11. Serial report sources, beginning in 1958 and originating from intelligence agencies, might offer an approach. A project at the Center for Contemporary Historical Research in Potsdam (Gieseke 2008) evaluated this possibility. It would be worth considering whether these reports could also be used for the perspective proposed here.

12. KgU Report, Gerhard Finn, 27 October 1954, Bundesarchiv B 289 SA 428/171-18/1.

13. KgU Protocol, 11 March 1954, Bundesarchiv B 289 VA 194/220-171/1.

14. Historian Rüdiger Bergien (2013) has presented thought-provoking reflections. He focuses on how the integration of people incriminated from the NS period worked in practice in the GDR. Unlike in the Federal Republic, the GDR had to reference an official antifascist discourse. The thematization of resistance or systemic opposition in the GDR also referred to this discourse, if it took place at all.

15. See also Fulbrook 2008 and Fulbrook and Port 2013.

16. In Suckut 2016, see chapter titled "References to National Socialism and Anti-Jewish Statements."

17. See the essay by Patrice Poutrus in this book.

References

Alisch, Steffen. 2014. *Strafvollzug im SED-Staat: Das Beispiel Cottbus*. Studien des Forschungsverbundes SED-Staat an der Freien Universität Berlin 20. Frankfurt a. M.

Allen, Keith R. 2013. *Befragung—Überprüfung—Kontrolle: die Aufnahme von DDR-Flüchtlingen in West-Berlin bis 1961*. Beiträge zur Geschichte von Mauer und Flucht. Berlin.

Ansorg, Leonore. 2005. *Politische Häftlinge im Strafvollzug der DDR: die Strafvollzugsanstalt Brandenburg*. Schriftenreihe der Stiftung Brandenburgische Gedenkstätten 15. Berlin.

Bästlein, Klaus. 2008. *Vom NS-Täter zum Opfer des Stalinismus: Dr. Walter Linse: ein deutscher Jurist im 20. Jahrhundert*. Schriftenreihe des Berliner Landesbeauftragten für die Unterlagen des Staatssicherheitsdienstes der ehemaligen DDR 27. Berlin.

Bergien, Rüdiger. 2013. "Das Schweigen der Kader: Ehemalige Nationalsozialisten im zentralen SED-Parteiapparat—eine Erkundung." In *Kontinuitäten und Diskontinuitäten: Der Nationalsozialismus in der Geschichte des 20. Jahrhunderts*, Beiträge zur Geschichte des Nationalsozialismus, edited by Birthe Kundrus and Sybille Steinbacher, 134–153. Göttingen.

Bergmann, Werner, Rainer Erb, and Albert Lichtblau, eds. 1995. *Schwieriges Erbe: Der Umgang mit Nationalsozialismus und Antisemitismus in Österreich, der DDR und der Bundesrepublik Deutschland*. Schriftenreihe des Zentrums für Antisemitismusforschung. Berlin.

Biddiscombe, Perry. 1999. "The End of the Freebooter Tradition: The Forgotten Freikorps Movement of 1944/45." *Central European History* 32, no. 1: 53–90.

———. 2004. *The Last Nazis: SS Werewolf Guerrilla Resistance in Europe 1944–1947*. Stroud.

Boghardt, Thomas. 2015. "Dirty Work? The Use of Nazi Informants by U.S. Army Intelligence in Postwar Europe." *Journal of Military History* 79, no. 2: 387–422.

Bösch, Frank, and Jens Gieseke. 2015. "Der Wandel des Politischen in Ost und West." In *Geteilte Geschichte: Ost- und Westdeutschland 1970–2000*, edited by Frank Bösch, 39–78. Göttingen.

Botsch, Gideon. 2012. "From Skinhead-Subculture to Radical Right Movement: The Development of a 'National Opposition' in East Germany." *Contemporary European History* 21, no. 4: 553–573.

Breitman, Richard, Norman J. W. Goda, Timothy Naftali, and Robert Wolfe. 2005. *U.S. Intelligence and the Nazis*. Cambridge.

Buschke, Heiko. 2003. *Deutsche Presse, Rechtsextremismus und nationalsozialistische Vergangenheit in der Ära Adenauer*. Frankfurt a. M.

Danyel, Jürgen. 2003. "Spätfolgen? Der ostdeutsche Rechtsextremismus als Hypothek der DDR-Vergangenheitspolitik und Erinnerungskultur." In *Fremde und Fremd-Sein in der DDR. Zu historischen Ursachen der Fremdenfeindlichkeit in Ostdeutschland*, edited by Jan C. Behrends, Thomas Lindenberger, and Patrice G. Poutrus, 23–40. Berlin.

Dudek, Peter, and Hans-Gerd Jaschke. 1984. *Entstehung und Entwicklung des Rechtsextremismus in der Bundesrepublik: Zur Tradition einer besonderen politischen Kultur*. Vol. 1. Opladen.

Fulbrook, Mary. 2008. *The People's State: East German Society from Hitler to Honecker*. New Haven.

———. 2016. "Die fehlende Mitte: Die DDR als postnazistischer Staat." In *Die DDR als Chance: Neue Perspektiven auf ein altes Thema*, edited by Ulrich Mählert, 89–97. Berlin.

Fulbrook, Mary, and Andrew I. Port. 2013. *Becoming East German: Socialist Structures and Sensibilities after Hitler*. New York.

Gieseke, Jens. 2008. "Bevölkerungsstimmungen in der geschlossenen Gesellschaft. MfS-Berichte an die DDR-Führung in den 1960er- und 1970er-Jahren." *Zeithistorische Forschungen* 5, no. 2: 36–257.

Hammerstein, Katrin. 2017. *Gemeinsame Vergangenheit—getrennte Erinnerung? Der Nationalsozialismus in Gedächtnisdiskursen und Identitätskonstruktionen von Bundesrepublik Deutschland, DDR und Österreich*. Diktaturen und ihre Überwindung im 20. und 21. Jahrhundert 11. Göttingen.

Heidenreich, Ronny, Daniela Münkel, and Elke Stadelmann-Wenz. 2016. *Geheimdienstkrieg in Deutschland: die Konfrontation von DDR-Staatssicherheit und Organisation Gehlen 1953*. Veröffentlichungen der Unabhängigen Historiker-kommission zur Erforschung der Geschichte des Bundesnachrichtendienstes 1945–1968. Berlin.

Heitzer, Enrico. 2008. *"Affäre Walter." Die vergessene Verhaftungswelle.* Berlin.

———. 2011. "Altenburg, Güstrow, Werdau und anderswo: die Kampfgruppe gegen Unmenschlichkeit (KgU) und der Jugendwiderstand in der SBZ und frühen DDR." In *"Wir sind das Volk:" Die Deutschen 1848 und 1989*, edited by Bundesarchiv-Erinnerungsstätte für die Freiheitsbewegungen in der deutschen Geschichte, 55–66. Rastatt.

———. 2015a. *Die Kampfgruppe gegen Unmenschlichkeit (KgU): Widerstand und Spionage im Kalten Krieg 1948–1959.* Zeithistorische Studien 53. Weimar.

———. 2015b. *Opposition und Widerstand in der Sowjetischen Besatzungszone und frühen DDR.* Erfurt.

Herf, Jeffrey. 1997. *Divided Memory: The Nazi Past in the Two Germanys.* Cambridge.

Hockerts, Hans Günter, ed. 1998. *Drei Wege deutscher Sozialstaatlichkeit: NS-Diktatur, Bundesrepublik und DDR im Vergleich.* Schriftenreihe der Vierteljahrshefte für Zeitgeschichte 76. Munich.

Jänicke, Christin, and Benjamin Paul-Siewert, eds. 2017. *30 Jahre Antifa in Ostdeutschland: Perspektiven auf eine eigenständige Bewegung.* 2nd edition. Münster.

Jarausch, Konrad H. 2004. *Die Umkehr: deutsche Wandlungen 1945–1995.* Munich.

Kisatsky, Deborah. 2005. *The United States and the European Right, 1945–1955.* Columbus.

Kowalczuk, Ilko-Sascha. 2009. *Endspiel: Die Revolution von 1989 in der DDR.* Bonn.

Kühling, Gerd. 2016. *Erinnerung an nationalsozialistische Verbrechen in Berlin: Verfolgte des Dritten Reiches und geschichtspolitisches Engagement im Kalten Krieg 1945–1979.* Berlin.

Maddrell, Paul. 2006. *Spying on Science: Western Intelligence in Divided Germany 1945–1961.* Oxford.

Maier, Charles S. 1981. "The Two Postwar Eras and the Conditions for Stability in Twentieth-Century Western Europe." *American Historical Review* 86, no. 2: 327–367.

———. 1987. *In Search of Stability: Explorations in Historical Political Economy.* New York.

Müller, Klaus-Dieter, Thomas Schaarschmidt, Mike Schmeitzner, and Andreas Weigelt. 2015. *Todesurteile sowjetischer Militärtribunale gegen Deutsche (1944–1947): Eine historisch-biografische Studie.* Schriften des Hannah-Arendt-Instituts für Totalitarismusforschung 56. Göttingen.

Neubert, Ehrhart. 1998. *Geschichte der Opposition in der DDR: 1949–1989.* 2nd edition. Bonn.

Pampel, Bert, and Siegfried Reiprich. 2013. "Heinz Brandt. Im Widerstand gegen Nationalsozialismus und Stalinismus." In *Damit wir nicht vergessen: Erinnerung an den Totalitarismus in Europa. Ein Lesebuch für Schüler höherer Klassen überall in Europa*, edited by Gillian Purves, 116–123. Prague.

Petrow, Nikita W., and Jan Foitzik. 2009. *Die sowjetischen Geheimdienste in der SBZ/DDR von 1945 bis 1953.* Texte und Materialien zur Zeitgeschichte 17. Berlin.

Reich, Ines, and Maria Schultz. 2015. *Sprechende Wände: Häftlingsinschriften im Gefängnis Leistikowstraße Potsdam.* Forschungsbeiträge und Materialien der Stiftung Brandenburgische Gedenkstätten 13. Berlin.

Reinhard, Oliver. 2012. "Neonazis: Wotansbrüder und Weimarer Front." *Die Zeit*, 20 August 2012. Accessed 11 February 2018, www.zeit.de/2012/08/DDR-Nazis/komplettansicht.

Schmidt, Monika. 2007. *Schändungen jüdischer Friedhöfe in der DDR: Eine Dokumentation.* Positionen, Perspektiven, Diagnosen 1. Berlin.

Stöver, Bernd. 2002. *Die Befreiung vom Kommunismus: Amerikanische Liberation Policy im Kalten Krieg 1947–1991.* Zeithistorische Studien 22. Cologne.

Suckut, Siegfried. 2016. *Volkes Stimmen: "Ehrlich, aber deutlich"—Privatbriefe an die DDR-Regierung.* Munich.

Waibel, Harry. 2011. *Diener vieler Herren: Ehemalige NS-Funktionäre in der SBZ/DDR.* Frankfurt a. M.

———. 2012. *Rassisten in Deutschland.* Frankfurt a. M.

———. 2014. *Der gescheiterte Anti-Faschismus der SED: Rassismus in der DDR.* Frankfurt a. M.

———. 2017. *Die braune Saat: Antisemitismus und Neonazismus in der DDR.* Stuttgart.

Weigelt, Andreas. 2015. "Fallgruppenübersicht und Erschließungsregister—Leitfaden für die biographische Dokumentation." In *Todesurteile sowjetischer Militärtribunale gegen Deutsche (1944–1947): Eine historisch-biografische Studie,* Schriften des Hannah-Arendt-Instituts für Totalitarismusforschung, edited by Andreas Weigelt, Klaus-Dieter Müller, Thomas Schaarschmidt, and Mike Schmeitzner, 159–416. Göttingen.

Weiß, Peter Ulrich. 2015. "Civil Society from the Underground: The Alternative Antifa Network in the GDR." *Journal of Urban History* 41, no. 4: 647–664.

Wierling, Dorothee. 2016. "Die DDR als Fall-Geschichte." In *Die DDR als Chance: Neue Perspektiven auf ein altes Thema,* edited by Ulrich Mählert, 205–213. Berlin.

Chapter 5

The GDR's Judgment against Hans Globke

On the Conviction of the Nazi Lawyer and Head of the Federal Chancellery under Konrad Adenauer by the Supreme Court of the GDR in the Summer of 1963

Klaus Bästlein

Hans Globke was the author of the most important addition to the National Socialist racial laws. He also played a leading role in devising the regulations relating to them, which included legal procedures for deportations. In 1949, Adenauer appointed Globke head of the Federal Chancellery. In this position, he ensured a thorough renazification of the Federal Republic of Germany (FRG) while coordinating secret services. In October 1963, Adenauer and Globke retired for age-related reasons. At the Eichmann trial in Jerusalem in 1961, for the first time, the international spotlight shined on Globke. Fritz Bauer, the chief public prosecutor in Frankfurt, wanted to bring charges against him, but ultimately failed. After the trial, the German Democratic Republic (GDR) prepared its own trial against Globke. The GDR's Supreme Court sentenced him to life imprisonment in absentia. The judgment was based on international law, was legally flawless, and went beyond extant German research into the murder of Jews. The Globke case leads us into the jungle of the myths and legends of German postwar history.

Globke: The Terrible Jurist

Hans Josef Maria Globke, son of a cloth wholesaler, was born in Düsseldorf in 1898 (Bevers 2009; Lommatzsch 2009; Strecker 1961). His strict Catholic family, which included five children, moved to Aachen. After graduating from high school in 1916, he served in an artillery unit on the Western Front. Beginning in late 1918, he studied law. Globke received his doctorate and sought an administrative position.

Globke joined the Catholic Center Party and became a district assessor (*Regierungsassessor*) in 1926. In December 1929, he was appointed to the Higher Civil Service and transferred to the Prussian Ministry of the Interior. Globke coauthored the law regulating names and, as early as 1932, drafted guidelines that were antisemitic in nature (more on these below). Despite his oath of service to democracy, he remained loyal to the National Socialists. At the end of 1933, he was appointed a senior civil servant (*Oberregierungsrat*).

Globke married in 1934 and began working in the Reich Ministry of the Interior in November that year. There he was responsible for name changes and shared responsibility for "race questions," coauthoring the "blood protection law." Globke was not directly involved in the enactment of the Nuremberg Laws. But together with his department head, Hans Stuckart, later a participant at the Wannsee Conference, Globke wrote a quasi-official addition to the laws (Stuckart and Globke 1936). He did not restrict antisemitic regulations but interpreted them very broadly.

This applied, for example, to the term "racial defilement" (*Rassenschande*). While Section 2 of the Law for the Protection of German Blood stated that "sexual intercourse" was punishable, Globke wrote, "Sexual intercourse is not only to be understood as coitus, i.e., the natural union of the genitals, but also similar acts, e.g., mutual masturbation" (Stuckart and Globke 1936: 112). The Supreme Court of the German Reich followed his line of thinking, and soon regarded even kissing or any show of tenderness as evidence of "racial defilement."

Globke's addition was legal pornography. With his construal of the term "sexual intercourse," he opened the door to unlimited interpretation. Globke wrote the most important ordinances on the Nuremberg Laws. The First Ordinance to the Reich Citizenship Law determined who was considered Jewish.[1] Globke also devised the introduction of the compulsory first names of "Sara" and "Israel." In 1938, he was promoted to undersecretary (*Ministerialrat*). In 1941, when deportations of Jews began, Globke wrote the Eleventh Ordinance to the Reich Citizenship Law. This meant that Jews became stateless when leaving the territory of the Reich, and their property "fell" to the Reich.[2]

Shortly before deportations of Europe's Jews began, Globke visited occupied countries and helped implement the ordinances. In 1941, he applied to the NSDAP but was rejected because of his earlier commitment to political Catholicism. Globke was not a Catholic resistance fighter, however (Bevers 2009: 67–69). After 1945, there were stories about his involvement in the 20 July 1944 attempt on Hitler's life. Yet Globke does not appear in any research on the subject.

Globke: Head of the Federal Chancellery

In August 1945, Hans Globke was interned by the Americans. At the trial at Nuremberg, he provided evidence of the Nazi euthanasia campaign. He joined the CDU, and in 1949 was promoted to vice president of the Regional Court of Audit of North Rhine-Westphalia. In the meantime, he got to know Adenauer, who had emerged from the National Socialist era with his reputation intact, unlike his soon-to-be loyal assistant. Adenauer could therefore rely on Globke's absolute loyalty.

Both came from the Rhineland, studied law, and were Catholics. Adenauer, however, was twenty-two years older than Globke and, unlike him, entered politics early in life. In 1917, he became the youngest mayor of a major city in the German Empire. The first chancellor of the Federal Republic was certainly no dyed-in-the-wool democrat. And while religious, he was no antisemite, unlike Globke. When Hitler visited Cologne on 18 February 1933, Adenauer refused to fly Nazi flags on public buildings. This was followed by his removal from office. During the Nazi period, he had to go into hiding several times to avoid arrest (Köhler 1994; Wagner 2017).

After 1945, Adenauer enjoyed a career in the CDU. Reconciliation with France made European unification possible. Germany's "economic miracle" overcame the hardships of the postwar period, and Adenauer ensured that refugees and displaced persons were integrated into society. He signed his first agreements with Israel. Yet under Adenauer's government, Nazi party members got a second chance, and, in allowing this to happen, the chancellor went much too far. Globke played a key role in this context. In 1951, Hitler's civil servants and employees were given the right to be "recycled" (Kirn 1972). Anticommunism became the West German ideology of integration. In 1953, Hans Globke was formally promoted to chief of staff of the Chancellery. He implemented policies, but it was Adenauer who made the decisions.

Globke also oversaw the Gehlen Organization, a Nazi secret service used by the Americans for spying against the Soviets. In 1956, it became the Federal Intelligence Service (Bundesnachrichtendienst / BND). Besides the BND, the Federal Office for the Protection of the Constitution (*Bundesamt für Verfassungsschutz* / BfV) was also directly subordinate to the chief of staff of the federal chancellery, Globke, who used both organizations to spy on opposition. The German magazine *Spiegel* wrote, "Pullach's rule of thumb: those who oppose Adenauer are communists" (Bevers 2009: 135). Dossiers were compiled on Willy Brandt's extramarital past and his fight against Hitler's Germany; even the coalition partner, the FDP, was spied on.

On 15 October 1963, Adenauer and Globke resigned. They had governed the new state in an autocratic and authoritarian manner. Globke's personnel policy meant that Hitler's former party supporters dominated politics, the administration, and the judiciary. It was not by chance that the Spiegel Affair, a conflict over media exposé of the democratic deficits of the Bonn Republic, came at the end of Adenauer and Globke's rule.

Globke in Jerusalem

Globke first drew international attention at the Eichmann trial in Jerusalem in 1961. His ordinances relating to the Reich Citizenship Law had laid the groundwork for deportations of Jews. GDR propaganda spoke of direct cooperation between Eichmann and Globke (Lemke 1995; Bästlein 1994: 408–410), yet the two men had never met. GDR star attorney Friedrich Karl Kaul acted in Jerusalem. The circumstances created by Globke offered an opportunity to present the Federal Republic as the state of Nazi perpetrators.[3]

GDR propaganda claimed, untruthfully, that the government of the FRG had contractually agreed with Israel to grant loans and arms deliveries if Globke was spared in the trial against Eichmann. There was no such agreement. However, Bonn delayed loans and arms deliveries in view of the Eichmann trial. GDR propagandists had correctly put two and two together.

The trial itself wrote legal history (Baumann 1963: 110–112). It took place before the Jerusalem District Court between 11 April and 15 December 1961. Charges were brought under the international criminal law of the London Agreement and Charter of August 1945. For the first time ever, the murder of European Jews was systematically dealt with and documented in court. Eichmann was sentenced to death. The Israeli Supreme Court upheld the sentence on 29 May 1962, and the death sentence was carried out two days later. In Germany today, the decision of the Israeli court is as unknown as the Globke ruling in East Berlin.

Adenauer was satisfied. Globke was mentioned in Israel, but only by the defense at the appeal trial; it hardly made waves. Treaties with Israel were concluded, and the vast majority of German citizens dismissed accusations against Globke as "communist propaganda."

Globke Accused by Fritz Bauer in Frankfurt am Main?

Globke also had opponents in the Federal Republic, in particular, chief public prosecutor in Frankfurt, Fritz Bauer, who took action against him (Steinke 2014; Wojak 2009). Bauer was an exception in the judiciary. He was influenced by his roots in Jewish culture, his social democratic convictions, and his exile in Denmark. He had survived thanks to the 1943 Danish rescue operation for Jews. At the time, Eichmann was beside himself at the thought that an entire people—from the king to farmers, factory workers, and fishermen via the church, banks, and political parties—was helping the Jews (Straede 1997; Yahil 1969; Cesarani 2004).

In 1949, Bauer returned to Germany, becoming chief public prosecutor in Braunschweig in 1950 and in Frankfurt am Main in 1956. In 1957, he was informed of Eichmann's whereabouts but did not alert the BND, the Federal Criminal Police Office, or the Foreign Office, because they protected Nazi mass murderers. Yet Bauer was not inactive; he notified the Mossad, the Israeli secret service. In the end it was Ben Gurion who gave the go-ahead for Eichmann to be abducted to Israel.

The origins of the Eichmann trial can thus be traced to Fritz Bauer's initiative. This was also true of the Frankfurt Auschwitz trial, which took place from 1963 to 1965, and the Globke trial in East Berlin in 1963. Bauer originally wanted to charge Globke in Frankfurt. He cooperated with the GDR's General Prosecutor's Office because it had the personnel files on Globke as well as the files of the NS Ministry of the Interior. While Bauer rejected the SED dictatorship, he worked with East Berlin when it came to addressing some of the most serious crimes in human history. This could have cost him his post; according to the political criminal law of the Federal Republic of Germany at the time, this constituted treason (Brüneck 1978).

Bauer's efforts to indict Globke in Frankfurt failed. When Adenauer learned of this, he intervened with Minister President Georg August Zinn (SPD).[4] However, Bauer's cooperation with the General Prosecutor's Office of the GDR did not disappear when the investigations against Globke in Frankfurt came to an end. There are indications that Bauer not only secretly passed his findings on Eichmann to the Israeli judiciary, but also those on Globke to the GDR Chief Public Prosecutor's Office (Foth 2006; Wieland 2002).

Preparing the Globke Trial in East Berlin

When Fritz Bauer's efforts failed, Albert Norden sought to hold a trial against Globke in East Berlin. The time to prepare for the trial was short, since it was supposed to take place while Globke was in office. The Ministry for State Security (Ministerium für Staatssicherheit / MfS) held preparatory conferences in Warsaw in 1962 and Berlin in January 1963. Representatives of the Supreme Court, the Chief Public Prosecutor's Office, and the MfS met on 3 April 1963. Agreements were made that contradicted the rule of law but proved common in such proceedings. In this case, however, the court, the chief public prosecutor's office, and the MfS obviously acted independently of one another. That the final report of the MfS was not simply adopted and that the content of the indictment was not paraphrased in the judgment have been completely overlooked in the literature to date.

Instead, Christian Dirks and Annette Weinke have placed the Globke trial in the history of the Oberländer trial.[5] Henry Leide did not even examine the trial as the most important NS proceeding. However, he wrote, "The trial was ... not suitable to make a contribution to the reappraisal ... of the genocide of the Jews" (Leide 2005: 82). The opposite is true. Jürgen Bevers (2009: 19–21), who produced the best Globke biography to date, discussed the trial only briefly, and GDR prosecutor Carlos Foth (2006) described its legal and factual bases but did not debate the judgment.

The trial began before the First Criminal Senate of the Supreme Court of the GDR on 8 July 1963. A long editorial by Albert Norden was published on 6 July 1963. He wrote, "This trial ... is something the authorities of the Federal Republic should actually have endeavored to hold for a long time." That was true. Norden explained that close cooperation between Globke and Eichmann would now come to light. The trial, he said, represented a "world court." Self-righteously, he continued: "The Supreme Court ... will act in the name of the good Germany, which has resolved and overcome the past."[6] The head of propaganda of the GDR thus set the agenda. On 8 July, he stated, "The world is looking to Berlin: ... The trial is regarded as a 'continuation of the Eichmann trial.'"[7]

Daniel Kloski's statement was presented on 15 July: "When the war began, I was with my parents in Grodno.... We ... had to wear yellow stars. In November 1941, the population was locked up in the ghetto.... At the end of 1942, the annihilation began.... In the beginning, five people were hanged in the main street of the ghetto as intimidation.... One of them was a young girl. She was left to hang there for three days.... On August 16, the order came to start with a small piece of luggage. That meant annihilation."[8] When asked, he answered, "I was 13 years old at the time."

Reporting by *Neues Deutschland* was completely geared to propaganda. Globke's "prejudgment" in GDR media was reminiscent of earlier show trials. Yet historical events receded behind phrases such as "world court" and Globke's work for Eichmann. The only exception was Daniel Kloski's statement. It showed what was possible. The trial offered a lesson but was turned into a vehicle for agitation.

The Judgment against Globke

In contrast to the exploitation of the trial for the purposes of propaganda, the judgment by the GDR Supreme Court is not objectionable. Only the representation of the GDR as the "better"—"antifascist"—German state appears problematic. Otherwise, the Supreme Court of the GDR used language objectively and represented the facts meticulously. The conviction was based on the London Statute of 8 August 1945 in conjunction with Article 5.1 of the GDR Constitution and Section 211 of the Criminal Code. The court thus applied international and German law (Rüter and de Mildt 2002: 70–71).

After presenting Globke's resume, the judgment detailed his activities. His contributions to antisemitic regulations began even before the Nazis seized power. A circular written by Globke dated 24 November 1932 prohibited the changing of "Jewish names." Later, Globke's Second Ordinance was added to the Law on the Alteration of Family and Personal Names of 17 August 1938, according to which Jews had to use the additional forenames of "Sara" and "Israel." He also drafted the First Ordinance to the Reich Citizenship Law of 14 November 1935, which defined who was to be considered Jewish.

Globke wrote the first addition to the "Nuremberg Laws." He interpreted the regulations excessively. His commentary also meant that in a trial, those affected by the laws were left with no way out. Women, for example, had to incriminate their sexual partners. A law drafted by Globke against abuse in marriage and adoption was targeted at Jews. They were not allowed to adopt "Aryan" children. Globke was also involved in regulations regarding the marking of the passports held by Jews with a "J."

Globke's Eleventh Ordinance to the Reich Citizenship Law of 25 November 1941 was decisive for the "Final Solution." Furniture and household effects were auctioned off to "ethnic Germans" (*deutsche Volksgenossen*). Tax offices used real estate, securities, and more for their own purposes. This model was also applied in occupied countries. The Thirteenth Ordinance meant that the property of Jews who died in the Reich could also be transferred to tax authorities. On 25 November 1944, Globke instructed registry offices to inform the tax offices of the deaths of Jews. He signed this decree.

When it came to anti-Jewish measures, the Supreme Court of the GDR consistently made correct historical assessments that went far beyond what was known in Germany at the time. That the legal principles and classifications of Nazi acts that were drafted by Globke were free of errors in the GDR's judgment should be stressed, given the level of GDR jurisprudence at that time.

The defendant's internal attitudes were then explored. Globke did not receive orders and was able to develop his own initiative. The court saw in him a "dogged antisemite" (Rüter and de Mildt 2002: 176). It stated that his relevant commentary confirmed "a malignant addiction to extending the racial laws." The court then subsumed the actions under international criminal law: "These mass crimes, by their very nature, had to be controlled by the state and carried out by the entire mechanism of the fascist dictatorship."

The murder of Jews was regarded as a process carried out according to the division of labor, in which various activities were intertwined under state control. Regarding the accused, Hans Josef Maria Globke, the judgment read, "The activity of the ministerial bureaucracy [played] an important role. . . . [It] coordinated the individual issues with each other and so often produced and concretized the 'Führer's will' and enforced it through to the ultimate consequence. The responsibility of superiors . . . cannot, therefore, absolve their subordinates . . . from their . . . responsibility" (Rüter and de Mildt 2002: 184–185).

The Supreme Court determined that the accused had (1) participated in the establishment of the Nazi dictatorship and the enforcement of the "Führer Principle"; (2) played a key role in the extermination of the Jews through the enactment of corresponding normative acts and their unrestricted interpretation; and (3) was involved in the policy of Germanization, especially in Eastern Europe but also in Western Europe. With regard to the first point, however, the Court of First Instance was unable to find any infringement of international or German criminal provisions that were not statute-barred.

The court then turned to more subjective matters. Globke was characterized as an "assiduous and overzealous official." It explained, "The genocide in which the accused participated . . . is . . . a crime, . . . which developed ... gradually.... The genocide ... increased dynamically until it culminated in the inferno of mass slaughter." It went on to say, "Just as gradually ... the intention of the accused, Globke, developed, too." And, "The murder was first committed by law before it was physically carried out to this extent" (Rüter and de Mildt 2002: 190). It remained unclear how Globke was involved in anti-Jewish activities leading up to and including genocide. He never had any contact with Eichmann. A gap in the evidence remained.[9]

When it came to sentencing, the court stated that the penalty had to come from the Criminal Code. The severest punishment appeared in the paragraph on murder, which only allowed for the death penalty or life imprisonment. A death sentence, however, would have met rejection in Western Europe. The judgment stated, "In the present case, it was not possible ... to completely ignore that the causes of the criminal activity of the accused were established by German imperialism in its most extreme form, that of fascism" (Rüter and de Mildt 2002: 194). Thus Globke ironically "benefited" from the GDR's fascism theory.[10]

False Historical Images in the East and West

The consequences of the policies of Adenauer and Globke were far-reaching. When they resigned in 1963, the judiciary, administration, and politics of the Federal Republic were influenced by former Nazi activists. According to several studies on ministries and authorities in the Federal Republic that have been conducted in the last decade, GDR data on renazification in the West was still understated.

Thus, among the nine thousand judges and prosecutors in 1953, two-thirds had served Hitler. Until 1970, 53 percent of senior staff in the Federal Ministry of Justice were ex-NSDAP members (Bösch and Wirsching 2015: 24; Raas 2016). The figure for the Federal Ministry of the Interior was 54 percent. At the Bundesnachrichtendienst (BND), more than half the staff had a Nazi past. The situation was even worse at the Federal Criminal Police Office (Bundeskriminalamt / BKA). At the end of the 1950s, two-thirds of management came from the SS, and about half were investigated for Nazi crimes. Ex-NS activists also dominated the police (Baumann et al. 2011).[11]

After 1945, homosexuals as well as Sinti and Roma were persecuted using NS stereotypes (Stümke and Finkler 1981; Stengel 2004). Nowhere else in Europe was there a ban on the Communist Party and persecution of sympathizers. The Federal Constitutional Court was considered a "foreign body." Protests against remilitarization were brutally suppressed;

the "Spiegel affair" threatened the freedom of the press. Police violence against students was excessive in 1967 and 1968, and multiple bans on employment of communist students undermined the constitution in the 1970s.

The prosecution of Nazi crimes in the Federal Republic of Germany remained mere camouflage; the men pulling the levers were not prosecuted. Only a few mid-level officials stood trial, and Nazi murderers received light sentences—"*Streichelstrafen*" (punishment by caresses) as Ernst Bloch put it. Hundreds of thousands of "minor subordinates" were prosecuted only if they had committed excesses (quoted in Bästlein 2016: 5–7).

The GDR, however, was not the "better Germany." A "post-fascist society" existed between the Elbe and Oder rivers too. Studies show that Nazis were also employed in the GDR bureaucracy, albeit not to the same extent as West Germany. By 1970, for example, about 20 percent of senior staff in the administrative department of the GDR Ministry of the Interior had belonged to the NSDAP. In the realm of internal security, the figure was only 7 percent; this comprised State Security, the Volkspolizei (the GDR's national police force), and the Command Sector in the Ministry of the Interior (Bösch and Wirsching 2015: 35).

In the People's Army (the GDR's Army), Hitler's generals and officers enjoyed careers that were as brilliant as those they had had in the Bundeswehr. The National Democratic Party of Germany was formed in 1949 to mobilize former Nazis. Even the official apparatus of the SED contained many former NSDAP supporters. In East Germany, too, entire village communities covered up for NS perpetrators. But the GDR had a systemic advantage over the West because the SED could be elected but not removed. NS crimes were thus pursued more intensively there than in the West.

No German historian or lawyer has seriously dealt with the Globke judgment. Only the Amsterdam-based professor of criminal law Christiaan Frederik Rüter, who, as a Dutchman, does not share the prejudices of the German academic community, has drawn attention to the details (de Mildt 2003).[12] As a result, it remains remarkable that a trial that was conducted for propagandistic purposes and prepared contrary to the rule of law led to a legally irreproachable judgment, the historical significance of which was considerable.

Hans Globke was a Nazi white-collar criminal. He created the legal conditions for the extermination of the Jews in Europe. Mass murder would not have been possible without the definition of who was considered a Jew and without rules on the exploitation of Jewish property. This applied to almost all occupied countries in Europe that, with the exception of Denmark, adopted Globke's specifications. In addition, there was his legal pornography regarding the interpretation of "racial defilement." On account of these acts, Globke was rightly convicted of crimes against humanity under international criminal law.

Globke should never have taken a leading position in the Federal Republic. His activity casts more than a mere shadow over Adenauer. Globke does not just represent a moral problem. The renazification he pursued left such a lasting impression on the young Federal Republic that it took decades before it was overcome. This is a dark chapter in West German history in two senses, but one that must no longer be ignored simply because of its unpleasantness for today's political class.

Klaus Bästlein, born in 1956, is a lawyer and holds a doctorate in history. He has worked for the German Resistance Memorial Center since 1983 and has been a research associate at the Hamburg Justice Department since 1990. Since 1994, he has worked at the Senate Administration for Justice in Berlin. In 2000, he began working on projects at the Free University of Berlin and the University of Karlsruhe. Since 2008, he has consulted on political and historical research at the Berlin State Commissioner for Stasi Documents (now Berlin Commissioner for Research on the SED Dictatorship).

Notes

This essay has been expanded into a book, *Der Fall Globke*, published in 2018 by Metropol-Verlag.

1. Ordinance of 14 November 1935, Reichsgesetzblatt (RGBl.) I, 1333.
2. Ordinance of 25 November 1941, RGBl. I, 722–723.
3. Albert Norden initiated the campaigns. As a communist of Jewish origin, he survived the Nazi terror in France and the United States. As of 1949, he worked for GDR propaganda. In late 1954, he became a Politburo member. From 1957 onward, Norden took the renazification of the Federal Republic of Germany to heart. In 1965, the famous *Braunbuch Nazi- und Kriegsverbrecher* (Brown book: War and Nazi criminals in the Federal Republic) was published containing names of over 1,800 Nazi offenders (Podewin 2003).
4. Zinn, however, had already agreed with Bauer to waive the proceedings against Globke. Otherwise, any further cooperation between the CDU and SPD would have been in question.
5. Contrary to what is often claimed, the proceedings against the Federal Minister for Refugees and Expellees, Oberländer, were not exemplary in this case. As early as 1923, Theodor Oberländer took part in Hitler's march to the Feldherrnhalle. A commission with Albert Norden, Minister of Justice Hilde Benjamin, Friedrich Karl Kaul, and Chief Public Prosecutor Josef Streit prepared the trial in

East Berlin in 1960. But the main accusations against Oberländer were inaccurate. He had not, for example, ordered the Nightingale Battalion to carry out Jewish massacres after the capture of Lvov in 1941. Nevertheless, on 29 April 1960, the Supreme Court of the GDR sentenced Oberländer to life imprisonment in absentia. Due to the false accusations, the problematic conduct of the case, and the legally inadequate judgment, the procedure turned into a fiasco. That is why it would not serve as a model for the Globke trial.

6. Quoted from *Neues Deutschland*, 6 July 1963, 1–2.
7. Quoted in *Neues Deutschland*, 8 July 1963.
8. Quoted in *Neues Deutschland*, 15 July 1963.
9. But this gap is easy to fill. Globke was taught by Hans Stuckart, the head of his department at the Ministry of Interior. Like Globke, Stuckart was a lawyer, took part in the Wannsee Conference, and held the next highest SS rank after the Reichsführer. When Himmler became Reich minister of the interior in 1943, Stuckart even conducted business on his behalf (Jasch 2012).
10. The author of the judgment was Dr. Heinrich Toeplitz, born in 1914. The First Ordinance to the Reich Citizenship Law had categorized him as "a half-Jew" and deprived him of any further education in 1937. After 1945, he enjoyed a career in the GDR as a CDU member; he became state secretary in the Ministry of Justice in 1950 and president of the Supreme Court in 1963. Toeplitz was always loyal to the SED as a *Blockflöte* (i.e., a member of one of the GDR bloc parties) and pronounced legally untenable verdicts against "refugees of the republic." In the Globke case, he demonstrated that he was quite a good lawyer (Wentker 2001: 278–279.).
11. To date, only individual studies on the West German police after 1945 are available (Noethen 2003; Weinhauer 2003).
12. See also the website Justice und NS-Verbrechen (Justice and NS crimes), accessed 12 December 2017, www.junsv.nl.

References

Bästlein, Klaus. 1994. "'Nazi-Blutrichter als Stützen des Adenauer-Regimes.' Die DDR-Kampagnen gegen NS-Richter und -Staatsanwälte, die Reaktionen der bundesdeutschen Justiz und ihre gescheiterte 'Selbstreinigung' 1957–1968." In *Die Normalität des Verbrechens*, edited by Helge Grabitz, Klaus Bästlein, and Johannes Tuchel, 408–443. Berlin.

———. 2016. "Zeitgeist und Justiz. Die Strafverfolgung von NS-Verbrechen im deutsch-deutschen Vergleich und im historischen Verlauf." *Zeitschrift für Geschichtswissenschaft* 64, no. 1: 5–28.

Baumann, Imanuel, Herbert Reinke, Andrej Stephan, Patrick Wagner, Deutschland Bundeskriminalamt (BKA). 2011. *Schatten der Vergangenheit. Das BKA und seine Gründungsgeneration in der frühen Bundesrepublik*. Cologne.

Baumann, Jürgen. 1963. "Gedanken zum Eichmann-Urteil." *Juristenzeitung* 18, no. 4: 110–121.

Bevers, Jürgen. 2009. *Der Mann hinter Adenauer. Hans Globkes Aufstieg vom NS-Juristen zur grauen Eminenz der Bonner Republik*. Berlin.

Bösch, Frank, and Andreas Wirsching. 2015. *Die Nachkriegsgeschichte des Bundesministeriums des Innern (BMI) und des Ministeriums des Innern der DDR (MdI) hinsichtlich möglicher personeller und sachlicher Kontinuitäten zur Zeit des Nationalsozialismus — Vorstudie*. N.p.
Brüneck, Alexander von. 1978. *Politische Justiz gegen Kommunisten in der Bundesrepublik Deutschland 1949–1968*. Frankfurt.
Cesarani, David. 2004. *Adolf Eichmann. Bürokrat und Massenmörder*. Berlin.
Foth, Carlos. 2006. "Die Nürnberger Gesetze und der Globke-Prozess in der DDR." *Bulletin für Faschismus- und Weltkriegsforschung* 27: 44–70.
Görtemaker, Manfred, and Christoph Safferling, eds. 2013. *Die Rosenburg. Das Bundesministerium der Justiz und die NS-Vergangenheit—eine Bestandsaufnahme*. Göttingen.
Jasch, Hans-Christian. 2012. *Staatssekretär Wilhelm Stuckart und die Judenpolitik. Der Mythos von der sauberen Verwaltung*. Munich.
Kirn, Michael. 1972. *Verfassungsumsturz oder Rechtskontinuität?: Die Stellung der Jurisprudenz nach 1945 zum Dritten Reich, insbesondere die Konflikte um die Kontinuität der Beamtenrechte und Art. 131 Grundgesetz*. Berlin.
Köhler, Henning. 1994. *Adenauer. Eine politische Biographie*. Berlin.
Leide, Henry. 2005. *NS-Verbrecher und Staatssicherheit. Die geheime Vergangenheitspolitik der DDR*. Göttingen.
Lemke, Michael. 1995. "Instrumentalisierter Antifaschismus und SED-Kampagnen-Politik im deutschen Sonderkonflikt 1960–1968." In *Die geteilte Vergangenheit. Zum Umgang mit Nationalsozialismus und Widerstand in beiden deutschen Staaten*, edited by Jürgen Danyel, 61–86. Berlin.
Lommatzsch, Erik. 2009. *Hans Globke (1898–1973). Beamter im Dritten Reich und Staatssekretär Adenauers*. Frankfurt a. M.
Noethen, Stefan. 2003. *Alte Kameraden und neue Kollegen. Polizei in Nordrhein-Westfalen 1945–1953*. Essen.
Podewin, Norbert. 2003. *Albert Norden. Der Rabbinersohn im Politbüro*. Berlin.
Raas, Christoph. 2016. *Das Sozialprofil des Bundesnachrichtendienstes. Von den Anfängen bis 1968*. Berlin.
Rottleuthner, Hubert. 2010. *Karrieren und Kontinuitäten deutscher Justizjuristen vor und nach 1945*. Berlin.
Rüter, Christiaan Frederik, and Dick W. de Mildt. 2002. *DDR-Justiz und NS-Verbrechen (DJuNSV). Registerband*. Amsterdam.
Steinke, Ronen. 2014. *Fritz Bauer: oder Auschwitz vor Gericht*. Munich.
Stengel, Katharina. 2004. *Tradierte Feindbilder: Die Entschädigung der Sinti und Roma in den fünfziger und sechziger Jahren*. Frankfurt a. M.
Straede, Therkel. 1997. *Die Menschenmauer: Dänemark im Oktober 1943: Die Rettung der Juden vor der Vernichtung*. Copenhagen.
Strecker, Reinhold. 1961. *Dr. Hans Globke. Dokumente*. Hamburg.
Stuckart, Wilhelm, and Hans Globke. 1936. *Reichsbürgergesetz, Blutschutzgesetz, Ehegesundheitsgesetz—Kommentar*. Munich.
Stümke, Hans-Georg, and Rudi Finkler. 1981. *Rosa Winkel, Rosa Listen. Homosexuelle und "Gesundes Volksempfinden" von Auschwitz bis heute*. Reinbek bei Hamburg.
Wagner, Rita, ed. 2017. *Konrad der Große. Die Adenauerzeit in Köln 1917 bis 1933*. Mainz.
Weinhauer, Klaus. 2003. *Schutzpolizei in der Bundesrepublik. Zwischen Bürgerkrieg und Innerer Sicherheit: Die turbulenten sechziger Jahre*. Paderborn.

Wentker, Hermann. 2001. *Justiz in der SBZ/DDR 1945–1953: Transformation und Rolle ihrer zentralen Institutionen*. Munich.
Wieland, Günter. 2002. "Die Ahndung von NS-Verbrechen in Ostdeutschland 1945–1990." In *DDR-Justiz und NS-Verbrechen (DJuNSV) Registerband*, edited by Christiaan Frederik Rüter and Dick W. de Mildt, 11–99. Amsterdam.
Wojak, Imtrud. 2009. *Fritz Bauer (1903–1968): Eine Biographie*. Munich.
Yahil, Leni. 1969. *The Rescue of Danish Jewry: Test of a Democracy*. Philadelphia.

Chapter 6

Might through Morality?

Some Comments on Antifascism in the GDR

Christoph Classen

"The past is not dead; it is not even past." So go the opening lines of Christa Wolf's 1976 semiautobiographical novel *Kindheitsmuster* (*Patterns of Childhood*) about her memories of childhood and her expulsion from home during the Nazi era. Little did she know that this aphorism by William Faulkner would slip into banality through constant use in a postmodern era obsessed with the past. Erroneous as this maxim may be if taken as a blanket statement, it does indeed fit the subject of Wolf's novel: the ever-present Nazi past in the German Democratic Republic (GDR). On the one hand, this past seemed "dead"—that is to say, officially defeated and publicly fixed in ritualized thought, clichéd language, and stone monuments. On the other hand, it continued to lead a life of its own, subliminally as it were, in the form of lives lived, memories, and continuities that were all but taboo in the public sphere. It was precisely this tension between a politically overdetermined public memory and a vastly different private memory that revealed, in Christa Wolf's view, the unfinished business of a difficult past.

Admittedly, the constant presence of the Nazi past was hardly limited to the GDR; it applied equally to the Federal Republic. Whereas representatives of the latter always viewed themselves in terms of the continuity of

German history, the GDR understood itself as the antithesis of German national history. Starting in the 1970s, the failed vision of German unification under the banner of communism and the resulting need to establish an "East German identity" gave rise to the selective use of certain "progressive" German traditions (buzzwords were "heritage and tradition"), none of which meant that the GDR accepted responsibility for crimes committed under Nazism. Nazi continuities were wholly attributed to West Germany. This was also the official reason that the GDR, unlike the Federal Republic, consistently refused to pay reparations to countries occupied by Germany during World War II or to representatives of the victims of persecution.

Instead, the GDR viewed itself as an "antifascist" state, resulting logically, as it were, from the "imperialist and fascist" experiences of German history. The founding of the East German state was accompanied by the purported break with political traditions. The history of war, suffering, and oppression were suddenly a thing of the past. On 8 May 1953, the anniversary of Liberation Day, East German radio proclaimed "that the Germany that . . . capitulated and perished on May 8, 1945 [was] the Germany of Fascists, big industry, big landowners, and Nazi generals."[1] Now—and this was unprecedented in German history—"liberated people"[2] were building a new future in the GDR. This promise of salvation in the form of mastering the past for the sake of a brighter, socialist future was typical of the early GDR.

In retrospect, the universal promise of progress and a better future are not the only aspects of socialism that seem bizarre. The idea of completely breaking with the past seems just as utopian. The GDR, too, had to be rebuilt primarily with the help of the existing population, who had been socialized before 1945 and who more or less went along with Nazism. Former members of the Nazi Party, the Wehrmacht, and the SS lived in the GDR just as they did in the West. It goes without saying that perceptions and mentalities survived for decades after the war, and national traditions could not simply be broken on a structural level, despite the emphasis on revolution. For this reason alone, the watershed of 1945 to 1949 was anything but a "zero hour," in East and West alike.

In this context, a paradoxical feature of the GDR's antifascist self-understanding becomes clear. It was a state that understood itself as a consequence of the immediate past while declaring this past to be over and done with, at least as far as its own sphere of rule was concerned. What the nationalist-conservative camp and others in West Germany long demanded to no avail—namely, a definitive "coming to terms" with the Nazi past—had somehow become reality in the East, where all references to the Nazi past primarily served as an apology for the socialist order.

But what distinguished the "antifascist" self-understanding of the GDR under these circumstances, and how did it change over time? How were the inevitable inconsistencies and paradoxes overcome? And how should we assess East Germany's antifascism from today's perspective? The normative standards of the present, applied often since 1990, are not sufficient to answer these questions. A historicizing perspective is needed that takes into account the strained and contradictory development of East German antifascism.

On the Perception of Fascism in the Communist Movement

Any understanding of antifascism in the GDR requires taking a look at the period before its inception and examining the communist movement's perception of right-wing mass movements that emerged in 1920s Europe. "Fascism," from a communist perspective, was by no means just a label used by the original movement under Mussolini in Italy. The term soon gained universal currency. It referred not only to other right-wing mass movements in Europe but, beginning in the mid-1930s, was broadened to include any political opponent that did not share the radical aims of proletarian revolution following the Soviet model (Luks 2017). In Germany, this seemed to rule out any moderate approaches, such as those espoused by Social Democracy, but also the policies of the liberal bourgeoisie, which were seen as hindering the goal of imminent revolution and thus "objectively" playing into the hands of capital. This explains the extension of the concept of fascism to include these groups as well, under the respective labels "national fascists" and "social fascists." The actual threat posed by right-wing movements was thus long underestimated, despite the occasional warning. The rise of Nazism and even Hitler's power grab did little to change this, perceived as they were as expressions of an existential crisis of capitalism that only improved the chances of a supposedly long overdue revolution.

From the beginning, "fascism" was more of a stereotype of a universal enemy than an empirical description of a new political phenomenon. The term was essentially absorbed in the established dichotomy of class struggle. Only well after the onset of Nazi rule in Germany (not to mention Fascist rule in Italy) did Moscow react with a change of strategy: the so-called Popular Front—that is, communist alliances with liberal and social-democratic forces. This required a revision of the concept of fascism (Bayerlein 1996: 103–122). In place of universalization came the "Dimitrov formula," named after the general secretary of the Comintern, according to which fascism was the "open, terrorist dictatorship of the most reactionary, most chauvinist, most imperialist elements of finance capital."[3] In practical terms, this was a compromise, allowing a focus on right-wing dictatorships as the "most decisive" form of imperialist rule and making room for strategic alliances without having to give up the previous definition based on class conflict and the end goal of revolution. Contrary to common opinion, the definition of fascism contained in the Dimitrov formula seems less ideological than strategic in its motivations.

Fascism and Antifascism as Foundational Historical Myths after 1945

The failure to grasp the peril posed by the Right in the 1930s and the strategic flexibility exhibited prior to the German-Soviet Non-Aggression Pact did not keep the myth of communist antifascism from spreading after World War II. A decisive factor here was the total material and moral bankruptcy of Nazism and Italian Fascism, which gave the myth plausibility after 1945. "Antifascism" was no longer just a political concept; it now referred to a concrete historical event: the putatively successful communist resistance against Nazi rule. It became a double category. On the one hand, the ideological and political agenda linked to it—tacitly or explicitly—remained the same: antifascism was espoused as (real) socialism, and fascism its adversary. The second dimension, its historical meaning, supported this political agenda, but could now be justified on the basis of "real" historical experiences and events. To put it abstractly, antifascism became a foundational historical myth (Dörner 1996: 35–37).

The strength of the strategic element could be seen in the Soviet Occupation Zone. In line with the tradition of Popular Front policy, the obligation to profess one's "antifascism" offered a compromise solution: a way of distancing oneself from the previous regime that conservatives and communists could generally agree on. This served at first as a way to secure the Soviet occupying power's control. Yet it also seemed advisable, with its Western allies in the frame, to integrate all relevant political groups, at least on the surface.

With the dissolution of the alliance of convenience between the Soviet Union and its Western allies and the resulting East-West conflict in the late 1940s, this consensus antifascism was soon a thing of the past. With the founding of the two German states at the latest, the twin terms "antifascism" and "fascism" denoted the dividing line between friend and foe, between those who belonged to society and those who did not. While the GDR declared itself a stronghold of antifascism, its political foes were now denoted by the closely related terms "fascism," "Nazism," "revanchism," "militarism," and "junkerdom." For the GDR, the main enemy was the competing German state in the West: the Federal Republic. But it was not infrequent for the terms to be applied in a general way to both camps of the Cold War: the Soviet bloc as a whole was thus "antifascist," whereas the West was labeled "fascist."

From the perspective of authorities in Moscow and East Berlin, implementing the new party line of asserting communist hegemony in strict compliance with the Soviet model required eliminating opposition and overcoming social resistance. The dual concepts of fascism and antifascism played a key role here. On the one hand, they were helpful in marginalizing bourgeois, social democratic, and national communist positions, while, on the other, they were meant to legitimize a strict policy of dissociation from the West.

The tone was correspondingly strident. The ratification of the Bonn-Paris conventions of 1955 was greeted in the Federal Republic by "howling hordes of fascists," whereas Western reception camps for migrants from the East were training "fascist rowdies" as agent provocateurs who would help in preparing "a new genocide against the peace-loving Soviet Union and the lands of people's democracies."[4] The old notion of "social fascism" had re-emerged during the Berlin crisis of 1948–1949 when it was claimed that the "Schumacher leadership" was "objectively [comprised] of neofascists and lackeys of imperialism," its anticommunism likened to Nazism.[5] "American imperialism," too, "was adopting all the traits of fascism—from ballot-rigging and election terror to the extermination of prisoners of war and the populations of occupied countries such as Korea, as well as the creation of a Gestapo and the establishment of concentration camps."[6]

"Fascism" thus reappeared as a universal enemy category with particular relevance to the present, having partly blended with class-related terms such as "imperialism" and "monopoly capitalism," and hence strongly resembling the way it was used in the period before 1934–1935. Its opposite, "antifascism," did not fare differently. Even in the immediate postwar years, survivors of concentration camps had a difficult time getting the public's attention. Now even the opposition to Nazism was being universalized and applied to the present. "Antifascist" frequently meant little more than whatever supported the latest party line against internal and external opponents. One Jewish communist resistance fighter got a taste of this when he was denied status as a Persecutee of the Nazi Regime on account of his refusal to toe the SED's policy line. Alluding to his past in the Nazi resistance, the denial was explained to him quite bluntly: "It is not about what you did back then; it's what you're doing now" (Niethammer, Plato, and Wierling 1991: 282).

With the founding of the GDR, a narrative was established that gave prominence to communist resistance during the Nazi era— indeed, it formed the centerpiece of the GDR's official antifascist culture of remembrance. But this struggle was integrated into a narrative of national advancement, a dramatic escalation, as it were, of class warfare between the working class and capital. The legacy of the sacrifices of this century-long struggle suggested the narrative was now made good by the founding of the GDR. Accordingly, the new state was a sort of Garden of Eden, the earthly liberation of humans from dependency and social adversity.

East German leaders used this secularized eschatology borrowed from the Christian model to create a founding myth that would help them combat a perceived lack of legitimacy. If German division was unpopular with the general population, then even more so Soviet hegemony and the SED rule that followed.[7] Even from a communist perspective, it was problematic that German socialism emerged not in prescribed fashion as a proletarian revolution, but through the victory of the Allied powers. The allegedly heroic—in any case, costly—antifascist struggle of German comrades proved helpful. The dead were elevated to the status of martyrs under the new system with suggestions that their suffering had served as a sort of midwife to the political project of the GDR, now bequeathed to the survivors, who, for their part, were entrusted with the task of executing this "will."

Ernst Thälmann became the human icon of this cult of the dead in the 1950s. For SED leaders, he was suited for this role for a number of reasons. Not only was he murdered in Buchenwald concentration camp, but as a participant in the Hamburg Uprising and a Moscow-loyal party chairman, he was one of the few leading figures in the German Communist Party (Kommunistische Partei Deutschlands / KPD) who could serve as a national symbol without arousing Moscow's suspicions of nationalist deviation. A veritable cult around Thälmann was established in the GDR in the years that followed, which was reflected in a variety of monuments, the Pioneer organization bearing his name, and countless streets, squares, and schools.

This narrative was literally carved into stone in the form of the Buchenwald memorial. Its 1958 dedication ceremony was a sacred enactment of the antifascist struggle, whose suffering was followed by salvation in the form of socialism. Very much in line with the Christian Passion narrative, visitors to the monument were supposed to experience the ascension from (fascist) darkness to (socialist) light (Knigge 1996: 324–326). This performance was an apparent attempt to lend the GDR an aura of holiness and make it unassailable. According to the logic of this symbolism, any criticism of the party line was tantamount to an offense against its saintly antifascist martyrs.

Apart from these forms of universalization and sacralization, specific historical references were intended to justify policy decisions. Typically, these were historical analogies connected to the wartime experiences of Germans and references to the specter of history repeating itself, possibly even worse than before. Thus, for example, personal experiences of victimhood in the firebombing of Dresden were compared to the atomic bombing of Hiroshima. "It was back when the war was just about to end, and for some crazy reason I was walking with my children down a country road . . . . Thirteen years after the demise of Dresden, I was sitting on a sickbed in the Hiroshima Atomic Hospital."[8] Attempts were made in this manner to make the threat of an atomic World War III sound plausible, a much-invoked scenario in the 1950s and 1960s, the United States being portrayed as the sole aggressor and the Eastern bloc as the guarantor of permanent peace.

There were also numerous references to continuities in the establishment of the Bonn Republic and frequent campaigns in the 1960s to expose such individuals as former Nazis (Lemke 1995: 61–86). These campaigns mainly targeted high-ranking officials such as Adenauer's undersecretary of state in the Federal Chancellery, Hans Globke, and federal president Heinrich Lübke, whose roles in the Nazi era were considered so scandalous because they seemed to offer proof of the unbroken continuity of fascist structures. Justifications of the Berlin Wall, the so-called "antifascist protective barrier" erected in 1961, also made use of historical references. This time, according to a radio address by Gerhart Eisler on 14 August (the day after the construction of the Berlin Wall), the interests of working people had been successfully defended against "big capitalists and militarists." "I only regret one thing: that German workers in 1933 did not have such a workers' army. Because then Hitler and his henchmen would have been destroyed, he wouldn't have seized power, and World War II could have been prevented."[9]

Indirectly, of course, examples like these point to the dangers of such inflationary references to historico-political myths. They often seemed arbitrary, which gradually eroded their effectiveness when used in the context of current affairs. Added to this was the codification of certain historical interpretations that at best corresponded to the experiences of communist leaders but not to the broad masses. Only certain groups of individuals found the opportunities attractive to become "antifascist" by participating in reconstruction. The majority perceived the end of the war as a demoralizing defeat and not as the dawn of a new and better era. To the German masses—that is to say, outside the ranks of the party—this official state-sanctioned history was a counternarrative that competed with the prevailing traditional paradigm of national history on the rise (and fall) of an indivisible German nation. In the language of cultural remembrance, one could say that the GDR was attempting to establish a cultural myth at a time when the population's personal, antagonistic memories remained very much alive—essentially a hopeless endeavor.[10] To be sure, the performance of the antifascist myth as the "end of history" is an indirect indication of how strongly certain individuals in the 1960s—at least in the GDR—still trusted in the cohesive power of the future promise of socialist utopia.

This changed in the 1970s and 1980s. With creeping stagnation and the sense of a loss of future, the past reemerged as a source of legitimation. By this time, however, antifascist pathos had acquired a thick patina. Those who had participated in the resistance, the Erich Honeckers and Erich Mielkes, were not only now in the minority but also had clearly passed the zenith of their careers. At best, a minority of the population could still appreciate ritualized celebrations and all too often hollow phrases (Käppner 1999). Given the state-centered and foundational character of the past, party leaders in the GDR did not succeed in opening up to new interpretations by the younger generation. This would have been the minimum requirement for successfully handing down the antifascist myth to the next generation. Instead, the promise of utopia was sometimes taken at face value, contrasted unfavorably with the real-socialist agony of the Honecker era. In her song "It Occurred to Me" (*Mir fällt ein*), the dissident singer-songwriter Bettina Wegener put it like this:

> Und ich denk an Thälmann
> und dann seh' ich was ist
> und das ist wie 'n Goldfisch gegen faulenden Fisch.
> Und ihr habt was versprochen
> und ihr hieltet es nicht
> und wer euch erinnert
> der kommt vor Gericht
> [And I think of Thälmann
> then look around me
> and it's like a goldfish compared to rotten fish
> And you promised something
> you didn't keep
> and those who remind you
> are taken to court] (Langenhahn 1997: 61).

A foundational myth had become a delegitimizing one.

Antifascism in Discussions after the End of the GDR

During the collapse of the SED regime in the fall of 1989, the "old system's last line of defense" was its allegedly consistent antifascism, as historian Stefan Wolle (2001: 144) noted. Party leaders tried to mobilize their followers against the demand for German reunification by playing up the danger of right-wing radicals. But even this did not preclude the debate about the GDR's legitimacy from focusing on its antifascist self-understanding. Understandably, critics from the ranks of the citizens' movement, but also West German politicians and scholars, were scandalized by the yawning gap between its moral claims and the instrumental character of historiography in the GDR being used to prop up the powers that be.

On the other hand, most representatives of the regime-loyal GDR elite were adamant about the importance of this antifascist self-understanding. You could "accuse this state and its social system of many things," wrote Günter Benser (1994: 150), a former historian at the Institute for Marxism-Leninism (IML), "but never that it stood on the wrong side [of history] in the battle between fascism and antifascism." Others saw in the supposedly dominant historiography of the victors, a "targeted insult and degradation of all resistance fighters," if not a "West German final solution to antifascism on the territory of the GDR" (Finker 1999: 11–13; Zorn 1996). For both sides, the German-German border was not least of all a moral line of demarcation between guilt and innocence. This made it particularly hard to abandon the "evaluational" scheme of deconstruction and opposition to it.

As necessary as it was to deconstruct the myth of antifascism, linking it to debates on the legitimacy of the GDR has done little to reveal the Janus-faced character of East German antifascism with its characteristic fusion of past and present-day political objectives. Since the semiofficial understanding of antifascism primarily saw the implementation of socialism as the most consistent means of fighting fascism, it was therefore wholly consistent from this perspective to view, for example, the social integration of countless Nazi fellow travelers and former perpetrators (van Melis 1999: 245–264) as practiced early on as "antifascist."

By 1990, however, this point could no longer be argued. The gradual erosion of the socialist project made it less convincing over time, so that when this project ultimately failed, it became the relict of a bygone era. In the ensuing debate, the GDR's policy of dealing with the past was judged according to present-day standards, which made its paradoxical nature seem quite scandalous. Its apologists found themselves on the defensive. The more problematic aspects were usually interpreted as exceptions, or as an expression of the Stalinist deformation of socialism. In some cases, counteraccusations were made by referring to equally scandalous examples of failures to deal with the Nazi past in West Germany.

From a Western perspective, the debate was about more than just the East German past. West Germans were negotiating the so-called "historians' dispute" (*Historikerstreit*), a relatively recent controversy between conservatives and liberals about the importance of anti-totalitarianism in the founding consensus of the old Federal Republic. Given the collapse of the Eastern bloc and fears of a reinvigorated German nation in the heart of Europe, the controversy entered a second round under different historical and political circumstances, this time about whether an anti-communist or anti-Nazi identity should form the basis of Germany's new identity.

Only in the aughts, when it became evident that the brief renaissance of the theory of totalitarianism did nothing to alter the debate on the collapse of communism, did the controversy over East German antifascism finally seem to have run its course. Against the backdrop of the democratic, mass media-based, and increasingly transnational culture of remembrance with regard to Germany's Nazi period, it ultimately seemed anachronistic. Its traditional focus, after all, was not the victims (least of all the Jewish ones) but the heroic communist resistance. It was not structured by the Western idea of a past that had now run its course serving as an orientation for the present, but the opposite: an ideological certainty that even the past had to bow to if necessary. Behind this lurked the teleology of historical materialism, a historico-philosophical concept inherited from the nineteenth century that was a poor fit for the postmodern Zeitgeist of the early twenty-first century.

Here lies the indirect answer to the question currently posed in the former Eastern states of Germany, given the sustained support for right-wing radicalism and populism. Why has the allegedly and thoroughly antifascist GDR had no lasting effect on the resurgence of nationalist and racist tendencies? The reason is plain enough. Without the historico-philosophical credo of socialism, this founding myth, as an integral part of the GDR's raison d'etre, would not have been viable. For more than four decades, it left no room for an open social appropriation and negotiation of history and remembrance. Contrary to the hopes of East German ideologues, the events of 1989–1990—the big protest demonstrations in autum 1989, the opening of the Berlin Wall, the breakdown of GDR dictatorship, the unification of the GDR and FRG, and the membership of the new FRG in the western alliance NATO—showed that history did not follow predetermined laws, and that the past could resist being reckoned with, even if German socialists had decided and proclaimed that it was.

Christoph Classen has been working at the Center for Contemporary Historical Research (ZZF) in Potsdam since 1997 and in the Department of Contemporary History of Media and Information Society since 2009. He teaches at the Free University of Berlin and the University of Potsdam. His scholarly work focuses on political and cultural history, European media history, the history of the Federal Republic of Germany and the GDR, and memory culture.

Notes

1. Fritz Beyling, Radio script "Kommentar des Tages," 11 April 1953 (Internationaler Befreiungstag), Deutsches Rundfunkarchiv Potsdam-Babelsberg (DRA), Historisches Archiv, Bestand Hörfunk. Kommentare 1945–49.

2. Herbert Gessner, Radio script "Kommentar zum 'Tag der Befreiung,'" 8 May 1953, DRA Potsdam, Historisches Archiv, Bestand Hörfunk. Kommentare 1945–49.

3. This definition was not penned by Dimitrov but came from the Thirteenth Plenary of the Executive Committee of the Communist International (Comintern) of November 1933. An abridged version of Dimitrov's speech at the Seventh World Congress of the Communist International can be found (in German) in Kühnl 1974: 57–75 (quote on 58).

4. Radio script "Das interessiert auch Sie!—Valka-Lager," Deutschlandsender, 17 February 1954, DRA Potsdam, Historisches Archiv, DS 54/251.

5. Jan Morel [pseudonym of Harald Hauser], Radio script "Das Wort hat Jan Morel. Churchill–Hitler, Schumacher–Göring," *Berliner Rundfunk*, 22 April 1949, DRA Potsdam, Historisches Archiv, B204-02-02/0278.

6. Karl-Eduard von Schnitzler, Radio script "Kommentar des Tages." Berlin I, II und III, 8 October 1952, DRA Potsdam, Historisches Archiv, Bestand Hörfunk, B 095-00-01/0112.

7. On the SED's reputation as the "Russian party," see Klemperer 1996, passim.

8. Herta Classen, Radio script "Kommentar des Tages," *Berliner Rundfunk* and *Berliner Welle*, 15 February 1960, DRA Potsdam, Historisches Archiv, Bestand Hörfunk, BR 60/1960.

9. Radio script "Kommentar des Tages," *Berliner Rundfunk*, 14 August 1961, DRA Berlin, Bestand Hörfunk, BR 61/915.

10. On the distinction between communicative and cultural memory, see Assmann 1991: 11–13.

References

Assmann, Aleida. 1991. *Kultur als Lebenswelt und Monument*. Frankfurt a. M.
Bayerlein, Bernhard H. 1996. "Einheitsfront- und Volksfrontmythos als Ursprungslegenden des Antifaschismus." In *Die Nacht hat zwölf Stunden, dann kommt schon der Tag. Antifaschismus—Geschichte und Neubewertung*, edited by Claudia Keller, 103–122. Berlin.

Benser, Günter. 1994. "Möglichkeiten und Grenzen einer antifaschistisch-demokratischen Erneuerung in Deutschland nach dem zweiten Weltkrieg." In *Ansichten zu einer Geschichte der DDR*, vol. 4, edited by Dietmar Keller, Hans Modrow, and Herbert Wolf, 137–152. Bonn.

Dörner, Andreas. 1996. *Politischer Mythos und symbolische Politik. Der Hermannmythos: zur Entstehung des Nationalbewußtseins der Deutschen*. Reinbek.

Finker, Kurt. 1999. "Antifaschistischer Widerstand. Kriterien. Spektrum Gewichte." In *Wider die Verfälschung deutscher Geschichte. Beiträge zum antifaschistischen Widerstand in Deutschland und zur Gründung der BRD und der DDR*, edited by Günter Judick and Hans Joachim Krusch, 11–30. Essen.

Käppner, Joachim. 1991. *Erstarrte Geschichte. Faschismus und Holocaust im Spiegel der Geschichtswissenschaft und Geschichtspropaganda der DDR*. Hamburg.

Klemperer, Victor. 1996. *So sitze ich denn zwischen allen Stühlen*. Vol. 1: *Tagebücher 1945–1949*, edited by Walter Nowojski. Berlin.

Knigge, Volkhard. 1996. "Die Gedenkstätte Buchenwald. Vom provisorischen Grabdenkmal zum Nationaldenkmal." In *Die Nacht hat zwölf Stunden, dann kommt schon der Tag. Antifaschismus—Geschichte und Neubewertung*, edited by Claudia Keller, 309–331. Berlin.

Kühnl, Reinhard, ed. 1974. *Texte zur Faschismusdiskussion*. Vol. 1: *Positionen und Kontroversen*. Reinbek.

Langenhahn, Sandra. 1997. "Ursprünge und Ausformung des Thälmannkults. Die DEFA-Filme 'Sohn seiner Klasse' und 'Führer seiner Klasse.'" In *Leit- und Feindbilder in DDR-Medien*, vol. 5, edited by Bundeszentrale für politische Bildung, 55–65. Bonn.

Lemke, Michael. 1995. "Instrumentalisierter Antifaschismus und SED-Kampagnenpolitik im deutschen Sonderkonflikt 1960–1968." In *Die geteilte Vergangenheit. Zum Umgang mit Nationalsozialismus und Widerstand in beiden deutschen Staaten*, edited by Jürgen Danyel, 61–86. Berlin.

Luks, Leonid. 2017. "Was ist Faschismus? Historische Betrachtungen über den inflationären Gebrauch eines Begriffs." *Die Kolumnisten*, 24 March 2017. Accessed on 7 December 2017, https://diekolumnisten.de/2017/03/24/was-ist-faschismus-historische-betrachtungen-ueber-den-inflationaeren-gebrauch-eines-begriffs/.

Niethammer, Lutz, Alexander von Plato, and Dorothee Wierling. 1991. *Die volkseigene Erfahrung. Eine Archäologie des Lebens in der Industrieprovinz. 30 biographische Eröffnungen*. Berlin.

van Melis, Damian. 1999. "Der große Freund der kleinen Nazis. Antifaschismus in den Farben der DDR." In *Die DDR. Erinnerungen an einen untergegangenen Staat*, edited by Heiner Timmermann, 245–264. Berlin.

Wolle, Stefan. 2001. "Staatsfeind Faschist." *Der Spiegel* 34: 144–150.

Zorn, Monika, ed. 1996. *Hitlers zweimal getötete Opfer. Westdeutsche Endlösung des Antifaschismus auf dem Gebiet der DDR*. Unerwünschte Bücher zum Faschismus 6. Freiburg.

Chapter 7

Toward a Sociology of Intelligence Agents

The GDR Foreign Intelligence Service as an Example

Helmut Müller-Enbergs

The terms "sociology" and "agents" form an odd couple and are rarely lumped together. Is it even possible to link them? A first step in answering this question would be to determine the meaning of each term. After agreeing on terminology, the next step would be to clarify whether conducting empirical social research on a highly invisible group—individuals working in intelligence—is even possible. Once that is confirmed, we can embark on a sociology of agents.

Current State of Research

Even the term "intelligence agent" is problematic. In the German context, an "agent" is a person active in or working for an intelligence service. The term, however, has multiple uses outside the intelligence field, which will be clarified later.

Sociology of Intelligence Agents

Researchers have indeed examined the "sociology of agents." Linguist Roland Mühlenbernd's 2013 dissertation, "Signals and the Structure of Societies" (submitted to the Department of Philosophy at the Eberhard Karls University in Tübingen) examines "agents that constitute the borders between language regions of signaling languages" (Mühlenbernd 2013, 134), not the type of agent discussed here.

While Hans Weber's (1971) dissertation discusses a "sociology of agents," it refers to civil liberties within rural communities in the Zurich region of Switzerland in the eighteenth century.

Jeffrey T. Richelson, David L. Blenkhorn, and Craig S. Fleisher have made relevant contributions. Richelson (1999: 6), an American political scientist, uses the term "sociological intelligence" to describe research conducted by intelligence services on social developments, social systems, and the dynamics between certain social groups to assess the stability of particular regions and their military dispositions. British marketing expert Blenkhorn and Fleischer (2005: 62), an American scholar, acknowledge the utility of these studies for competitive intelligence within the global economy.

Georg Herbstritt (2007) comes closest to what we mean here. Analyzing five hundred indictments made against West German citizens who spied for East Germany, he presents a portrait of a group and examines the social structure of the West German network of "Inoffizieller Mitarbeiter (IM)," or unofficial collaborators. Herbstritt examines their professional qualifications and family relations. One quarter worked in the West German civil service, 11 percent were self-employed, 5 percent were journalists, and 4 percent were homemakers. Since one third of these collaborators had an academic degree, Herbstritt (2007: 115–117) claimed that they were preferred targets. Unfortunately, his pioneering study included only individuals against whom the indictments had a chance of success, which was often influenced by the absence of reliable documents. Therefore, his sample is not representative of the whole.

Sociology of Intelligence Officers

There are studies on full-time intelligence officers in the German Democratic Republic (GDR). Jens Gieseke's (2000) dissertation laid the groundwork for this research. Gieske also investigated the personnel organization and living conditions of full-time employees of the East German Ministerium für Staatssicherheit (MfS). His work sheds light on what he calls the "Chekist milieu" (Gieseke 2000: 544–546)— "Chekists" being the name given to members of the secret services in Soviet satellite states.

Working together, Uwe Krähnke, Matthias Finster, Philipp Reimann, and Anja Zschirpe (2017) produced an in-depth sociological examination of the self-image of full-time employees (*Hauptamtliche Mitarbeiter*) of the

MfS. The authors interviewed former MfS officers; from a total of sixty-three "usable interviews," their analysis focuses on ten.

This approach was not new: Ariane Riecker, Annett Schwarz, and Dirk Schneider (1990) published ten interviews as early as 1990, when there were hardly any biographical narratives. The same goes for the interview collection by Christina Wilkening (1990), also published that year, and former Hauptamtliche Wanja Abramowski's (1992: 212–214) "Im Labyrinth der Macht. Innenansichten aus dem Stasi-Apparat," whose twenty-two-page analysis remains unmatched, especially when it comes to her breakdown of groups within the MfS.

In choosing "prototypical lives," Krahnke et al. (2017) highlighted cases that contrast with others in terms of "belonging to a particular generation or sex, positions of power, range of activities within the organization, mental dispositions and ways of habit, as well as experiences made after German Reunification." However, one group is missing from their analysis: the important cohort of Hauptamtlichen who were active in the years 1928 to 1948.

Their study is based on a handful of interviews, which makes it nearly impossible to generalize from the little available knowledge there is. Even the reduced number of Hauptamtlichen, from 91,015 to 78,000, a figure freshly calculated by the authors, does not enhance the size of the representative sample. From the newly calculated figure of 71,000 Hauptamtlichen, 13,000 temporary noncommissioned MfS officers serving three years in the guard division Feliks Dzerzynski were subtracted. According to the authors, including them would not have "made any sense," since "almost all the examined traits did not apply." But excluding this subgroup means that an important control was left out of the investigation: the cohort of those who decided not to continue working with the MfS after their term of duty ended. This particular guard division, according to the authors, was "primarily" a recruiting field for the MfS.

In the end, the logic of modern society with its prescribed role expectations crept into the MfS, sublimating the entire personality of agents into the corps when viewed through a sociological lens. This intrusion into the personalities of employees could be easily attributed to the material benefits that MfS agents received, although these were declared to be "intrinsically motivated." In other words: recruits voluntarily submitted themselves to the MfS, subordinating themselves completely.

At the same time, they understood themselves—as they were required—as "Top Level Comrades." The "Avantgarde of the Avantgarde" showed an "authoritarian and conformist" attitude, which, truth be told, is generally seen in military organizations, and should not be seen as particular to MfS. Krahnke et al. (2017) also claim their subjects were politically in line, elevated themselves to heroic stature, and yet were socially isolated. The essence of the study can be summarized in the words of the authors:

> When individuals willingly and voluntarily accede to the intrusion of an organization or institution, when they habitually 'incorporate' and even dogmatize the respective ideology, the danger lurks that the resulting mentality and lifestyle acquire a life of their own, and appear to be part of the system. This is a gateway to the annihilation of individualism, pluralism, and the allowance for all eventualities—in short, for totalitarianism. (Krähnke et al. 2017: 300)

Christoph Rass (2016) studied the social profile of the Bundesnachrichtendienst BND, the German foreign intelligence service for the period up to 1968. From a total of 11,567 files, he selected 2,689 personnel files and 951 security clearance files for further scrutiny, about a third of the total. He focused on former connections to Nazi organizations and discovered that three-quarters of the 1948 cohort belonged to this group, and in 1965 more than half (Rass 2016: 250–252).

In these studies, comparisons are seldom made between so-called "voluntary" agents who were regularly used in "enemy" countries abroad and "official" full-time intelligence officers. Our focus, the sociology of intelligence agents, has not received sufficient critical attention. So once again we ask, how do we approach this subject?

Nazi Traditions?

For decades, the argument was that the MfS engaged former members of the Nazi secret services within their formal organization and adopted their methods (Untersuchungsausschuss freiheitlicher Juristen, n.d.; Kappelt 1981: 207–208). Occasionally, there was talk of a "Red Gestapo" (Sagolla 1952). In his 1997 essay "Erst braun, dann rot?," Gieseke (1997: 129–131) dismantles that theory. From the beginning, the MfS excluded known members of the NSDAP, individuals who were found to be members of law enforcement ("Mitarbeiter der Vollzugsorgane") and active officers of the Hitler Youth ("aktive Funktionäre der Hitlerjugend") (Gieseke 1997: 133). Gieseke summarizes his findings:

> Within the ranks of the Ministry for State Security there were indeed individual cases of former soldiers of the Wehrmacht, former members of the Hitlerjugend, including those who had joined the NSDAP in the late phase of WWII while very young; there were also cases of former NSDAP members who kept silent about their membership, who were exposed in time, and almost always expelled from the MfS. But not a single case exists

as compelling evidence for the claim that there is unbroken continuity in personnel from the Nazi terror organizations to the Hauptamtlichen of the MfS. There does not even seem to be any corresponding strategy to recruit cadre for the MfS from former organs of the Nazi state. (Giesecke 1997: 147)

The majority of the Hauptamtlichen hired were between twenty-one and twenty-five years old, and were generally from the working class (Giesecke 2000: 11–13).

For the so-called unofficial network of the MfS, especially the foreign intelligence service—the HV A (Hauptverwaltung Aufklärung)—a different picture emerges. In its ranks, we find a long list of former Nazis: the former police informant Paul Reckzeh, a member of the Gestapo in Saxony; former heads of an SD branch, such as Erwin Rogalsky-Wedekind and Ernst Schwarzwäller; the SS bureaucrat Kurt Harder; chief squad leader (Hauptscharführer) in the SS special task force Erich Mauthe; plus the convicted war criminal August Moritz (Leide 2005: 195–197). The unofficial network of the MfS in West Germany reflected, on the one hand, personal careers of former National Socialists and, on the other, their desire to ensure—by assisting the intelligence efforts of the GDR— that they would not fall victim to the workings of the SED's relentless intelligence machinery. Historian Henry Leide (2005: 415) concluded, "The NS cadre could easily be put under pressure; they possessed a high degree of social capital which would enable them to infiltrate any enemy environment, and many of them already could call on their professional experience in intelligence work . . . but in truth, the willingness of many to co-operate was grounded in tactical arguments and self-protection." While there are quite a few examples, these represent just a selection. It is therefore necessary to embed them in a systematic sociology of agents, which is undertaken in the following section.

Definitions

Agent

The term "agent" has various definitions in German. Essentially, it refers to someone who acts, or someone who is given a task to complete. The term encompasses a range that includes the fictive subject in economics, the representative of an agency, an employee at a call center, a lobbyist, a middleman in a business transaction, and a sales representative. These definitions are all linked through the concept of acting on one's own.

In the present context, however, an "agent" means an actor within the intelligence services who essentially remains unknown or undercover in his actions in the foreign country where he is active and who attempts to obtain access to relevant information. This agent is often a full-time officer within an intelligence service (Roewer, Schäfer, and Uhl 2003: 18–19). But this does not always apply to everyone, which is demonstrated in the files of the MfS, where "unofficial collaborators" or "*inoffiziellen Mitarbeiter* (IM)" are often discussed.

For decades, the HV A of the MfS relied on the following definition: "Unofficial employees are such persons who are engaged by the Ministry for State Security to work secretly, and who must meet certain criteria in order to carry out their assigned operations and given tasks" (Müller-Enbergs 1998: 14). But this definition offers only an outline of duties; under scrutiny, it becomes quite vague.

Only one segment of the IM matches most of the characteristics outlined in the HV A description of the IM. The definition applies only to IM who have declared themselves willing to carry out assigned operations for the MfS, in written or another binding form, specifying time, date, and locality. Only officers in Special Operations (Offizieren im besonderen Einsatz OibE), full-time informal informants (hauptamtlichen IM HIM), and "volunteers" (ehrenamtliche ID) in the "operational area" are known to have provided an explicit indication of their willingness to work with the MfS. The HV A preferred such a binding commitment, which was often accompanied by a swearing-in ceremony. In practice, however, recruitment to informal cooperation was seen as a multistep process in which the case officer secured a commitment and cemented his relationship to a contact. It was left to the case officer's discretion to determine when a contact was ready to begin unofficial work for the MfS.

During the recruitment process, assessing information delivered by an IM recruit was only of limited significance since this was considered part of the relationship development process. First, public information was accepted and worthless tidbits were delivered in the hope of receiving valuable information at a later point. To the case officer, this process may have seemed like crossing a threshold, while the supposed IM often saw it as acting on a whim, neither compromising nor committing him to additional work. Among many prospective IM (PIM) were students who were motivated by professional prospects and whose relationship with the case officer was based on trust, without, however, knowing the officer's real background or intentions, and in spite of receiving no information of substance from the officer.

The HV A definition of an IM left an unanswered question: for whom was the recruit offering to carry out secret operations? Not knowing the identity of the recruiter posed difficulties for the HV A. Certainly, a clear and conscious commitment to work for the MfS was better than the recruit assuming he was working for a Western intelligence service or unofficially for a real or fictional organization, or unwittingly giving away secrets to a trusted confidant. It is not of particular relevance here that those who were recruited under a false flag or cover were filed as IM; they are not to be included among the "peace scouts" (*Kundschafter des Friedens*, a euphemism for GDR spies). More relevant is the fact that from a legal perspective, these individuals cannot be considered IM of the MfS unless evidence shows that the named person knew who his recruiter was.

A commitment to the MfS, declared and then rescinded verbally or through one's actions, does not constitute membership in the MfS either, since the HV A insisted on accepting and accomplishing various tasks and operations as proof of engagement; thus the documented membership status is often in question (Müller-Enbergs 1998: 14–15).

Sociology

Just as we have seen with the term "agents," the academic discipline "sociology" can also assume various meanings. In the present context, the focus is on political sociology in the widest sense, a field located between sociology and political science that examines the relationship between politics and society. It considers the prerequisites for a political system and political activity as well as the structure and function of political institutions. Finally, it takes into account political decision-making processes and their implications for society (Pappi 2000: 535–537). How can research on political sociology be linked to the shadowy world of intelligence agents?

Sociology of Intelligence Agents

Rainer Rupp (born 1945) offers one way. While studying economics, he veered to the political left, taking part in demonstrations against the US war in Vietnam. GDR foreign intelligence services saw his potential and approached him from a political angle.

Rupp believed in the concept of bipolarity—a world order of competing systems—and East versus West justified the need for intelligence work. Abandoning plans to become a development worker, he assiduously sought to penetrate NATO headquarters, where he was employed. Operating under the code name "Mosel," and later as "Topas," beginning in 1977 he worked in the policy-setting department of the NATO Economic Desk and delivered reams of information to the HV A, a total of 1,064 documents (Eichner and Rehbaum 2013; Müller-Enbergs 2011: 193–194). Rupp knowingly delivered input that helped shape the policy frameworks of the GDR and Warsaw Pact alliance members, including the structure and function of political institutions and decision-making processes. In the long run, he had an impact on political decision-making and its effects on social structures.

Beyond a doubt, intelligence agents constitute a group in a sociological context, yet because of the confidential nature of their work, their members were not aware of one another. Group members remain unknown, not only to inquiring researchers but also to the states they worked for and against. Given the dearth of empirical sources, it is any wonder that in-depth studies are not available? This prompts the question, what sources are available?

Current Research Resources

Often referred to as "Rosenholz," a pool of written records from the HV A offers a tool for scrutinizing the sociology of agents. The Rosenholz files are a compilation of statistics for internal use regarding the operational intelligence network in the so-called area of operations. The file contains statistics on individuals, including their professions and assets. Produced in December 1988, it provides details on about two thousand West German citizens. Amendments to this data were carried out by case officers who maintained the files to varying degrees. The files were highly controversial within the HV A, which remained keenly aware, based on collected data, of the danger that its methods would be discovered. While some of the files cannot be seen as reliable, they are currently the best material available to researchers (Müller-Enbergs 2007). The Rosenholz files have an additional advantage; to some extent, they have solved the "agent" problem by including both the IM and *"Kontaktpersonen."* Beyond Rosenholz, analysis written by the HV A about its operational procedures also sheds light on the matter (Förster 1996, 1997, 1998, 2001).

Sociological Profile of Agents of the HV A (1988)

A person's social status determines the respect they receive. This may be granted due to outward social characteristics, including their profession, abilities, power, privileges, or wealth. Pierre Bourdieu (1982) calls this economic, cultural, and social capital.

A Profession as Social Capital

Rosenholz contains information on 1,890 unofficial collaborators and contacts of the HV A. For seventy-one unofficial collaborators and contacts, a second profession is reported (see table 7.1). For example, "Alexander" is listed as a journalist and as having a managerial position. The HV A

Table 7.1. Professions of West German IM/KP of the HV A (as of December 1988).[1]

Profession	Number (n)	Share in percent
Employees	635	34
Laborers	72	4
Unemployed/Not working	23	1
Trainees	3	0
Civil Servants	158	8
Diplomats	5	0
Managers	133	7
Wives of IM, not working	128	7
Tradesmen	16	1
Housewives	43	2
Journalists	74	4
Artists	10	1
Military	50	3
IT workers	35	2
R+D workers	89	5
Pensioners	106	6
Secretaries	47	2
Self-employed/Professionals	228	12
Students	141	7
Civilian employee within military	27	1

used twenty-two classifications. These were not discrete categories but rather reflected an interest in certain professions. Thus, finding five persons listed as diplomats and civil servants, we must assume that most diplomats were civil servants. Only certain trends in professions can be ascertained, and, as a result, we can conclude that the working class was not a significant intelligence target for the HV A. Only seventy-two individuals (or 4 percent) are classified as laborers or factory workers. Even if an additional twenty-three individuals listed as unemployed or with no occupation are added to this total, only 5 percent in this class carried out intelligence tasks. The majority of recruits for the HV A were company employees; 34 percent were categorized as such. The second largest group were self-employed individuals or professionals, with 12 percent, followed by 158 civil servants (8 percent). It is thus apparent that the HV A focused mainly on what Bourdieu (1989) called "la noblesse d'etat," the state elite—namely, employees, civil servants, and the legal profession. In a narrower sense, this meant state-employed teachers were counted among civil servants, and commercial traders and sales representatives among professionals and lawyers.

Secretaries

Three targeted professions are especially noteworthy: secretaries, students, and journalists. Forty-seven women were classified as secretaries in the Rosenholz files, while an additional 141 students and seventy-four journalists are listed. Among secretaries, those who captured the most interest in operational terms were chief secretaries, who generally worked independently. They were expected to develop a close relationship with their bosses, becoming their indispensable "right hands." It has been shown that this close relationship allowed for lax security, thus making it easier to access internal documents. Additionally, they often understood how the boss thought, which enabled them to gauge his reactions or opinions. In the training materials of the HV A, the "exploitation of typical feminine behavior and emotions" was emphasized when establishing contact with this group:

> The development of close friendships and love affairs has always been and will continue to be a consistent, stable, and proven successful basis for the operative work with IM secretaries. It has been shown again and again that the female IM first dedicates herself to the person she respects or loves, and only as an afterthought commits herself to the actual task that he brings her. For the recruiter, it is therefore of primary interest that he maintains a cautious, sensitive approach and that he is able to dedicate substantial time to the interests and preoccupations of the woman involved, that "he is there for her," and gives her a secure sense of being his equal partner, cherished and loved.[2]

The HV A estimated that 30 percent of secretaries working in party or government structures were single or divorced, thus one can assume that most of the secretaries contacted by the HV A did not have a steady partner. They were targeted by recruiters, and it was assumed that for many IM secretaries, a decisive or "stabilizing" factor was their intimate relationship with their recruiter. Yet additional methods to assure loyalty among female recruits were sought. The increased use of female recruiters was discussed within the HV A.[3] Yet there are no known examples of such. A number of spectacular cases involving secretaries, which were grotesquely dubbed "Romeo Traps," achieved notoriety. From 1949 to 1987, a total of fifty-eight IM secretaries in West Germany were uncovered by the counterintelligence unit of the Office for the Protection of the Constitution (Bayerisches Staatsministerium des Inneren 1988: 184–185).

Students

In the 1970s in the West, operational approaches sought various ways of getting a foot in the door with students, making use of this group's socioeconomic structure. An internal HV A study concluded that students, hoping for social advancement after their diploma, tended to hide their "lower" social heritage, which would hamper their career chances. Students from lower but up-and-coming classes seemed to realize that, despite the gradual lowering of entry barriers to the "state elite," they would "soon be disappointed." Under these circumstances, students, according to the study, would "quite often" be willing to become enemies of the "government." The HV A was mainly interested in the students who came from blue-collar and lower- and middle-class families of civil servants and employees.[4]

Journalists

As its training materials explain, the HV A considered journalists a group with privileged access to internal information due to their numerous contacts. On the one hand, journalists could cover topics of interest without arousing suspicion. Even their professional attributes and character were to some degree "similar" to those associated with intelligence activities. On the other hand, these journalists were in the "spotlight of imperialist intelligence services" and could readily discern "operative work methods." For these reasons, the HV A saw a need to recruit journalists under a "false flag," and target young adults for the journalistic profession in view of building them up as perspective IMs.[5]

Wealth as Economic Capital

HV A files detailing unofficial collaborators and contact persons also contain data regarding their financial situation, at least at the time of their recruitment. Some 1,890 files offer insight. From the total, 461 (or 24 percent) owned their own house, and an additional 282 owned their own apartment (15 percent), bringing the subset of property owners to 39 percent of the total. But the majority were renters (1,067), and 147 were even listed as subtenants.[6] This suggests a significant gap in financial assets between unofficial collaborators and contact persons. A hint of this discrepancy can be viewed in table 7.2, where we find the owners of three buses, four

Table 7.2. Economic capital of West German IM/KP der HV A (as of December 1988).[7]

Economic capital	Number (n)	Share in percent
Own car	1.347	71
Renter	1.067	56
House owner	461	24
Owner of apartment	282	15
Subtenant	147	8
Own office	136	7
Weekend property	66	3
Own truck	21	1
Own motorcycle	12	1
Own motorboat	10	1
Own airplane	4	0
Own bus	3	0

airplanes, ten motorboats, and twenty-one trucks. Yet this sample is too limited to provide an overall picture of the social profile of the IMs and contact persons of the HV A. Still, one can say that the middle class was more represented among the ranks of intelligence agents than the working class.

Conclusion

Putting together an odd couple—"sociology" and "agents"—has allowed for empirical research into a largely invisible group, as intelligence agents must be in principle. Beyond the statistical files of the HV A from 1988—and perhaps the survey conducted by Georg Herbstritt that would contribute to building a social profile of GDR intelligence agents—hardly any data is available. It is possible to conclude that the unofficial collaborator network and pool of contact persons of the foreign intelligence unit HV A were largely employees, and that a smaller segment were professionals and self-employed as well as civil servants. It appears that espionage was not a matter for the working class. This conclusion is underscored by the fact that more than a third owned a house or an apartment at the time of their recruitment.

Helmut Müller-Enbergs is a political scientist and GDR researcher. Since 1992, he has worked as a research assistant at the Federal Commissioner for the Stasi Files. He has been an honorary professor at the Faculty of Humanities of the Syddansk Universitet in Odense (Denmark) since 2010. From 2012 to 2014, he was an honorary professor at the Faculty of History of Högskolan på Gotland in Visby (Sweden). His research focuses on unofficial staff and the MfS Headquarters Enlightenment (HV A) as well as on espionage and intelligence psychology. One of his publications, authored with Cornelia Jabs, revealed that the West Berlin policeman Karl-Heinz Kurras was an SED member and Stasi-IM "Otto Bohl."

Notes

1. Multiple answers were given by 1,890 persons.
2. Schulungsmaterial. Einige ausgewählte Erkenntnissen und Erfahrungen zur Berufsgruppe der Sekretärinnen in der BRD, BStU, MfS, BV Gera, Abt. XV 282, 40.
3. Ibid., 39–45.
4. Major Hermann, Schulungsmaterial (Entwurf): Die zielgerichtete Bestimmung und operative Analyse operativ interessierender Personengruppen im Operationsgebiet Westdeutschland. Potsdam 1972, BStU, MfS, BV Gera, Abt. XV 367/6, 49–61; Klaus Rösler, Psychologische Bedingungen der inoffiziellen Arbeit in das und im Operationsgebiet. Potsdam 1972, BStU, MfS, JHS 21819, 55–63.
5. Schulungsmaterial: Einige ausgewählte Erkenntnisse und Erfahrungen zur Berufsgruppe der Journalisten in der BRD. Potsdam 1984, BStU, MfS, BV Gera, Abt. XV 467/4, 46–50; Schulungsmaterial: Aktuelle Erfahrungen und Probleme der Arbeit einiger Diensteinheiten der Aufklärung des MfS mit der Methode der Abschöpfung. Potsdam 1986, BStU, MfS, BV Gera, Abt. XV 367/4, 20–22.
6. The total is 103 percent, which is likely due to the fact that one individual could possess various items.
7. Multiple answers were given by 1,890 persons.

References

Abramowski, Wanja. 1992. "Im Labyrinth der Macht. Innenansichten aus dem Stasi-Apparat." In *Die Ohnmacht der Allmächtigen. Geheimdienste und politische Polizei in der modernen Gesellschaft*, edited by Bernd Florath, Armin Mitter, and Stefan Wolle, 212–233. Berlin.
Bayrisches Staatsministerium des Inneren. 1988. *Verfassungsschutzbericht Bayern 1987*. Munich.
Blenkhorn, David L., and Craig S. Fleisher, eds. 2005. *Competitive Intelligence and Global Business*. London.
Bourdieu, Pierre. 1982. *Die feinen Unterschiede*. Frankfurt a. M.
———. 1989. *La Noblesse d'Etat: Grandes écoles et esprit de corps*. Paris.
Dennis, Mike, and Norman Laporte. 2014. *The Stasi: Myth and Reality*. New York.

Eichner, Klaus, and Karl Rehbaum. 2013. *Deckname Topas. Der Spion Rainer Rupp in Selbstzeugnissen*. Berlin.
Förster, Günter. 1996. *Die Juristische Hochschule des Ministeriums für Staatssicherheit*. Berlin.
———. 1997. *Die Dissertationen an der "Juristischen Hochschule" des MfS. Eine annotierte Bibliographie*. Berlin.
———. 1998. *Bibliographie der Diplomarbeiten und Abschlussarbeiten an der Hochschule des MfS*. Berlin.
———. 2001. *Die Juristische Hochschule des Ministeriums für Staatssicherheit. Die Sozialstruktur ihrer Promovenden*. Münster.
Gieseke, Jens. 1997. "Erst braun, dann rot? Zur Frage der Beschäftigung ehemaliger Nationalsozialisten als hauptamtliche Mitarbeiter des MfS." In *Staatspartei und Staatssicherheit. Zum Verhältnis von SED und MfS*, edited by Siegfried Suckut and Walter Süß, 311–324. Berlin.
———. 2000. *Die hauptamtlichen Mitarbeiter der Staatssicherheit. Personalstruktur und Lebenswelt 1950–1989/90*. Berlin.
Herbstritt, Georg. 2007. *Bundesbürger im Dienst der DDR-Spionage. Eine analytische Studie*. Göttingen.
Hertle, Hans-Hermann. 1999. *Der Fall der Mauer. Die unbeabsichtigte Selbstauflösung des SED-Staates*. Opladen.
Kappelt, Olaf. 1981. *Braunbuch DDR*. Herford.
Krähnke, Uwe, Matthias Finster, Philipp Reimann, and Anja Zschirpe. 2017. *Im Dienst der Staatssicherheit. Eine soziologische Studie über die hauptamtlichen Mitarbeiter des DDR-Geheimdienstes*. Frankfurt a. M.
Leide, Henry. 2005. *NS-Verbrecher und Staatssicherheit. Die geheime ergangenheitspolitik der DDR*. Göttingen.
Mühlenbernd, Roland. 2013. "Signals and the Structure of Societies." PhD diss., Eberhard Karls University, Tübingen.
Müller-Enbergs, Helmut. 1998. *Inoffizielle Mitarbeiter des Ministeriums für Staatssicherheit*.
Part 2: *Anleitungen für die Arbeit mit Agenten, Kundschaftern und Spionen in der Bundesrepublik Deutschland*. Berlin.
———. 2007. *"Rosenholz." Eine Quellenkritik*. Berlin.
———. 2011. *Hauptverwaltung A. Aufgaben – Strukturen – Quellen*. Berlin.
Pappi, Franz. 2000. "Politische Soziologie." In *Politik-Lexikon*, edited by Everhard Holtmann, 535–538. Munich.
Rass, Christoph. 2016. *Das Sozialprofil des Bundesnachrichtendienstes. Von den Anfängen bis 1968*. Berlin.
Richelson, Jeffrey T. 1999. *The U.S. Intelligence Community*. Boulder.
Riecker, Ariane, Annett Schwarz, and Dirk Schneider. 1990. *Stasi intim. Gespräche mit ehemaligen MfS-Angehörigen*. Leipzig.
Roewer, Helmut, Stefan Schäfer, and Matthias Uhl. 2003. *Lexikon der Geheimdienste im 20. Jahrhundert*. Munich.
Sagolla, Bernhard. 1952. *Die Rote Gestapo. Der Staatssicherheitsdienst in der Sowjetzone*. Berlin.
Süß, Walter. 1999. *Staatssicherheit am Ende. Warum es den Mächtigen nicht gelang, 1989 eine Revolution zu verhindern*. Berlin.
Untersuchungsausschuss Freiheitlicher Juristen, ed. (undated). *Ehemalige Nationalsozialisten in Pankows Diensten*. N.p.

Weber, Hans. 1971. *Die zürcherischen Landgemeinden in der Helvetik 1798–1803*. Zurich.
Wilkening, Christina. 1990. *Staat im Staate. Auskünfte ehemaliger Stasi-Mitarbeiter*. Berlin.

Chapter 8

At War with Israel

Anti-Zionism in East Germany from the 1960s to the 1980s

Jeffrey Herf

One of the most remarkable episodes in the history of Communism and the radical left in Germany and in Europe after World War II is also one that has received much less attention than it deserves. I refer to the decision by leaders of the German Democratic Republic (GDR), or East Germany, to participate in the Soviet bloc campaign of antagonism to the state of Israel, especially from the mid-1960s to the end of the Cold War in 1989 (Herf 2016). By "antagonism," I refer to a continuum of actions. They included hostile propaganda aimed at the delegitimation of Israel's moral standing, which the East Germans published and broadcast in their official press and media and which they repeated in the United Nations and other international venues. The East German regime described Zionism as racism; depicted every one of Israel's efforts to defend itself against its Arab adversaries as acts of aggression and, on occasion, mass murder; called Israel a "spearhead of American imperialism"; celebrated Arab and Palestinian armed attacks on Israel as legitimate elements of an anti-colonial and anti-imperialist struggle. The East German dictatorship never accepted any of Israel's factual assertions about events, said nothing about terrorist attacks on Israeli civilians, and never criticized antisemitic—that is, anti-Jewish—propaganda coming from the Arab governments and Palestinian terror organizations aimed at Israel and Zionism. As Israel civilians were killed in terrorist attacks, the East Germans and the Soviet bloc insisted all of this had nothing to do with antisemitism, as if the murder of civilians was acceptable if it were not due to that ideological tradition.

Yet the East German government did not limit its antagonism toward Israel to propaganda and diplomacy. As the archives of the East German Defense Ministry, the Ministry of State Security (MfS), commonly known as the Stasi, and the files of the governing Politburo document, the GDR enthusiastically joined the Soviet Union and its Warsaw Pact allies in offering military training and weapons to both the Arab states and to Palestinian terrorist organizations engaged in armed attacks on Israel. Had its policies succeeded, it is probable that the Jewish state would have been destroyed in the 1970s or 1980s. To be sure, the GDR's antagonism pales when compared to the Holocaust. Yet despite the relative neglect of the topic by too many historians, the hostility of a German and Communist regime to Israel was not and is not an insignificant fact. The East German Communist leaders convinced themselves that a campaign of "anti-imperialist solidarity" placed them on the correct side of a dialectic of imperialism and revolution and that the Jewish state deserved opprobrium because it was on the wrong side of that global conflict.

In 1997, in the volume *Divided Memory*, I wrote a history of the anticosmopolitan purges of the early postwar years in East Germany. The East German chapter of a campaign more famously associated with the Doctors' Plot in Moscow and the Slansky Trial in Prague led to an identical shift in the policies of the Communist regimes. Their solidarity with the Jews in Europe and the Soviet Union's and Czechoslovakia's consequential support for the Zionists from 1945 to 1948 vanished and was replaced by denunciations of Zionism filled with classic antisemitic conspiracy theories about the power of the Jews and their links to American imperialism. The ascendant Stalinists marginalized, arrested, or drove into exile those Communists, such as Paul Merker and Leo Zuckerman, who thought that the logical outcome of wartime antifascism should be support for the Jewish state against the reactionary Arab oligarchies and also against the Islamists and Arab nationalists who had supported the Nazis during World War II. Marxist-Leninist ideology about the global anti-imperialist struggle fit well with the conventional power political interests of an East German regime that was desperate for diplomatic recognition from states outside the Warsaw Pact.

From the mid-1950s to the spectacularly successful diplomatic breakthrough of spring and summer 1969, Walter Ulbricht, his successor Erich Honecker, and their diplomats led by Foreign Minister Otto Winzer realized that the single most powerful card they had to play in order to break West Germany's effort to prevent such recognition (called the Hallstein Doctrine) was the GDR's well-deserved reputation for antagonism to Israel and for support for the Arab states during and after the Six Day War of 1967. In 1969, Iraq, Syria, Yemen, and Egypt became the first non-Communist regimes to establish diplomatic relations with the GDR. In 1970 in East Berlin, it became the first state in the Soviet bloc to open a Consulate for the Palestinian Liberation Organization (PLO). In the coming decade, the GDR became a popular member of the third worldist majority in the UN General Assembly as well as an active member of the Committee for the Exercise of the Inalienable Rights of the Palestinian People.

In the present contribution, I first want to underscore the enormous enthusiasm, initiative, and passion with which the GDR threw itself and its modest but nevertheless real political, ideological, and military resources into the battle against what became a hated and despised Zionist enemy. To be sure, the driving force of Soviet bloc anti-Zionism was the Kremlin leadership, but the GDR was not a reluctant participant. Quite the contrary, it took as leading a role as was possible to for a small state with a population of seventeen million people and an economy that was very far from the myth of being the world's eleventh largest. The GDR took its anti-Zionist position because after the anti-cosmopolitan purges of 1949–1953, Communism and anti-Zionism became synonymous. Only with great difficulty could a supporter of Israel's right to exist as a Jewish state remain in a Communist party or support a Communist regime movement. As my work in the archives indicates, the public, familiar denunciations of Zionism that came from East Berlin expressed the genuine ideological passion that the GDR leadership voiced in private when they spoke to one another, to their fellow Communist allies, to Arab states, and to the Palestinian terror organizations.

My second point concerns the fact that the East German dictatorship was a government and as such it had the attributes of a dictatorship's sovereignty, including armed forces, a controlled press, embassies and consulates around the world, and justly famous secret police and intelligence agencies. It had, in short, the sinews of war, and it employed them in support of Israel's Arab adversaries. Although, on a few occasions, the East Germans contemplated sending East German soldiers to fight the Israelis, the Soviet leaders and perhaps some East German Communists as well understood that few outside the Arab states, the PLO, and its many armed factions and radical leftist terrorist organizations would understand or support Germans, no matter if they were Communists from East Germany, who were aiming guns and bombs at the citizens of Israel. While East German soldiers did not appear on the battlefield shooting at the Israelis, their support for the Arab and Palestinian terrorist wars with Israel extended from propaganda to extensive military training, intelligence cooperation, and delivery of weapons.

East Germany's partisanship for the Arab states and its denunciation of Israel and Zionism long preceded the Six Day War of 1967. The war was less a turning point than a manifestation of by then well-established views. On 7 June 1967, two days after the Six Day War began, the Politburo of the Socialist Unity Party, the ruling party of Communist East Germany, met to consider the events in the Middle East. Among its members were Walter Ulbricht, Friedrich Ebert, Gerhard Grüneberg, Fritz Hager, Erich Honekker, Herman Matern, Gunter Mittag, Albert Norden, and Will Stoph. Otto Winzer, Wolfgang Kiesewetter, Gerhard Weiss, and Paul Markowski from the Foreign Ministry were in attendance.[1] The group sent messages to Gamal Abdul Nasser and Hafez al Assad in which "the GDR offered material support to both states in connection with the Israeli aggression." Foreign Minister Otto Winzer was assigned to contact the general secretary of the Arab League and to condemn Israeli aggression and express solidarity with the Arab states and to convey these sentiments to the members of the Arab League. The Politburo ordered its Agitation Division (Abteilung Agitation) to inform the press about the events in the Middle East. Special emphasis was to be placed on "the international legal position of the Arab states, Israel's aggressive role and its conspiracy with the USA, Great Britain and West Germany," and "the GDR's anti-imperialist stance."[2] The National Council of the National Front, led by Albert Norden, was to publish "statements by Jewish citizens of the GDR which express indignation about the Israeli aggression and the Israel-Washington-Bonn conspiracy."[3]

The Politburo then ordered Willi Stoph, the chairman of the Minsters Council to see that East German "weapons and equipment now in the UAR [United Arab Republic]" could be "used according to their (the Egyptian and Syrian governments) own judgment," and to "give priority to fulfilling the requests of the UAR and the Syrian Arab Republic for deliveries of goods in the non-civilian"—that is, military "area."[4] Stoph was to send medical supplies to Egypt and Syria, make preparations for accepting their wounded soldiers and children "whose parents were victims of Israeli aggression," and send unspecified specialists from the GDR to support the Arab states. Finally the German-Arab Society, in collaboration with the Foreign Ministry, was ordered "to organize measures of solidarity with the Arab peoples."[5]

On 15 June 1967, Walter Ulbricht delivered a major address in Leipzig that became a classic statement of Communist anti-Zionism. It was front page news in *Neues Deutschland* (Epstein 2003; Herf 1997). Whereas Islamists have incorporated the conspiracy theories of European antisemitism, theories that place an international Jewish conspiracy at the center of their hatreds, Ulbricht placed "US imperialism" and its "global strategy" at the center of his concerns. He wrote that, along with the war in Vietnam, the imperialists were conducting "another, no less criminal military aggression in the Middle East" (Bator and Bator 1984: 115). The causes of the war did not lie in Arab threats to destroy Israel, movements of Arab armies closer to Israel's borders, demands that UN peacekeeping forces be withdrawn from the Sinai, or Nasser's decision to blockade the Gulf of Aqaba. Instead, they lay in the desire of "imperialist colonial rulers" to prevent the Arab countries from attaining economic independence and to secure "imperialist exploitation" of the riches of the region—that is, access to its oil. The Israeli government had made itself into a "tool of a new, despicable imperialist aggression" and had "brought shame and disgrace on itself by playing the role of an imperialist aggressor against the Arab states" (Bator and Bator 1984: 115).

Ulbricht attacked West German restitution payments to Israel (Ulbricht 1967: 515–538). Israel had been "pumped full" of military goods by the United States and West Germany, including "several hundred million dollars" of goods sent by West Germany as "restitution" for "the Jewish citizens of Poland, Czechoslovakia and many other countries murdered by the Nazi regime" (Ulbricht 1967: 520). The Six Day War, he continued, was not a matter of "the survival of the Jews." Rather, it was about a "class conflict between monopolistic oil interests and their imperialist governments on the one hand, and the Arab peoples, on the other." The imperialists wanted to prevent Egypt, Syria, Algeria, and other Arab states from following a "non-capitalist" path. It was both shameful and "tragic" that Israel placed itself in the service of such "imperialist aggression," he said, because many people in Israel "have our sympathy" in view of what they endured under Nazism. Rather than have regard for human rights, he asserted, "the government and militarists of the state of Israel [then still led by the Labor Party] are apparently struck with blindness, due to chauvinism, racial madness and *Klassendünkel*" so that they "believe that they can violate the demands of international law" (Ulbricht 1967: 525).

Actually, in 1967, the United States was not a major weapons supplier of Israel, a fact that did not deter Ulbricht from claiming that US imperialists had helped to "prepare the aggression as part of US global strategy" and had even "fixed the date of the aggression" as well. Had the United States "told its war-loving tool [German *kriegslüsternes Werkzeug*] Israel that a war could not take place, then the Israeli militarists and their government would have had to abandon the aggression" (Ulbricht 1967: 528). The war could not have taken place "against the will of USA imperialism." Conversely, the Soviet Union had "done everything" it could to prevent a war. Ulbricht expressed thanks to the Soviet Union for its "great sense of responsibility" that led it to try to "stop the aggression," end the fighting, and bring about a withdrawal of Israeli troops.

He further claimed that Egypt and Nasser had not wanted war either—that there "was no military threat to Israel" (Bator and Bator 1984: 117–118). Now, in the interest of world peace, "the Middle East aggressor" must be held in check. "The world cannot accept that a quarter century after the Second World War, the aggressor Israel and its men behind the scenes (German *Hintermänner*) are createing a 'Sinai protectorate' or a 'General government of Jordan' for renewed colonial oppression of the Arab peoples" (Bator and Bator 1984: 118). By using terms such as "Sinai protectorate" and the "General government of Jordan," Ulbricht evoked language that he knew his listeners would associate with Nazi Germany's policies in Eastern Europe in World War II. The association of Israel with Nazi Germany remained an element of Communist, Arab, Palestinian, and West German and West European leftist anti-Zionism.

Following the Six Day War, Soviet leaders decided on a program of rearmament and intensified training of the armed forces of the Arab states and of the PLO. They concluded that the cause of the debacle of 1967 did not lie in the inferiority of Soviet weaponry. On the contrary, they asserted that Soviet weapons were superior to those in Israel's arsenal. The problems lay instead with deficiencies in leadership and training in the Arab states. In order to facilitate a victory in the next war, the Brezhnev regime decided to intensify military training both in the Soviet Union and in its Warsaw Pact allies. East Germany was to play a central role in this effort. It was manifest in a series of bilateral agreements for weapons deliveries, military training of officers in East German military academies, and regular consultations between high-ranking officers.

By 1969, Ulbricht's passionate support for the Palestinians extended to proposing in a letter to Leonid Brezhnev that East German "volunteers" join in a "war of attrition" against Israel. Ulbricht shared the letter with the Politburo members, as well as with Erich Mielke, head of the Ministry for State Security, and General Heinz Hoffmann, head of the East German Defense Ministry. On 24 October, Erich Honecker wrote to Ulbricht to report that both the Politburo and Mielke and Hoffmann agreed with Ulbricht. Writing to "Dear Comrade Leonid!," Ulbricht informed the leader of the Soviet Union that the Central Committee of the SED in its Politburo meeting of 7 October 1969 agreed "with your suggestions." As Israel, in association with the USA and the West German Federal Republic, was "systematically engaged in a war of attrition against the Arab states," he said, "it is necessary to conduct a comprehensive international political action and a war of attrition against the Israeli troops in the occupied territories."⁶ The East German Politburo supported a common declaration of the Communist parties that declared that, in the occupied territories, Israel was "conducting a policy of colonial exploitation, oppression and violence against the Arab population" and called for withdrawal of Israeli troops from those areas. He proposed sending "volunteers from the socialist countries" to serve as "flyers, tank commanders (drivers) and special forces" in fighting the Israelis.⁷ Brezhnev appears to have understood the propaganda disaster that East German soldiers fighting against Israel would have entailed. As far as I know, nothing came of it, at least then. In her important 1994 work, *Hammer, Zirkel, Davidstern: Das gestörte Verhältnis der DDR zu Zionismus und der Staat Israel*, Angelika Timm included the text of Ulbricht's remarkable offer to have East German soldiers participate in military action against Israel—that is, to have German soldiers shooting at Jews for the first time since 1945. In the fifteen years since its publication, Timm's revelation aroused remarkably little if any interest and commentary among the by then growing number of German historians and historians of Germany and post-1945 Europe.

Perhaps East Germany's diplomatic successes of the spring and summer of 1969 reinforced the Central Committee's enthusiasm in October 1969 for sending young Germans to fight against Israel. For it was in spring and summer 1969 that the anti-Zionist card paid big political dividends. On 30 April 1969, Iraq became the first non-Communist government to establish diplomatic relations with the GDR (Timm 1997, chapters 7–9). The breakthrough was due in part to the persistent efforts of East Germany's foreign minister, Otto Winzer. He displayed his hostility to Zionism, and to placing priority on the memory of the Holocaust, during the anti-cosmopolitan purges in East Berlin in 1953 (Herf 1997: 130–132). The joint declaration issued by Winzer and Iraqi foreign minister Abdul Karim al-Sheikhly on 10 May 1969 at the conclusion of Winzer's successful week in Bagdad made a clear connection between Iraq's decision to establish diplomatic relations—and thus break with the Hallstein doctrine—and East Germany's position regarding Israel. The two foreign ministers stressed the "commonalities of struggle of both friendly regimes and peoples against the forces of imperialism, neo-Nazism, colonialism and Zionism and stress[ed] the need for closer cooperation of both states and peoples as well as all anti-imperialist forces in order to check the maneuvers of imperialism and Zionism." The ministers denounced Israel's "terror, campaigns of repression and forced evacuations against the Arab people." Israel, they proclaimed, "is racist, imperialist, reactionary and aggressive." It was the "spearhead of imperialism in the Arab world and threatened peace and international security." "The peoples of the GDR and Iraq," they asserted, "will struggle fiercely in a common front against this situation." Winzer and Scheikhly also denounced the military and political support for Israel by the United States and West Germany. The East Germans underscored "the sympathy of the regime and the people of the GDR for the just struggle of the Palestinian Arab peoples against Israeli aggression" and recognized the rights of the Palestinians for "self-determination and resistance against Israeli occupation" (Bator and Bator 1984: 147).

The description of Israel as a racist state, an "imperialist spearhead," and even as a state similar to Nazi Germany was thus embedded in the beginnings of diplomatic relations between the two states in 1969, six years before the United Nations "Zionism is racism" resolution of November 1975. In recognizing the Palestinian "right of resistance against Israeli occupation," the joint declaration also legitimized Palestinian terrorism not only against the Israeli forces in the West Bank and Gaza, but also against Israel proper. The charter of the Palestine Liberation Organization called for the replacement that is, destruction, of the Jewish state and a right of return of Palestinian refugees, which also would have meant the end of Israel. The East Germans never publicly called for the destruction of Israel, but neither did they ever publicly reject calls to do so by others.

The anti-Zionist/anti-Israeli card shattered the Hallstein doctrine as diplomatic recognition was granted by Sudan on 3 June 1969, Assad's Syria on 5 June 1969, and Nasser's Egypt as well as with South Yemen on 10 July 1969 (Bator and Bator 194: 153–169). In view of East Germany's economic and military assistance to the Assad regime in the following twenty years, it is important to note the phrasing of the statements that accompanied the establishment of diplomatic relations in 1969. Winzer stated that the establishment of relations between East Germany and Syria would be "an effective blow against the alliance of the forces of imperialism and Zionism in the Middle East, and especially against the alliance of aggressive West German imperialism with aggressive Israel" (Bator and Bator 1984: 155). In contrast to West Germany's "anti-Arab policies," the GDR had been a "reliable friend of the Arab states," evident in its denunciation of "Israeli aggression" in 1967 and subsequent solidarity with the Arab states. Israel's "aggression" not only endangered peace and security in the Middle East but "in the most serious manner also endangers world peace." The notion that Israel endangered not just regional but "world" peace remained a constant theme of Communist anti-Zionism.

Winzer accurately stated that "in the twenty years of its existence, the GDR had always supported the just cause of the Arab peoples. This [pro-Arab] stance forced the stabile foundation for her [the GDR's] close friendship with the SAR [Syrian Arab Republic]." Moreover, he said, the GDR was the home of the "centuries old humanistic tradition of German-Arab friendship." The establishment of diplomatic relations would contribute to world peace and European security, which was not possible without the recognition of the GDR (Bator and Bator 1984: 155). Winzer did not elaborate on which humanistic tradition he had in mind, as the most recent forms of "German-Arab friendship" included Wilheminian Germany's efforts to foster jihad against Britain and France during World War I and, more famously, Nazi Germany's cooperation with Haj Amin al-Husseini and Rashid al-Kilani during World War II and the Holocaust. Be that as it may, Winzer clearly articulated the connection between East German antagonism to Israel and support for the Arab states and the Palestinians at war with it, and the reasons for Arab willingness to antagonize West Germany and establish diplomatic relations with the GDR.

All of these statements were published in the pages of *Neues Deutschland*. Despite the remarkable importance that antagonism to "Zionism" and Israel had for what was one of the more important diplomatic developments—maybe the most important—in the history of the regime, the topic of the mélange of anti-Zionism and its relationship to antisemitism has remained a marginal theme in the scholarship on the history of East Germany and, I also think, in the history of the Cold War. This lack of interest has not been due to inaccessible archives. Many of the key documents, as those I have just cited, were on the front pages, or sometimes on the second or third pages, of *Neues Deutschland*. Why did so many scholars, journalists, and politicians who showed great interest in remembering the murders of Europe's Jews manifest so much less interest in a second German dictatorship that was helping states and organizations at war with the Jewish state? For the West German left, especially after 1967, these anti-Israeli sentiments emerged as a conventional wisdom evident in the terrorist organizations but also in the plethora of Marxist-Leninist organizations and the less orthodox successors to the Socialist German Student Union (Sozialistischer Deutscher Studentenbund, SDS) in the 1970s. For today, suffice it to say that it became an important element of West German public life and exerted an enduring impact on left-wing and left-liberal politics and journalism. Far from antagonism of Israel being taboo, it was state policy in the GDR.

The files of the East German Defense Ministry are now in the German Federal Archive in Freiburg. The office files of Defense Minister Heinz Hoffmann (1910–1985) are central to the history of the East German military alliance with the Arab states, first and foremost Hafez al Assad's Syrian Baath dictatorship. Hoffmann joined the German Communist Party in 1930, fought in the Spanish Civil War, survived the Nazi years in the Soviet Union, returned to East Berlin in 1946, and worked with Ulbricht and Politburo member Wilhelm Pieck. He studied at General Staff Academy in the Soviet Union (1955–1957), became deputy minister of defense in 1957 and army chief of staff in 1958. He served the GDR Defense Ministry from 1960 to 1985 and was one of the central figures in the military alliance between the GDR, the Arab states, and the PLO. From 1973 until his death in 1985, he was a member of the SED Politburo, the most important decision-making body in the GDR. The files of Hoffmann's office are essential for understanding the military dimensions of GDR alliance with Syria, PLO, and, at times, Egypt and Iraq.

I am not yet able to assess the extent of East German arms shipments compared with those coming from the Soviet Union or other Warsaw Pact states. Klaus Storkmann's recently published *Geheime Solidarität: Militärbeziehungen und Militärhilfen der DDR an die "Dritte Welt"* and the remarkable declassified files of the Central Intelligence Agency in the CREST system at the US National Archives in College Park will be important for arriving at accurate figures on the role the GDR played in the overall policy of the Soviet bloc (Stockmann 2012).[8] Nevertheless, a memo from Hoffmann's office of fall 1969 indicates that the GDR was already in contact with the Egyptian Air Force and Navy and was repairing MiG-21 jets. In 1971, the GDR exports to Egypt included 29,000 machine pistols, 85,000 pairs of protective clothing, and twelve kits of repair parts for the MiG-21. The machine pistols and protective clothing were delivered with "special credit" arrangements between the GDR and Egypt, while the other materials were paid with letters of credit.[9]

Two years later, in October 1971, Heinz Hoffmann led an East German military delegation on a trip to Iraq, Egypt, and, most importantly, to Hafez al-Assad's Syria. There he met with Assad, as well as with the chief of the Syrian general staff, Mustafa Tlass. Tlass informed Hoffmann of his "unlimited admiration of fascist Blitzkrieg strategy and of the actual accomplishments of the bourgeois German military" ("die rückhaltlose Bewunderung der faschistischen Blitzkriegsstrategie und der sachlichen Leistungen der bürgerlichen deutschen Militärs").[10] He expressed Syria's interest in delivery of Warsaw Pact tanks and MiG fighter jets. In an interview with Syrian journalists, Hoffmann said that the Syrians would "be victorious in your battle against the common enemy." "We are fighting against a common enemy!," he proclaimed; "The American imperialist support our enemies in Europe and give Israel money and weapons to protect their imperialist interests."[11] He continued:

> In reality, both of our peoples are fighting together against the imperialist and Zionist forces. We in the GDR fight on our border against our enemy, the NATO countries. This enemy is the strongest partner of the American imperialists in Europe. The American imperialists always stand behind

West Germany. In just the same way, you here fight against Israel, that is also a partner of the USA. Israel in fact is a bridge [*Brückenkopf*] for the imperialists in the Middle East. That is why the American imperialists support Israel and give Israel everything it needs (money, weapons) and thus it can play its imperialist role. Therefore I assert that we are conducting a common struggle against the imperialist and Zionist forces. Can we defeat this common enemy? Naturally we can, if we place all of our effort toward that end but together with the help of our friends in the world we will finally defeat our common enemy because the fighting people will always win in the end. In your country, we are certain that the Arab peoples be victorious over their enemy so that he will have to pull his troops back from occupied Arab territories.[12]

The relationship between the GDR and Syria and between Hoffman and Tlass deepened in the next decade. At the end of his visit to Damascus in May 1983, Hoffmann raised a toast to the Syrians and to Tlass.[13] Following the familiar standard denunciations of Israel, imperialism, and Zionism, Hoffmann extolled the Syrian and GDR friendship, as well as "the community borne of struggle [*Kampfgemeinschaft*] among soldiers of the Syrian armed forces and the National Peoples' Army of the GDR, to the health of all members of the Syrian armed forces and to its Minister of Defense, comrade General Mustafa Tlass!"[14]

GDR and PLO

In 1970, the Palestine Liberation Organization, whose charter called for a one-state solution that would eliminate the Jewish state, and whose activity consisted of terrorist attacks on Israel and, in some of its groups, in Western Europe and on international civil aviation, opened an office in East Berlin. Over the next two decades, the relationship between the GDR and the PLO became central for both parties. For the GDR it was evidence of its global revolutionary commitments, and for the PLO it served as a source of weapons, economic aid, military training, and political and diplomatic support. In the years in which the PLO was engaged in armed attacks on Israeli civilians, Yassir Arafat's photo appeared frequently on the front page of *Neues Deutschland* literally embracing a smiling Erich Honecker, visiting the memorial to victims of fascism in East Berlin, and sitting across the table from Honecker and other members of the East German Politburo. The East Germans worked closely with the Arab and Palestinian delegations at the United Nations to deflect criticisms about terrorism or human rights abuses in the Arab states and to redefine the meaning of words such as "terrorism."

Arafat visited East Berlin for the first time from 30 October to 2 November 1971 at the invitation of the GDR's Afro-Asian Solidarity Committee (AASK) (Timm 1997: 269–275). In 1973, Arafat traveled to East Berlin for the second time and met with Politburo member Herman Axen. In June 1973, he had an official conversation with Gerhard Grüneberg, who emerged over the sixteen years as the key contact in the Politburo with the PLO. In August 1973, Arafat was celebrated as a major attraction of the "World Youth Festival" in East Berlin. He then met Erich Honecker for the first of what would turn out to be many visits. East Germany was the first of the Communist states to open a PLO consulate and did so a year before the Soviet Union did. The common "struggle against imperialism and Zionism" was incorporated into the 1973 agreement that accompanied the opening of the consulate.[15] Though Winzer denied that the agreement included military assistance and training, in fact the agreement signed by Arafat and Grüneberg on 2 August 1973 included the GDR's agreement "to support the Palestinian Liberation Organization with deliveries of equipment of a non-civilian nature."[16] The agreement between the SED and the PLO in 1975 for 1976/1977, states that the "GDR continues its solidarity and support for the Palestinian people and give the PLO solidarity materials [Solidaritätsgüter]" in civilian goods valued at five million Marks, and material from the "non-civilian" area will take place according to "special" yet unspecified agreements. De facto, the GDR thus supported military actions against Israel even when it distanced itself from terrorism. The public denunciation of individual terrorist acts went hand in hand with descriptions of PLO attacks on Israel as "armed liberation struggle" and thus not terrorism.[17]

Shortly after the massacre of the Israeli wrestling team at the Munich Olympics by terrorists of the Black September organization on 5 September 1972, Arafat publicly denied that the PLO was involved. On 17 September 1972, Arafat wrote a long and interesting letter in the name of the PLO Executive Committee to Honecker about what he called "the action in Munich," and about what he called Israeli aerial attacks on "Palestinian refugee camps" on 6 September. He said that the PLO "was not responsible for the organization Black September" but did not directly say that he and the PLO had nothing to do with the attack. The absence of a firmer denial must have suggested to Honecker and his comrades that Arafat and the PLO leadership were somehow involved. In any case, Arafat did not criticize the attack in Munich. He was sending the note because "we [the Executive Committee of the PLO] approve, treasure, are proud of and take hope and strength from the sincere friendship for our cause and your sympathy that you have shown us as well as your recognition of our right in struggle." He reminded Honecker that two days earlier the PLO issued an official statement that "it is not responsible for the Black September Organization"—the group which carried out the attack in Munich. Arafat urged "understanding of the action in Munich from the viewpoint of the general problem and its historical events with all of their political, national and human dimensions. If one wants to really distinguish between the deep causes and the peripheral and secondary events," he wrote, "it is futile and useless to view the action apart from the stream of events and from their whole historical framework."[18]

Arafat's appeal for understanding the Munich attack was a clear message to Honecker and the SED leadership that he viewed terrorism as a fully justified means of achieving his political ends. Not only did the letter not contain a hint of remorse over the murders of the Jewish athletes; it took Israel to task for "claiming" that an act of terrorism was, in fact, an act of terrorism, and for using the event to unleash a "war of annihilation" and a global campaign of murder against the Palestinians. With the receipt of this letter, Honecker and the SED leadership knew that Arafat justified terrorism directed against Israelis. This was a man with whom Honecker and the SED were in the process of developing a close and enduring bond that lasted until the regime fell in 1989.

On 27 November 1972, Honecker sent a public letter of greetings to the Arab People's Conference in Support of the Palestinian Revolution, which was taking place in Beirut. The text, composed a few days earlier in the Division of International Relations in the SED's Central Committee, was printed in *Neues Deutschland* and distributed by the GDR's press agency.[19] In the name of the SED's Central Committee and "of the whole people" of the GDR, he sent "warm greetings" to the conference, which he called an expression of "strengthening of the unity and determination of broad strata of the Arab peoples in struggle against imperialism, Zionism and reaction." While Honecker did not mention the Munich massacre, he did assert that what he called "the string of recent Israeli acts of aggression against the Republic of Lebanon and the Syrian Arab Republic demonstrate yet again that Israel, with the support of the USA and other imperialist states is not ready to agree to a peaceful settlement of the Middle East conflict."[20]

Honecker condemned "the efforts of imperialism and all reactionary forces to rob the Palestinian people of their right to self-determination and [those] engaged in reactionary conspiracies to split and attack the Palestinian liberation movement." The "history of the world-wide confrontation with imperialism" had shown that the unity of the "anti-imperialist front" led by the Soviet Union and the "socialist community of states" lay behind "every success in the struggle for self-determination and social progress." The GDR, "in the future as in the past," stood "firmly on the side of the

Arabic-Palestinian people [and] its resistance movement," and supported its right to self-determination.[21]

The GDR's Intelligence Cooperation with the PLO and Its Eurocentric Definition of Counterterrorism

In June 1979, Erich Mielke, the director of Stasi, signed an agreement of cooperation with Abu Ayad, the head of the counterpart institutions of the PLO intelligence service. In August, Mielke and Ayad further agreed that a representative of the PLO intelligence service would be sent to work in East Berlin.[22] From then until the collapse of the regime in 1989, Ayad or his second in command Amin al-Hindi met several times a year with Mielke or with Gerhard Neiber, the director of the Ministry of State Security's (MfS) Division XXII, the office for *Terror Bekämpfung*, which is roughly translated as "fighting terrorism" or more colloquially as "counterterrorism." The agreement called for *"operative Zusammenwirkens"* or "operational cooperation" in the GDR. Not long after the 1979 agreement, on 15 July 1980, Abu Ayad met with officials in Division XXII to discuss "terrorist forces and their activities."[23] Before offering a detailed assessment of various terrorist organizations (the memo is twenty pages long), Ayad explained the meaning of some important terms. His comments were striking in their candor. The PLO, he said, distinguished between "right-wing terrorism," "left-wing adventurers" and "terrorist forces that are active in the interest of the Palestinian resistance movement." While it rejected both "right-wing terrorists" and "left-wing adventurers," the "PLO supported the other terrorist forces and at times worked together with them" ("unterstütze die PLO die anderen terroristischen Kräfte, bzw. arbeitete teilweisemit ihnen zusammen").[24] Ayad's discussion with the MfS officials was striking for its absence of euphemism. He did not refer to "anti-imperialist resistance fighters" or say that "one's man's terrorist is another man's freedom fighter." Instead, he understood terrorism to be the intentional targeting of civilians, and that it was distinct from acts of war carried out against military forces. While in public both the PLO and the GDR, as well as the Soviet bloc states in general, denounced Western attacks on "international terrorism" as imperialist propaganda, when speaking frankly to one another, officials understood the nature of terrorism and were equally frank about supporting it.

The MfS officials, probably Neiber and perhaps Mielke as well, replied that they "could support a certain toleration of left-oriented terrorist forces so long as it preserves strict secrecy, obedience to [East German] law, and it precludes any kind of political or any other kind of damage for the GDR and its allies."[25] Ayad assured his counterparts that the PLO agreed with the MfS on this matter. He suggested that agreement about these issues was a basis on which "the exchange of information could continue to be improved," then offered "details about terrorist groups and forces to which the PLO had contacts and connections."[26] The groups in question included the Carlos group, Abu Nidal, Saddam Hussein, former members of the Wadi Haddad group, the Armenian Liberation Front, and the Japanese Red Army. Regarding "terrorist groups in the FRG" (Federal Republic of Germany or West Germany), Ayad said that the PLO had no contact with the 2 June Movement or the Red Army Faction (RAF). It had developed contacts with the Revolutionary Cells, the group that participated in the hijacking of an Air France flight to Entebbe, Uganda, in 1976. In 1981, Ayad told the MfS officials that the PLO was, in fact, working with the Revolutionary Cells and "intended to expand the connections to the so-called 'Revolutionary Cells' in the Federal Republic and eventually to use it to carry out particular armed actions." Ayad offered to give the names of members of "these terrorist organizations" in West Germany to the MfS. The ministry officials suggested that he give them the names before the PLO established close connections to them so the Stasi could examine them first. "Abu Ayad accepted the offer with gratitude."[27]

These are the kinds of conversations that take place only among close, trusting, and firm political allies who are involved in a very special relationship and alliance of great import. The goals of the cooperation included intelligence about and measures to prevent "subversive plans and intentions" that would endanger the state and security of the GDR; intelligence about "terrorist and extremist forces" working in West Germany and West Berlin that could negatively affect the GDR; "creation of positions and possibilities of influence among Palestinian citizens for fulfilling the operational tasks of the MfS"—that is, seeking agents among Palestinians to work for the Stasi; and influencing "Palestinians, Arabs and other foreigners working with them to obey the laws and state regulations of the GDR (passports and visa rules, customs and currency regulations, registration orders, drug laws)."[28] This last goal concerned the efforts of the Stasi to keep track of Palestinian, Arab, and West European terrorists who lived in or traveled to and from East Germany. The official, whose name is blacked out in the Stasi files, would be given press credentials of the WAFA, the Palestinian news agency, as a cover and would have ongoing contact with Division XXII led by Neiber. The East German government would cover expenses for an apartment and office in East Berlin.

The Stasi had no objections to Palestinian terror attacks on Israel. Its concern was preventing Arab and Palestinian terrorists from using East German territory to launch attacks in West Germany and Western Europe.

On 3 January 1983, for example, MfS officers asked Abu Ayad a series of very detailed questions about the aftereffects of the "Israeli aggression," that is, Israel's invasion of Lebanon in 1982. Were there splinter organizations that placed "armed struggle" at the center of their activities? "In what form and extent would armed actions be conducted outside the Arab region, especially in Western Europe?" Would "territories or citizens of the socialist states be involved in such actions?" What did he know about "terrorist groups and forces" in the aftermath of the Lebanon war and "to which ones did the PLO have connections?" The questions indicate that the MfS was familiar with groups named Abu Nidal, Carlo, Abu Mohammed, Abu Ibrahim, and Carlos as well. What were their plans? Did they intend to establish bases in East Germany and engage in terrorist activities in Western Europe? Mielke, Neiber, and their staff made clear that there should be no terrorist bases in the GDR, saying, "Our experiences in recent years confirm that difficulties are to be expected due to lack of discipline [and] violation of agreements among individual functionaries of the PLO."[29]

The emerging policy in the 1970s was what can be called East Germany's Eurocentric counterterrorism policy—that is, support for terrorism waged against Israel but opposition to terrorist attacks waged against West Germany and Western Europe. That said, the links between the MfS and the RAF in West Germany were important. For example, the East German government gave members of the RAF who fled from West German authorities new names, apartments, and employment and thus protected them from arrest by the West German authorities (Jander 2006: 712). The Stasi kept a close eye on them and on Arabs and Palestinians living in East Germany who might use the GDR as a base to launch terrorist attacks on West Germany and Western Europe. Such attacks could be traced back to the GDR and destroy support in West Germany and Western Europe for the lucrative financial support coming to East Germany from West Germany under the terms of détente. In short, the Stasi officials knew very well that "international terrorists"—that is, radical Arabs and Palestinians as well as their West German and West European collaborators—were flying into East Berlin from the Middle East with false passports and then traveling to West Berlin where they were carrying out terrorist attacks. As the Western intelligence services knew this as well, the problem facing the East German regime was obvious: how could it claim to be an advocate of peace, détente, and better relations with the West—thus bringing large cash donations from the West German government—if it was tolerating and, who knows, perhaps assisting terrorist groups waging attacks in West Germany and Western Europe? How, in other words, could it avoid confirming Western suspicions that it was a state sponsor of international terrorism? Thus, the Stasi, which was aiding the PLO as well as terrorist groups on its left wing such as the Popular Front for the Liberation of Palestine (PFLP) and the Democratic Popular Front for the Liberation of Palestine (PDFLP), in carrying out terrorist attacks against Israel and perhaps elsewhere in the world, also worked with the PLO to prevent those same organizations from carrying out terrorist attacks in West Germany and Western Europe, attacks that could be traced to the GDR, the Soviet Union, and the other Communist regimes in Eastern Europe. This combination of support for terrorism waged against Israel but opposition to terrorism waged in Western Europe if based in the Soviet bloc became the meaning of the term "counterterrorism" (*Terrorismusbekämpfung*) assigned to Division XXII and was central to the Eurocentric meaning and the hypocrisies of East German counterterrorism policy.[30]

Weapons Deliveries

Establishing the amount and kinds of weapons that the East German regime delivered to the Arab states at war with Israel, to the Palestinian Liberation Organization, and to splinter groups such as the PFLP, which engaged in airplane hijacking, bombings, and assassinations in the Middle East and in Western Europe, is a task for ongoing research. Public assertions remained at the level of generalities about solidarity with anti-imperialist forces. In the fall of 1989, significant amounts of document destruction took place within the offices of the MfS and probably within those of the Defense Ministry as well. Surviving files indicated weapons shipments to other states, such as Yemen, which may have included shipments to the PLO and its member organizations. With these qualifications in mind, however, significant evidence about the directly military nature of the alliance between the GDR, the Arab states, and the PLO has survived in the archives of both the MfS and the National People's Army (NVA). The evidence in the Stasi's Division of Weapons and Chemical Services (Bewaffnung und Chemischer Dienst / BCD) includes receipts and records of weapons deliveries and records of military training to officers in the PLO and from Syria, Iraq, and Yemen in military training institutes in East Germany. They were colleagues with officers from Angola, Vietnam, the Congo, El Salvador, Ethiopia, Laos, Libya, Nicaragua, Mozambique, and Zanzibar. There may also be evidence about East German assistance to Syria in constructing an arsenal of chemical weapons. The evidence in the Defense Ministry files details shipments not only to the PLO but also to Arab states, first and foremost to Syria in the 1970s and 1980s. As we will see, the weapons sent to the PLO were those most useful for terrorism and guerilla war.

Given the secrecy that surrounded the East German weapons programs, it is possible that additional arms shipments were recorded in files under code names or were in files that were destroyed as the regime was collapsing in fall 1989. Weapons in East Germany's "Operation Friendship" program went to many armed leftist movements in newly industrialized nations, especially to Yemen, where Palestinian terror organizations had bases. Weapons shipped to those other destinations may have found their way into the arsenals of Al Fatah, the PFLP, PDFLP, and other Palestinian armed organizations. Most of the larger weapons systems, such as tanks, MiG fighter jets, Katuysha rocket launchers, and artillery, that East Germany shipped to the armed forces of Egypt, Syria, Iraq, and Libya were produced in the Soviet Union. Following the Politburo's decision of 1969 to expand military support to states and movements around the world, however, East Germany began to manufacture its own version of the Kalashnikov assault weapon, hand grenades, cartridges, and landmines.

The following is summary of the information in the now-available East German archives of the total amount and kinds of weapons that East Germany gave as "solidarity" goods free of charge or sold to the Arab states and the Palestinian armed organizations at war with Israel from 1967 to 1989: 750,000 Kalashinikov assault weapons; 120 MiG Fighter jets; 180 thousand antipersonnel land mines; 235 thousand grenades; 25 thousand rocket-propelled grenade (RPG) launchers; and 25 million cartridges of various sizes. In addition, during these years, East German technicians repaired and serviced 350 MiG fighter jets for the air forces of Iraq and Syria. From 1972 to 1989, more than three thousand military personnel received training in East Germany military institutes, including several hundred from Syria, Iraq, Libya, and the PLO. A long list of other equipment with military purposes includes binoculars, tents, parachutes, radio equipment, field hospitals, equipment for chemical warfare, sniper rifles, carbines, fuses, and explosives (Herf 2016: 453). While Soviet armed forces fought in battle against Israel, I have not found evidence that East Germans did so.

Conclusion

Hatred of Israel and the willingness to support its armed enemies was not a peculiarity of East German Communism. Rather, antagonism, efforts to de-legitimize it, and ideological rejection of Zionism was the norm among Communist governments and parties everywhere in the world after the anti-cosmopolitan purges of 1949 to 1953. East Germany was not exceptional in associating Zionism with racism and imperialism. After the purges, it was impossible everywhere to remain a Communist and simultaneously support the existence of Israel as a Jewish state. It was Marxism-Leninism, not the aftereffects of Nazism, that inspired the Communist attack on Israel. The most important source of weapons was the Soviet Union, though small East Germany made remarkable contributions. East Germany's enthusiastic participation in this effort was an example of the unity of Marxist-Leninist theory with political practice. The shipment of weapons to Syria and weapons training for the PLO was the logical consequence of a Marxist-Leninist interpretation of global politics and of the place of Israel in the world system.

Yet it was only in Germany after the Nazis that the antagonism to Israel smashed the implicit and unspoken eleventh commandment followed by the West German government to do no more harm to the Jews. It was only in Germany that turning against Israel came with the supposed benefit of liberation from the burdens of German history after the Holocaust, what the West Berlin leader of the 2 June Movement, Dieter Kunzelmann, derisively called "the Jewish complex." The eagerness with which East German Communists and West German leftists called the Israelis Nazis suggested that a different kind of relief and liberation was at work, one in which these Germans thought of themselves as the "good Germans" whose goodness lay in attacking the Jewish state, in finding common ground with its Arab and Palestinian Arab enemies, and oddly achieving freedom from the burdens of German history after Nazism.

In the immediate aftermath of World War II and the Holocaust, anti-Zionism was correctly associated with the ideology and policies of the Nazi regime (Herf 2009). Part of the historical importance of the Communist turn against Zionism and Israel during the Cold War was to lend the global prestige of leftist antifascism to the association of Zionism and Israel with racism and imperialism. That was a connection that neither neo-Nazis nor their collaborators among Islamists could have spread as an element of leftist politics around the world. In that sense, they both contributed greatly to the persistence of an antisemitism of consequences, and at times of intentions, that persists to our own time. In the era of the undeclared wars and terrorism aimed at Israel, the East German reversal of the meaning of antifascism led to a bizarre outcome: a self-described antifascist regime in East Berlin denounced the leaders of the Jewish state as Nazis. The East German Communists indignantly rejected any suggestion that their willingness to believe the worst about Israel and to impute murderous and even genocidal aims to its leaders had anything to do with 1,900 years of European anti-Judaism and its repeated associations of the Jews with violence and murder (Nirenberg 2013). The more they insisted that anti-Zionism had nothing to do with hatred of Jews or Judaism, the less they reflected on the fact that they were participating in an effort to bring yet more misery, death, and destruction to the Jews living in Israel.

Jeffrey Herf, born in 1947, is an American historian and Distinguished University Professor at the University of Maryland, College Park, where he is a professor of modern European and German history. Herf graduated with honors in history from the University of Wisconsin-Madison in 1969 and received a PhD in sociology from Brandeis University in 1981. He taught at Harvard University and Ohio University before joining the faculty of the University of Maryland in 2000. His publications include *Reactionary Modernism: Technology, Culture and Politics in Weimar and the Third Reich* (Cambridge University Press, 1984); *War by Other Means: Soviet Power, West German Resistance and the Battle of the Euromissiles* (The Free Press, 1991); *Divided Memory: The Nazi Past in the Two Germanys* (Harvard University Press, 1997); *Zweierlei Erinnerung: Die NS Vergangenheit im Geteilten Deutschland* (Ullstein/Propylaen Verlag, 1998); *The Jewish Enemy: Nazi Propaganda during World War II and the Holocaust* (Harvard University Press, 2006); *Nazi Propaganda for the Arab World* (Yale University Press, 2009); *Undeclared Wars with Israel: East Germany and the West German Far Left, 1967–1989* (Cambridge University Press, 2016); and *Unerklaerte Kriege gegen Israel: Die DDR und die westdeutsche Linke, 1967–1989* (Wallstein Verlag, 2019). He is currently working on a book titled *Israel's Moment: Support and Opposition in the United States and Europe, 1945–1949*.

Notes

This essay refers to my 2016 book *Undeclared Wars with Israel: East Germany and the West German Far Left, 1967–1989*. The book also deals with the Left's hostility toward Israel in the Federal Republic of Germany.

1. "Protokoll Nr. 7/67 der Sitzung des Politbuüros des Zentralkomitees am 7. Juli 1967," Bundesarchiv Berlin (hereafter BAB), Stiftung Archiv der Parteien und Massenorganisationen der DDR im Bundesarchiv (hereafter SAPMO) DY 30/J IV 2/2/1117, 1.
2. "Anlage Nr. 1 zum Protokoll Nr. 7/67 vom 7 August 1967; Betr.: Maβnahmen im Zusammenhang mit der Situation im Nahen und Mittleren Osten," BAB, SAPMO DY 30/J IV 22/1117, 7–8.
3. Ibid., 8–9.
4. Ibid., 9.
5. Ibid.
6. Walter Ulrbricht to Leonid Brezhnew, "An den Generalsekretär des ZK der KPdSU Genossen Leonid Iljitische Breshnew," 17 October 1969, BAB, SAPMO, Büro Walter Ulbricht, DY 30/3666, 114–120.

7. Ibid., 118–120. Also see W. Ulbricht to P.A. Abrassimow, Berlin, 3 February 1970, BAB, SAPMO, Büro Walter Ulbricht, DY 30/3666, 159; Timm 1997: 234.

8. The CIA has declassified millions of files. They are available via searches that need to be conducted on computers at the US National Archives in College Park.

9. "Arabische Republik Ägypten (ARÄ): Beziehungen der speziellen Außenwirtschaft zu den militärischen Organen der ARÄ," Bundesarchiv Militärarchiv (hereafter BAMA) DVW1/ 115671, Ministerium für Nationale Verteidigung (hereafter MfNV), Sekr. D. Ministers. Unterlagen zur Vorbereitung d. Militärdelegation in den arabischen Staaten, 37–38.

10. Ibid., 17.

11. Heinz Hoffman interview with Jaych-Ach-Chaab (Damascus, October 1971), MfNV. Schriftverkehr des Ministers, Militärdelegation der DDR nach Syrien, Ägypten, Irak, BAMA DVW1/115673, 4. The German reads as follows: "Wir sind überzeugt, daß Sie in Ihrem Kampf gegen den Feind siegen werden. Wir kämpfen gegen einen gemeinsamen Feind! Die amerikanischen Imperialisten unterstützen unsere Feinde in Europa und geben Israel Geld und Waffen, um ihre imperialistischen Interessenzuschützen."

12. Ibid., 5–6.

13. Heinz Hoffmann, "Empfang in der Botschaft der DDR," MfNVSekr. Des Ministers. Militärdelegation der DDR nach Syrien, Ägypten, Irak., BAMA DVW1/115673.

14. Ibid., 4, 10.

15. Ibid., 276.

16. Gerhard Grüneberg and Yassir Arafat, "Vereinbarung zwischen der Sozialistischen Einheitspartie Deutschlands und der Palästinensischen Befreiungsorganisationen (PLO) für die Jahre 1976/1977," [East] Berlin (1 December 1975), BAB SAPMO DY 30/ 9529, Büro des Politbüro des ZK der SED 1972–1989, 1–3.

17. Ibid.

18. Yassir Arafat to Erich Honecker (17 September 1972), "Notzen und Schreiben außenpolitischen Charakters zwischen der DDR und der Palästinensischen Befreiungsbewegung zur Unterstützung der PLO durch die DDR, 1972, 1974, 1978–1979," Politisches Archiv des Auswärtigen Amtes (hereafter PAAA), Ministerium für auswätige Angelegenheiten (hereafter MFAA), Abt. Naher-und Mittlerer Osten, MfAA, C 7.667 (ZR 2040/01), 48–49.

19. Abteilung Internationale Verbindungen, "Entwurf eines Grußschreibens: An die arabische Volkskonferenz zur Unterstützung der palästinensischen Revolution," Berlin (24 November 1972), 1–2. Also see "Kongreß zur Unterstutzung des palästinensischen Volkes eröffnet: Delegation der DDR überbrachte Grüße des ZK der SED," *Neues Deutschland*, 28 November 1972, BAB, ZK der SED, DY 30 9529, 1.

20. Abteilung Internationale Verbindungen, "Entwurf eines Grußschreibens: An die arabische Volkskonferenz zur Unterstützung der palästinensischen Revolution," Berlin (24 November 1972), 1–2.

21. Ibid., 2.

22. Gerhard Neiber, "Vorlage zum Einsatz eine Vertreters der Vereinigen PLO-Sicherheit in der DDR," Berlin (1980), Bundesbeauftragter für die Stasi Unterlagen

(hereafter BStU), Archiv der Zentralstelle, Ministerium für Staatssicherheit (hereafter MfS) Hauptabteilung (HA) XXII, Nr. 17508, 67–69.

23. "Bericht über das Gespräch mit dem Leiter der 'Vereinigten PLO-Sicherheit' — ABU AYAD — am 15.7.1980 zu terroristischen Kräften und ihren Aktivitäten," [East] Berlin (18 June 1980), BStU, Zentralachiv (hereafter ZA), HA XXII, Nr. 17508, 304–323.

24. Ibid., 304.

25. Ibid., 304.

26. Ibid., 305.

27. Ibid., 319.

28. Ibid., 68.

29. Abteilung XXII, "Konzeption für die Gespräch mit dem Leiter der 'Vereinigten PLO-Sicherheit' Abu Ayad für Linie XXII," [East] Berlin (3 January 1983), BStU ZA HA XXII, Nr. 17508, 178–81.

30. Given the clandestine nature of all terrorist activity and the fact that there was considerable destruction of documents in the files of the Ministry of State Security during the collapse of the East German regime in the fall and winter of 1989–90, active support of West German terrorism by the Stasi cannot be ruled out. What is clear is that the stated policy of the Stasi as expressed in important official memos opposed such terrorist attacks due to the damage they would do to East German and Soviet bloc interests. On document destruction, see Winkler 2013: 490–491. For a detailed account of the Eurocentric counterterrorism policy, see Herf 2016, chapters 8 and 11.

References

Bator, Wolfgang, and Angelika Bator, eds. 1984. *Die DDR und die arabischen Staaten. Dokumente 1956–1982*. Berlin.

Epstein, Catherine. 2003. *The Last Revolutionaries: German Communists and Their Century* Cambridge, MA.

Herf, Jeffrey. 1997. *Divided Memory: The Nazi Past in the Two Germanys*. Cambridge.

———. 1998. *Zweierlei Erinnerung: Die NS-Vergangenheit im geteilten Deutschland*. Berlin.

———. 2009. *Nazi Propaganda for the Arab World*. New Haven.

———. 2016. *Undeclared Wars with Israel: East Germany and the West German Far Left, 1967–1989*. New York.

———. 2017. "The Anti-Zionist Bridge: The East German Communist Contribution to the Revival of Antisemitism after the Holocaust." *Antisemitism Studies* 1, no. 1: 130–156.

Jander, Martin. 2006. "Differenzen im antiimperialistischen Kampf." In *Die RAF und der linke Terrorismus*, vol. 1, edited by Wolfgang Kraushaar, 696–713. Hamburg.

Nirenberg, David. 2013. *Anti-Judaism: The Western Tradition*. New York.

Storkmann, Klaus. 2012. *Geheime Solidarität: Militärbeziehungen und Militärhilfen der DDR in die "Dritte Welt."* Berlin.

Timm, Angelika. 1997. *Hammer, Zirkel, Davidstern: Das gestörte Verhältnis der DDR zu Zionismus und Staat Israel*. Bonn.

Ulbricht, Walter. 1967. "Rede des Vorsitzenden des Staatsrates der Deutschen Demokratischen Republik, Walter Ulbricht, auf einer Wahlversammlung in Leipzig am 15. Juni 1967, zu Fragen der Lage im Nahen Osten und zur westdeutschen Expansionspolitik im Rahmen der USA-Globalstrategie (Auszug)." In *Staatsverlag der Deutschen Demokratischen Republik (1970): Dokumente zur Außenpolitik der Deutschen Demokratischen Republik 1967*, vol. 15, edited by Institut für internationale Beziehungen, Deutsche Demokratische Republik. Ministerium für auswärtige Angelegenheiten, 515–538. Berlin.

Winkler, Heinrich August. 2013. *Germany: The Long Road West*. Vol. 2: *1933–1990*. Oxford.

Wolf, Markus. 1997. *Man without a Face: The Autobiography of Communism's Greatest Spymaster*. New York.

Chapter 9

Holocaust Lite?

Fiction in Works by Christa Wolf and Fred Wander

Agnes C. Mueller

This essay demonstrates how works by Christa Wolf and Fred Wander—both celebrated authors in the German Democratic Republic (GDR)—present and negotiate themes such as the Holocaust, dealing with the German past, and the memory of National Socialism. While Wolf's fiction and essays supposedly grapple with Holocaust trauma, Jewish identity, and perpetrator guilt, I argue that the relevance of these themes remains hidden for subsequent generations of readers. Examining Wolf's strategies of emotionalizing, I draw in part on theories of social realism alongside texts by Fred Wander. Wander's work offers explicit descriptions of experiences in the camps, not obstructed in any way in their directness, whereas Wolf's texts present more remote figures, themes, and motives. With Wander's work, we encounter a mode of representation that runs the risk of being received as "kitsch," or, to be exact, "Holocaust-Kitsch," and this would limit the effectiveness of his texts. Meanwhile, Wolf's remoteness and seclusion in dealing with the German past can invite us to look away rather than confront German National Socialism and the Holocaust. Given persistent claims that the GDR was the "better" Germany, purportedly free of fascism, Nazism, and thus antisemitism, fictionalizing and emotionalizing strategies in the literary works of prominent GDR authors are relevant for the history of Holocaust memory and dealing with the National Socialist past. The ways in which memory is negotiated must be re-evaluated, especially in light of newer, post-1990 texts, such as work by Benjamin Stein.

Christa Wolf's highly lauded 1976 autobiographical novel *Kindheitsmuster* is key to this analysis.[1] The text is often cited when it comes to showing how intensely Wolf supposedly dealt with Holocaust memory in the GDR. But neither Jews nor the Holocaust are explicitly mentioned or referenced in her novel even though it covers 1939 to the immediate postwar period, narrated through the experiences of Nelly Johnson. A comment from Wolf sheds light on this omission: "When I wrote *Kindheitsmuster*, it did not occur to me to draw any parallels between German fascism and Soviet Stalinism. I looked at these phenomena, despite their similarities in appearance, as fundamentally different" (Rechtien 2012: 123).[2]

This statement reflects the core of Wolf's work, which is marked by techniques of disguising and encoding any encounters with Jews, survivors of the Shoah, or perpetrator narratives. Just as it did not occur to Wolf to draw parallels between fascism and Stalinism, it did not occur to her to directly name the Holocaust. As Renate Rechtien shows, all attempts at "dealing with the past" fail in *Kindheitsmuster*, though it is not clear from Rechtien's discussion to what extent this might be connected to subliminal anxieties resulting from what might be called guilt-rejection antisemitism (Rechtien 2012: 123–125; for antisemitism resulting from guilt rejection, also see Mueller, *The Inability to Love*).

According to Rechtien, the failure of German dealing with the past is the result of German division and the two political regimes approaching their respective artists with different expectations. This is a position also maintained by Wolf. The recognition that there were before 1989/90 two historically and politically separate German ways of dealing with the memory of the past is not new, and has been the subject of scholarly study (Schaumann 2008; Klocke 2014). The most prominent and, for historians, relevant example is Jeffrey Herf's (1997) *Divided Memory*. What has not been looked at closely, however, and where we will find new material by reading work by Wander[3] and Wolf, are the Jewish figures in their texts, or figures who are purposely represented as Jewish. In what ways do Wolf and Wander contribute as GDR writers to German Jewish identity? How does dealing with the representation of Holocaust memory by individuals work beyond public and political discourse?

Literature and the Analysis of Holocaust Memory

Literary works often deal with representing and depicting emotional events and changes taking place within individuals, like the case of Nelly in *Kindheitsmuster*: "Where Nelly was most involved, dedicated, self-sacrificing, the details that would matter are erased. Step by step, one has to conclude, and it is not difficult to guess why: the loss must have resulted from a deeply disturbed and insecure consciousness, which, as we know, can give effective directives behind its own back, for example this one: No longer think of it. Directives that were diligently followed over the years. Avoiding certain memories. Not talking about it. Not allowing words, phrases, trains of thought that could evoke them. Not asking certain questions among peers. Because it is unbearable to have to think at the mention of 'Auschwitz' the small word 'I.' 'I' in past subjunctive: I should have, I could have, I would have. Done. Obeyed" (Wolf 1976: 270).

Yet, the "unbearable" Auschwitz discourse continues to be concealed. The "never think of it again" that the narrator criticizes is represented in precisely this form—namely, missing or as silence in her literary work. While formulated differently and less fictionalized and artistically constructed, this silence can be found in Christa Wolf's essay on Fred Wander, where it is justified in ways that are problematic.

Christa Wolf and Fred Wander

In her 1972 "Nachwort" (epilogue), republished in the 1985 Luchterhand edition of Fred Wander's most popular work, *Der siebente Brunnen*, Wolf (1972, 1985) makes a few predictable observations and others that are more surprising. That Wolf praises the fiction of Fred Wander, a friend and fellow comrade in the project of elevating socialist realist—or GDR—fiction, is to be expected. Perhaps less expected is that she invokes a well-known and potentially troubling label that is ascribed to various Holocaust narratives. Using Wander's text as testimony, Christa Wolf asserts that only those on the "inside," only those personally affected, who were incarcerated in the camps and lived to tell their story—true survivors—can speak about the Holocaust. Others are thereby rendered mute.

This inside/outside binary is of course neither new to the discourse of Holocaust memory nor is it limited to experiences of the Shoah. Any experience, and in particular trauma, is more credible when recounted by someone who knows firsthand what it was like. Authenticity is important, and exponentially more so when it comes to narratives about the largest and most horrific genocide in human history.

Desires for authenticity, however, apply to literature writ large, even to fiction, alongside other more documentary styles. Without this presupposition (and I will not invoke Dilthey's theories or distinctions between representations of *Erlebnis* and *Erfahrung*), hermeneutics would not have evolved as a field. Wolf's declaration that only those who were there, who lived through the horrors of the camps, can "really" know seems like a reasonable claim, and one that in East Germany in 1971 might have not raised too many eyebrows. The need for authentic, accurate, and trustworthy Holocaust survivor testimony takes precedence over desires to overcome binary oppositions, and with good reason.

Yet our understandings of the ways in which Holocaust remembrance and taboo are intertwined have evolved since then. These considerations become even more complex when accounting for the GDR as a political entity, as well as lingering discourses of guilt and shame that prevented engagement with the Shoah in both Germanies for decades after 1945. The "divided memory" (Herf 1997, 1998) of East and West Germany adds layers of emotional baggage to the already fraught project of rendering Holocaust memory visible and fresh for younger generations. While in the West the myth of the "zero hour" and ensuing "re-education" by the Allied Forces might have silenced Holocaust memory, the lore of the GDR as the "better Germany," free of ties to National Socialism and, by association, to the genocidal murder of the Jews, had a similar effect. It might not seem surprising that in 1971, in the wake of the 1968 movement and during the second generation's public outcry against the *Tätergeneration* of their fathers, we are presented with a narrative that renders an unambiguous view from the inside and commentary that insists that only this insider view can relate lived experience.

Fred Wander

Wander's recollections of moments in and around the camps are fictionalized but offer authentic testimonies that seek to grip the reader with strong emotive vocabulary and vivid renditions of gruesome sufferings. At the same time, we as readers stay detached. This is because Wander's stories offer nothing about the characters' pasts. Instead of fully developed types, Thadeusz Moll or Mendel Teichmann remain somewhat abstract figures, painted in broad strokes as fragmented people with characteristics but without identities. But to say they are thin, flat, and abstract is not a putdown—even if this runs counter to the conventions of socialist realism. They are abstract in the sense of Picasso's figures in *Guernica*. This abstract narrative style results from the unusual combination of impressions that belong to individual figures. For example, "Tadeusz feels his feet going numb. In his hands, which he can't move, it pierces like a thousand needles. But then he loses feeling in his hands too" (Wander 2005: 126). Here, narration and forgetting are thematized in the figure of Mendel Teichmann: "He died a senseless undignified death, let me be silent about it.

Forgotten are his verses, his ashes are scattered all over Polish forests and fields" (Wander 2005: 16).

Karl Müller's essay takes a related tack. It celebrates Wander's poetics of remembering and seeing. He notes that it is reminiscent of an X-ray while commenting on Wander's unusual poetics of testimony about the camps. Wander's poetics of X-rays, of seeing, brings them into clear if also abstracted view (Müller 2006: 249–267). Related to this idea of an X-ray view, I would suggest that Wander's prose offers "glimpses," since it is not a full view presented by his narrative but a segment, a fragment, of a full life. Poetologically, this is also reflected in the abrupt ways in which the narrative moves from one character's story to the next, and in the short sentences, the back-and-forth between direct speech and related speech, and other stylistic devices. Müller (2006: 249–267) notes in particular how Christa Wolf has praised Wander's style. Erin McGlothlin (2005: 97–118) aptly describes the prose in *Der siebente Brunnen* as located somewhere on the spectrum from autobiography to fiction. This makes perfect sense, I would say, insofar as both forms are narrative and thus acts of imagination. To remember is to imagine. McGlothlin also remarks on how the distanced and distancing narrative voice often leaves critics uncomfortable when trying to discern the autobiographical content in Wander's prose — that is, the truth-content — as if fiction were lacking in truth. Yet, according to McGlothlin, it is precisely this "closed-off" narrative perspective that renders the witnessing of Holocaust experiences meaningful — which is to say, authentic. Since we as "outsiders" (the outside perspective according to Wolf) can't fully grasp the actual experiences of living through the horrors of the camps, the narrative creates this gap rather than making experience palpable and easy to grasp.

Witnessing

According to Wolf, not everyone is allowed to speak about the Shoah. Witnessing requires privileged or star witnesses to make the experience come to life, and Wolf seeks to make such a star of Wander. Ruth Klüger's (2005) essay, which was published later, falls into a similar category. Wander's (1982: 21–27) often cited letter to Primo Levi unabashedly praises him as a star witness. But where is the center of gravity? How much difference does it make that Wander is located in the East German camp of socialist realism? Consider the difference with photographers. How much do we care about the backgrounds of photographers who captured the liberation of the camps? Their politics do not make a difference like a writer's.

The task of witnessing seems more neutral for a photographer, though we know that style is of paramount importance. But the photographer is always an outsider, whereas Wander—like Primo Levi or Jean Améry—has the status of insider and, possibly, star witness. James E. Young's (1988) *Writing and Rewriting the Holocaust* was an important development in the politics of witnessing. Witness and testimony became questions about *how* witnessing took place, and not only for the GDR. With any mode of representation, there came an interpretation.

In Wander's (1971) *Der siebente Brunnen*, the fragmentation in poetic style and character representation, alongside the outsider/insider binary, enacts the very experience of negotiation between reader and text. The writer, or key witness, provides us with glimpses or broken shards of lived experience—while stylistically pointing to the broken shards. Just as a witness (unlike a photographer) transcends the boundaries of inside versus outside, so do the poetics of Wander's text. It is therefore—and this is what makes Wolf's commentary problematic—not the goal of Wander's text to keep the reader on the outside. Worse still, Wolf legitimizes the silence of bystanders and perpetrators; by limiting the possibility of authentic witnessing to actual survivors, she allows entire generations of perpetrators and bystanders to remain silent and not engage with the memory of the Shoah at all. Such a reading of their texts was not intended by Wander or Wolf. Yet it is at least feasible, and, considering the visibility of Wolf's commentary, we need to take it seriously and ask what might lead her and potential readers to this outcome. This is especially the case since Wolf, in delivering direct citations from Wander's text, almost exclusively cites the voices of perpetrators. The significance of this reading is underscored by the fact that in her essay, in rare moments when she evokes the victims in Wander's text, she does not talk about Jews. Neither does Wolf quote any Jewish protagonists directly, with one exception: an old Ukrainian peasant who is murdered by the SS guard. But then the SS perpetrators are cited for more than a page. The only victim's voice quoted in Wolf's commentary is Mendel Teichmann, who at the end of the essay struggles to find words. "And Mendel saw it and looked at her with his sad, inquisitive eyes, tried to understand, tried, for every beating, for every humiliation, for the laughter in the face of our torturers and for the obscene jokes in the face of our death, Mendel tried to find a form, a saving word" (Wolf 1985b: 159). Jews are, it seems, silenced by Wolf twice over: once because only one gets to speak and cannot find his own words, and then again, because even this moment of speech is defined by the acts of the perpetrators (beatings, humiliations, laughter, jokes). Jews and Jewish voices are thus not present in Wolf's account, even while

Fred Wander is put on the pedestal of star witness. Imre Kertesz (2013: 67) described a similar situation in Hungary, where no one wanted to hear the voices of Jews, since they did not fit the official communist party line. The GDR is, of course, even more complex due to German complicity with the Nazi perpetrators.

In the first chapter of *Der siebente Brunnen*, the narrator asks his fellow inmate Mendel Teichmann an important question about how one learns to tell stories. This moment of narratological self-reflection gains traction later, when it turns out that storytelling is a means for survival. This is a trope in the literature on the memory of the Shoah that Wolf (1972: 155), too, *almost* recognizes when she writes, "This narrative style exactly represents the process that is taking place behind the 'actual content': the process of the author's self-liberation."

Wander, Wolf, and the GDR Reception of the Holocaust

What exactly is the author—in this case, Fred Wander—supposed to be liberated from? From the memory of the Shoah? From the dogmatic constraints of socialist realism? Because of the narratological self-reflection, there is more at stake in the text than the author's liberation or survival. That Wolf fails to recognize this seems to be a failure not of the poetics of the text or of Christa Wolf as a critic, but rather of the conditions of the GDR reception of Holocaust remembrance. Even Wander (1982: 22) falls prey to this paradigm in his admiring letter to Primo Levi, when he states, "In the GDR, fascism was done away with thoroughly, the administrative and bureaucratic apparatus of the Nazi regime was destroyed. As a Jew and as a former camp inmate I would like to note that as opposed to the FRG, where explanations by German Jews increase, the problem of antisemitism is, for now, solved here (in the GDR)." The binary of the FRG versus the GDR, where the GDR represents the better Germany when it comes to addressing the Nazi past, is as widely known as it is insidious.

In his 2006 essay on Holocaust representation in the of the GDR, Thomas Schmidt (2006: 83–109, 403–425) states that we need to bear two parameters in mind: first, the category of history, where the GDR's self-representation did not allow for taking historical, political, or moral responsibility; and, second, literature, which was sanctioned to serve GDR self-representation, in which projecting a socialist utopia (socialist realism) was the main goal, thus severely restricting literary production. In Wander's work, these two parameters are apparent in the ways in which the texts sidestep and ultimately subvert socialist realism. As Schmidt (2006:

83–109, 403–425) points out, the textual self-referentiality in *Der siebente Brunnen* invokes Judaism *not* by asking about modes of representation of the Holocaust but rather by emphasizing—in its self-referentiality—the humanizing quality of the text and the ways in which searching for words and narrative style is reminiscent of interpretations of the Torah instead of a literary style that follows the norms of socialist realist fiction (or another normative category). Socialist realism and Marxist doctrine allow literature and history to be self-referential only if they depict a political utopia. Clearly, Wander's prose and his flattened, highly fragmented, and even abstract invocations of human suffering are far from depicting any socialist or socialist realist utopia. Yet, paradoxically, this fact is not only not recognized in Wolf's exuberant celebration of Wander the author, it is further muted by the fact that many—East and West German as well as post-unification—critics continue to cite Wolf's commentary without pointing out its shortcomings.

Wolf's praise is therefore paradigmatic both for the ways in which Wander's prose has been celebrated in the context of the author as a star witness, but also for the troubling premises of GDR Holocaust remembrance. The text, on the other hand, points to its own powers of referencing memory by invoking a self-referential construct that allows the narrative (and not only the author or the narrator!) to survive allegorically. The final scene in the last chapter in *Der siebente Brunnen* constructs this mimetic pact between text and reader. Joschko did not experience liberation from the camps but he knew all about it. This is enacted when Naftali, the youngest of Joschko's brothers, dreams: "Joschko carefully stroked the boy's face . . . . With the spoon, with my spoon, he spilled a few drops on the mouth of the dreamer" (Wander 1971: 150). The few drops from the narrator's spoon are the drops of memory that we as readers need.

The poetics of Holocaust remembrance in Fred Wander's *Der siebente Brunnen* are thus more complex than the reception by Christa Wolf (and others) may suggest at first glance. We can no longer think in terms of an inside versus outside binary when it comes to speaking about the Shoah, nor can we accept a muting of the Jewish voice. A reader today might be strangely moved by Wander's allegorical and poetic styles that seek to bear witness in a way that is authentic on the one hand, but that appears highly fictionalized and fragmented on the other. The estrangement that we feel vis-à-vis the protagonists might be more unsettling. Looking for the author as a witness, however, might be more obfuscating than enlightening. The conditions of GDR writing have yet to be fully illuminated so that the actual achievements of the texts invoking the memory of the Shoah may be excavated to let their subversive powers shine.

Agnes C. Mueller

Epilogue: Benjamin Stein

To be clear, it is important to note that the goal of this analysis is not to call out individual authors and make them responsible for something that needs to be read as part of a large, highly complex political-historical discourse on the memory of the Shoah. To show that the silence about Jews and the perpetrator past of Germans (in East and West Germany) is not a limited phenomenon of the 1970s, it might be helpful to also consider the more recent novel by Benjamin Stein (2010a), *Die Leinwand* (*The Canvas*). As Beatrice Sandberg[4] described in great detail, the text that forms the foundation of Stein's novel—the hotly debated and ultimately fraudulent "memoirs" of Binjamin Wilkomirski (1995, 1997)—reveal traces of Wander's *Der siebente Brunnen*.

In other words, Wilkomirski (alias Bruno Doessekker) used passages from Wander's works that had been clearly marked as fiction to legitimize his supposedly authentic survivor accounts. The case of Wilkomirski is interesting for this particular analysis, since we are confronted with an author who claims to have been an eyewitness without actually having been an eyewitness. The case of Wilkomirski is extremely well documented among scholars of the memory of the Shoah, so there is no need to reiterate the details here (see Horstkotte 2014). It is merely important to note that the fraudulent memoir's success is far more important for our evaluation of the discourse on the memory of the Shoah than the question of potential motifs and intentions on the part of Bruno Doessekker/Binyamin Wilkomirski. The fact that such a fraud could be so successful even though, or perhaps because, it uses a work of fiction (as proven for Wander's text by Sandberg and could probably be shown for other fictional works) must compel us to reconsider the parameters of our understanding of fiction and testimony in the context of Holocaust memory.

Benjamin Stein, a younger writer (born in 1970) who grew up in the GDR and converted to Judaism as an adult, thematizes the case of Wilkomirski in a complex and sophisticated novel. Two Jewish protagonists, the ultra-orthodox Amnon Zichroni and the conservative-orthodox Jan Wechsler, are bound up in a crime story about a lost memory. It is not entirely clear which of the two figures is invented and which one is "real" (on the level of the plot). This directly refers to Wilkomirski's memoir, which tricks readers into thinking that a writer's memory is authentic even when it is not. The paratextual elements in Stein's novel are geared toward educating his readers about Judaism, and in the novel there are numerous references to the Jewish faith, Jewish religion, and Jewish culture. This is in direct contrast to the works of Wander and Wolf, in which Jewish characters, in as much as they appear at all, are not identified with particularly Jewish attributes. In the context of the reception of Auschwitz in the GDR, especially post-unification, it is interesting to note that neither of the novel's two main protagonists displays a connection to Judaism or lives their Jewish faith in a meaningful way. Instead, Judaism appears stuck onto the plot of the novel in an attempt to educate the German public and to build a reference to Holocaust discourse. Both characters, especially since they are so heavily fictionalized in Stein's novel, could also be read metonymically for the German-German division.

Jeffrey Herf's "divided memory" is thus still inscribed into this contemporary version of Holocaust memory, especially as it is problematized in fiction. Stein (2010b: 47) has this to say on the subject: "For my Judaism ... I don't need Zionism and I don't need the Holocaust. Those play a role, but are entirely exterior. When someone comes to me in search of their Jewish identity, I tell them: Try and light candles on Shabbat. See what that does to you." Wander's answer to this suggestion, as poetologically enacted in *Der siebente Brunnen*, might be that just as Stein does not need the Holocaust for his Jewish identity, he does not need Judaism for his testimonial renderings of the memory of the Shoah.

The more than unsatisfactory ending of *The Canvas*, where we never find out which protagonist survives and which was invented, suggests that the transgenerational self-perpetuating reception of Auschwitz in the GDR is all but in the past. While Christa Wolf's texts, mostly motivated by a political position but also by the cultural context of her era, evoke silence and a silencing of Jewish victims, Fred Wander's prose marks a different trajectory. Wander's Jewish victims are visible and speak to the horrors of life in the camps, even if their Jewish identity is often not front and center. Benjamin Stein's text makes Jewish identity the main theme. Yet here the memory of the Holocaust appears, due to the many levels of fiction, and the generationally specific story is removed. The Shoah or recollections of life in the camps are merely referenced in Stein's novel and are no longer the events of the text. And this is where Wander's prose gains currency, especially today, when the memory of the Shoah has become both tangible (in the context of GDR history) and removed (due to the passage of time). Wander's poetics in *Der siebente Brunnen* vividly display those important parts of our cultural memory that might otherwise be inaccessible.

Agnes C. Mueller is Professor of German and Comparative Literature at the University of South Carolina in the US, where she is also the College of Arts & Sciences Distinguished Professor of the Humanities. Her recent work deals with German-Jewish literature, emotions in literature, and literature since 1945, especially contemporary literature. Mueller completed her MA in comparative literature at the University of Munich in 1993 and her PhD at Vanderbilt University in Nashville, Tennessee, in 1997. Since she joined the University of South Carolina, Mueller has held multiple academic leadership positions, most recently, Director of the Program in Global Studies. Her 2015 monograph, *The Inability to Love*, was published in German as *Die Unfähigkeit zu lieben* (Würzburg, 2017). In 2018, Professor Mueller co-edited *German Jewish Literature since 1990* (with Katja Garloff). Her current book project has the working title *Holocaust Migration: Jewish Fiction in Today's Germany*.

Notes

1. Christa Wolf was born 18 March 1929 in Landsberg/Warthe. Her parents, Herta and Otto Ihlenfeld were merchants, and she had a brother three years younger. In 1945, the family fled to Mecklenburg. Starting in 1947, they lived in Bad Frankenhausen in Thuringia. Wolf finished her high school diploma (*Abitur*) in 1949. After studying German literature in Jena and Leipzig, she worked in Berlin with the Writer's Guild as a critic and reviewer and as editor-in-chief of the journal *Neue deutsche Literatur*. In 1951, she married Gerhard Wolf (born 1928), and their daughters were born in 1952 and 1957. Between 1959 and 1962, the family lived in Halle, where Wolf worked as editor for the Mitteldeutscher Verlag. In 1962, the family moved to Kleinmachnow near Potsdam, and since then Wolf has worked as a writer. She wrote and published numerous books, novels, essays, screenplays, and edited volumes. From 1976 on, the Wolfs lived in Berlin and Mecklenburg. Christa Wolf died on 1 December 2011 in Berlin.

2. When sources are in German, translations are mine.

3. Fred Wander grew up poor, the son of immigrants from Galicia. He went to elementary school in Vienna and worked as an apprentice in the textile industry and in other trade professions. After the Nazis took over Austria, he fled to France and was interned as a "hostile foreigner." In 1942, he was apprehended trying to flee to Switzerland. He was eventually deported to Auschwitz. In April 1945, he was liberated from Buchenwald. His parents were murdered in Auschwitz. After his return to Austria, he worked as a journalist and photographer. In 1950, he joined the Communist Party. The following year, he joined the GDR creative writing institute in Leipzig and, in 1956, married Maxie Brunner. The couple moved in 1958 to Kleinmachnow in the GDR, where he worked as a freelance author, and in 1977, Maxie died. In 1982, he married Susanne and, in 1983, left the GDR permanently with her to live in Vienna. He died on 10 July 2006. His writings deal with his experiences in German concentration camps and with the Nazis. In addition to novels and short stories, he published plays, travel literature, and young adult literature. *Der siebente Brunnen* is considered his main work.

4. Unpublished lecture by Beatrice Sandberg during the international Fred Wander Symposium at the Technische Universität Dortmund in November 2017.

References

Herf, Jeffrey. 1997. *Divided Memory: The Nazi Past in the Two Germanies*. Cambridge.
Horstkotte, Silke. 2014. "Ich bin woran ich mich erinnere. Benjamin Steins Die Leinwand und der Fall Wilkomirski." In *Der Nationalsozialismus und die Shoah in der deutschsprachigen Gegenwartsliteratur* (Amsterdamer Beiträge zur neueren Germanistik 84), edited by Torben Fischer, Philipp Hammermeister, and Sven Kramer, 115–132. Amsterdam.
Kertesz, Imre. 2013. *Dossier K. A Memoir*. Translated by Tim Wilkinson. New York.
Klocke, Sonja E. 2014. "The Triumph of the Obituary: Constructing Christa Wolf for the Berlin Republic." *German Studies Review* 37, no. 2: 317–336.
Klüger, Ruth. 2005. "Nachwort." In *Fred Wander: Der siebente Brunnen*. Göttingen.
McGlothlin, Erin. 2005. "Das eigene Leid begreift man nicht: Fred Wanders, Der siebente Brunnen und die Geschichte des Selbst." In *Fred Wander. Leben und Werk*, edited by Walter Grünzweig and Ursula Seeber, 97–118. Vienna.
Mueller, Agnes C. 2015. *The Inability to Love: Jews, Gender, and America in Recent German Literature*. Evanston, IL.
Müller, Karl. 2006. "Es ist eine Welt und ich lebe weiter im Exil: Zu einigen Bausteinen der Poetik Fred Wanders." In *Echo des Exils: Das Werk emigrierter österreichischer Schriftsteller nach 1945*, edited by Jörg Thunecke, 249–267. Wuppertal.
Rechtien, Renate. 2012. "From Vergangenheitsbewältigung to Living with Ghosts: Christa Wolf's Kindheitsmuster and Leibhaftig." In *The Self in Transition: East German Autobiographical Writing before and after Unification; Essays in Honour of Dennis Tate*, edited by David Clarke and Axel Goodbody, 123–143. Amsterdam.
Schaumann, Caroline. 2008. *Memory Matters: Generational Responses to Germany's Nazi Past in Recent Women's Literature*. Berlin.
Schmidt, Thomas. 2006. "Unsere Geschichte? Probleme der Holocaust Darstellung unter DDR-Bedingungen: Peter Edel, Fred Wander, Jurek Becker (Part I/Part II)." *Monatshefte* 98, no. 1: 83–109 and 403–425.
Stein, Benjamin. 2010a. *Die Leinwand*. Munich.
———. 2010b. "Religion ist kein Wunschkonzert." Interview by Ijoma Mangold. *Die Zeit* 15 (8 April 2010): 47.
Wander, Fred. 1971. *Der siebente Brunnen. Erzählung*. Berlin: Aufbau.
———. 1982. "Brief an Primo Levi." In *Sammlung: Jahrbuch für antifaschistische Literatur und Kunst*, 21–27. Frankfurt.
———. 1985. *Der siebente Brunnen*. Neuwied: Luchterhand. With an epilogue by Christa Wolf. Neuwied.
———. 2005. *Der siebente Brunnen*. With an epilogue by von Ruth Klüger. Göttingen.
Wilkomirski, Binjamin. 1995. *Bruchstücke: Aus einer Kindheit 1939–1948*. Frankfurt.
———. 1997. *Fragments: Memories of a Wartime Childhood*. Translated by Carol Brown Janeway. New York.
Wolf, Christa. 1972. "Nachwort." In *Der siebente Brunnen. Erzählung*, by Fred Wander, 147–159. Darmstadt.
———. 1976. *Kindheitsmuster*. Berlin.
———. 1985. "Fred Wander: Der siebente Brunnen." In *Lesen und Schreiben. Neue Sammlung. Essays, Aufsätze, Reden by Christa Wolf*, 191–197. Darmstadt.
———. 2003. *Ein Tag im Jahr: 1960–2000*. Munich.
Young, James E. 1988. *Writing and Rewriting the Holocaust*. Bloomington, IN.

Chapter 10

The Stigma of "Asociality" in the GDR

Reconstructing the Language of Marginalization

Katharina Lenski

In both East and West German postwar societies, the remainders of National Socialism were dealt with through suppression and denunciation in equal measure.[1] In the German Democratic Republic (GDR), everyday practices from the National Socialist period were given little thought and continued under the guise of a "new beginning." Old thinking and behavioral patterns lingered inconspicuously in society (Judt 2006: 965; Stone 2014; Feinberg 2015: 274–275.). This can be seen in the stigmatization of so-called asocials (Ayaß 1995; Lieske 2016).

The stereotype of the "asocial" was not subject to critical scrutiny after 1989 but persisted, unchallenged, and was hardly addressed in discussions of the "reappraisal" of the past. For example, only a handful of researchers (Korzilius 2009: 209–222; zur Nieden 2003: 155–161) have analyzed ascriptions that were brought to attention by failed rehabilitation attempts (Wierling 1997: 223–240; Wierling 1994: 404–425). In the lexicon of the Ministry for State Security, "asociality" and "political-ideological deviation" were interconnected (Suckut 2001: 57–58). It stipulated that anyone who dressed or styled themselves out of the ordinary was to be considered a political enemy (Wierling 1994: 410–411). The aim was to create a homogenous lifestyle through intense surveillance and the use of violent and exclusionary practices. The manner in which the clampdown took place demonstrates how an individual became—and remained—"asocial" in the GDR.

The Haircut: A Symbolic Act of Power

The GDR was founded as a society of inner and outer boundaries—a dictatorship of exclusion and isolation (Lindenberger 2016). Youth politics, therefore, meant much more than responsibility for the next generation. Rather, (East German) youth were a canvas for concepts about the past and future, which they were then linked to. Even after the youth communiqué of 1963, youths' "bad behavior" was a hot topic among members of the Politburo, all the way to the highest echelons of the Soviet Union (Wierling 1993: 29–37; Kötzing 2016; Fürst 2010: chapters 5 and 6).

To discipline and humiliate people by cutting their hair is a well-known practice that goes back many centuries. While it was used to stigmatize "fallen women" in the early modern period, National Socialists used it in various ways; after 1945 it was collaborators across Europe that had their hair shorn (for a comprehensive overview, see Frevert 2017; for the years after 1945, see Lowe 2012: 210–220; Shore 2013: 27–43).

One would expect that the antifascist state revised this practice after 1945. Their handling of youth issues, however, raises doubts. In the GDR, neither youth at young people's homes nor young army recruits were spared from having their heads shaved. In the 1960s, the police chased young people with scissors in what can only be likened to a hunt.

This essay highlights the contradictions between propaganda and social practice in a state that was purportedly in the process of "normalization."[2] Nonconformist youths served as enemy objects. Politics and propaganda linked cultural deviation to fears of criminality. Disciplinary measures often crossed the line into brutal violence. In the autumn of 1965, Max Stiller, editor of the party newspaper *Neues Deutschland*, stoked aggression against "long-haired people." One needs to fight "the beginnings,"[3] wrote Stiller, referring to National Socialism, which was to be stopped. He continued that long hair would lead to immorality. Furthermore, hooliganism,[4] which was paired with an aversion to work, would inevitably lead to political decline. Hairstyles, he explained, were not an expression of personal style, but weakened one's ability to work and provoked violence. Chiming in on this matter, Stiller was agreeing with state leadership (Wierling 1993).

The links between authority, power relations, rhetorical devices, and actions against long-haired—and therefore enemy—youths will be demonstrated in the following sections, which explore the "Beat demonstration" in Leipzig in 1965 and the Pößneck Haircut Act of 1969. While the first took place at a moment of legal experimentation, the second occurred shortly after the criminal code of 1968 was issued and following Mielke's order on monitoring youths in 1966.

Becoming "Asocial": From the Restriction on Movement of 1961 to the Penal Code of 1968

Created by GDR lawmakers after the erection of the Berlin Wall and issued on 24 August 1961, the Order on the Restriction of Movement was an important instrument that paved the way for the "pseudo-legalization" of dehumanizing practices: "Work-shy people can be forced into re-education measures by order of local state institutions" (Lindenberger 2002: 208). This "re-education" corresponded with forced internment in work camps.[5] In 1968, paragraphs on "asociality" (paragraph 249) and "hooliganism" (paragraph 215) were embedded in the GDR criminal code. After the Helsinki Agreements, these same paragraphs were used by the courts to cover up human rights violations.[6]

Initially, 1963 was a hopeful moment. Walter Ulbricht had placed "trust and responsibility" in GDR youth, which the party newspaper confirmed: "It is up to the youth to choose the beat, so long as they stay in time!"[7] The "youth communiqué" no longer regarded youth culture, its features and images, as a product of the class enemy. But this period of creative freedom ended almost as quickly as it began as ideas were quickly "axed" at the Socialist Unity Party's (SED's) eleventh Central Committee Plenary Meeting in December 1965 (Agde 1991). The stigmatization of youth culture was quickly followed by new laws. Bands were no longer allowed to perform without special licenses; playing music in public without permission was deemed unlawful (Lipp 2016).

The youth communiqué included a reference to delinquent youths and "hooligans," which offered anti-reformists an opening. In July 1965, in Walter Ulbricht's absence, the SED Central Committee passed a motion on "the emergence of groups of criminal and at-risk youths in the GDR."[8] This was passed by the Honecker faction, which saw even the pettiest of disputes as an indication that youth criminality was rising, when in fact it had fallen (Kaiser 1997: 170). These arguments were backed up by obscure statistics that should have been easy to see through. Yet even universities in the GDR supported the branding of youths by undertaking research to justify official statistics (Lenski 2017a: 102–111). These were reinforced by Western discourses on youth criminality, which also reported rising rates but sought to respond with other solutions (Kebbedies 2000).

In August 1965, after young rock music fans in West Berlin destroyed the Waldbühne (Forest Stage) at a Rolling Stones concert, Erich Honecker used this as an excuse to go after "dropouts, longhairs, and loiterers" (Wierling 1993: 30; Mählert 2001: 60). These three terms completed the ensemble of arguments against so-called outsiders. Lifestyle, clothing, and hairstyles were symbols and criteria for and against belonging to the socialist community.

On 11 October 1965, the SED Central Committee secretariat, once again with Walter Ulbricht absent, decided to curtail existing freedoms and to solve the "Beat problem" (Rauhut 2002: 31–32). Honecker toughened the original sentence by ordering a "referral to work camps" in writing (Rauhut 2002: 31–32). One week later, in the *Neues Deutschland* (*ND*), Max Stiller denounced a group of "amateur dropouts from Lichtenberg" as having an aversion to work and education and being fetid and filthy. In so doing, he not only drowned out moderate statements in the satirical paper *Eulenspiegel*, which had recently suggested "brushing it off,"[9] but also launched a Cold War–style tirade against youths who did not fit the established mold. While the *Eulenspiegel* spoke of "teething troubles," the *ND* called for the exclusion of *community aliens*: "They don't wash, they stink, their shaggy manes are matted and filthy, they avoid work and education."[10] Reports on public humiliations of longhaired people in workplaces and schools to the tune of "use soap, my friend" followed: the newly shaved were said to have belonged to the animal kingdom (Wolle 2011: 123–125). This example demonstrates how old patterns of thinking were left unchallenged.

As shown by the example in Leipzig, the Central Committee's campaign was taken up by all subsidiary bodies.[11] Shortly after the Central Committee Decree of 11 October 1965, numerous bands in the district of Leipzig were banned from performing.[12] On 31 October, youths gathered in large numbers for the "Beat demonstration," which was violently dispersed. After arresting 267 demonstrators, the police cudgeled more than half onto lorries and swiftly sentenced them to weeks of hard labor in the coal mines. But first they all had their hair shaved (Wierling 1994: 408–413; Rauhut 2002: 34). Simultaneously, the Free German Youth banned individuals with "Beatles haircuts" from their 1965 guitar competition (Mählert 2001: 60).

The eleventh plenary of the Central Committee of the Socialist Unity Party from 16 to 18 December 1965 would go down in history as a major setback. The leadership reversed cultural freedoms and effectively gave criminal law the green light to tighten youth legislation. The minister for state security acted quickly: the topic of sociocultural deviation appeared in Order 11/66 and Directive 4/66, disguised in political-ideological and socio-racist categories.[13] Order 11/66 argued that the high number of youths involved in "criminal and state-opposed incidents" proved that the "enemy" was trying to disrupt socialist progress. In Directive 4/66, Mielke ordered a crackdown on *possible* threats, using diverse political party, secret service, police, and administrative organizations to gather "seamless" information on the next generation (preemptively!) and to use the 1961 order on "re-education through work."[14] Biannual reports called "youth analyses" were commissioned.[15] Henceforth, the local Ministry for State Security offices would regularly report back to directors with lists of allegedly subversive groups and individuals. The purported threat was generally nothing more than the length of hair, Western alterations to clothing, and an interest in new music. Order 11/66 came into effect two years before the GDR penal code was reformed in 1968. From this point on, youths were transformed into the "inner enemy" (Wierling 1994). Their lifestyles were labeled hostile and put into a context that justified surveillance, punishment, and criminalization. In 1968, laws were passed sanctioning hooliganism (§ 215) and asociality (§ 249). This was the early climax to a process in which bureaucracy, surveillance institutions, research, and publicity worked together to justify the exclusion of all those who wanted to live, work, or look a different way.

The "Asociality" Argument: Pößneck 1969

In 1969, the Ministry for State Security youth analysis reports included details of a "haircut operation" in Pößneck in Thuringia, locally dubbed "Aktion Schniegelscher" (Operation spruce yourself up).[16] Pößneck was no anomaly, however. Haircut campaigns were being used to intimidate youths across the country.[17]

In August 1969, on the occasion of the twentieth anniversary of the founding of the GDR state, the SED second district secretary wrote to his comrades in Pößneck, summoning them to ban longhaired youths from appearing in public (Best and Mestrup 2003: 663). They were alleged to pose a threat to festivities if they were to walk down the street with their portable radios.

The SED district office decided to summon "underperforming" youths to face-to-face meetings.[18] "Group gatherings" were to be dissolved by the police henceforth, and longhaired people were banned from playing in bands. They were even stopped from shopping or dancing in public. The

Free German Youth and other educational organizations were instructed to join these discriminatory efforts.[19]

On the evening of 20 October 1969, the second district secretary of the Socialist Unity Party in Pößneck called a meeting with his key party and Free German Youth secretaries to inform them of the secret plans for the next day (Best and Mestrup 2003: 699–700): "The times in which we debated with our youth are now officially over. From now on, we are going to start a process of clarification via the Free German Youth order groups by cutting off the youths' hair."[20]

This was not the only measure discussed by officials. "Longhairs" were not to be served in restaurants or shops: "These youths need to feel that they are outsiders."[21] On 23 October 1969, Ministry for State Security reports confirmed successes in "most shops, restaurants, etc.,"[22] even while positing an antifascist identity.

Initially, the SED district office succeeded in implementing its plans. On the morning of 21 October 1969, Free German Youth representatives from the companies were called into the town hall, where they were advised that "surely half a dozen workers' fists will manage to bring one youth to the hairdresser."[23] Shortly after, FDJ marshals entered local schools[24] in an especially "boorish" manner (Best and Mestrup 2003: 278). The assault reached a climax at around three o'clock in the afternoon at the main train station in Pößneck, as apprentices and workers started their commute home after the end of their shifts. Forty youths were humiliated at the train station with a forced haircut:

> [FDJ] marshals infiltrated the crowds, picked out the youths with long hair and forced them aside. Altogether, sixty-eight FDJ officials were deployed to demand that the youths have their hair cut. To emphasize the official nature of the campaign, police joined the efforts and requested to see their identification. If anyone showed resistance, additional FDJ marshals jumped in and held the youths down.[25]

Since youths had to hand in their ID cards to the police, they not only had their details taken but also faced losing their identification and having to live with a "replacement ID card," which would stigmatize them as "asocial" and restrict future opportunities.

Onlookers were largely supportive of the campaign.[26] A few, however, argued that it was not right to "be so forceful." The party leadership at the Plastunion firm in Triptis even lodged a complaint, but this opposition soon died down.[27] Even inquiries made by the regional SED control commission did not question the assault on the youths' personal integrity, although they requested that "young people should be able to have something to spend their money on." The party leadership in Pößneck remained undeterred (Best and Mestrup 2003: 278).

On 22 October, they were in for a surprise. After "thirty-eight friends and comrades"[28] spent the afternoon chasing longhaired youths in the town, a hundred young people gathered on the market square in the evening to hold a protest (Best and Mestrup 2003: 278). Alarmed officials and police tried to debate "progressively" but instead earned a barrage of catcalls that referred to the GDR constitution and argued that the campaign was reminiscent of the persecution of the Jews.[29] This appeal was ignored in all but one aspect: the party control commission demanded that the party secretary in Pößneck withdraw the ban on sales to longhairs (Best and Mestrup 2003: 279–280). District leadership and the Ministry for State Security failed to listen, however, and concluded that the young people had not understood *why* their hair had been cut. Longhaired youths remained barred from public dances, and anyone who did not have a Prussian haircut during police inspections was forced to reapply for a passport with a new photo.[30]

On Thursday, 23 October 1969, pupils wore black armbands and held a silent protest at school. Around two hundred demonstrators gathered on the market square. The SED and Ministry for State Security district heads assessed the situation personally but did not give in. They simply let thirty-nine youths be taken into custody.[31] Later, party secretaries in Pößneck were asked to explain why they had let crowds gather (Best and Mestrup 2003: 280). The district committee held meetings until Saturday (Enkelmann 2000: 6). Although the ban on sales had officially been lifted, it took on a life of its own. Discriminatory practices were passed on, and older citizens were much more likely to support the exclusion of young people than to show compassion for them (Best and Mestrup 2003: 281). The night of 24 October, the police woke up a local hairdresser, who was urgently instructed to cut two youths' hair (Enkelmann 2000: 6).

In early November, it became clear that the haircut campaign had not hit "loiterers and dropouts" but apprentices, pupils, and workers.[32] On 3 November, the district party announced at their conference that while political-ideological persuasion was at the heart of their work, brute force was not.[33] Honecker, on the other hand, did not criticize the brutal crackdown. His aim was to assert his system of rule. Party and public authorities had been slighted, for which the heads of the police and the Ministry for State Security district offices had been disciplined and SED heads were made to step down. Honecker responded that haircut campaigns had also taken place in Halle and Berlin; unlike Pößneck, however, there had been no opportunity for protest, since the police loaded "rioters and hooligans into police vans and sent them off to work."[34] By reducing the affected people to "rioters and hooligans," Honecker turned facts on their head. It was not the "longhairs" who had acted like brutal "hooligans," but FDJ marshals, officials, and the police—all of whom remained far from ready to take responsibility for their actions (Best and Mestrup 2003: 699–700, 714).

The following February, the Ministry for Security reported on a flyer from the "Longhaired Club," a sign of protest against the clampdown.[35] But by then, the violence had been legitimized, confirmed, and stabilized through the 1968 paragraph against "asocials" and "hooligans" and with the relabeling of those affected.

Staying "Asocial": Aftereffects

In Pößneck, "Aktion Schniegelscher" was met with little opposition. The same applied to the nearby towns of Neustadt/Orla and Triptis, where similar operations took place the very same week. The stigmatization of those affected became even more burdensome with time, as the exact events leading to their ostracization faded from memory. In the workplace, colleagues continued to assault longhaired people, chasing and humiliating them with scissors. Anyone who enacted "the law" had nothing to fear. Many youths reported that they were refused their trade proficiency certificate due to having long hair (Ohse 2003: 322). They were frequently barred from shops and dances, while on the streets they were pursued by the police, entering a downward spiral as "asocials."

Historian Dorothee Wierling retraced the steps of a young man who was arrested as part of the 1965 Beat demonstration in Leipzig. The seventeen-year-old stood on the sidelines, waiting to see what would happen. When he saw the water cannon, he tried to escape through a housing complex, but the police forced him back into the town center, where he was loaded onto a lorry and sentenced to labor in the coal mines. After weeks of penal labor, he was released and told that he now had a "clean record." Nevertheless, the man, who was born in 1948, later had the impression that his career was being blocked. When he applied for rehabilitation after 1989, he was declined because of his "criminal" record. The authorities had not seen any of his files, since they were destroyed; the only record they had was an index card from the prosecution, which classified him as criminal and asocial in 1965 (Wierling 1997: 234–238; Lenski 2014: 116–136; see Lenski 2017b: 165–169)! His application for rehabilitation was rejected based on these official sources, without even taking his perspective into account. The unjust stereotyping and degradation therefore continued after the fall of the Wall.[36] This example demonstrates why so few people have spoken out after 1989. The framing of the discourse leaves few opportunities to those whose life stories do not align with the hegemonic heroicized narrative. The stigmatization of "asocials" and "hooligans" carried on; they were marginalized at the edges of society, not just in the short-term but also far beyond it.

Conclusion

The practices described in this chapter show links to elements of National Socialism. Although the exclusionary practices changed, certain features persisted. The forced haircut was one of many disciplinary measures aimed at people with nonconformist lifestyles. Their labeling as "asocial" was an easy (pretend) solution that avoided facing reality. New laws and their associated institutions helped create a system of exclusion in the GDR.

But the system of exclusion neither helped stop criminality nor did it prevent lifestyles that were seen as threatening to society. Rather, it created a framework for disambiguation and criminalization in which neighbors, work colleagues, and impatient citizens could humiliate weaker members of society, giving rise to a horizontal power network. Press reports and party-led operations, carried out by the police and security groups, successfully aided the exclusion and degradation of anyone "different." This resonated with existing power structures and helped in turn to stabilize them.

Although these structures broke down after 1989, the consequences are still felt, for the fall of the Wall did not tear down the inner borders or eliminate long-existing prejudices. Friend-or-foe thinking was directed at those who were still easily excludable and who had few material or cultural resources to help. This is reflected in present-day rehabilitation practices and indicates the ambiguity of research on the margins of mainstream discourse.

Katharina Lenski is a historian, sociologist, and educator. Her work as a postdoctoral fellow at the Jena Research Group "The GDR and the European Dictatorships after 1945 from a Comparative and Historical Perspective" focuses on "asociality." In 2016, she conducted research at the Imre-Kertész-Kolleg in Jena on exclusion in state socialism from a transnational perspective, looking at the continuing effects of stereotypes and their social practices before and after 1945. She received highest honors for her doctorate in 2015, and her dissertation "Geheime Kommunikationsräume: Die Staatssicherheit an der Jenaer Universität" was published by Campus. Katharina Lenski has initiated and conducted numerous research projects on the history of the GDR and socialist state bureaucracies, on the history of universities and education, on the history of youth cultures, and on the role of the church after 1945. She currently coordinates the interdisciplinary Research Network on the Stigma of "Asociality." Since 1991, she has built one of the most important social archives on dissidence in the GDR: the Thuringian Matthias Domaschk Archive for Contemporary History, which she directed until 2011. Previously, she studied medicine in the GDR, was exmatriculated for political reasons, and was subsequently active in dissident groups in Berlin. Following her rehabilitation in 2001, she completed her master's degree in 2008.

Notes

1. The German version of this essay was published in Enrico Heitzer et al. (eds.), *Nach Auschwitz. Schwieriges Erbe DDR, Plädoyer für einen Paradigmenwechsel in der DDR-Zeitgeschichtsforschung* (Schwalbach/Ts., 2018), 162–175. I give thanks to Dorothee Wierling and the editors for their comments and suggestions. Translation by Jenny Price.

2. As explained by Mary Fulbrook (2009, 2016: 89–97), "normalization" was not, as so often suggested, used to create normality but was rather a hidden power practice.

3. Max Stiller, "Die Amateur Gammler," *Neues Deutschland*, 17 October 1965.

4. The East German term for hooligan was *Rowdy*; hooliganism was called *Rowdytum*. This chapter will use the English translation.

5. For more on the tradition of "re-education through work" in West Germany, see, e.g., Kebbedies 2000.

6. For example, against those wishing to exit the country and punks. Lindenberger 2002: 209.

7. "Der Jugend Vertrauen und Verantwortung. Kommuniqué," *Neues Deutschland*, 21 September 1963, 1–3.

8. Beschluss Sekretariat ZK der SED 7 July 1965, in Kaiser 1997: 170.

9. "Die Harkleine von Lichtenberg," *Eulenspiegel*, 14 October 1965.

10. Max Stiller, "Die Amateur-Gammler von Lichtenberg," *Neues Deutschland*, 17 October 1965.

11. "Ständige Kommission Jugendfragen des Bezirkstages Leipzig: Dem Mißbrauch der Jugend keinen Raum!," *Leipziger Volkszeitung*, 20 October 1965; Wierling 1994: 408–413; Renft 1997.

12. Renft 1997. There are some inconsistencies in the reported number of bands. Wierling (1994: 409) says fifty-four out of fifty-eight bands were banned from playing; Rauhut (2002: 34) says forty-four bands were banned; Liebing (2005: 67) says nine out of fifty-six bands were allowed to play.

13. From the perspective of a former youth prosecutor: Dieter Plath 1991: 32–39; Befehl 11/66 and DA 4/66 in Engelmann and Joestel 2004: 153–173.

14. Bundesbeauftragter für die Stasi Unterlagen (BStU), Ministerium für Staatssicherheit (MfS), Büro der Leitung (BdL) Dok. 1083, 23 (*Dienstanweisung* 4/66).
15. Ibid., 25.
16. BStU, MfS, Bezirksverwaltung (BV) Gera, Kreisdienststelle (KD) Jena 001837, 127–128.
17. See Sammlung Parteien und Massenorganisation im Bundesarchiv (SAPMO-BA) DY 30/IVA2/16/173: Unpublished letter to *BZ am Abend*, 17 July 1967, in Rauhut 2002: 37. Regarding the campaign, see Ohse 2003: 321–322; Enkelmann 2000, 2008: 32–36.
18. Thüringer Staatsarchiv Rudolstadt Bezirksparteiarchiv (ThStA Rud BPA) SED Gera, Bezirksleitung (BL) Gera IV B—2/5/378: Beschlussentwurf SED-Kreisleitung (KL) 25 September 1969.
19. Ibid.
20. ThSTA Rud BPA SED Gera, KL Pößneck IV B 4.08–55, Sitzung 25 October 1969; Best and Mestrup 2003: 275–276.
21. ThSTA Rud BPA SED Gera, KL Pößneck IV B 4.08–55, Sitzung 25 October 1969
22. BStU, MfS, Bezirksverwaltung (BV) Gera, Abt. XV 1180, 21.
23. Memory minutes, Burkhard Kunze, 27 October 1979, in author's collection.
24. The director of the Karl Marx Factory in Pößneck called twenty apprentices to his office for meetings in which he instructed them to have their hair cut within the hour. ThStA Rud BPA SED Gera, BL Gera IV B—2/5/378: BV Gera des MfS 22 October 1969: Maßnahmen. Hunts took place in the Pößneck community center, in restaurants, the cinema, and in the Heinz Kapelle Factory. In nearby Triptis, twenty-five youths were affected; in Neustadt it was twenty: BStU, MfS, BV Gera, Abteilung (Abt) XV 1180, 22.
25. BStU, MfS, BV Gera, Abt XV 1180, 21-23.
26. Ibid., 23.
27. Ibid.
28. BStU, MfS, BV Gera, Abt. XV 180, 21.
29. Ibid., 24; ThSTA Rud BPA SED Gera, BL Gera IV B—2/5/378: BV Gera des Mfs, 22 October 1969.
30. BStU, MfS, BV Gera, Abt. XV 1180, 24–25; Ohse 2003: 122.
31. The youth analysis report lists forty youths. BStU, MfS, BV Gera, KD Jena 001837, 128.
32. ThStA Rud BPA SED Gera, BL Gera IV B—2/5/378: Einschätzung 31 October 1969.
33. ThStA Rud BPA SED Gera, BL Gera IV 2/2-24. See Best and Mestrup 2003: 283, who say 700 delegates took part.
34. ThStA Rud BPA SED Gera, BL Gera IV B—2/5/378: Niederschrift 5 November 1969.
35. BStU, MfS, BV Gera, Abt. XV 1180, 45, IM "Heinz Halter," n.d. (flyer from February 1970).
36. See Inga Markovits 2006, esp. chapter 7; thanks to Enrico Heitzer for the reminder of earlier interpretations. See Markovits 2008: 43–59.

References

Agde, Günter, ed. 1991. *Kahlschlag. Das 11. Plenum des ZK der SED 1965, Studien und Dokumente.* Berlin.
Ayaß, Wolfgang. 1995. *"Asoziale" im Nationalsozialismus.* Stuttgart.
Best, Heinrich, and Heinz Mestrup, eds. 2003. *Die Ersten und Zweiten Sekretäre der SED. Machtstrukturen und Herrschaftspraxis in den thüringischen Bezirken der DDR.* Weimar.
Engelmann, Roger, and Frank Joestel. 2004. *Grundsatzdokumente des Ministeriums für Staatssicherheit (MfS-Handbuch).* Vol. 5: *Anatomie der Staatssicherheit. Geschichte, Struktur und Methoden.* Edited by Klaus-Dietmar Henke, Siegfried Sukkut, and Thomas Großbölting. Berlin.
Enkelmann, Hans Walter. 2000. *Die Haarschneideaktion von 1969.* Erfurt.
———. 2008. "Unnatürlich lange Haare. Die Haarschneideaktion im Kreis Pößneck 1969." *Horch und Guck*, no. 61: 32–36.
Feinberg, Melissa. 2015. "Book Review: Dan Stone, Goodbye to All That? The Story of Europe since 1945." *Central European History* 48, no. 2: 274–275.
Frevert, Ute. 2017. *Die Politik der Demütigung. Schauplätze von Macht und Ohnmacht.* Frankfurt a. M.
Fulbrook, Mary, ed. 2009. *Power and Society in the GDR, 1961–1979: The "Normalisation of Rule."* New York.
———. 2016. "Die fehlende Mitte. Die DDR als postnazistischer Staat." In *Die DDR als Chance*, edited by Ulrich Mählert, 89–97. Berlin.
Fürst, Juliane. 2010. *Stalin's Last Generation: Soviet Post-War Youth and the Emergence of Mature Socialism.* Oxford.
Judt, Tony. 2005. *Postwar: A History of Europe since 1945.* New York.
———. 2006. *Geschichte Europas von 1945 bis zur Gegenwart. Aus dem Englischen von Matthias Fienbork und Hainer Kober.* Vienna.
Kaiser, Monika. 1997. *Machtwechsel von Ulbricht zu Honecker. Funktionsmechanismen der SED-Diktatur in Konfliktsituationen 1962 bis 1972.* Berlin.
Kebbedies, Frank. 2000. *Außer Kontrolle. Jugendkriminalpolitik in der NS-Zeit und der frühen Nachkriegszeit.* Essen.
Korzilius, Sven. 2009. "Arbeitsethik, Sozialdisziplinierung und Strafrecht in der SBZ und in der DDR—Kontinuität oder Diskontinuität?" In *Ausgesteuert—ausgegrenzt... angeblich asozial*, edited by Anne Allex and Dietrich Kalken, 209–222. Ulm.
Kötzing, Andreas. 2016. "Grünes Licht aus Moskau. Die SED-Führung am Vorabend des 'Kahlschlag'–Plenums." *Deutschland Archiv*, 10 June 2016. Accessed 23 January 2018, www.bpb.de/228714.
Lenski, Katharina. 2014. "Der zerbrochene Spiegel. Methodische Überlegungen zum Umgang mit Stasi-Akten." In *Die Securitate in Siebenbürgen*, edited by Joachim von Puttkamer, Stefan Sienerth, and Ulrich A. Wien, 116–136. Cologne.
———. 2017. *Geheime Kommunikationsräume? Die Staatssicherheit an der Jenaer Universität.* Frankfurt.
———. 2017b. "Im Schweigekreis. Der Tod von Matthias Domaschk zwischen strafrechtlicher Aufarbeitung und offenen Fragen." In *Recht und Gerechtigkeit. Die strafrechtliche Aufarbeitung von Diktaturen in Europa*, edited by Jörg Ganzenmüller, 131–169. Cologne.

Liebing, Yvonne. 2005. *All You Need Is Beat: Jugendsubkultur in Leipzig 1957–1968*. Leipzig.
Lieske, Dagmar. 2016. *Unbequeme Opfer? "Berufsverbrecher" als Häftlinge im KZ Sachsenhausen*. Berlin.
Lindenberger, Thomas. 2002. "Diktatur der Grenze(n). Die eingemauerte Gesellschaft und ihre Feinde." In *Mauerbau und Mauerfall. Ursachen—Verlauf—Auswirkungen*, edited by Hans-Hermann Hertle, Konrad H. Jarausch, and Christoph Kleßmann, 203–213. Berlin.
———. 2016. "Das Land der begrenzten Möglichkeiten." *Deutschland Archiv*, 10 August 2016. Accessed 23 January 2018, www.bpb.de/geschichte/zeitgeschichte/deutschlandarchiv/232099/das-land-der-begrenzten-moeglichkeiten-machtraeume-und-eigen-sinn-der-ddr-gesellschaft.
Lipp, Florian. 2016. "'Keinerlei Textverständlichkeit—Keyboard oft nicht rhythmisch.' Staatliche Einstufungspraxis in der späten DDR am Beispiel von Punk- und New-Wave-Bands." *Deutschland Archiv*, 2 June 2016. Accessed 23 January 2018, www.bpb.de/228328.
Lowe, Keith. 2012. *Savage Continent: Europe in the Aftermath of World War II*. London.
———. 2016. *Der wilde Kontinent. Europa in den Jahren der Anarchie*. Stuttgart.
Mählert, Ulrich. 2001. *FDJ. 1946–1989*. Erfurt.
Markovits, Inga. 2006. *Gerechtigkeit in Lüritz*. Munich.
———. 2008. "Rechtssoziologie für Außenseiter." In *Wie wirkt Recht? Ausgewählte Beiträge zum ersten gemeinsamen Kongress der deutschsprachigen Rechtssoziologie-Vereinigungen*, edited by Michelle Cottier, Josef Estermann, and Michael Wrase, 43–59. Lucerne.
Ohse, Marc-Dietrich. 2003. *Jugend nach dem Mauerbau. Anpassung, Protest, Eigensinn (DDR 1961–1974)*. Berlin.
Plath, Dieter. 1991. "Über Kriminalität und innere Sicherheit." In *Kahlschlag*, edited by Günter Agde, 32–39. Berlin.
Rauhut, Michael. 2002. *Rock in der DDR. 1964 bis 1989*. Berlin.
Renft, Klaus. 1997. *Zwischen Liebe und Zorn. Die Autobiographie*. Berlin.
Shore, Marci. 2013. *The Taste of Ashes: The Afterlife of Totalitarianism in Eastern Europe*. New York.
Stone, Dan. 2014. *Goodbye to All That? The Story of Europe since 1945*. Oxford.
Suckut, Siegfried, ed. 2001. *Das Wörterbuch der Staatssicherheit. Definitionen zur "politisch-operativen Arbeit."* Berlin.
Wierling, Dorothee. 1993. "'Negative Erscheinungen'—Zu einigen Sprach- und Argumentationsmustern in der Auseinandersetzung mit der Jugendsubkultur in der DDR der 60er Jahre." *WerkstattGeschichte* 5: 29–37.
Wierling, Dorothee. 1994. "Die Jugend als innerer Feind. Konflikte in der Erziehungsdiktatur der sechziger Jahre." In *Sozialgeschichte der DDR*, edited by Hartmut Kaelble, Jürgen Kocka, and Hartmut Zwahr, 404–425. Stuttgart.
Wierling, Dorothee. 1997. "Der Staat, die Jugend und der Westen." In *Akten. Eingaben. Schaufenster. Die DDR und ihre Texte. Erkundungen zu Herrschaft und Alltag*, edited by Alf Lüdtke and Peter Becker, 223–240. Berlin.
Wolle, Stefan. 2011. "Erfrorene Melodien." In *Woodstock am Karpfenteich. Die Jazzwerkstatt Peitz*, edited by Uli Blobel, 116–141. Berlin.
zur Nieden, Susanne. 2003. *Unwürdige Opfer. Die Aberkennung von NS-Verfolgten in Berlin 1945 bis 1949*. Berlin.

Chapter 11

Lesbians and Gays in the GDR

Self-Organizing, Politics of Remembrance,
Discrimination, and Public Silencing

Christiane Leidinger and Heike Radvan

The history of the lesbian and gay movement as well as the history of their emancipation have not garnered the attention of society. This is evident even after a quick glance at schoolbooks, which fail to mention the movement's history and the long-term battles it has waged. This historical silencing is not particular to the lesbian and gay past or to the German Democratic Republic (GDR). The grassroot successes (and downfalls) of marginalized groups are not represented in the FRG or the GDR, even after 1989. Today, while there is greater visibility of the lesbian and gay movements, and legal equality was implemented through same sex marriage in 2017, lesbian, gay, bisexual, trans*, and inter* persons (LGBTI)[1] are still perceived as "others" and as a social minority. The situation for those living outside larger cities, especially in rural areas, is particularly precarious (Radvan and Schondelmayer 2017).

This chapter traces official state treatment of lesbians and gays in the GDR. One aspect of this story—the homophobic elements of anti-Jewish persecution in the 1950s—has been shunned in national memory discourses on the GDR. This contribution focuses on self-organizing, beginning in the 1970s, and attempts to commemorate lesbian and gay victims of fascism in the 1980s. These initiatives contradicted the often unilateral official commemorations of the communist struggle for resistance. Like other groups in several cities from the 1970s onward, whose members from Jewish communities and churches remembered Jewish victims in "bottom-up" commemorations (Amadeu Antonio Stiftung 2010: 128–129), lesbians and gays were also surveilled and frequently impeded by the Ministerium für Staatssicherheit and the Volkspolizei. Initiatives and activities carried out by lesbians and gays demonstrate how self-organization was exercised in a democratic manner. Even within broadly based civil rights movements, confronting National Socialism and its legacies was a nonissue or a profoundly marginalized one. Hence, the critical question arises: Why have lesbian-gay political initiatives and activities for remembrance been widely overlooked within public discourse?

(Futile) Hopes

Following liberation from Nazi dictatorship, the establishment of the Soviet occupation zone and the GDR raised hopes for a life without discrimination and persecution for lesbians and gays within the emerging socialist system. Ever since the turn of the previous century or, rather, since the German Empire, Socialists and Communists alike had campaigned against the criminalization of gay people in penal law paragraph 175 RStGB[2] (Grumbach 1995: 21–29) and against efforts to extend its scope to lesbians.

The humanistic ideas of Marxist and even Leninist theory may have also fostered hopes for equality for citizens with different lifestyles and sexual orientations under socialism.[3] These included the right to freely express one's personality and the notion of actively contributing toward a socialist society for all. Derogatory, hostile perceptions of LGT*[4] were socially and structurally widespread and rooted within the Soviet Union and other Eastern Bloc states, as well as in Western capitalist countries. Accordingly, in 1945, "zero hour" did not begin. Indeed, in both German states, there were continuities in penal prosecution and societal discrimination.[5]

In 1968, the GDR excluded §175 StGB from its criminal law code, departing from the FRG when it came to LGBTI* rights. Legal discrimination, however, continued until August 1987[6] in the form of §151 StGB, which established a different age of consent for heterosexual contact. For the first time, lesbian acts also became punishable. In principle, the exclusion of §175 StGB led neither to recognition nor equality for lesbians and gays within society (Grau 1995: 120). As early as 1947, the physician and communist Rudolf Klimmer (1905–1977) campaigned against legal discrimination in the GDR. To this day, his tireless dedication is hardly present in public discourse. Occasional appreciation and recollections of his achievements are limited to the communities in question (Kowalski 1987; Grau 1998).

The fact that early 1950s persecution within the SED state had homophobic elements is also suppressed. Alongside antisemitic persecution (1952/1953), individuals were discredited and discharged from executive positions by means of homophobic stigmata and the application of §175a StGB (Evans 2014: 347–348). Homosexuality was considered bourgeois and decadent: a manifestation of capitalism and a threat to socialism.[7] Pro-family policies that complemented the (heterosexual) model of a nuclear family were reinforced (Notz 2015: 148–158). In this homophobic atmosphere, the founder of state security Wilhelm Zaisser (1893–1958) and Minister of Justice Max Fechner (1892–1973), both opponents of Walter Ulbricht, were removed from office. They were vilified "not only politically, but also morally degenerated" (cited in Fischer 2015; Evans 2014: 347). Until now, hardly any research exists that questions the role alleged (or real) homosexuality played in denunciations in the (state) persecution of unpopular persons. It has yet to be shown if there were connections to other virulent enemy images, such as anti-Jewish attributions. If nothing else, anti-homosexual discrimination and persecution continues to be overlooked. The standard literature—*Wer war wer in der DDR?* (Who was who in the GDR?)—contains no references to the examples mentioned above (Müller-Enbergs, Wielgohs, and Hoffmann 2006: 201, 946–947).

Self-Organizing

Focusing on persecution, repression, and discrimination, official historiography directs marginal attention to forms of resistance and protest. In the spirit of political empowerment, and from the perspective of democratization, it is imperative to examine self-organizing, in this case, by lesbians and gays within the GDR.

Since the end of the nineteenth century, a homosexual and trans* subculture developed, comprising a wide-ranging, semi-public infrastructure that included meeting places, bars, clubs, associations, and shops, especially within metropoles along the Elbe, Spree, and Rhine. This subculture experienced its heyday in the Weimar Republic and was crushed in 1933. In the postwar period, there was said to have been a lesbian bar in East Berlin within the Soviet Occupation Zone. It was established in 1945 by leaders of the subculture in the Weimar era such as Lotte Hahm (1890–1967) and Kati R. Reinhard (also Reinhardt, biographical data unknown).

But this bar existed for only one and a half years (Leidinger 2015a: 45, 48). While the history of this postwar subculture has yet to be written, a remarkable number of contributions have focused on self-organizing and key figures within the GDR, mostly by researchers linked to the movement (for lesbians, see outline in Dennert, Leidinger, and Rauchut 2007; documentation in Kenawi 1995; Leidinger 2017a).

New attempts at self-organizing, beyond social spaces such as bars that were popular with the subculture, emerged in the 1970s. Accordingly, the first initiative in 1972 or 1973 came from a private circle that used the name Homosexual Interest Group Berlin (HIB) from 1973/ 1974 onward (Kowalski 1987: 53; Dennert, Leidinger, and Rauchut 2007: 96, 98). Men and women organized regular meetings, parties, and discussion panels and promoted the use of public spaces, such as youth clubs, by lesbians and gays. The HIB had knowledge of dominant discourses in the gay movement in West Berlin[8] and was evidently inspired by ideas of emancipation and self-help. Following one woman's initiative, a homosexual self-help group was founded 1976 in Leipzig, in which mostly gays debated one another (Leidinger 2017b: 38).

After a 1976 discussion between the Protestant church and the state, which resulted in increased independence (Beyer 2014), numerous (work) groups were founded in various cities under auspices of the church[9] beginning in 1982. Among these were the following: AK Homosexuality in Leipzig, AK Gays in Church-Homosexual Self-Help Berlin, and AK Lesbians in Church in Berlin.[10] Beyond the church, new groups cropped up: HIB evolved into the Sonntagsklub, and other spin-offs followed (Tammer 2013: 32).

Self-help, including support for coming out, was a common practice for most groups—for example, in lesbian groups in Erfurt, Halle, and Jena (Kenawi 1995: 135, 173, 193). A pivotal principle within the women's and lesbian movement in the FRG, self-help was disseminated through the transnational transfer of feminist ideas (Leidinger 2015b: 8, 68–69). To date, little research on self-organizing by trans* people within the GDR exists; starting in the 1970s, meetings at the Gründerzeit Museum of Charlotte von Mahlsdorf (1928–2002) in Berlin offered trans* people a venue and opportunities to interact with one another (Mahlsdorf 1995: 175–176, 192).

Commemoration of Lesbian and Gay Victims of Fascism

These groups were engaged in diverse activities, but one area in particular shows the tenacity of their initiatives and organizers: lesbian and gay commemorations of the neglected victims of fascism[11] and corresponding activities that took place from 1983 to at least 1986.

Unlike in the FRG, where resistance fighters were still seen as traitors to their country after 1945 (Nußberger 2014), in the GDR, resistance against the dictatorship was regarded positively, and the commemoration of communist resistance represented a top priority for its official commemorative culture. It formed a central component of both antifascist identity and state doctrine. This went hand in hand with a dismissal of the persecution of various afflicted groups. Similar to the FRG, lesbians and gays persecuted by the National Socialists were not recognized as victims of fascism (*Opfer des Faschismus*). Particularly in the years after the war, to be gay or lesbian remained a stigma that entailed degradation and exclusion. Acknowledging persecution or compensation for the injustices they suffered seemed inconceivable. Persecuted individuals were denied the social support measures offered to officially recognized *Opfer des Faschismus*, such as pensions, spas, and free public transport. Lesbians and gays were not mentioned in the public culture of commemoration. The discrimination, repression, and persecution they experienced were not researched or remembered, and instead were officially repressed.[12]

From 1983 onward, self-organized groups took up the matter of suppression and attempted to set political examples at memorial sites. They were monitored by the Volkspolizei or Staatssicherheit. The latter tried to restrict their activities, since autonomous commemoration was not desirable for the state. Eduard Stapel (1953–2017), a gay activist since the 1980s, noted the state's counterarguments: "Tributes to specific groups of victims" were "not historically justifiable" and "not permissible from a Marxist-Leninist point of view." "Furthermore, gay people were not active fighters against fascism" (Stapel 1999: 96). This allegation also affected other groups of victims, especially Jewish people. Distinctions between "victims" and "fighters" and different assessments of these groups were evidenced in varying pension payments, the implication being that "victims" had simply not defended themselves or fought. To date, the effects of debasing those who were "merely victims" has barely been examined. This not only includes Jewish people but also lesbians and gays who were persecuted, particularly if they showed resistance.

The first self-organized lesbian-gay commemoration was scheduled for 22 May 1983 inside the national memorial site Sachsenhausen. The event was not officially registered and was to take place without a wreath-laying ceremony. The group was stopped by the police at the S-Bahn station Oranienburg, claiming—falsely—that a private function was being held at the memorial site (Krautz 2009: 65). A few weeks later, a group managed to commemorate homosexual victims at the memorial site Buchenwald by keeping the event a surprise, and thus it proceeded unregulated. This shifted in subsequent years as the Ministerium für Staatssicherheit attempted to monitor the preparatory work of all groups and simultaneously inhibited their activities. Thus, wreath-laying ceremonies were forbidden, or wreaths were removed after events. On 10 March 1984, eighteen women (Krautz 2009: 65) visited the memorial site Ravensbrück (Kenawi 2007), where they were officially registered for a guided tour and wreath-laying ceremony. Their wreath and a ribbon displaying "AK Homosexual Self-Help Berlin Lesbians in Church 8 March 1984" were immediately taken from the group following their visit. Their entry in the guest book was erased. Following another removal of a guest book entry a few days later, the group decided to draft a submission to the Kulturministerium, which was in charge of memorials. The women successfully fought for their right to collectively visit, at the Ministry's invitation, since initially only one person was approved. Thus, as Samirah Kenawi (2007: 119–120) suggests, the interdisciplinary work group Homosexuality at the Humboldt University was formed in autumn 1984 after taking previous measures. This group "supported and recommended the admission of interest groups and reference points, proclaiming them as fundamentally conducive to Socialist Society" (as cited in Beyer 2014). What's more, the scientific advisory council believed that discrimination against homosexuals was irreconcilable with the socialist social order and its characteristics of "collectivity, solidarity, tolerance" (Dennert, Leidinger, and Rauchut 2007: 100).

The party's (ostensible) great fear of memorial activities became apparent in April 1985, when the Ministerium für Staatssicherheit learned about another undertaking by the group from a florist. The ribbon bearing the phrase "Commemorating those lesbian women who suffered in Ravensbrück" was forbidden. On 20 April 1985, eleven women who were on their way to the (official) memorial service were arrested at the train station, detained for several hours while interrogated separately, and finally released on the condition that they would not enter the premises of the memorial site (Kenawi 2007: 120).

Although initially the effect appeared to be limited, in hindsight, these activities ushered in small successes: in September 1985 a coalition of lesbian, gay, ecological, peace, and human rights groups laid a wreath at the memorial site at Sachsenhausen while a representative delivered a speech remembering homosexual victims (Kenawi 1995: 445); and on 20 April 1986 at Ravensbrück, the women were guided through the museum by the head of the memorial site. That said, their entry in the guest book was again in vain, since shortly after their visit a new book took its place. Nevertheless, the women had forced the comrades to engage with a disagreeable topic. Their dedication had also facilitated the emergence of new (work) groups as well as publications, films, and discussion forums (Kenawi 2007: 121).

Institutional and Structural Discrimination

Control, surveillance, and repression of lesbian and gay (and trans*) self-organizing, which aimed at preventing or disturbing group (founding) processes, connections between groups, and activities, must still be examined in detail. But these measures can be regarded as forms of institutional discrimination by the state. The term institutional discrimination implies that "practices of degradation, discrimination, and exclusion exerted by social groups and their members are examined at the level of an organization and the professions acting herein" (Gomolla 2017: 134). Institutional and structural forms of discrimination are embedded in power structures, which are historical. Structural discrimination refers to "a historical and sociostructural concentration of discrimination, which can no longer be explicitly traced back to a specific institution" (Gomolla 2017: 149). The demonstrable medical, psychological, and sexual pathologization of lesbians, gays, trans*, and inter* persons (e.g. Kowalski 1987; Borowski 2015; Klöppel 2012) in both the FRG and the GDR—offering just one example of discrimination that had persisted since end of the nineteenth century—was reproduced and reflected within the health care system. On a sociostructural level, this means that there was no provision of medical care in the area of consultation for LGBTI people, and this is still the case today. Researchers have yet to conduct interviews to determine the extent to which deep-seated prejudices against LGBTI, representing another form of structural discrimination, were present in daily life in the GDR.

Public Silence on Commemoration "From Below": A Summary

In the end, the way the state handled attempts to establish a lesbian-gay commemoration culture for the victims of National Socialism is by no means a singular case, which points to the GDR's lack of sovereignty. Further instances of commemoration took place, occasioning hour-long interrogations by state police in advance of a lesbian get-together and celebration in Berlin in 1978 (Kenawi 1995: 435). In hindsight, the amount of energy and personal resources mobilized by the surveillance apparatus to respond to lesbian and gay activities appears downright absurd.

At the same time, lesbian and gay alignments in the 1980s expose the democratic nature of these processes of self-organizing.[13] The establishment of these groups was not only intrinsically connected to gradual emancipation and empowerment, but also to an awareness of and resistance to discrimination. With their commemorative strategies and political activism, these groups succeeded in offering an alternative to the often abstract and ideologically rigid memories of "the communist fight of resistance." One can cautiously claim that lesbian-gay groups, along with other initiatives, irritated official remembrance, opening it up to new possibilities for action and initiating the concurrent debate on commemoration "from below." Regarding other groups of victims, this shift was confirmed on the fiftieth anniversary of the Pogromnacht in 1988, when for the first time, documents dealing with regional Jewish history were published. The SED's preoccupation with Jewish history, however, was instrumental, with foreign policy interests serving as the main motives for their focus on "Jewish topics"—and the associated antisemitic images should not be overlooked (Amadeu Antonio Stiftung 2010: 128–130). And yet, a careful expansion of commemoration culture within the GDR had been initiated.

In post-1989 discourses, numerous activities and successes achieved by lesbian-gay self-organizing have only been mentioned when lesbians and gays have been able to raise their voices (in person). It is striking that self-organized lesbian and gay commemoration activities are not mentioned in existing reflections on the causes that led to silencing of lesbian and gay activities within the civil rights movement of the GDR (Lautmann 2008). There are four considerations here. Perhaps (1) this phenomenon conveys that politics and democracy from below are not taken seriously, since neither the previously demonstrated self-organized political processes nor the above-named forms of self-organization and their activities fit into parliamentary democracy, since they do not belong to established groups in the FRG such as NGOs and *Vereine*, or citizens initiatives. Moreover, (2) various types of marginalization potentially reinforce one another at this point: the silence of society as a whole regarding lesbian, gay, and trans* lifestyles is accompanied by a disregard for their everyday resistance and protest. Both aspects thwart the already slighted commemoration of their history of discrimination, violence, and persecution. Furthermore, (3) this phenomenon may represent a general display of arrogant Western disinterest in GDR history ("from below"). At the same time, (4) lesbian and gay commemorative initiatives in the GDR are disregarded while discussions of a culture of remembrance of lesbian and gay victims of the Nazi dictatorship within these communities remain abundant.

Christiane Leidinger is a political scientist and sociologist. She currently holds a professorship in sociology with a focus on gender studies at the University of Applied Sciences Duesseldorf in the Faculty of Social Sciences and Cultural Studies, where she began working in 2018. Previously, she worked as a guest professor and freelancer, mainly in the fields of pedagogy, research, and political education. Her current research interests include political sociology and the historiography of old and new social movements, protest research, political biographies, theories and practices of empowerment, and discrimination and violence. Her monographs include *Media—Governance—Globalization* (2003), *No Daughter of a Good House—Johanna Elberskirchen (1864–1943)* (2008), and *Theory of Political Actions* (2015).

Heike Radvan is a social worker and educationalist with a doctorate in educational science. In 2017, she began working as a professor of methods and theories of social work at the Brandenburg Technical University Cottbus. She completed her doctoral thesis on "Pedagogical Action and Antisemitism" at the Freie Universität Berlin in 2009. In the next fifteen years, she conducted research and project development at the Amadeu Antonio Foundation (Berlin), including project conception and coordination of the exhibitions of the Amadeu Antonio Foundation "Das hat's bei uns nicht gegeben! Antisemitism in der DDR" (2007) and "Germany after 1945: A Society Confronts Antisemitism, Racism and Neo-nazism" (2012). During this period, she established and managed the Foundation's Gender and Right-Wing Extremism Unit. Her research focuses on the following areas: reconstructive social research, educational action and antisemitism, gender and the prevention of right-wing extremism, rural diversity in the new federal states, intercultural education, and antisemitism in the GDR.

Notes

1. Persons who cannot or do not wish to identify with the gender given to them at birth and whose body and/or self-conception as inter*person cannot be integrated within the gender binary distinction of "man or woman" call themselves trans*, the asterisk signaling a broader definition of the term. LGBTI do not form discrete groups, since sexual and gender identities are interconnected and at times overlap thus, for example trans* persons can identify as lesbian.

2. Criminal Code of the German Empire.

3. Beyond the valid critique of its dogmatism and violence, here we are referring to Leninist theory and practices, particularly within the realm of pedagogy: the focus here is on, for example, systematic learning (versus appropriation of knowledge by memory), egalitarian education policies such as extracurricular literacy, the establishment of libraries, reading rooms, and further reform of peda-

gogical approaches regarding pupils' self-administration (e.g., Anweiler 1990: 102, 108, 110).

4. Persons who identify as lesbian, gay, and trans*, for further specification see footnote 1.

5. Section 175 of the German criminal code was exploited by the National Socialists in 1935 and maintained in both the Western (Allied) Occupation zones and the FRG until 1969, or rather 1973; its complete abolition took place as late as 1994 (Burgi and Wolff 2016: 22–37).

6. As early as August 1987, the Supreme Court decided that §151 of the GDR penal code should no longer be applied. Following the fifth criminal law amendment act in December 1988, the section was abolished, which took effect in July 1989 (Burgi and Wolff 2016: 25).

7. By contrast, in the West, homosexuality was regarded as specifically communist, especially in the context of espionage (Leidinger 2015a: 26).

8. On the importance of exchange between organizations in East and West, see Tammer 2013: 22–30.

9. It should be noted that these groups organizing themselves under auspices of the church were by no means excluded from constraints such as repression and censorship (Kenawi 1995: 24, 439).

10. AK is the abbreviation of the German term *Arbeitskreis*, meaning task force or work group.

11. Representatives made use of the phrase "victims of fascism" (partly until today: Kenawi 2007: 118), which was familiar in the GDR and considered opportune.

12. The state of research regarding discrimination and state prosecution of lesbians under the National Socialist regime is still controversial, like the commemoration of lesbian victims. Most recently, this was evidenced in the debate on a memorial plaque for lesbians in Ravensbrück. Elli Smula and Margarete Rosenberg were two women's names specified on a list from the concentration camp Ravensbrück stating "political" as their reason for arrest, which also had the annotation "lesbian." Unfortunately, the inadequate state of research on lesbians does not preclude claims that state persecution of lesbians within National Socialism was nonexistent. This occurs regardless of older and newer source material proving otherwise, such as in the national archive in Berlin and suggested research programs (e.g., Boxhammer and Leidinger 2014). It is undoubtedly true that lesbian women (or those labeled as such) were not persecuted by a particular section of criminal law as with §175 RStGB, which referred only to male homosexuality and, accordingly, gays. Further research is required to determine specific forms of persecution. Whether it is possible or insightful to attempt a strict division between "woman" and "lesbian" when considering the persecution of lesbians is questionable given prevailing social norms. In addition, the division neglects intersectional research on discrimination. These show specific forms of discrimination, violence, and persecution targeted at lesbians under National Socialism.

13. Naturally, right-wing or even extreme right-wing organizations also exist. Here, however, we are referring exclusively to those who wish to have an emancipatory effect inside and out.

References

Amadeu Antonio Stiftung. 2010. *"Das hat's bei uns nicht gegeben." Antisemitismus in der DDR. Das Buch zur Ausstellung*. Berlin.

Anweiler, Oskar. 1990. *Wissenschaftliches Interesse und politische Verantwortung: Dimensionenvergleichender Bildungsforschung*. Opladen.

Beyer, Irene. 2014. "Lesben in der DDR—vom Tabu zum Aufbruch, 19 March 2014." Accessed 15 June 2020, http://lernen-aus-der-geschichte de/Lernen-und-Lehren/content/11669.

Boxhammer, Ingeborg, and Christiane Leidinger. 2014. "Sexismus, Heteronormativität und (staatliche)Öffentlichkeit im Nationalsozialismus." In *Homosexuelle im Nationalsozialismus*, edited by M. Schwartz, 93–100. Munich.

Borowski, Maria. 2015. "Schwule und Lesben in der frühen DDR—Verlierer der Moderne?" In *Gewinner und Verlierer Beiträge zur Geschichte der Homosexualität in Deutschland im 20 Jahrhundert*, edited by Norman Domeier, 63–78. Berlin.

Burgi, Martin, and Wolff, Daniel. 2016. *Rehabilitierung der nach § 175 StGB verurteilten homosexuellen Männer Auftrag. Optionen und verfassungsrechtlicher Rahmen Im Auftrag der Antidiskriminierungsstelle des Bundes*. Baden-Baden.

Dennert, Gabriele, Christiane Leidinger, and Franziska Rauchut, eds. 2007. *In Bewegung bleiben 100 Jahre Politik, Kultur und Geschichte von Lesben*. Berlin.

Evans, Jennifer. 2014. "Homosexuality and the Politics of Masculinity in East Germany." In *Gender and the Long Postwar: The United States and the Two Germanys, 1945–1989*, edited by Karen Hagemann and Sonya Michel, 343–362. Washington, DC.

Fischer, Susanne. 2015. "Max Fechner—Opfer oder Täter der Justiz der Deutschen Demokratischen Republik?" *Deutschland Archiv*, 10 December 2015. Accessed 15 June 2020, www.bpb.de/217123.

Gomolla, Mechtild. 2017. "Direkte und indirekte, institutionelle und strukturelle Diskriminierung." In *Handbuch Diskriminierung*, edited by Albert Scherr, Aladin El-Mafaalani, and Yüksel Gökçen, 133–155. Wiesbaden.

Grau, Günter. 1995. "Sozialistische Moral und Homosexualität Die Politik der SED und das Homosexuellenstrafrecht 1945 bis 1989." In *Die Linke und das Laster*, edited by Detlef Grumbach, 85–141. Hamburg.

———. 1998. "Leben im Kampf gegen den Paragraphen 175 Zum Wirken des Dresdener Arztes Rudolf Klimmer 1905–1977." In *100 Jahre Schwulenbewegung. Dokumentation einer Vortragsreihe in der Akademie der Künste Berlin*, edited by Manfred Herzer, 47–64. Berlin.

Grumbach, Detlef. 1995. "Die Linke und das Laster Arbeiterbewegung und Homosexualität zwischen 1870 und 1933." In *Die Linke und das Laster*, edited by D. Grumbach, 17–37. Hamburg.

Haury, Thomas. 2014. "Antifaschismus und Schuldabwehr in der frühen DDR." *Lernen aus der Geschichte*, 21 May 2014. Accessed 15 June 2020, http://lernen-aus-der-geschichte.de/Lernen-und-Lehren/content/11759.

Kenawi, Samirah. 1995. *Frauengruppen in der DDR der 80er Jahre: eine Dokumentation*. Edited by GrauZone Dokumentationsstelle zur nichtstaatlichen Frauenbewegung in der DDR. Berlin.

———. 2007. "Konfrontation mit dem DDR-Staat—Politische Eingaben und Aktionen von Lesben am Beispiel Ravensbrück." In *In Bewegung bleiben*, edited by Gabriele Dennert, Christiane Leidinger, and Franziska Rauchut, 118–122. Berlin.

———. 2008. "Die Ersten werden die Letzten sein. Thesen zur Lesbenbewegung der DDR." In *Lesben und Schwule in der DDR Tagungsdokumentation*, edited by Heinrich Böll Stiftung Sachsen-Anhalt and LSVD Sachsen-Anhalt, 57–66. Halle.

Klöppel, Ulrike. 2012. "Die 'Verfügung zur Geschlechtsumwandlung von Transsexualisten' im Spiegel der Sexualpolitik der DDR." In *Trans*homo Differenzen, Allianzen, Widersprüche*, edited by Justin Time and Jannik Franzen, 67–172. Berlin.

Kowalski, Gudrun. 1987. *Homosexualität in der DDR—ein historischer Abriss*. Marburg.

Krautz, Stefanie. 2009. *Lesbisches Engagement in Ost-Berlin 1978–1989*. Marburg.

Lautmann, Rüdiger. 2008. "Warum vergisst die Geschichtsschreibung zur späten DDR den Beitrag der Lesben und Schwulen?" In *Lesben und Schwule in der DDR Tagungsdokumentation*, edited by Heinrich Böll Stiftung Sachsen-Anhalt and LSVD Sachsen-Anhalt, 117–136, Halle.

Leidinger, Christiane. 2015a. *Lesbische Existenz 1945–1969. Expertise erstellt im Auftrag der Senatsverwaltung für Arbeit, Integration und Frauen*. Schriften der Landesstelle für Gleichbehandlung—gegen Diskriminierung (LADS) 34. Berlin.

———. 2015b. *Zur Theorie politischer Aktionen. Eine Einführung*. Münster.

———. 2017a. *Auswahlbibliographie zu LSBTI-Geschichte vom Ende des 19Jahrhunderts bis zum Beginn der neuen Lesben- und Schwulenbewegungen Anfang der 1970er Jahre*. In *State of Research*, in cooperation with Julia Roßhart, edited by Senatsverwaltung für Justiz, Verbraucherschutz und Antidiskriminierung. Berlin.

———. 2017b. *LSBTI-Geschichte entdecken! Leitfaden für Archive und Bibliotheken zur Geschichte von Lesben, Schwulen, Bisexuellen, trans- und intergeschlechtlichen Menschen*, edited by Senatsverwaltung für Justiz, Verbraucherschutz und Antidiskriminierung. Berlin.

Mahlsdorf, Charlotte von. 1995. *Ich bin meine eigene Frau*. Munich.

Müller-Enbergs, Helmut, Jan Wielgohs, and D. Hoffmann. 2006. *Wer war wer in der DDR? Ein biographisches Lexikon*. Berlin.

Notz, Gisela. 2015. *Kritik des Familismus*. Stuttgart.

Nußberger, Angelika. 2014. "Widerstand im Nationalsozialismus—eine aktuelle Botschaft aus einem vergangenen Jahrhundert." Accessed 15 June 2020, www.bpb.de/apuz/186868/widerstand-im-nationalsozialismus-eine-aktuelle-botschaft?p=all.

Radvan, Heike, and Anne Schondelmayer. 2016. *"Ich hab mich normal gefühlt, ich war ja verliebt, aber für die andern ist man anders." Homo- und Trans*feindlichkeit in Mecklenburg-Vorpommern*. Eine Expertise des Vereins Lola für Demokratie in Mecklenburg-Vorpommern e V. Berlin.

Schenk, Christian. 2008. "Die Partei(en) in der DDR Ihre Politik und ihre Ideologie(n) im Blick auf lesbische Lebenswelten." In *Lesben und Schwule in der DDR Tagungsdokumentation*, edited by Heinrich Böll Stiftung Sachsen-Anhalt and LSVD Sachsen-Anhalt, 35–56. Halle.

Stapel, Eduard. 1999. *Warme Brüder gegen Kalte Krieger. Schwulenbewegung in der DDR im Visier der Staatssicherheit*. Magdeburg.

Tammer, Teresa. 2013. "Schwul bis über die Mauer Die Westkontakte der Ost-Berliner Schwulenbewegung in den 1970er und 1980er Jahren." MA thesis, Institut für Geschichtswissenschaften, Humboldt Universität Berlin, Berlin.

Chapter 12

Have We Learned the "Right" Lessons from History?

Antigypsyism and How the GDR Dealt with Sinti and Roma

Ingrid Bettwieser and Tobias von Borcke

Across Europe during the Nazi era, hundreds of thousands of Sinti and Roma were deported to and murdered in concentration and extermination camps, in mass shootings, and by forced labor (Fings 2015). But the ideological foundations for persecution and mass murder did not begin in 1933. For centuries, antigypsyism, as a specific form of racism, was deeply rooted in disparate European societies.[1] This tradition was far from interrupted in 1945. In many cases, the survivors of the genocide and their descendants were once again confronted with ostracism and discrimination. Continuing racism and societal ignorance about the crimes of the Nazi era proved to be mutually reinforcing. In the Federal Republic of Germany (FRG), the German Sinti and Roma civil rights movement articulated opposition to this state of affairs. Launching major initiatives in the 1980s, it made social and political issues of both the genocide and ongoing discrimination. In 1982, the Central Council of German Sinti and Roma was created to campaign for the concerns of the minority and to provide a counterpoint to mainstream discourses. Today, it continues its work in the political sphere.[2]

In the German Democratic Republic (GDR), there was no comparable movement. In fact, there continues to be sparse documentation about Sinti and Roma in the GDR, and this is presumably attributable to more than the small number of Sinti living there.[3] Below, we begin by characterizing the situation of genocide survivors in the Soviet Occupation Zone (SBZ) and the subsequent GDR. We shall then address the question of how *Neues Deutschland* (*ND*), the daily newspaper of the Socialist Unity Party of Germany (SED), wrote about "gypsies"[4] and the genocide carried out against Sinti and Roma. This is followed by thoughts on the role of the history of Sinti and Roma in the GDR's memorialization culture and schools. In conclusion, we discuss unresolved questions and present some theses on the effects of how the GDR has dealt with the genocide and with Sinti and Roma up until the present day.

How Survivors in the SBZ and Former GDR Were Dealt With

One indicator of engagement with the genocide and its underlying ideologies is the treatment of survivors by government agencies in the SBZ/GDR. One dramatic case was recorded in Wurzen, a town in Saxony, where in July 1947, survivor Josef Wasungen applied for a residence permit for five persons and himself (Müller 2014: 119–121).[5] After his application was rejected by the town council, he contacted the Resettlement Agency, which requested a statement from Wurzen, only to reiterate and justify the refusal.

The determining factor behind this rejection was not actual or alleged misconduct by Wasungen, but that in Wurzen, "a sizeable number of" Wasungen's "uncontrollable clan members" had turned up, thus creating "a veritable gypsy encampment" (Schmohl 2016: 98). Though members of the Sinti minority had suffered severely under Nazi persecution, explained the ruling, the town's residents could "not be expected to look on as these people lazed around, especially as due to their unverifiable income they are able to lead a life of luxury" (Schmohl 2016: 98).[6] What's striking about this response is not only the lack of empathy but also the readiness to resort to stereotypes in support of an official ruling. On 1 August 1947, Wasungen was issued a residence ban for Wurzen. Together with other Sinti, he was expelled from the town.

For survivors, institutional recognition as a victim of fascism (VoF) was extremely important. Viewed as a form of social approval, it was linked to higher pension payments and other benefits. Sinti and Roma were at first categorically excluded from this status. Beginning in 1946, recognition was possible on principle. This was conditional on the survivors—to quote relevant guidelines—"having after 1945 been recorded by the employment office responsible, and having maintained an anti-Fascist /democratic attitude."[7] Thus recognition was not derived exclusively from persecution suffered in the Nazi era but was coupled with politically and morally desired behavior and conformity with societal norms after 1945. While an "antifascist/democratic attitude" was a fundamental precondition for recognition as a VoF, the necessity of registering with an employment office, by contrast, applied only to Sinti and Roma (Hölscher 2002: 78–80).

This highlights the survival of ancient stereotypes whereby Sinti and Roma were regarded as inherently work-shy. In fact, the VoF status of Sinti and Roma was a source of repeated conflict. Documented examples show how Sinti and Roma—deemed "work-shy" and thus rendered guilty of "behavior unbecoming of a VoF"—were stripped of VoF status (Reuss 2015: 145).

For surviving Sinti and Roma, creating a new existence for themselves after 1945 was extremely difficult, since many were neither physically nor mentally able to hold down a "regular job." This resulted in official harassment that sometimes extended as far as being committed to workhouses. Accordingly, most surviving Sinti and Roma left the SBZ/GDR by emigrating to the FRG (Zimmermann 2007: 45; Reuss 2015: 150).

For other reasons, policeman Ewald Hanstein, a Sinto and survivor of the Auschwitz and Dora-Mittelbau concentration camps, emigrated to the West. Following a deployment near the border with West Berlin, he was accused by two colleagues of illegal border crossing. He spent ten months remanded in custody but was ultimately acquitted. Yet he was dismissed from the police force and expelled from the Association of Victims of the Nazi Regime (VVN) and the SED. It is unclear whether the accusations against Hanstein were racially motivated. But what's indisputable is what this period meant to him: "The prison in Magdeburg-Sudenburg was not comparable to Auschwitz, but it was horrible enough for me to feel as if I had suddenly been transported back to the Nazi era" (Hanstein 2005: 95). After his release from prison, Hanstein started to plan his escape. The triggering moment was a confrontation in February 1954 with one of his former colleagues: "In a restaurant, I met the small, aging railway policeman who had got me sent to prison. As soon as I saw him, I flew into such a rage that I threw overboard all good resolutions and abandoned all caution. I gave him a real dressing-down. Probably I also called him a Nazi, and all his fellow-policemen as well" (Hanstein 2005: 122).

While Hanstein turned his back on the GDR, the FRG was, in his perception, also characterized by racist continuities. Regarding protracted disputes over compensation payments, he wrote, "In the Nazi era, we were persecuted, tortured and exterminated, and have had to fight for a minuscule pension for twenty years. And those who are responsible for our sufferings are pocketing huge pensions, which are forwarded to them if they live abroad. I've been opposing this injustice since my return to Bremen. And for as long as nothing has really changed in this regard, Germany is and remains a nation of perpetrators, which doesn't even grant the victims any reasonable compensation" (Hanstein 2005: 150). Neither of the two German states actively endeavored to assist survivors of the genocide or helped Ewald Hanstein to feel that he was welcome as an equal among equals. In the FRG, it was at least possible for him to socialize with other Sinti and to fight in the civil rights movement to attain equality for Sinti and Roma.

The SED and the "Gypsies": *Neues Deutschland* (1946–1990)

In the GDR, the political leadership's attitudes towards Sinti and Roma can be reconstructed with particular clarity using articles that appeared in the SED-controlled daily newspaper *Neues Deutschland*. In his instructions for authoring newspaper articles, SED Chairman Otto Grotewohl called for a rhetorical idiom designed to serve the "political struggle" and "the influencing of the masses" (Ciesla 2012). The task of guiding the "masses" in line with party policies was primarily assigned to *ND*, the main media organ in the Soviet Occupation Zone (SBZ) and subsequently, the GDR.

In the GDR, a "land of newspaper readers" (Fiedler and Meyen 2012), the newspaper functioned (between 1946 and 1990) as a vehicle for announcements and as an agitation instrument for the SED. It was popular for its low price, high circulation, local pages, format, and absorbent paper. The GDR's citizens read it primarily for local coverage, to keep up with SED policies, and to know what was permissible to say at that time (Ciesla 2012; Fiedler and Meyen 2011a, 2011b, 2012; Richter 2011; Wilke 2011).

Between 1946 and 1990, the term "gypsy" can be found 384 times in issues of the *ND*.[8] The low number of hits indicates that the topic was regarded by the state as relatively unimportant for the population. These articles, reports, reviews, and event announcements can be divided into five categories. Articles, reports on trips, events, serialized novels, and book reviews that feature romanticized antigypsyism are among the most frequent mentions. Hackneyed clichés are not questioned but rather consigned to the past, and thus transmuted into a tool to demarcate the socialist present and future. With the establishment of socialism, "gypsiness" is transmogrified from the alleged lifestyle of a social group to mere folklore.

"Gypsies" are even assigned a role in building socialism. This is adumbrated in a 1967 article titled "Nomads from Bulgaria Settle Down":

> Gypsies, fortune-tellers, illiteracy, that all belongs together in Bulgaria as well.... Since the people came to power ... there are already 480 gypsies with a university degree in Bulgaria. They are working as teachers, doctors, agronomists, engineers.... The nomadic lifestyle and peddling are things of the past.... The new emphases in the life of Bulgaria's gypsies are not intended to rob them of their distinctive culture. Their cheerfulness, their love of music, and their dances survive in lay collectives in various parts of the country.[9]

Event announcements represent the next highest number of hits, around forty, primarily for performances of the opera *The Gypsy Baron* by Johann Strauss. Radio, television, and cinema programs were also advertised.

A mere twenty-eight articles appearing in between 1946 and 1990, most of them placed inconspicuously in the paper, address persecution and extermination during the Nazi era. The genocide of Sinti and Roma is briefly mentioned in the context of an article on the Nuremberg trials.[10] In December 1946, a report, "Inconceivable Cruelties," concerning "seawater experiments on 50 gypsies conducted in 1944"[11] in the concentration camp at Dachau, appeared in a report on the Nuremberg doctors' trial.[12] At least some of these early articles demonstrate empathy with the victims.

Only sporadic mentions appear of the persecution of Sinti and Roma and the genocide they suffered. This reflects the institutionalization of antifascist memorialization in 1958.[13] The content of *ND* was increasingly used to justify the GDR and distinguish it from the FRG, with the proceedings against Hans Globke receiving special attention (Baetz, Herzog, and Mengersen 2007). Continuities between National Socialism and the FRG were emphasized: "Bonn's rat's nest of war—Hitler's wartime judges are regrouping. New power for the Jew-murderer Globke."[14] The daily's enumerations of Nazi crimes feature formulaic references to the genocide suffered by Sinti and Roma in addition to the murder of the Jews.[15]

Between 1960 and 1969, three brief reports appeared, revealing the same agenda: criticism of discriminatory practices in West Germany. In 1960, the *ND* reported,

> Because he resembled a gypsy, the Swedish businessman Erik Taikon was refused entry by West German border police.... [They] cited as justification the racially discriminatory Immigration Police Ordinance even today fully applicable in West Germany ... from 22 August 1938.... The Swedish businessman ... was subjected to shouts of ... "We don't want any

gypsies!" . . . The West German border police assumed that . . . [Taikon] was a gypsy merely because his profession was stated in his passport as "coppersmith," and because . . . [his] baggage . . . included some camping equipment. . . . The officers justified their action by citing their administrative instructions under the Immigration Police Ordinance, which stipulated: "Foreign gypsies must be turned away if they attempt to enter federal territory."[16]

The message conveyed by such reports, which did not have to be spelled out in the *ND*, was that incidents of this kind would not be possible in the GDR. In 1969, the *ND* even let activists from the minority (indirectly) have their say for the first time for disseminating the paper's anti-West message: "In West Germany, the discriminatory Nuremberg race laws of the Nazis still apply for gypsies." This statement came from Rudolf Karway, chairman of the International Gypsies' Rights Commission, in an interview with the Hamburg-based magazine *Stern*. Especially for gypsies, said Karway, the Bonn government is applying entry restrictions and bans. "Many gypsies never registered compensation claims as Nazi victims with the relevant government agencies."[17]

Occasional mentions of the civil rights movement of Sinti and Roma in Germany and Europe and critical reports on violence against members of this minority can be found starting in 1979. The large-scale demonstration on the premises of the former Bergen-Belsen concentration camp in 1979 and hunger strike at the Dachau Memorial in 1980—two preeminent events in the history of the civil rights movement—are at least briefly mentioned.[18]

Yet it is also illuminating to note what is *not* reported. For example, the *ND* did not think it worthwhile to cover the foundation of the Central Council of German Sinti and Roma in February 1982 or, one month later, the recognition of the genocide by Helmut Schmidt. The recognition of this genocide, in particular, constitutes one of the paramount successes won by West Germany's civil rights movement.

There was hardly anything published in the *ND* about the lives of Sinti and Roma in the GDR. Most mentions are to be found in the culture section. Romantic "gypsy" sentimentality was also emphasized in the socialist GDR. The Nazi persecution of Sinti and Roma, together with antigypsyism, were (with exceptions in the early years) covered only when there were distinctions to be drawn in the context of competing systems. But here, too, the propaganda value was obviously low. Mentions are correspondingly scarce.

The only article in the *ND* that covered the GDR's dealings with Sinti and Roma survivors of Nazi persecution appeared in 1949. Reporting on a VoF support center, it demonstrates the narrative involving the "successful model" adopted for the socialist integration of "gypsies." One section reads, "A small black gypsy turns up who, simply because he didn't have a Nordic profile and blond Wagnerian locks, had spent three excruciating years in Auschwitz and Buchenwald concentration camps. He asks for work. A telephone call suffices. Janosch will perhaps next month already be able to bring his first month's wages home to his little Saffi."[19]

Antifascist Memorials and the School System

For the political self-image of the GDR, engagement with National Socialism was fundamental. It was designed to represent the communist resistance and to build a socialist society in its spirit. Memorials located at former concentration camps were designed to foster, anchor, and communicate relevant interpretations of history.

In contrast to the FRG, these memorials were not the work of grassroots movements, a constituent of critical engagement with the history of National Socialism. As national memorials (Nationale Mahn- und Gedenkstatte Sachsenhausen / NMGS), Buchenwald, Sachsenhausen, and Ravensbrück were governmental projects right from the start. While Sinti and Roma were inmates at these camps, they were almost ignored in the exhibitions, events, and the publications of the NMGS.

The 1980s marked a period of gradual change. In 1985, Sinti and Roma were explicitly mentioned for the first time in the permanent exhibition of the Buchenwald Memorial. This mention, however, remained subordinate to the antifascist narratives of the communist resistance and camp solidarity.[20]

The situation was not very different in the schools of the GDR. Here, too, broad coverage was given to the communist resistance to National Socialism, keeping in line with the state-fostered myth of antifascism, while the mass murders of Jews and Sinti and Roma received peripheral mentions at best. Similar to the memorials, however, Roma, Sinti, and Jews sometimes were mentioned explicitly in the 1980s (Baetz, Herzog, and Mengersen 2007: 88–90).[21]

Schools in the GDR could have provided critical coverage of antigypsyism through the young adult book *Ede and Unku*. Published by Grete Weiskopf under the pseudonym "Alex Wedding," the book first appeared in 1931, and was reprinted several times in the GDR. Petra Josting (2017: 83) surmises that since 1954, when the book was reprinted for the first time in the GDR in a new edition, every school child has read it. Weiskopf's book is not free of stereotypes; Sinti are portrayed as a traveling group. Still, the story of friendship between the young Sintezza Unku and the working-class youth Ede Sperling delivers on the author's anti-racist aspirations. "Gypsies" appear not as enemies or threats but as allies to the protagonists. Unku and her family help a communist evade the clutches of the police.[22]

The genocide suffered by the Sinti and Roma is not mentioned in *Ede and Unku* simply because the book first appeared in 1931. But Grete Weiskopf addressed Nazi persecution in an afterword to the new edition in 1954. This afterword was not, however, included in numerous subsequent editions. Following the institutionalization of memorial policy in 1958, thematization of the genocide was not officially desired and was viewed as inimical to the primacy of antifascism.[23]

In this context, it is also important to note that the fictional figure of Unku was inspired by a real person. Grete Weiskopf was personally acquainted with the Sintezza Erna Lauenburger, who was deported in 1943 to Auschwitz, where all traces of her were lost.[24] Keeping alive the memory of Erna Lauenburger and the Sinti and Roma minority and anchoring them in the collective consciousness were among the primary concerns of author and activist Reimar Gilsenbach.

Triggered by the letter of a Sintezza reader to *Wochenpost* magazine, for which Gilsenbach was a writer, he began in the mid-1960s to address the genocide and situation of Sinti and Roma in the GDR. Gilsenbach wrote numerous articles on the history and the present-day lives of Sinti and Roma, though many of them appeared only in West Germany.[25]

Gilsenbach also campaigned for the erection of monuments in Berlin and Magdeburg at the locations of former Nazi forced-labor camps for Sinti and Roma. Additionally, he sought to have a memorial fountain built, designed to thematize the genocide as exemplified by the story of Erna Lauenburger. In the GDR, only a commemorative stone for the forced-labor camp in Berlin-Marzahn was introduced in 1986. The inscription on the memorial stone was so biased in favor of the GDR's political take on history that Gilsenbach expressed vehement criticism (Baetz, Herzog, and Mengersen 2007: 113). A monument for the forced-labor camp in Magdeburg was not inaugurated until 1998. The texts of Reimar Gilsenbach, and in particular his literary estate, preserved at the Documentation and Cultural Center of German Sinti and Roma in Heidelberg, rank among the most important sources for the history of Sinti and Roma in the GDR.

Antigypsyism: A Parallel between the Two German States?

Different as the GDR and FRG were, similarities appear when taking into account social attitudes toward the Nazi genocide of Sinti and Roma and the continuation of antigypsyism. In both states, a publicly discernible engagement with the genocide emerged rather late: in the FRG with a large-scale demonstration on the site of the former Bergen-Belsen concentration camp in 1979, and in the GDR during a cautious liberalization of memorialization culture in the mid-1980s.[26] In neither state was there a committed engagement with the long history and presence of antigypsyism after 1945, at least not with any broad impact. One significant difference can be discerned with regard to continuities in the police force after 1945. In the GDR, as in the FRG, files from the Nazi era continued to be stored on police premises instead of in archives, and some files contained unequivocally racist entries. There are no indications, however, of a continued blanket registration for members of the minority, as practiced in the FRG by CID officers serving in what were called Traveler Centers, and who often had Nazi pasts. It is also indicative of the postwar situation in the FRG that definitional sovereignty regarding the events of the Nazi era was for a long time vested in the perpetrators, who were able to legitimize their actions *ex post facto* and to exculpate one another, taking an active part in compensation proceedings against survivors, for example (Reuter 2012). Comparable developments in the GDR were not possible (Baetz, Herzog, and Mengersen: 144–146).

Differences are also apparent regarding the situation of survivors, which was less than easy in both states. In the FRG, many were forced into a socially marginalized life "on the outskirts of the cities."[27] Severe pressure to conform, which was prevalent in the SBZ/GDR, meant that many survivors emigrated to the West. Yet it needs to be clarified whether this pressure made it easier for Sinti remaining in the GDR to participate in society—for example, in the field of formal education, which in West Germany was not without difficulties.[28]

The effects of the absence of a self-determined civil rights movement of Sinti and Roma in the GDR continue today. While a political lobby for the minority emerged in the FRG, comparable structures in the former GDR are practically nonexistent. The only organization that represents the autochthonous minority of German Sinti and Roma on the territory of the former GDR is the State Association of German Sinti and Roma Berlin-Brandenburg.[29]

There are hardly any organizations of immigrant Roma either. The Leipzig-based association Romano Sumnal, which campaigns proactively for the concerns of Roma in Saxony, is noteworthy.[30] The lack of self-representation for Sinti and Roma, due to the political culture of the GDR, has weakened the position of the minority in the five new states of reunited Germany.

Several studies have examined the situation of Sinti and Roma in the GDR and the persistence of antigypsyism in socialist Germany. But further research is required to obtain a more complete picture. Regional studies, for example, could provide information on commonalities and differences in disparate parts of the GDR and thus on the influence of local protagonists. One shortcoming of the sources that scholars have investigated is that many come from government agencies, reflecting a dominant, mainstream perspective. To illuminate, for example, the above-mentioned issue of societal participation and assimilation, oral history research would be an obvious option. Finally, we hardly know anything about Roma who came to the GDR from other socialist countries to work, and may not even have been perceived as Roma.

The task remains to understand the life stories of Sinti and Roma as a part of German history, not least before and after National Socialism. In this context, questions emerge regarding social exclusion and the participation and rights of minorities. Finally, it must be stated that antifascism in the GDR has not led to the disappearance of racist bogeymen. This was evidenced not least by antigypsyist rabble-rousing in the run-up to the August 1992 pogrom in Rostock-Lichtenhagen.[31] On this point, however, the old FRG and the former GDR are all too similar; enduring racism directed at Roma and Sinti continues to pose challenges to society.

Ingrid Bettwieser, born in 1979 in Göttingen, Germany, studied history, literature, and teacher training at the Freie Universität Berlin. She has worked freelance at the Sachsenhausen Memorial and Museum since 2012 and has been an employee of the Ravensbrück Memorial since 2017.

Tobias von Borcke completed his studies in sociology, philosophy, and educational sciences at the University of Münster with a master's thesis on antigypsyism in the FRG against the backdrop of the Nazi genocide of Sinti and Roma. He is active in the field of historical-political education (e.g., Memorial and Museum Sachsenhausen, Topography of Terror) and since summer 2016 has worked as a project collaborator in the Berlin office of the Documentation and Cultural Center of German Sinti and Roma. His publications are devoted mainly to tsiganology and the relationship between memorial pedagogy and educational work that is critical of antigypsyism.

Notes

1. The complex story of this resentment has not yet been written. See the introductory remarks in Reuter 2014. For a theoretical approach, see End 2011 and 2016.

2. For the history of the civil rights movement, see Rose 1987 and Wippermann 2005: 71–82. In 2016, the Central Council of German Sinti and Roma organized an exhibition on this subject; the catalog can be retrieved online (*45 Jahre Bürgerrechtsarbeit deutscher Sinti und roma / 45 Years of Civil Rights Work of German Sinti and Roma*, Zentralrat Deutscher Sinti und Roma, Heidelberg, 2017, accessed 1 February 2018, http://zentralrat.sintiundroma.de/download/6102). At Heidelberg University's Antigypsyism Research Unit, Daniela Gress is working on a dissertation addressing this topic.

3. There are no reliable statistics. Zimmermann estimates that at first, there were about 600 Sinti living in the GDR and subsequently, "hardly more than 200" (Zimmermann 2007: 45).

4. The self-designation "Sinti and Roma" was used in the *ND* for the first time in May 1985. "Zentralrat der Juden verurteilt Bitburg-Programm," *Neues Deutschland* 104, 4 May 1985, 1 (Allgemeiner Deutscher Nachrichtendienst, ADN).

5. For purposes of anonymization, Kai Müller uses altered names, which are also adopted here.

6. Schmohl likewise references the work of Müller (2014).

7. This formulation is drawn from the "Guidelines for Recognition as Victims of the Nazi Regime" dated 10 February 1950. These constitute a revised version of regulations that were already applicable from 1946 onward (Schmohl 2016: 96).

8. The number of hits comes from the "DDR-Presse" database at the Berlin State Library, set up in conjunction with the Center for Contemporary History Research (ZZF). Access to digitized issues of the *ND* is not complete. Some issues and pages, especially from the year 1947, are missing. (See "Liste nicht beschaffbarer Ausgaben / fehlender Seiten," Staatsbibliothek zu Berlin, accessed 19 January 2018, http://zefys.staatsbibliothek-berlin.de/ddr-presse/nicht-beschaffbare-ausgaben-und-seiten). Consequently, our figures do not claim to be complete.

9. Joachim Römer, 1967, "Nomaden in Bulgarien sesshaft. Zigeuner auf neuen Wegen," *Neues Deutschland* 22, 9 December 1967, 15.

10. "Rudenkos Anklagerede — Todesstrafe für eine Verbrecherbande," *Neues Deutschland* 83, 31 July 1946, 3.

11. "Unfassbare Grausamkeiten — Weitere Aussagen im Nürnberger Ärzteprozess," *Neues Deutschland* 203, 19 December 1946, 2 (ADN).

12. In the following year, a brief report appeared in which compulsory sterilizations of Sinti and Roma were mentioned in the context of the Hamburg doctors' trial. "Dramatischer Zwischenfall," *Neues Deutschland* 148, 28 June 1947, 2 (ADN).

13. Between 1958 and 1990, only twelve articles appeared in the *ND* on the subject of memorialization in which "gypsies" were mentioned. Regarding the National Memorials at Buchenwald, Sachsenhausen, and Ravensbrück, only three appeared. Two concern Ravensbrück and one Sachsenhausen ("Unser aller Müttern und Schwestern — Zur Einweihung der Gedenkstätte Ravensbrück," *Neues Deutschland* 251, 12 September 1959, 9; Otto Gotschke, "Ehre und

Menetekel," *Neues Deutschland* 154, 6 June 1961, 2). It may be assumed that the "women's camp" at Ravensbrück would be seen as suitable for mentioning supposedly deviant "gypsy prisoners." Buchenwald, as the focus for the GDR's antifascism, was portrayed in the GDR's narrative as communist, heroic, and normatively male (Knigge 1993 and 2009; Tillack 2012). There was no place here for "gypsies."

14. "Das Bonner Rattennest des Krieges—Hitlers Kriegsrichter sammeln sich /Neue Macht für Judenmörder Globke," *Neues Deutschland* 285, 15 October 1960, 3.

15. See "Das Bonner Rattennest des Krieges—Hitlers Kriegsrichter sammeln sich/Neue Macht für Judenmörder Globke," *Neues Deutschland* 285, 15 October 1960, 3; "Neues Belastungsmaterial gegen den Bonner Judenmörder—Völker Afrikas und Asiens sind für Globke 'Untermenschen,'" *Neues Deutschland* 123, 5 May 1961, 12; Werner Keimer, "Aufsehenerregende Pressekonferenz in Warschau: Neues Beweismaterial für Globkes Blutschuld," *Neues Deutschland* 347, 18 December 1962, 2; "Anklageschrift gegen Staatssekretär Globke," *Neues Deutschland* 164, 18 June 1963, 5; "Die Blutspur des Mörders—Auszüge aus der Anklagerede des Generalstaatsanwalts Josef Streit im Prozeß gegen Globke," *Neues Deutschland* 185, 9 July 1963, 5; Unsere Prozeßberichterstatter, "Globke in schwarzer Uniform—Am fünften Verhandlungstag am obersten Gericht der GDR," *Neues Deutschland* 189, 13 July 1963, 2 (ADN-Korr); "Globke—Verbrechen am polnischen Volk. Neue Enthüllungen auf internationaler Pressekonferenz in Warschau," *Neues Deutschland* 34, 3 February 1962, 5.

16. "Westzonenpolizei wies Schweden ab—Nazirassengesetz wird noch heute in Westdeutschland angewandt," *Neues Deutschland* 331, 30 November 1960, 2 (ADN).

17. "Gegen Zigeuner gelten noch die Nürnberger Gesetze," *Neues Deutschland* 24, 24 January 1969, 7 (ADN).

18. "Zigeuner fordern das Ende ihrer Diskriminierung," *Neues Deutschland* 34, 29 October 1979, 5 (ADN); "Hungerstreik in Dachau (Hunger Strike in Dachau)," *Neues Deutschland* 81, 5 April 1980, 5 (ADN).

19. "Wo ein Wille ist, da ist auch ein Weg. Es ist viel wiedergutzumachen/ Eine verbindliche OdF-Beratungsstelle," *Neues Deutschland* 52, 3 March 1949, 4.

20. There was of course research on the Nazi persecution of Sinti and Roma in the context of the memorials, but they were always projects carried out by individuals, for which official support was refused or even prohibited.

21. A 1990 history curriculum shows that treatment of the "persecution of Sinti and Roma" was singled out as a subject for lessons, so there would have been an opportunity for a broader thematization. With the unification of the two German states, however, this curriculum was no longer valid. It is notable that here, for the first time in a GDR curriculum, the term "Sinti and Roma" was used instead of "gypsies" (Baetz, Herzog, and Mengersen 2007: 87).

22. In this estimation, we are following Petra Josting (2017). A similar verdict is advanced by Michail Krausnick (2000). In terms of reproducing stereotypes and at the risk of blanket judgments, these passages are not without their dangers, and may have to be thematized during reading. Still, there is a difference between an

approach of this kind and an essentialization that interprets deviant behavior as "inherent" and thus not amenable to change. However, the book was commonly perceived as focusing not on racism or the situation of Sinti and Roma, but on proletarian solidarity and the class struggle.

23. In the GDR's film version of the book, produced in 1980, there was at least one allusion to genocide. The film's final shot shows an empty square on which Unku's family lived until recently. On a wall in the background, a swastika can be seen, accompanied with the following text: "Jews and Gypsies Out" (Josting 2017: 105). The coupling of "Jews" and "gypsies" would have sufficed for contemporary audiences to interpret the allusion.

24. Erna Lauenburger's life story also formed the basis for the film *What Really Happened to Unku*, a project by the AJZ Dessau e.V. In addition to the search for traces of Erna Lauenburger, it included interviews with contemporary witnesses. See www.amadeu-antonio-stiftung.de/aktuelles/2009/filmpremiere-dessau, accessed 31 January 2018. See also *Ede und Unku – Die Wahre Geschichte* (Ede and Unku: The true story), by Janko Lauenberger, a relative of Erna Lauenburger (with Juliane von Wedemeyer, 2018). It covers their life stories and Janko Lauenberger's experiences as a Sinto in the GDR. The announcement can be retrieved online at www.randomhouse.de/Buch/Ede-und-Unku-die-wahre-Geschichte/Janko-Lauenberger/Guetersloher-Verlagshaus/e530681.rhd, accessed 1 February 2018. There is also a biographical essay on Erna Lauenburger; see Neubauer 2007.

25. Noteworthy here is the "Global Chronicles of the Gypsies," a projected four-volume edition (ultimately only two volumes) that were published in Frankfurt a. M. (Gilsenbach 1994; Gilsenbach 1998). Two additional volumes that have already been completed remain unpublished.

26. In both cases, these initiatives did not originate with the government. The demonstration in Bergen-Belsen was organized by the predecessor organizations of the Central Council of German Sinti and Roma in conjunction with the Society for Threatened Peoples; in the GDR the involvement of Reimar Gilsenbach and a few others was crucial. The newspaper articles cited here, in which genocide was mentioned, were publicly available. They did not, however, have any discernible social effects.

27. This is the title of a study by Peter Widmann (2001) that addresses this issue.

28. This question is also noteworthy because it has the potential to generate new insights into the experiences of Sinti and Roma in the GDR, unlike the current approach, which focuses on conflicts and problems. Wolfgang Wippermann's (2015: 99) verdict that "the relatively few Sinti and Roma in the GDR were completely assimilated, and integrated into mainstream society" is too generalized and lacks substantiation. Wippermann goes as far as to claim there was no discrimination and across-the-board recognition as VoFs. That is contradicted in general by the examples listed in this text and numerous others.

29. However, it originated in West Berlin.

30. Information on the work of the two organizations can be found on the internet at www.sinti-roma-berlin.de and www.romano-sumnal.com, accessed on 2 February 2018.

31. For the antigypsyist dimension of this rabble-rousing, see Geelhaar, Marz, and Prenzel 2013.

References

Baetz, Michaela, Heike Herzog, and Oliver von Mengersen. 2007. *Die Rezeption des nationalsozialistischen Völkermords an den Sinti und Roma in der sowjetischen Besatzungszone und der DDR. Eine Dokumentation zur politischen Bildung.* Heidelberg.
Ciesla, Burghard. 2012. "Zur Geschichte des *Neues Deutschland.*" *DDR-Presse: Articles and Materials.* Accessed 28 October 2017, http://pressegeschichte.docupedia.de/wiki/Neues_Deutschland_Version_1.0 _Burghard_Ciesla.
Ciesla, Burghard, and Dirk Külow. 2009. *Zwischen den Zeilen. Geschichte der Zeitung "Neues Deutschland."* Berlin.
End, Markus. 2011. "Bilder und Sinnstruktur des Antiziganismus." *Aus Politik und Zeitgeschichte* 64, nos. 22–23: 15–21.
———. 2016. "Die Dialektik der Aufklärung als Antiziganismuskritik. Thesen zu einer kritischen Theorie des Antiziganismus." In *Konstellationen des Antiziganismus. Theoretische Grundlagen, empirische Forschung und Vorschläge für die Praxis*, edited by Wolfram Stender, 53–94. Wiesbaden.
Fiedler, Anne, and Michael Meyen. 2011a. "Entwurf einer Geschichte der DDR-Tagespresse." *DDR-Presse: Articles and Materials.* Accessed 28 October 2017, http://pressegeschichte.docupedia.de/wiki/Neues_Deutschland_Version_1.0_Anke_ Fiedler_Michael _Meyen.
———, eds. 2011b. *Fiktionen für das Volk: DDR-Zeitungen als PR-Instrument. Fallstudien zu den Zentralorganen Neues Deutschland, Junge Welt, Neue Zeit und Der Morgen.* Berlin.
———. 2012. "Zeitungslesen in der DDR." *DDR-Presse: Articles and Materials.* Accessed 28 October 2017, https://pressegeschichte.docupedia.de/wiki/Zeitung lesen_in_der_DDR.html.
Fings, Karola. 2015. "Der Völkermord an den Sinti und Roma im Nationalsozialismus. Lokale Vorstöße, zentrale Initiativen und europäische Dimension." In *Sinti und Roma. Eine europäische Minderheit zwischen Diskriminierung und Emanzipation*, edited by Oliver von Mengersen, 101–123. Bonn.
Geelhaar, Stephan, Ulrike Marz, and Thomas Prenzel. 2013. "'. . . und du wirst sehen, die Leute, die hier wohnen, werden aus den Fenstern schauen und Beifall klatschen.' Rostock-Lichtenhagen as an Antigypsyist Pogrom and Conformist Revolt." In *Antiziganistische Zustände 2. Kritische Positionen gegen gewaltvolle Verhältnisse*, edited by Alexandra Bartels, Tobias von Borcke, Markus End, and Anna Friedrich, 140–161. Münster.
Gilsenbach, Reimar. 1993. *Oh Django, sing deinen Zorn. Sinti und Roma unter den Deutschen.* Berlin.
———. 1994. *Weltchronik der Zigeuner.* Vol. 1: *Von den Anfängen bis 1499.* Frankfurt a. M.
———. 1998. *Weltchronik der Zigeuner.* Vol. 4: *Von 1930 bis 1960.* Frankfurt a. M.
Hanstein, Ewald. 2005. *Meine hundert Leben. Erinnerungen eines deutschen Sinto.* Recorded by Ralf Lorenzen. Bremen.

Hölscher, Christoph. 2002. *NS-Verfolgte im "antifaschistischen Staat." Vereinnahmung und Ausgrenzung in der ostdeutschen Wiedergutmachung (1945–1989)*. Berlin.
Jäckel, Michael. 2002. *Medienwirkungen. Ein Studienbuch zur Einführung*. Wiesbaden.
Josting, Petra. 2017. "Arm, aber selbstbewusst und solidarisch. Das 'Zigeuner'-Motiv im Medienverbund Ede und Unku." In *"Denn sie rauben sehr geschwind jedes böse Gassenkind." "Zigeuner"-Bilder in Kinder- und Jugendmedien*, edited by Caroline Roeder, Frank Reuter, and Ute Wolters, 79–112. Göttingen.
Knigge, Volkhard. 1993. "Antifaschistischer Widerstand und Holocaust. Zur Geschichte der KZ-Gedenkstätten in der DDR." In *Erinnerung. Zur Gegenwart des Holocaust in Deutschland-West und Deutschland-Ost*, edited by Bernhard Moltmann, Doron Kiesel, Cilly Kugelmann, Hanno Loewy, and Dietrich Neuhaus, 67–77. Frankfurt.
———. 2009. "Buchenwald." In *Erinnerungsorte der DDR*, edited by Martin Sabrow, 118–128. Munich.
Krausnick, Michail. 2000. "Das Bild der Sinti in der Kinder- und Jugendliteratur." In *Zigeunerbilder in der Kinder- und Jugendliteratur*, edited by Anita Awosusi, 31–46. Heidelberg.
Meyen, Michael. 2003. *Denver Clan und Neues Deutschland: Mediennutzung in der DDR*. Berlin.
Müller, Kai. 2014. "Die Verfolgung der Sinti und Roma in der Kreishauptmannschaft/ Regierungsbezirk." MA thesis, Modern German and European History, Hagen Open University, Leipzig.
Neubauer, Rahel Rosa. 2007. "Erna Lauenburger, genannt Unku. Das Schicksal der Titelheldin des Romans Ede und Unku." In *Alex Wedding (1905–1966) und die proletarische Kinder- und Jugendliteratur*, edited by Susanne Blumesberger and Ernst Seibert, 123–142. Vienna.
Reuss, Anja. 2015. *Kontinuitäten der Stigmatisierung. Sinti und Roma in der deutschen Nachkriegszeit*. Berlin.
Reuter, Frank. 2012. "Die Deutungsmacht der Täter. Zur Rezeption des NS-Völkermordes an den Sinti und Roma in Norddeutschland." In *Die Verfolgung der Sinti und Roma im Nationalsozialismus*, edited by Neuengamme Concentration Camp Memorial, 127–143. Bremen.
———. 2014. *Der Bann des Fremden. Die fotografische Konstruktion des "Zigeuners."* Göttingen.
Richter, Sigrun. 2011. "Die Volkskorrespondenten im Pressesystem der DDR." *DDR-Presse: Articles and Materials*. Accessed 28 October 2017, https://pressegeschichte.docupedia.de/wiki/Volkskorrespondenten_Version_1.html
Rose, Romani. 1987. *Bürgerrechte für Sinti und Roma. Das Buch zum Rassismus in Deutschland*. Heidelberg.
Schmohl, Daniela. 2016. "Rom_nja und Sint_ezze in der SBZ und DDR. Ausgrenzung, (Nicht-)Entschädigung und Wahrnehmung." In *"Viele Kämpfe und vielleicht einige Siege." Texte über Antiromaismus und historische Lokalrecherchen zu und von Roma, Romnja, Sinti und Sintezze in Sachsen, Sachsen-Anhalt und Tschechien*, edited by Kathrin Krahl and Antje Meichsner, 93–99. Dresden.
Tillack, Anne-Kathleen. 2012. *Erinnerungspolitik der DDR. Dargestellt an der Berichterstattung der Tageszeitung "Neues Deutschland" über die Nationalen Mahn- und Gedenkstätten Buchenwald, Ravensbrück und Sachsenhausen*. Frankfurt a. M.
Wilke, Jürgen. 2011. "Presseanweisungen, Organisation, Themen, Akteure, Sprechakte." *DDR-Presse: Articles and Materials*. Accessed 28 October 2017, https://pressegeschichte.docupedia.de/wiki/Presseanweisungen_Version_1.html.

Widmann, Peter. 2001. *An den Rändern der Städte. Sinti und Jenische in der deutschen Kommunalpolitik*. Berlin.
Wippermann, Wolfgang. 2005. *"Auserwählte Opfer?" Shoah und Porrajmos im Vergleich, eine Kontroverse*. Berlin.
———. 2015. *Niemand ist ein Zigeuner. Zur Ächtung eines europäischen Vorurteils*. Hamburg.
Zimmermann, Michael. 2007. "Zigeunerpolitik und Zigeunerdiskurse im Europa des 20. Jahrhunderts. Eine Einführung." In *Zwischen Erziehung und Vernichtung. Zigeunerpolitik und Zigeunerforschung im Europa des 20. Jahrhunderts*, edited by Michael Zimmerman, 13–70. Stuttgart.

Chapter 13

The GDR People's Chamber Declaration of 12 April 1990

Ending the "Universalization" of the Holocaust

Martin Jander

To "universalize" Nazi crimes is to deny the uniqueness of the Holocaust and the murder of the Jewish people by dissolving it into one universal story or another, from "man's inhumanity to man" to the "barbarism of capitalism." It is a form of denial and can be an expression of contemporary antisemitism. This essay examines the history of the universalizing of the crimes of National Socialism by the German Democratic Republic's ruling party, the Socialist Unity Party of Germany (SED), and the GDR's spotty record when it came to challenging this phenomenon and what Jeffrey Herf has called the GDR's "wars against Israel." This essay then highlights brave figures in the GDR, Christian and Jewish, who took a stand and prepared the ground for the adoption of the historic "commitment to the responsibility and complicity for past and future" by the newly elected People's Chamber on 12 April 1990.

On 12 April 1990, shortly before the demise of the state, the first (and last) freely elected parliament of the GDR accepted responsibility and accountability for the Germans' crimes against humanity.[1] On that day, the Volkskammer (People's Chamber) voted to pass a commitment to the responsibility and complicity for past and future (Bundesministerium für innerdeutsche Beziehungen 1991: 158). The commitment was initiated by Konrad Weiß (Aktion Sühnezeichen) and accepted by all 409 members of parliament, with twenty-one abstentions. The commitment admitted the "responsibility of the Germans in the GDR for their past and future" (Jander 2001, 2003)[2] and accepted that during National Socialism, "immeasurable harm was inflicted upon the people of the world" and that "nationalism and racial fanaticism" resulted in "genocide, particularly affecting Jews from all European countries, the people of the Soviet Union and the Polish people, as well as Sinti and Roma."

From this guilt derived a "responsibility for the future." The People's Chamber admitted "joint responsibility for the humiliation, persecution, displacement, and murder of Jewish women, men, and children." They confessed sorrow and shame and took responsibility for "the burden of German history," asking Jews around the world for forgiveness. They asked the state of Israel for forgiveness for "the hypocrisy and animosity of official GDR policy" as well as "for the persecution and debasement of Jews even after 1945 in the GDR." The gathered members suggested their responsibility to contribute everything in their power "to achieve the healing of the psychological and physical wounds of the survivors and to advocate for a just reparation for material losses."

In the same declaration, lawmakers assured citizens of the Soviet Union that they "hadn't forgotten the horrible suffering that the Germans had inflicted on the people of the Soviet Union during the Second World War." In addition, they acknowledged joint responsibility for crushing the Prague Spring in 1968. "The unjust military intervention" caused the people in Czechoslovakia "great suffering, postponing the democratization process in Eastern Europe for twenty years." The lawmakers also pledged to recognize "German borders with all neighboring countries, drawn as a result of the Second World War, without conditions." The Polish people in particular were to know that "Germany won't challenge its right to secure borders by claiming territory, neither now nor in the future."

The People's Chamber Declaration of 12 April 1990 showed a historic conscience that was especially lacking in previous declarations by East German dissident groups. This article examines the universalizing of the crimes of National Socialism by the SED, and the spotty record of East German dissent when it came to challenging the state, highlighting figures who failed to take a stand and others who did, preparing the ground for the vote of 12 April 1990.

1945–1989: East German Communism and the Universalization of the Holocaust

During the postwar transformation of the Soviet Occupation Zone (SBZ) and then the GDR into a Soviet-type dictatorship, National Socialist elites were certainly deprived of power (Mlynar 1982–1989). But there was no reconstruction of democracy and no assumption of responsibility and liability by the GDR for the crimes of the Germans. Support for surviving victims of National Socialism inside and outside the GDR remained inadequate (Mertens 1995: 194–211). By contrast, in the Federal Republic of Germany (FRG), after National Socialism's military defeat, the Western Allies forced a recognition of Nazi crimes and supervised the construction of a constitutional democracy, a treaty with Israel, and the integration of German industrial and military potential into the constitutional process of a democratic Europe (Schwartz 1991). The GDR, with the support of the Soviet Union, took a different path, opting to "universalize" Nazi crimes, as the sociologist Mario Rainer Lepsius (1993: 229–248) put it. The term captures the tendency to relativize the the uniqueness of the Shoah by characterizing it as one example of "mass murder" or "man's inhumanity to man."

In the GDR, National Socialism was officially regarded as a product of capitalism, which had been destroyed in the GDR by the socialization of the means of production, the establishment of a "people's democracy," and a comprehensive process of educating the population to become "socialist personalities." Subsumed under the categories "fascism" and "capitalism," National Socialism was classified as a problem specific to capitalist Western societies and to the United States and Israel (Wistrich 2017: 37–50). With very few changes, the ruling SED in the GDR maintained this attitude until its downfall in 1989.

With the exception of two studies by historian Jeffrey Herf (1997, 2016) on GDR history, a study by Thomas Haury (2002), and smaller contributions on particular aspects of this story, a comprehensive analysis of the history and society of the GDR in the context of the "universalization" of German crimes is still lacking (Bergmann 1995). As a contribution to that history, this article highlights a range of individuals and organizations from the world of East German dissent, showing that although some opponents did little more than repeat the orthodoxy of the SED, others, especially in the Christian organization Aktion Sühnezeichen (Weiß 1998) and among left-wing Jewish intellectuals, who helped prepare the ground for the rupture with the politics of the SED on 12 April 1990 (Offenberg 1998: 267).

Robert Havemann and Wolf Biermann: Left-Wing Dissidents Who Also "Universalized" National Socialism

For those GDR dissidents who saw themselves as communists, socialists, or social democrats, the issues of National Socialism, antisemitism, and Israel did not loom large. In fact, the most important representatives of the leftist GDR opposition in the 1960s and 1970s, Robert Havemann and Wolf Biermann, tended to *reproduce* the GDR leadership's universalizing criticism of fascism.[3]

The chemist Robert Havemann had already approached the German Communist Party (KPD) before National Socialism and founded the Europäische Union (European Union) resistance group with friends in 1943.[4] The group set up a communications network for forced laborers who had been abducted to Germany, and helped threatened Jews flee the country. Together with some friends, Havemann was arrested in 1943 and sentenced to death. He was able to escape the death penalty through the intervention of other chemists, who claimed his research was vital to the war effort. Havemann became an important figure for the GDR's left-wing opposition because, after Stalin's death, he turned away from Stalinism and declared that he had made a mistake.[5] Because of his public criticism of Soviet dictatorships, Havemann was barred from employment. With the help of friends, he published his books in the FRG, from where they were smuggled back into the GDR or became known via discussions on West German radio and television.

Havemann's ideas also reached an audience in the GDR through the songs of Wolf Biermann, who was born in Hamburg in 1936 (Rosselini 1992). Biermann's father was arrested for resistance as a Jewish communist and killed in Auschwitz in 1943. Wolf Biermann was sent by his mother and her communist friends to study in the GDR after the war, but instead of devoting himself to economics, he frequented Bertolt Brecht's theater, founded his own theater, and soon became famous for his irreverent songs and poems. He also published in the FRG. In 1964, the Socialist German Student Organization (SDS) arranged a tour of West Germany for the songwriter. As a result, beginning in December 1965, the SED banned Biermann from performing in the GDR. His songs and poems continued to be heard in the FRG and spread even more quickly in critical circles in the GDR. In November 1976, he was expatriated; invited to perform in the FRG in November 1976, Biermann was given permission by the SED to leave but not to return.

Solidarity with Jews in the GDR and Israel or with Holocaust survivors in other states hardly registered for Havemann or Biermann.[6] Havemann's 1972 book *Fragen, Antworten, Fragen,* for example, claims that

National Socialism ended only in the GDR while it continued to be present in West Germany and in all Western democracies. Hitler's political power may have collapsed, but Havemann (1972: 240) argued, "We communists knew that German fascism was only a particularly grisly variation on a political element that was colored by specific national characteristics; yet, it doesn't have its roots in the German constitution but in the contradictions inherent in capitalist society." Havemann attributed the genocide of the Jews entirely to "racism" and "bourgeois ideology." It's a matter of the "biological justification of social injustice," he wrote. He presumed that racism in Germany was directed toward the Jews only because the country lacked a larger minority, such as African Americans in the United States. He claimed that "in the US . . . Jews took part in the persecution and oppression of negroes as well."

Havemann did not consider the socialist world, particularly the GDR, entirely free of its Nazi past. He even explained that "an immense number of domestic political conditions and events in the GDR" produced "new versions of fascist behavioral norms and mindsets." The power of a single party, the "synchronized media," the "dominance of the secret police," and a "parliament without opposition" also belonged to it. He believed that all this deserved condemnation. Despite these phenomena, however, Havemann believed that the GDR constituted "essential progress in German history," having contributed to the defeat of "capitalism and fascism in Germany." Havemann held on to this mode of interpretation until the end of his life.[7] A version of it can be found in his last book, *Morgen* (Morning) (Havemann 1982).

Taking a Stand

The Protestant Bishops: "The History of God with the People of Israel"

When East German civil rights groups formulated their platforms in 1989, they drew on Christian traditions that are traceable to the Bekennende Kirche (Confessing Church), or, more precisely, to Dietrich Bonhoeffer, and many of their ideas came from the various meetings of the Ökumenische Versammlung für Gerechtigkeit, Frieden und Bewahrung der Schöpfung (Ecumenical Assembly for Justice, Peace, and the Integrity of Creation), which had begun meeting in February 1988 in Dresden and Magdeburg.[8] As with Biermann and Havemann, however, National Socialism, antisemitism, and Israel were largely absent from the concerns of Christian reform groups in the GDR, which tended to focus on the repercussions of "the Wall," the destruction of art and culture, demilitarization, pedagogy in national education that evoked feelings of hatred and fear, the treatment of people with different beliefs, the demise of forests due to pollution, and issues of German identity and everyday racism (Jander and Voß 1995: 896).

But there were Christian voices in the GDR that confronted the country's refusal to accept responsibility for National Socialism and antisemitism, as well as the regime's obsessive "anti-Zionism" and violent hostility toward Israel. On 27 November 1975, East German Protestant bishops distanced themselves from a UN resolution that described Zionism as "a form of racism and racial discrimination."[9] The bishops of the GDR spoke out in response: "We must not forget: as Christians we are, according to the testimony of the Bible, placed in the history of God with the people of Israel; as Germans we have in the past denied the right of the Jewish people to exist to an alarming degree; as churches in the GDR we have emphatically supported the program of the World Council to Combat Racism" (Hartewig 2000: 544). Unfortunately, this attitude was not found in the decisions of the ecumenical assemblies of 1988 or the programs of opposition groups in 1989.

Lothar Kreyssig: "A Sacrilegious Revolt against God"

Individual Protestants, however, did criticize the GDR leadership's "universalization" of Nazi crimes and its "anti-Zionist" policies. In 1958, a decade before the Protestant churches of East Germany separated from the Protestant churches of West Germany, the lawyer and Nazi dissident Lothar Kreyssig founded Aktion Sühnezeichen (Action Atonement Sign) (Weiß 1998: 329).[10] Kreyssig was the first to admit guilt, responsibility, and accountability for Nazi crimes against humanity. An evangelical Christian born in Saxony in 1898, he studied law in Leipzig and volunteered for World War I. After graduating from university, he served as a judge in Leipzig and became a member of the Association of National Socialist Lawyers. In a 1940 letter to the minister of justice, he was the only lawyer to voice his suspicion that mentally ill German patients were being mass murdered (Klee 2005: 340). As a result, Hitler ordered him retired. Because of the absence of constitutional legality in the GDR, Kreyssig did not resume his judicial profession after the war. In 1952, he briefly headed up the chancery of the Evangelical Church of the Old Prussian Union. That same year, he became its president, a position he held until 1970.

While traveling to the United States by boat, Kreyssig wrote down his thoughts, which later became the motto of Aktion Sühnezeichen: "We ask for peace. We Germans started the Second World War and have already, more than others, caused immense suffering to mankind: Germans killed millions of Jews in a sacrilegious revolt against God. Those of us survivors who did not want this, did not do enough to prevent it. . . . We ask the peoples who have suffered violence from us to allow us to do something good with our hands and with our means in their country; to build a village, a settlement, a church, a hospital or whatever else they want for the common good, as a sign of atonement. Let us begin with Poland, Russia and Israel . . ." (Weiß 1998: 330). Young Christians who joined the organization first applied their beliefs in Norway, the Netherlands, Great Britain, France, and Greece.

Helmut Eschwege: "Operativer Vorgang Zionist"

In contrast to Havemann and Biermann, some left-wing dissidents did criticize the anti-Zionist policies of the GDR. Helmut Eschwege, a leftwing Jew, expressed especially clear criticism of the GDR's remembrance policy and the regime's "anti-Zionist" obsession (Eschwege 1991).[11]

Born in Hanover in 1913, Eschwege grew up in Hamburg, where he also joined the Social Democratic Party (SPD). After the rise of the Nazis, he managed to flee to British Palestine with his mother and siblings. Eschwege worked as a civilian employee in the British army and became a member of the Palestine Communist Party (PCP). After the end of National Socialism, Eschwege left for the Soviet Occupation Zone and became a member of the SED. He stayed there until the end of the GDR, despite the party's antisemitic campaign.

Eschwege wrote about Jewish history and the history of the Shoah, despite the many restrictions in the GDR. (The Ministry for State Security [Stasi] spied on him as part of its Operativer Vorgang Zionist.)[12] Together with evangelical pastor Siegfried Theodor Arndt, Eschwege was honored in 1984 by the FRG for his promotion of Christian-Jewish dialogue (Löffler 2011: 112). After the collapse of the SED, Eschwege was one of the founders of the Social Democratic Party of the GDR (SDP) in the city of Dresden and prepared his memoirs for publication. His best-known books are *Kennzeichen J* (Code Word J; 1966), *Die Synagoge in der deutschen Geschichte* (Synagogues in German history; 1980), and *Selbstbehauptung und Widerstand. Deutsche Juden im Kampf um Existenz und Menschenwürde 1933–1945* (Self-assertion and resistance: German Jews and their fight for existence and human dignity; Eschwege and Kwiet 1984). The latter was coauthored with the historian Konrad Kwiet and was published only in the FRG.

Starting in the mid-1960s, Eschwege gave talks to Jewish communities, Protestant congregations, and evangelical theologians, as well as to the Society for Christian-Jewish Collaboration. Later, he also became honorary chairman of the Society's Dresden branch. Eschwege not only lectured on the history of the Jews and antisemitism; he also talked about recent history and the persecution of Jews in the GDR, Stalin's antisemitism, the refusal to return property and assets to GDR Jews, and other taboo topics. Nor did he forget to discuss Martin Luther's antisemitism, which was not the favorite topic among Protestant Christians in the GDR.[13] Whenever he was given the opportunity, Eschwege also criticized the GDR's policies toward Israel and support for the war against Palestinians.[14] With these publications and lectures, claims Karin Hartewig (2000: 186), Eschwege took "cultural politics in his own hands."

The GDR Round Table of 1989–90

Demonstrations broke out in the GDR in the summer of 1989, triggered by the escape of its citizens to the Federal Republic after the opening of the Hungarian border. The successful refugees' movements and the visit of Mikhail Gorbachev to the GDR on 7 October 1989 spurred hopes of change. But as oppositional movements emerged, advocacy for the assumption of responsibility and liability for the crimes of National Socialism by the Germans played no discernible part. On 15 November 1989, Israeli Prime Minister Yitzhak Shamir expressed his concern to an American TV station that the Germans could once again become "the strongest country in Europe and perhaps the world" and take this opportunity to kill millions of Jews (Winkler 2000: 524). Not surprisingly, the GDR and West Germany condemned Shamir's announcement. Later, the Central Council of Jews demanded that Germany include the remembrance of its unparalleled crimes against humanity and its obligation toward its victims in the unification treaty (Lehmann 1997: 409). This demand was rejected.

On 30 January 1990, employees of the Foreign Office of Israel and the GDR met in Copenhagen as the GDR leadership tried to reach a diplomatic relationship with Israel behind the scenes. The effort failed (Deutschkron 1991: 455).[15] Instead, the office of the Palestine Liberation Organization (PLO), which was established in East Berlin in 1973, was transformed into a Palestinian embassy.[16]

The SED did not apologize for its forty-year anti-Zionist policy or for its political and military support of the wars against Israel (Herf 2016). While the SED rehabilitated Walter Janka, a communist imprisoned in 1957 after a show trial for allegedly engaging in a counterrevolutionary conspiracy (Jander 2002: 224–229), it did not rehabilitate Paul Merker, a communist condemned in 1955. Merker was accused of having worked for years as a "Zionist agent" to carry out the "plunder of Germany" and the "shifting of German national wealth" in favor of American and "Jewish monopoly capitalists" (Kießling 1994; Herf 1997). His conviction and expulsion from the SED occurred at the height of the GDR's antisemitic campaign in 1952. As part of that campaign, many Jews were expelled from the GDR as the state pursued aggressive internal and external "anti-Zionist" policies.

It is troubling that even the civil rights groups that tried to negotiate a peaceful democratization of the GDR with the SED and its block parties failed to address these issues in 1989. None of the declarations of civil society oppositional groups—Neues Forum, Demokratie Jetzt, Demokratischer Aufbruch, Social Demokratische Partei, Böhlener Plattform, and the Grüne Partei—referenced National Socialism, antisemitism, Jews, or Israel, though a few of the declarations did at least mention the rise of the radical right (Schüddekopf 1990: 125).[17]

The Für unser Land (For Our Country) appeal in November 1989 was typical (Schüddekopf 1990: 240). Its signatories, including Stefan Heym and Christa Wolf, demanded that socialism, as an alternative to capitalism, be defended and that antifascism in the GDR be maintained. The signatories advocated for an independent path for the GDR, demanding a socialist alternative to West Germany that would remember the GDR's "anti-fascist and humanist ideals" (Weiß 2000: 52).

After talks between the opposition and government representatives to negotiate a peaceful transition to democracy, a Round Table began in the GDR in December 1989, and reform demands became more precise. Although appeals like Für unser Land and the platforms of civil rights groups had neglected to tackle National Socialism, antisemitism, and Israel, the meaning of "anti-fascist and humanist ideals" appeared self-evident to many civil society activists. As a result, on 12 February 1990 they unanimously supported a petition from the Jüdischer Kulturverein (Jewish Cultural Society) to the Round Table that demanded asylum for Soviet Jews in the GDR and to forward the petition to the GDR government (Offenberg 1998: 267).

The group making this demand was founded by survivors of Jewish origin, former emigrants, resistance fighters, and their adult children, including many scientists and cultural workers, most of whom were neither religious nor members of the religious community. The group included Irene Runge, Vincent von Wroblewsky, Anetta Kahane, Salomea Genin, Barbara Honigmann, and her husband Peter. Together, partly shamefaced and partly anxious, they had begun in 1986 to rediscover the Jewish traditions hidden in their families (Bachmann 2009).

In its petition to the Round Table, the Jewish Cultural Society pointed out the Germans' responsibility for the Shoah and demanded solidarity with persecuted Jews in the Soviet Union: "Considering that the whole world watched as German fascism persecuted and decimated the Jews, we demand not to repeat the German opprobrium of the past. The Talmudic law holds: (Lo tamood dam reecha peku ach nefesh doche et kol hatorah culah.) We must break all laws if one life can be saved" (Thaysen 2000: 781).

The guideline passed by the GDR's Council of Ministers did not make it into the unification treaty, but the commissioner for foreigners of East Berlin, Anetta Kahane, persuaded the federal state of Berlin to accelerate the admission of Jews. On 9 January 1991, the first conference of secretaries of interior of the states of Germany after unification met and decided that Jews from the Soviet Union would be accepted as "quota refugees" (Kahane 2004: 186). This regulation changed German society for years to come.[18] Approximately two hundred thousand people arrived (Peck 2006: 6).

Conclusion: The Meaning of 1989

A *Wirtschafts- und Sozialunion* (economic and social union) of the two German states was agreed on in the summer of 1990. At the same time, the Einigungsvertrag (Unification Treaty) between the two German states was being drafted. One part of the draft treaty regulated the return of property that National Socialists had taken from the Jews between 1933 and 1945. *The GDR had not returned this property to the former owners or their heirs.* The declaration by the Volkskammer in April 1990 was attached to the Unification Treaty. In addition, the four Allies—the United States, USSR, Great Britain, and France—had to agree with the Germans on the transfer of all sovereignty rights. On 3 October 1990, the GDR joined the constitution of the Federal Republic, and on 2 December 1990, a first joint parliament was elected.

With the decision of the Round Table of 12 February 1990 to invite Jews who had been discriminated against and persecuted in the Soviet Union to immigrate to the GDR, and the adoption of the Declaration of 12 April 1990 in the newly elected People's Chamber, the GDR's leftist, Jewish, and Christian dissidents gave the collapse of the GDR and the unification of the two German states a special character. With these decisions, which do not appear in many descriptions of the demise of the GDR (Kowalczuk 2009), the GDR, and later the five new federal states, departed from the "universalization" of German crimes during National Socialism.

The collapse of the GDR in 1989–1990 and the unification of the two German states are often seen as a revolution in the tradition of the failed German revolutions of 1848 or 1918 (Eisenfeld 2004: 808). I see it more as a process of catching up to something that was refused in 1945 (Habermas 1990). A restoration of democracy in Germany after 1945 was not possible without punishment of the Nazi perpetrators, compensation for the Nazi victims, and recognition of responsibility and liability for the crimes, and without the attempt to help the surviving victims as best as possible. These steps failed to materialize in large part in the SBZ/GDR after 1945. They were restarted in 1989–90.

The antifascist policies of the GDR negated and suppressed many noncommunist traditions of resistance and opposition to National Socialism. Despite the repressive policies of the GDR, two of the anti-Nazi traditions continued to exist on the margins of society. Jewish and Christian opposition to National Socialism gave the collapse of the GDR in 1989–90 a democratic and universalist face. The decision of the Round Table of 12 February 1990 and the declaration of the People's Chamber of 12 April 1990 are possibly the two most important documents from the collapse of the GDR and its subsequent accession to the Basic Law of the Federal Republic of Germany.

Martin Jander, born in 1955 in Freiburg, is a historian, lecturer, and journalist and teaches German and European history at Stanford University (Berlin), New York University (Berlin), and in the Freie Universität Berlin European Studies Program. He completed his dissertation in 1995 on "Formation and Crisis of the GDR Opposition" at the Otto Suhr Institute of the Freie Universität Berlin. Until 2017, he chronicled left-wing terrorism, a project sponsored by the Hamburg Foundation for the Advancement of Science and Culture, some of which has been published. In addition to his teaching and research, Jander works as an adult educator in the trade unions, produces teaching materials for school curricula, and offers guided tours of Berlin and Potsdam (www.unwrapping-history.de). His most recent publication, with Enrico Heitzer, Martin Jander, Anetta Kahane, and Patrice G. Poutrus (eds.), is *Nach Auschwitz: Schwieriges Erbe DDR* (Frankfurt, 2018).

Notes

I want to thank Jeffrey Herf and Alan Johnson for their very helpful comments and critical remarks. See also the German version of this essay: Enrico Heitzer, Martin Jander, Patrice Poutrus, and Anetta Kahane, eds., *Nach Auschwitz: Schwieriges Erbe DDR* (Frankfurt: Wochenschau-Verlag, 2018). The English version of this article, titled "Ending the 'Universalisation' of the Holocaust and the Wars against Israel: The GDR People's Chamber Declaration of 12 April 1990," was first published in *Fathom*, December 2018, http://fathomjournal.org/ending-the-universalisation-of-the-holocaust-and-the-wars-against-israel-the-gdr-peoples-chamber-declaration-of-12-april-1990/.

1. The Declaration was included in the Agreement of 23 September 1990 between the governments of the Federal Republic of Germany and the German Democratic Republic on the implementation and interpretation of the Unification Treaty (Einigungsvertrag 1990: 544).

2. Following my request, Konrad Weiß tried to remember and asked friends. In contrast to our interview, he is now certain that Harald Schneider from the Christian Democratic Union (CDU) contributed the formation of the People's Chamber's declaration. Among its contributors were also Lothar Klein from the German Social Union (DSU) and Walter Romberg, a representative of the Social Democratic Party (SPD), according to an email from Konrad Weiß to me (Martin Jander) on 1 December 2017.

3. Rudolf Bahro and Jürgen Fuchs should also be mentioned here. But since neither influenced the GDR's opposition program like Havemann (Florath 2016), they are not dealt with here.

4. The best short description of the activities of the "European Union" and its work can be found in "The Righteous among the Nations Database," Yad Vashem: The World Holocaust Remembrance Center, http://db.yadvashem.org/righteous/family.html?language=en&itemId=5419419. The story is also dealt with in detail in a Hannemann 2001.

5. See Robert Havemann, "Ja, ich hatte unrecht," *Die Zeit*, 7 May 1965, accessed 15 June 2020, https://www.zeit.de/1965/19/ja-ich-hatte-unrecht.

6. Solidarity with Jews played an important role for Havemann during National Socialism. The Yad Vashem memorial in Jerusalem honors him as "righteous among the nations." See "The Righteous among the Nations Database," accessed 1 October 2017, http://db.yadvashem.org/righteous/family.html?language=en&itemId=5419422. The tribute took place after his death and after the fall of the GDR in November 2005. Biermann (2016: 397–399) discovered the topic through his friend Arno Lustiger after 1988.

7. Until his expatriation in November 1976, Wolf Bierman often poeticized Havemann's political ideas, yet his approach to the GDR differed somewhat from that of Havemann (Biermann 2016). He defended the GDR as part of the dreams of his father, who was killed in Auschwitz. In *Wintermärchen*, which was based on Heinrich Heine, he sang for his "Comrade Dagobert Biermann" whose "ashes were eternally dispersed over all seas and people." His Jewish-communist father was being killed anew every day, Biermann (1972: 66) continued, listing a series of personalities, including Eldridge Cleaver and Alexander Dubček. After the demise of the GDR, Biermann changed his position. Under the influence of the historian Arno Lustiger, he started to directly criticize antisemitism and warfare against Israel (Biermann 2016: 454–456).

8. In 1934, facing the imminent threat of war, Dietrich Bonhoeffer made an appeal to an ecumenical assembly on a Danish island to urge countries under the authority of a church council to make peace. Members of the Protestant church used Bonhoeffer's appeal as a model, initiating the "ecumenical conferences" in 1988 (Neubert 1997: 174).

9. Quoted in UN Resolution 3379 of the General Assembly, 10 November 1975, in *Resolutions by the General Assembly during Its Thirtieth Session*, accessed 27 November 2017, www.un.org/documents/ga/res/30/ares30.htm.

10. The Yad Vashem World Holocaust Remembrance Center has honored Lothar Kreyssig and his wife as "righteous among the nations" in March 2017. See "Liste der Gerechten unter den Völkern aus Deutschland," Wikipedia, accessed 16 November 2017, https://de.wikipedia.org/wiki/Liste_der_Gerechten_unter_den_Völkern_aus_Deutschland.

11. Worth mentioning are also Rudolf Schottlaender and Victor Klemperer. But because they were less influential for GDR dissents than Helmut Eschwege, they are not discussed here.

12. Helmut Eschwege's two short-term commitments to the Ministry of State Security (code names "Bock" and "Ferdinand") and his many years of being spied on in the "OV Zionist" have not yet been described in detail (Hartewig 2000: 189).

13. Eschwege was closely connected to Eugen Golomb (Elijokum Getzel), the long-time chairman of the Jewish community of Leipzig (Löffler 2011: 46).

14. The civil rights activist Konrad Weiß, who initiated the GDR's People's Chamber declaration of 12 April 1990, encountered Eschwege as a speaker at one of these conferences.

15. In a letter to Israel, the GDR's prime minister who was in office on 8 February 8 1990 at least acknowledged the responsibility of all Germans for committing crimes against humanity (Weiss and Gorelik 2012: 381).

16. See "Botschaft des Staates Palästina in der DDR." *Neues Deutschland*, 17 January 1989, 1.

17. Civil rights activist Konrad Weiß tried but failed to include a requirement giving asylum to persecuted Jews to the Round Table's draft of the constitution (Thaysen 2000: 1112).

18. On 11 March 1992, Konrad Weiß petitioned the Federal Parliament (Bundestag) on behalf of Bündnis 90/Die Grünen to allow for the unlimited emigration of Jews from the Commonwealth of Independent States to Germany. While his petition was debated on 10 September 1992, it was not adopted. The Israeli government asked that the petition be withdrawn because it saw it as its own genuine duty to provide a home for persecuted Jews (Conversation with the author Konrad Weiß on 9 November 2017).

References

Bachmann, Ralf, and Irene Runge, eds. 2009. *WIR—Der Jüdische Kulturverein e. V. 1989*. Mannheim.
Bergmann, Werner, Rainer Erb, and Albert Lichtblau, eds. 1995. *Schwieriges Erbe. Der Umgang mit Nationalsozialismus und Antisemitismus in Österreich, der DDR und der Bundesrepublik Deutschland*. Frankfurt.
Biermann, Wolf. 1972. *Deutschland. Ein Wintermärchen*. Berlin.
———. 2016. *Warte nicht auf bessre Zeiten*. Berlin.
Bundesministerium für innerdeutsche Beziehungen. 1991. *Texte zur Deutschlandpolitik*, vol. 3/8a. Bonn.
Deutschkron, Inge. 1991. *Israel und die Deutschen*. Cologne.
Einigungsvertrag. 1990. *Sonderdruck aus der Sammlung "Das deutsche Bundesrecht."* Bonn.
Eisenfeld, Bernd, Ilko S. Kowalczuk, and Erhhart Neubert. 2004. *Die verdrängte Revolution. Der Platz des 17. Juni 1953 in der deutschen Geschichte*. Bremen.

Eschwege, Helmut. 1966. *Kennzeichen J: Bilder, Dokumente, Berichte.* Berlin.
———. 1980. *Die Synagoge in der deutschen Geschichte.* Dresden.
———. 1991. *Fremd unter Meinesgleichen. Erinnerungen eines Dresdner Juden.* Berlin.
Eschwege, Helmut, and Konrad Kwiet. 1984. *Selbstbehauptung und Widerstand: Deutsche Juden im Kampf um Existenz und Menschenwürde 1933–1945.* Hamburg.
Florath, Bernd, ed. 2016. *Annäherungen an Robert Havemann.* Göttingen.
Hartewig, Karin. 2000. *Zurückgekehrt: Die Geschichte der judischen Kommunisten in der DDR.* Weimar.
Habermas, Jürgen. 1990. *Die nachholende Revolution.* Frankfurt.
Hannemann, Simone. 2001. *Robert Havemann und die Widerstandsgruppe "Europäische Union."* Berlin.
Haury, Thomas. 2002. *Antisemitismus von links. Kommunistische Ideologie, Nationalismus und Antizionismus in frühen DDR.* Hamburg.
Herf, Jeffrey. 1997. *Divided Memory: The Nazi Past in the Two Germanys.* Cambridge, MA.
———. 2016. *Undeclared Wars with Israel: East Germany and the West German Far Left 1967–1989.* Cambridge, MA.
Havemann, Robert. 1972. *Fragen, Antworten, Fragen – Aus der Biographie eines deutschen Marxisten.* Hamburg.
———. 1982. *Morgen: Die Industriegesellschaft am Scheideweg. Kritik und reale Utopie.* Frankfurt.
Jander, Martin. 2001. "Das war keine spontane Entscheidung" (Interview with Konrad Weiß). *Deutschlandarchiv,* no. 5: 768–778.
———. 2002. "Walter Janka." In *Opposition und Widerstand in der DDR. Politische Lebensbilder,* edited by Karl Wilhelm Fricke, Peter Steinbach, and Johannes Tuchel, 224–229. Munich.
———. 2003. "Eine Fahrt nach Auschwitz" (Interview with Konrad Weiß). *Horch und Guck,* no. 44: 1–8.
Jander, Martin, and Thomas Voß. 1995. "Die besondere Rolle des politischen Selbstverständnisses bei der Herausbildung einer politischen Opposition in der DDR außerhalb der SED und ihrer Massenorganisationen seit den 70er Jahren." In *Materialien der Enquete-Kommission "Aufarbeitung von Geschichte und Folgen der SED-Diktatur in Deutschland,"* edited by Deutscher Bundestag, 896–986. Baden-Baden.
Kahane, Anetta. 2004. *Ich sehe was, was du nicht siehst.* Berlin.
Kießling, Wolfgang. 1994. *Partner im "Narrenparadies." Der Freundeskreis um Noel Field und Paul Merker.* Berlin.
Klee, Ernst. 2005. *Das Personenlexikon zum Dritten Reich.* Frankfurt.
Kowalczuk, Ilko-Sascha. 2009. *Endspiel. Die Revolution von 1989 in der DDR.* Munich.
Lehmann, Ines. 1997. *Die deutsche Vereinigung von außen gesehen: Angst, Bedenken und Erwartungen in der ausländischen Presse.* Vol. 2: *Die Presse Dänemarks, der Niederlande, Belgiens . . . und jüdische Reaktionen.* Frankfurt.
Lepsius, M. Rainer. 1993. "Das Erbe des Nationalsozialismus und die politische Kultur der Nachfolgestaaten des 'Großdeutschen Reiches.'" In *Demokratie in Deutschland,* edited by M. Rainer Lepsius, 229–248. Göttingen.
Löffler, Katrin. 2011. *Keine billige Gnade: Siegfried Theodor Arndt und das christlichjüdische Gespräch in der DDR.* Hildesheim.
Mertens, Lothar. 1995. Die SED und die NS-Vergangenheit. In *Schwieriges Erbe,* edited by Werner Bergmann, Rainer Erb, and Albert Lichtblau, 194–211. Frankfurt.

Mlynar, Zdenek, ed. 1982–1989. *Krisen in den Systemen sowjetischen Typs* (Schriftenreihe). Vienna.
Neubert, Ehrhart. 1997. *Geschichte der Opposition in der DDR 1949–1989*. Bonn.
Offenberg, Ulrike. 1998. *Seid vorsichtig gegen die Machthaber*. Berlin.
Peck, Jeffrey M. 2006. *Being Jewish in the New Germany*. New Brunswick, NJ.
Rosellini, Jay. 1992. *Wolf Biermann*. Munich.
Schüddekopf, Charles. 1990. *"Wir sind das Volk!" Flugschriften, Aufrufe und Texte einer deutschen Revolution*. Reinbek.
Schwartz, Thomas Allan. 1991. *America's Germany: John J. McCloy and the Federal Republic of Germany*. London.
Thaysen, Uwe. 2000. *Der Zentrale Runde Tisch der DDR—Wortprotokoll und Dokumente*. 5 volumes. Wiesbaden.
Weiss, Yfaat, and Lena Gorelik. 2012. "Die russisch-jüdische Zuwanderung." In *Geschichte der Juden in Deutschland*, edited by Michael Brenner, 379-418. Munich.
Weiß, Konrad. 2000. "Was macht ihr, wenn ihr die Macht habt?" In *Eine Revolution und ihre Folgen*, edited by Eckhard Jesse, 42–58. Berlin.
———. 1998. *Lothar Kreyssig*. Gerlingen.
Winkler, Heinrich August. 2000. *Der lange Weg nach Westen*. Vol. 2: *Deutsche Geschichte vom "Dritten Reich" bis zur Wiedervereinigung*. Munich.
Wistrich, Robert Salomon. 2017. "Antisemitism and Holocaust Inversion." In *Antisemitism before and since the Holocaust: Altered Contexts and Recent Perspectives*, edited by Anthony McElligott and Jeffrey Herf, 37–50. Cham, Switzerland.

Part II

Federal Republic of Germany

Chapter 14

Understanding Silence

On an Ongoing Search for People, Things, and Connections Not Really Unknown

Regina Scheer

In the 1970s, I began methodically talking to inhabitants of a particular street in the middle of Berlin, mostly old women, asking what they knew about a certain house. It was the Jewish hospital, built in 1861, which after 1915 became a Jewish refugee hostel, and then an AHAWAH orphanage.[2] This was not public knowledge back then, and I had no access to information about the building. From old address books I managed to find at the public library, I learned which institutions were housed at Auguststraße 15/16 since 1861.

The building was familiar to me; it was my school. In 1945 it accommodated a well-known secondary school, later named after Max Planck. I graduated in 1968 and often wondered about the history contained within these old walls. Through the windows you could see the ruins of a synagogue. Because when I attended school, antifascism was one of the goals of education, we visited the neighboring Große Hamburger street every year, on the day commemorating the victims of fascism, and held a tribute, placing flowers for the Jewish victims of fascism. Our own schoolhouse did not seem to be connected to this in any way. No teacher knew anything; only a cleaning lady who had grown up in this neighborhood once told me we should have placed a wreath at our own door as well.

When I found the entries in the address books, I began making inquiries. But the neighbors, many of whom had resided there for decades, claimed they knew nothing about this house. They had not noticed that since 1915, up to 120 children had lived here, went to school here, played in this garden. They also knew nothing of the whereabouts of these children. I often went to Auguststraße and gradually got to know many of the neighbors. They were not reluctant to talk to me; the people in this area of Berlin were not that uncommunicative. But in long conversations in kitchens or living rooms, where I questioned them about their life stories, I learned nothing about this Jewish house for the longest time. It was a forgotten house, which I wrote about in a book published in 1993 (Scheer 1993). Today, in a changed social context, it is hard to imagine how extensive the forgetting—the denial of memory was—even decades after the war ended.

But the women from Auguststraße, Hamburger Straße, and Koppenplatz talked readily—almost grateful to heard—about their own lives, their deceased, their losses and worries during the war and after. And about their difficult, modest lives. For years, they insisted they knew nothing about the AHAWAH. At times, it felt like I was researching a phantom, as if this orphanage had never existed. But an old woman from Linienstraße, an outsider—a heavy drinker who collected garbage—told me that she had seen the children and saw them being deported. And the nuns from St. Hedwig Hospital remembered that as well.

In 1988, during the military campaign-like preparations for the fiftieth anniversary of the November pogroms, as it became clear that East Germany's views of Jewish history were shifting, I received a visa allowing me to enter West Berlin for several days so I could conduct research in the chief finance president's archive. There, I found evidence that after the deportation of the last orphans, the house on Auguststraße became a collection point for the elderly. Thousands of old men and women, many of them sick and dying, came through here, deported "East" from this house. Of course, the neighbors knew about this. They also knew that in 1943, a forced labor camp was set up here for workers building the bunker at Koppenplatz and clearing the rubble from bombed official buildings. In that house on Auguststraße, Hitler Youth were trained for the final battle. The neighbors were aware of this, naturally. They had lied to me. Or lied to themselves.

But after I visited them for years, after I had become familiar with their life stories, some began to talk. What baffled me was the undercurrent to their stories—as if they had been the actual victims, even though they were uninvolved, by virtue of witnessing something so awful, so alarming.

I thought for a long time and again and again about these repressed memories, and for the longest time did not understand the alleged forgetting, this strange sense of victimization. Hardly any of these women had been Nazis; they were not callous—they had compassion, a humane view toward others in their lives. Only after so-called reunification did I understand what I had experienced there. I watched as people, after 1989, tried on a massive scale to deny their participation in something that was coming to an end. Overnight, new interpretations of individual lives emerged. Responsibility was basically shifted to *those at the top*.

Journalists and social scientists, but also teachers who I knew well—who were greater conformists than they needed to be, who hurried to obey and bent to accommodate—suddenly claimed they did this under pressure and were ready to subjugate themselves to new masters. It annoyed me that, for a short period, it was even unclear who these new masters actually were. Indignation broke out after the so-called revelations in the media on the reputed life of luxury in Wandlitz. Many people threw away their membership cards to political parties and mass organizations. The revelations of the true state of things had opened their eyes, so they could no longer go along with it. But nothing of what became known was really unknown before. Of course, you could not verify rumors of arms deals, but every person living in East Germany was aware of the daily corruption, the absence of democracy, the gradual and systematic erosion of socialist values, the everyday lies.

Yet the majority of people, as Immanuel Kant knew, are made of such crooked timber. As I observed this phenomenon in the first months after reunification—as things began to spin so quickly, as had happened only two or three times in the past century—I understood that on Auguststraße, silence and keeping silent was not so unusual. Today, I think that the women in the 1930s and 1940s felt their powerlessness, maybe, as something akin to shame. But they saw no room for action and instinctively sensed the threat to their own lives if they got too involved in the pain of others.

That's exactly how most people in East Germany behaved—to avoid any misunderstandings. In East Germany, no crimes comparable to the organized killings of Jews took place. Yet there was a daily loss of a humane sensibility, and only a few individuals were willing and able to recognize this. And they paid a high price for it: even if they only withdrew into their private sphere, their peace of mind was disturbed. Those who went against the current not only lost their peace of mind, but also career prospects, opportunities for the educational advancement of their children, or even their home.

Not looking too closely can be a survival strategy. I, for example, was sometimes told in East Germany about the appalling conditions in prisons and correctional facilities. But I could not confirm this. And what was I supposed to do? I simply repressed it. Only after reunification, when citizens' committees published reports on the situation in prisons, did I have a sense of shame, did I feel guilty. But I never would have said that to anyone who reproached me, self-righteously, especially not someone from another reality.

The women of Auguststraße, when I asked what they knew about the Jewish orphanage, suspected the reproach in my question. To justify their passivity, they would have had to do a lot of explaining, but could they be sure that someone like me, born after the war, would understand them?

The Israeli author Amos Oz once said that everyone knows black from white. It was all about the different shades, the gray areas. The women of Auguststraße had lived in different gray areas. Their lives were not white, by no means, but also not black. And when I questioned them, the subject of the murder of Jews in East Germany had apparently already been dealt with. It took place in Auschwitz and Majdanek, and not at the house next door. "Hitler was never seen at Auguststraße," a woman once said to me. There were no words for what actually happened on Auguststraße, because there was no readiness to hear and understand them.

As chance would have it, in the 1990s, I did similar work in the Prenzlauer Berg neighborhood. For the book *Leben mit der Erinnerung* (Living with memories), published by the Prenzlauer Berg Museum, I researched the streets surrounding the water tower (Scheer 1997). Except for the fact that very few witnesses were still alive, their readiness to speak about their Jewish neighbors was very apparent. So much time had gone by, even East Germany was a thing of the past, and the subject was no longer taboo. Quite the opposite, the silence had been broken by a flood of films, books, and exhibitions. Sometimes, I encountered only unsuspecting, chatty, harmless memories of the Jewish neighbors, and I thought of the denied memories of the women from the 1970s, and now it seemed this inability to put things into words, this frozen memory, was a sign of an inner concern they did not know how to articulate.

Between 1987 and 1989, together with the historian Annette Leo (and also on my own), I worked on a series of interviews with former prisoners of the concentration camp Sachsenhausen. These were well prepared, methodical life history interviews—not random, although intense, encounters like on Auguststraße. The subjects were men who were recognized resistance fighters, who could be proud of their biographies. We did not want to hear what had been written in *Neues Deutschland*, but asked about the personal memories behind the big words. For many people we interviewed, this was the first time they had been posed questions like this about their lives. It was clear that the interviews were not going to be published in the foreseeable future. Maybe that is why almost all of the interviewees opened up like never before. Another factor was that they were old men, felt death approaching, and, perhaps, even though they refused to believe it, the imminent end of East Germany.[3] During this project, not only did I learn more than ever about German history, I also felt the limitations of any sophisticated theoretical method. Our questions alone did not yield any answers. We, ourselves, had to recognize what we thought and felt—and also express it. Judgments, even condemnations, were simply not tolerated; I wanted to know what had happened and was grateful for the readiness to delve into these questions. In the interviews with former prisoners, I began to understand something about the purpose and meaning of a confession.

One does not always encounter such traumatic memories in life history interviews. But even every "normal" biography has its points of pain, unresolved and maybe unresolvable moments. There are interviewers who develop almost criminological methods to get to the truth behind the events, using hidden questions, trick questions, and so on. But for me, the most important basis of any true exchange was respect. An interview about the history of someone's life was also an exchange; if it wasn't, you could simply set the tape recorder in front of the interviewee and have him or her answer a list of questions. Respecting the other person is the key requirement, as well as the readiness to accept their truth, even if only for the duration of the interview. Even if I believe I know better, if my knowledge of history or experience with other statements by witnesses tells me differently, it is still the story of the person sitting across from me.

And if I engage with them, try to understand them, I will maybe also understand the reasons for the silence, repression, and twisting of events. Apart from the fact that there are the most incredible coincidences, where something can happen that is totally improbable, I am not a judge, someone examining the life history of my dialogue partner, weighing its objective truth content. Maybe this is different in the case of certain fact-based interviews. But when a person tells me he heard screams from the gas chamber, then I do not allow myself to raise an objection, even an unspoken one, claiming the gas chambers were too far from the barracks for screams to be heard. He heard them, just maybe not with his ears.

And when a man says he spent years in the hospital, and I know from documents that it was only four months, for him these four months were years. And I have to respect that. A completely different question is how I deal with this truth, whether I can justify taking it on as my own truth.

I need to know that what is remembered, how it is remembered, depends on the circumstances of someone's life. What I understand depends on my own circumstances. I was often startled when I listened to the tape-recorded interviews I had conducted. In a different context, perhaps with new insights or interests, I suddenly heard things—allusions, situations I had not even noticed during the interview. Sometimes I heard a pause, a silence, and was sorry that during the interview I had not detected it. I was already working on my next question or was too concerned with the facts the person I was talking to was offering me. Especially in this hesitation, in this silence, something essential might have been concealed.

When an older person remembers the younger version of themselves, a dialogue between the generations takes place. The older person no longer understands the younger one, or understands them even better than before. And a seventy-year-old remains a seventy-year-old. Even when he looks back on his thirty-year-old self, he is still seeing with the eyes of his seventy years.

However, I also saw in an interview people change the tone of their voice, take on a different expression, even a different language, when they stepped into their memories. Almost all the interviews were conducted with much older individuals. I have little experience with younger interviewees. This generation gap played a crucial role. Frequently, I took on the role of a daughter to whom certain experiences were being handed down. This often led to great intimacy between interviewer and interviewee, a deep trust, as if I were their own child. Again and again, I discovered details about the life of the person I was talking to that even the closest relatives did not know.

Sometimes, historical and personal distance was required to understand the extent of something that happened in the twentieth century. And living closely within the family protected the silence and kept at bay an explosion of uncontrolled feelings. Even when keeping silent becomes keeping a secret, the children or grandchildren stake their claim to it, for the unspoken is still there and passed on, sometimes as unconscious experience. It almost seems like a law of human coexistence that some things can only be said out loud to the grandchildren. But the grandchildren also become mothers and fathers. I think it is not about asking our next of kin about guilt or responsibility, but posing those questions to ourselves. To understand our own history, it is necessary to listen to those in front of us. And to hear their silence between the words.

Regina Scheer was born in Berlin in 1950. She graduated from Humboldt University with a degree in theater and cultural studies. Since the age of sixteen, she has been publishing poems, lyrics, and prose in magazines and anthologies. After receiving her degree, she worked as an editor at *FORUM* until the office closed due to "counter-revolutionary tendencies." Since 1976, she has been a freelance author, working between the realms of documentation and literature. She has contributed to diverse magazines, among them *TEMPERAMENTE* and *Blätter für junge Literatur*. After 1990, she focused on documentary films and exhibitions, conducting research on National Socialist history and on Nazi resistance. Since 1992, she has devoted herself mainly to literary work and publishing several books, most on recent German-Jewish history. She has published two novels: *Machandel* (2014) and *Gott wohnt im Wedding* (2019).

Notes

1. Until the thirties "AHAWAH" stood over the door of a house in the Auguststraße 15/16 in Berlin. (The hebrew word *ahawah* means love.) At that time it was a Jewish children's home with extraordinary social and educational concerns. Then it became a collection point for the transportation of Jewish people to the concentration camps. Later it seemed to have no past. Regina Scheer published an entire book about the history of that house (Scheer 1993).

2. The close to thirty interviews were not published until today. They are available in the archive of the former KZ Sachsenhausen.

References

Scheer, Regina. 1993. *AHAWAH. Das vergessene Haus*. Berlin.

———. 1997. "Leben mit der Erinnerung." In *Jüdische Geschichte in Prenzlauer Berg*, edited by Kulturamt Prenzlauer Berg, Museum für Heimatgeschichte Prenzlauer Berg, 16–38. Berlin.

Chapter 15

"A Reassessment of European History?"

Developments, Trends, and Problems of a
Culture of Remembrance in Europe

Günter Morsch

Under the heading "Celebrating the Events of 1989 also Means Remembering 1939," an announcement appeared in a national German weekly newspaper in August 2009 at the instigation of, among others, the Federal Commissioner for the Records of the State Security of the former German Democratic Republic. Included in the long list of signatures were those of many historians, particularly from the left-liberal end of the political spectrum.[1] Initially, the text suggested that the signatories were seeking to remind citizens—amid a multimedia maelstrom on the occasion of the twentieth anniversary of the fall of the Berlin Wall, the anniversary of which has been celebrated every year since at least 2009—that they should not forget the seventieth anniversary of the start of World War I, a date that is by no means insignificant. But for those hoping for such signals, the rest of the text was a disappointment.

The announcement appeared on the seventieth anniversary of the Hitler-Stalin Pact of 23 August 1939. The text contained many balanced, sensitive, and correct statements regarding the historical significance of this pact between the two dictators. The politics associated with the declaration, however, were introduced in the final sentence and only in passing. In April, the declaration said, the European Parliament acknowledged, for the first time ever, its responsibility for developing a responsible culture of remembrance that sensitizes future generations to any new authoritarian and dictatorial developments. This idea, it said, should be pursued further.

Like it or not, we must assume that the signatories, by putting their names on the announcement, knew precisely what politics of remembrance they were endorsing. Yet it must be said that only a small minority of experts in Europe who grapple with issues of remembrance and commemoration are familiar with the astonishing and important—almost paradigmatic—resolution of the European Parliament.

In April 2009, just before new elections, the European Parliament adopted, by a large majority, a resolution to make 23 August a day of remembrance for the victims of totalitarian and authoritarian regimes.[2] The resolution, introduced mainly by Baltic, Czech, and Polish parliamentarians of Christian Democratic, Liberal, and national factions and adopted—not coincidentally—during the presidency of the council by Prime Minister Václav Klaus, demanded, among other things, "a comprehensive reassessment of European history."[3] "Europe," the resolution states, "will not be united unless it is able to form a common view of its history, recognises Nazism, Stalinism and fascist and Communist regimes as a common legacy and brings about an honest and thorough debate on their crimes in the past century."[4] To achieve this objective, the European Parliament called for "the establishment of a Platform of European Memory and Conscience to provide support for networking and cooperation among national research institutes specialising in the subject of totalitarian history, and for the creation of a pan-European documentation centre/memorial for the victims of all totalitarian regimes."[5]

Backed by numerous statements of historical principles and reflecting ambitious political intentions, this relatively comprehensive resolution was full of moral verdicts and judgments. Demanding political action, it brought to a climax the opinion-forming process in the European Parliament that began in January 1993, almost sixteen years earlier. In February 1993, the European Parliament had adopted a resolution on the European and international protection of Nazi concentration camps as historical monuments.[6] In this resolution, barely a half-page long and limited to a few points, the parliamentarians, concerned about the future of national memorials in the former German Democratic Republic, demanded the preservation of authentic sites under European and international protection. In their almost unanimous statement, the initiative by the presidents of international prisoners' associations firmly rejected "all arbitrary correlations between the reality of the Nazi camps and the uses to which they may have been put after the war,"[7] referring above all to the Soviet special camps in Sachsenhausen and Buchenwald.

A Shift in the Culture of Remembrance

Comparing these two resolutions illustrates profound and enormous changes in the culture of remembrance in Europe in recent years. In just sixteen years, fundamental positions regarding key issues have undergone a nearly complete about-face. In my view, this process of change can be attributed to two developments. First, contrary to what former Latvian foreign minister Sandra Kalniete feared in October 2007 (Kalniete 2008: 133)—that the "long road to achieving a certain equality in the European culture of remembrance" between the two totalitarian dictatorships would not be fulfilled—it appears to have been. The integration of specific memories from more than four decades of communist oppression into a pan-European culture of remembrance, which the new member states of the EU in Central and Eastern Europe have demanded, not wrongly, no longer lies in doubt.

The second, and by no means less important, shift in recent years has been the growing will in many European countries and the European Parliament to unite different cultures of remembrance by means of a new form of politics of memory based on a European master narrative, thus instrumentalizing the past for current political goals much more strongly and unambiguously than before. What are the reasons for this rapid process of change, and what are its consequences?

A New "Age of Remembrance"

In the early 1990s, French cultural historian Pierre Nora invoked a new "age of remembrance." This striking *"Konjunktur des Gedächtnisses"* (Cornelißen 2003: 548) is described by some historians as a memory boom. It took place not only on European soil. In the United States, many South American countries, Korea, Japan, Cambodia, elsewhere in Asia, and then in many African countries, debates on history and memory gathered momentum, especially when it came to the consequences of war and tyranny. Fabrice Larat refers to a "global market of the politics of remembrance" (Larat 2008: 51), Andrew H. Beattie points to "cosmopolitan memory" (Beattie 2007: 12), while Henry Rousso has described a "global regime of historicity" (Rousso 2007: 4). Other authors, turning to recent economic developments, simply speak of the globalized politics of remembrance.

These names and authors reflect the rise of a branch of history and cultural studies that has produced an abundance of literature for a new global market in just a few years. Where discussions concerning the legacy of dictatorships and state violence are socially relevant, museums and memorials on contemporary history are created—surprisingly quickly. These museums and memorials commemorate the victims but also present large and impressive exhibitions that document historical events using a variety of media.

Thus it seems obvious that with the end of the Cold War, the collapse of old ideological fronts, and the development of global communications and economics, a "memory boom" set in for societies and states alike. As a consequence, crimes that were long kept secret are being revealed; forgotten and discredited victims are publicly honored; relatives are discovering information about the graves of their deceased; survivors are finally receiving recognition; and perpetrators are being held accountable for their crimes, even decades later. In many countries, this memory boom has led to a fundamental shift in the culture of remembrance, which has primarily benefited memorial sites that had long received little attention or recognition.

As taboos and silence has come to an end, a bitter battle of interpretation has emerged. The old concepts of the enemy are once again emerging; cracks have opened between social groups, ethnic groups, and states. Rivalries among victims are growing while parties and governments transform resentments that once again, have erupted over the politics of memory and the past. History is becoming a weapon and, in extreme cases, such as in the processes of disintegration of the former Yugoslavia and the Soviet Union, real shots have been fired. Imre Kertész (2007: 6), Nobel Prize laureate and survivor of several concentration and extermination camps, writes with horror about "Europe's oppressive inheritance": "Who would have believed that for the peoples of Eastern Europe the so-called 'Velvet Revolution' would prove to be a time machine that would set off, not forward, but backward in time for them to carry on their petty games from roughly where they had left off in about 1919, at the end of the First World War?"

The revival of national myths, illusions, and fears is by no means limited to the new accession countries of the EU. During the conflict between the "old" and "new" Europe over the War in Iraq, the memory of a continental blockade between Great Britain and France was invoked. The Napoleonic wars and the Congress of Vienna were suddenly recalled to draw lines and discredit different positions in current conflicts. In Spain, the reappraisal of reciprocal crimes committed during the Civil War has had especially violent consequences seventy years after the victory of the Falangists under Franco. Another example of a process of social division over questions of memory is the Belgian debate on the establishment of a museum in Mechelen dedicated to the persecution of Jews. In discussions of whether "Transit Mechelen" should be a "classical Holocaust museum," or a place where the entire history of persecution and genocide of past centuries is dealt with, there have been the usual rivalries among victims but also in-depth debates about national historical images and identity (Verbeeck 2008). The search for a clear, unified, transnational, and morally unassailable framework for the interpretation and explanation of wars and crimes, particularly in the history of the twentieth century, is what unites these disparate battlefields where remembrance politics take place.

Battlefield of Europe?

In view of increasing conflicts over the politics of remembrance in Europe, the attempt to force the constitution of a uniform European culture of remembrance by decree and from the top down appears obvious. German political scientist Claus Leggewie (2009) recently identified seven circles of "transnational memories" on what he calls the "battlefield of Europe." These memories compete to form a collective European memory or must be integrated into it. Undoubtedly, the two most important and influential master narratives are so-called Holocaust education and the theory of totalitarianism.

The 2000 Stockholm Declaration, which appeared in connection with the establishment of a Task Force for International Cooperation on Holocaust Education, Remembrance and Research, was especially significant given the presence of forty-seven heads of government and other important state representatives, including the American president. The new foundation of Europe would be attempted "on the basis of the worst" (Rousso 2004: 365). Reflecting the singularity thesis, the genocide of the European Jews as the absolute evil was declared a negative fixed point in a unified European and global culture of remembrance. In a series of conferences, experts and diplomats defined pedagogical and didactic standards, developed practical instructions for action to combat antisemitism and racism, and transplanted Holocaust museums, some of which were privately financed, to various countries.

For the broader European public, the introduction of 27 January as "Holocaust Remembrance Day" has proved highly effective. But what was supposed to be a negative founding consensus in Europe has become for the countries of Eastern Europe, an entry ticket to the European Union.[8] That is where resistance stirred, where experiences of the terror of the communist system were felt to be much more oppressive. Other Western and Northern European states on the periphery of the genocidal process did not find that their national memories were represented by

Holocaust education. Finally, historians and other experts have criticized the decontextualization of genocide, its causal reduction to antisemitism, the erasure of other victim groups, and a tendency toward anthropologization that is associated with the universalization of Auschwitz.

The revival of totalitarianism theory, which was developed during the Cold War, amounted to more than an attempt to integrate the historical experiences of new member states into European memory. Who would doubt that the millions of victims of communist terror should have the same right to commemoration and remembrance as the victims of the Nazis? Unlike Holocaust education, however, totalitarianism theory claims to synthesize the memory of the concentration camp with the memory of the Gulag. Here, it is not a matter of the scientifically legitimate—even indispensable—comparison of genocide and crime. Rather, it is a matter of equating them a priori, despite all the denials in soapbox speeches. While officially there is no intention to set the sufferings of the victims against each other to allow for the emergence of first- and second-class victims, there is a search for historical analogies to prove essential similarities between the crimes. From the perspectives of the victims, as stated in the European Parliament Resolution on European Conscience and Totalitarianism,[9] the particular regime that deprived them of liberty and tortured or murdered them for whatever reasons becomes irrelevant.

Strategic Decontextualization

If the devastation of Warsaw in 1944 and the murder of hundreds of thousands of people, for instance, are considered the worst example of "cooperative destruction" (Snyder 2008: 36) between the Soviet Union and Nazi Germany, or if shootings of Polish officers by the Soviet secret service in Katyń and the mass murders of representatives of the Polish elite carried out by the SS and Wehrmacht are seen as the result of a common or at least consistent plan, then the analysis of historical contexts and causes takes a backseat to moral verdicts. No longer is it a question of explaining and justifying historical events and processes but only of commemorating and condemning them. This decontextualization can lead to a reassessment of crimes in comparisons of Stalinism and National Socialism. British historian Norman Davies writes in this vein in *Heart of Europe: The Past in Poland's Present*:

> Indeed, in the light of the subsequent reversal of policy, it could be argued that at this stage [1939–41] the Soviet terror in many ways exceeded that of the Nazis. The Stalinist system had a head start on the Nazis with

regard to the techniques and logistics of terror, having built up the necessary machinery during the recent purges in its own country. At a time when the Germans were still refining their preparations for Auschwitz or Treblinka, the Soviets could accommodate a few million Polish and West Ukrainian additions to the population of their "Gulag archipelago" with relative ease. Although they preferred to condemn their victims to a long slow death from cold and starvation, in contrast to Nazi methods of summary murder—and who is to say which was the more humane?—the effect was much of the same.

Not only does the acclaimed British historian gloss over the entire prehistory of the concentration camp system, from Dachau to Buchenwald, Flossenbürg, and Mauthausen via Sachsenhausen, but he also conceals that most of the victims of the Holocaust were literally slaughtered by task forces. He comes disturbingly close to the self-assessment of the mass murderers who claimed that with the gas chambers, they had invented a more "humane" form of human extermination.

The Compulsion to Standardize

Following this logic, the Sachsenhausen Memorial, for example, renders insignificant whether the terrible mass deaths suffered by prisoners of the Soviet special camps from 1945 to 1950—as a result of starvation and illness on account of prison conditions that could be designated criminal—are interpreted as the result of a plan of premeditated murder, or if typical Stalinist indifference to human lives against the backdrop of a famine devastating large parts of Central and Eastern Europe is to blame. Anyone who mentions such differences and qualifies them as distinguishing features is regarded suspiciously not only by victim support organizations and interest groups, but also by parts of the public and political spheres.

The compulsion to standardize events is of course particularly strong in places with multiple histories of suffering. In Sachsenhausen, for example, between 1936 and 1945, the National Socialist concentration camp served as the administrative center of the entire concentration camp system, as well as Berlin's nearby SS model and training camp. It was followed in 1945 by the largest Soviet special camp, and for a long time, there was no way to achieve an overarching, common commemoration of victims of different dictatorships that did not once again tear open deep rifts and wounds, even—or especially when—it was endorsed by the state. In these conditions, even science finds it difficult to assert itself against instrumentalization and appropriation. The multicausal history of the special camps and the extraordinary heterogeneity in the composition of the prisoner population cannot be grasped with simple explanatory models that are politically and morally desired.

The complexity of real historical events breaks down as a result of a seemingly overpowering need for clear and unambiguous systems of guilt, assessment, and evaluation. On the one hand, special camps were sites of detention for Nazi perpetrators, and on the other, a German branch of the Soviet Gulag system. The results produce suspicion, mutual recrimination, and insults. The more the process of unifying remembrance and commemoration is forced for political reasons, the more violent the conflicts will be. Only through the unfettered juxtaposition of historical narratives is it possible to gradually and slowly achieve—as has been the experience at Sachsenhausen—an understanding of commonalities and differences between the various crimes committed there.

Example of 23 August 1939

The problematic consequences of establishing a standard European culture of remembrance by decree can be illustrated by the introduction of 23 August as a day of remembrance for the victims of totalitarian and authoritarian dictatorships.

Selecting the day on which the so-called Hitler-Stalin Pact was signed runs the risk of dislodging the beginning of World War II from its context and dissolving it into a new historical construct. This creates the impression that after 1 September 1939, war and genocide were the result of a conflict between totalitarian dictatorships and democratically liberal states.

Yet nothing could be further from the truth. For the most part, the decision by the National Socialists to invade Poland was established by 1933 at the very latest, owing to the racist and antisemitic ideology of *Lebensraum*. Meanwhile, the Soviet Union, at least until the Munich Agreement, negotiated a serious agreement not only with the Western powers but also with Poland. And, finally, Poland at the time was an authoritarian, partly nationalistic, and antisemitic state. Shortly before the pact, it participated in the so-called dismemberment of the only democratic and liberal Eastern European state—Czechoslovakia—which, unlike Poland, had given refuge and protection to German exiles and resistance fighters. Poland was, therefore, anything but the antithesis of a totalitarian dictatorship.

In the interest of not being misunderstood, I would like to add that we must also confront with great acceptance and understanding the subjective experiences of suffering that Andrzej Wajda (2007) captured in his recent award-winning film *Katyń*. Both invaders attacked Poland, and in particular the Polish elite, using similar terror and committing countless crimes. Alaida Assmann (2006: 269) rightly warns that any insight into historical events must not silence the truth of selective experience. But experience must be contextualized. Memorial sites must not stop at merely presenting and interpreting experiences of suffering if they do not wish to encourage an irreconcilable solipsism. Thus, the European Parliament's attempt to establish an anti-totalitarian culture of remembrance in Europe by decree accepts a precarious decontextualization—the consequences of which are not yet foreseeable—at the expense of blurring clear historical causalities and unambiguous responsibilities.

The "comprehensive reassessment of European history" in the explanatory statement makes clear just how serious the authors of the resolution on Europe's conscience really are.[10] Their aim is not only to pay tribute to the victims of communist terror—for which the October Revolution might have been more fitting as a day of remembrance—but also to elevate a political theory to the status of master narrative that is binding for Europe and relegates competing explanatory models to the sidelines.

Contested Sites in the "Battle of Remembrance"

Many authors and scholars describe the emergence of a new collective European culture of remembrance using warlike terms: "battlefields," "battles of interpretation," "weapons," "mobilization," "enemies," "dividing lines," "trenches," or—as Harald Welzer (2007) puts it—the "war of remembrance." Other military terms are used to characterize conflicts around the European politics of remembrance. As the head of a memorial foundation, long exposed to the conflicts and rivalries of remembrance, I understand the choice of vocabulary. As representatives of memorial sites and museums of contemporary history, we must be clear that our place in this "battle" for Europe's remembrance, according to the wishes of governments, parties, and interest groups, should forge a considerable part of the weaponry with which it is conducted. Where interpretations of the past become an instrument of political influence, museums and memorial sites are founded, expanded, or redesigned in quick succession to freeze an interpretation of history in stone, concrete, or glass.

What is striking is that a large number of these newly founded history museums—such as the House of Terror Museum founded by the conservative-liberal Fidesz government in Budapest in 2001, or the Warsaw Rising Museum established by Kaczynski, the city's mayor at the time—work by staging history, apparently hoping to generate simple answers rather than questions regarding the past. These are adventure museums, where visitors can stand behind machine guns and assume the role of heroes who combat evil. In contrast to most earlier memorials, these museums have been designed to overwhelm the public and thus hardly offer any alternative view of history. They do not promote the development of independent judgment and do not shy away from using creative or financial means to convey to visitors the preconceived and unambiguous doctrines of the politics of remembrance. This is one reason why they have proved extremely popular with the public.

From the perspective of memorial pedagogy, decontextualization and dedifferentiation in favor of historical or even anthropological themes that are to encompass different criminal episodes must be questioned. Can all the evil in the world really be traced to the differences between totalitarian and open societies? Accordingly, are the victims of (nontotalitarian) military dictatorships, for example, second-class victims? And are the casualties of World War I third-class victims? To which category do the dead of the massacres of Srebrenica or Darfur belong? Is it even worth remembering the fifteen thousand victims of the Sétif massacre, perpetrated against the Algerian population by French troops on 8 May 1945?

Finally, one must ask to what extent master narratives—whether Holocaust education or totalitarian theory—are suitable as a transnational hermeneutic. How much did the history of Germany, after the unprocessed trauma of World War I, contribute to the expansionist policies of National Socialism, and how much is explained by the totalitarian structures of the Nazi system? How much of the subjugation of East-Central Europe by the Soviet Union after the end of World War II derived from Russian power politics, and what part did the Stalinist system play? The strength of the theory of totalitarianism lies, in my opinion, in explaining internal social processes in dictatorships. But as far as the changing relationships between European states in the twentieth century is concerned, both master narratives seem to have too little explanatory power.

An Apple of Discord: The Center Against Expulsions

In Germany, Poland, and the Czech Republic, heated debates on the planned Center Against Expulsions offer additional proof that the attempt to recontextualize through Europeanization does not mitigate explosive problems. Demands from liberals and critics to embed this topic in a European context in hopes of defusing highly emotional conflicts that endanger transnational and neighborly relations threaten to turn into the opposite of what was originally intended. From a discourse enriched with different histories of expulsion in Europe, a new explanatory model is emerging, according to which ethnic cleansing has been carried out by all sides in the process of nation building, at least since the nineteenth century. In this light, the brutal expulsions of millions of Germans after the end of World War II appear less as a primary consequence of Nazi crimes. Instead, according to some—conservative historians, in particular—these expulsions were opportunities to carry out long-planned ethnic cleansing. Of course, there is no lack of references to the interplay of totalitarian dictatorships, which many people in Central and Eastern European countries now seem willing to swallow (Kittel and Möller 2006).

Memorials and Their Tasks: Nine Principles

Memorial sites shoulder great responsibility. They must defend the dignity of victims against any appropriation and keep the interpretation of the past open if they wish to stimulate more critical, independent contemplations of history rather than affirming the alleged lessons of history. My view is therefore that memorial sites and museums of modern history must communicate nationally and internationally. Only by working together can they overcome efforts at political instrumentalization in Europe that seek to overcome a profound crisis of purpose and identity through the historico-political setting of new and collective cultures of remembrance that have been partly created by decree, and which in turn aggravate struggles for interpretation and rivalries between groups of victims. The organizational framework required for this international association has already been created. The International Committee of Memorial Sites in Remembrance of the Victims of Public Crimes (IC-MEMO), founded a few years ago, is being incorporated into the International Council of Museums (ICOM), which is committed to the general ethical and political principles contained in the UN Charter, universal human and civil rights, and the careful preservation of traditional cultural heritage.

IC-MEMO encompasses diverse memorial sites for the victims of state tyranny. These are located in Asia, Europe, Africa, and the United States. This international association of memorial sites offers new possibilities to influence macro-level political decisions. This became clear in the German Bundestag's discussions of a motion for a resolution regarding the further development of the memorial site concept. An initiative associated with a former Bundestag CDU member and construed by most Nazi victim organizations and memorial experts as an attempt to blend different persecution complexes was successfully averted with international assistance, which was largely initiated by IC-MEMO.

While memorial sites need to share a common organization and enjoy better international networking, they should also agree on general principles of remembrance and commemoration. It cannot be a matter of enshrining a "DIY standard of remembrance," as Timothy Garton Ash has stated, but rather of initiating a European or international process to which memorial sites voluntarily commit. An international memorial charter, based on both the UN Declaration and the ethical principles of ICOM, might be helpful. In the following paragraphs, I will try to formulate some general principles that I think are useful to stimulating a common discussion among international memorial sites:

1. A common European culture of remembrance cannot and must not be decreed. In light of different historical experiences, memorial sites profess a juxtaposition of remembrance imperatives. Seeking a pluralist culture of remembrance, memorial sites serve as places where these remembrance imperatives join together in dialogue but not in a struggle for interpretation or suppression. If it makes any sense at all, a common European culture of remembrance might slowly emerge from the bottom up, from a multitude of decentralized initiatives.

2. The pluralist culture of remembrance needs a common positive-value framework. This already exists in the Universal Declaration of Human Rights. Further conclusions about, or even creations of, a sense of value are not required.

3. Memorials and museums of contemporary history remind people above all of state crimes committed predominantly against minorities. States and governments, therefore, have a special responsibility for memorials, whose existence they must guarantee alongside their independence from political directives. At the same time, memorial sites must be anchored as broadly as possible in civil society, and minorities in particular must be integrated.

4. Modern memorials are museums of contemporary history with special humanitarian and educational tasks. Only when a certain internationally recognized level of qualitative work and personnel

organization has been achieved can memorial sites hold their own against representatives of the political sphere and interest groups.

5. Basic decisions regarding the memorial site's content, pedagogy, and design should be made primarily on the basis of open, non-hierarchical, and pluralistic discussion with survivors, academics, stakeholders, and committed social groups. As much as possible, state institutions and private sponsors should not influence these opinion-forming and coordination processes.

6. When communicating historical events in exhibitions, publications, and educational projects, empathy with victims should be encouraged without activating the "malignant potential of memories in the form of revenge, hatred, resentment" (Assmann 2006: 267).

7. Historical experiences must be placed in historical context, without relativizing the personal suffering of the individual person. The classification of historical events takes place at the level of modern contemporary historical research and is committed to the scientific principles of discursivity and multiperspectivity. This includes the views of perpetrators of crimes who are not demonized, but whose actions are to be explained on the basis of their ideologies, goals, and motives. The ability to question one's own point of view includes a willingness to include what Reinhart Koselleck calls "negative history" (2002: 25)—that is, taking one's crimes and self-perceptions into account when representing the "other."

8. Memorials at historically authentic sites of crimes open up great potential and risks for historico-political education. Memorials should, therefore, gear their educational work less to content than common principles, as formulated, for example, in 1976 in the so-called "Beutelsbach Consensus" (Widmaier and Zorn: 2016). These, above all, prohibit overwhelming and indoctrinating the pupil, preserve the individual's subject position, and maintain the rule of controversiality.

9. Memorial sites and museums of contemporary history are in danger of reflecting currents in the Zeitgeist and thus codifying presentist interpretations of the past instead of historical events. They should therefore always reflect self-critically on their own history, which should be embedded in a history of the respective culture of remembrance.

The "Bequest" of the Survivors

This year, on Remembrance Day of the Victims of National Socialism (27 January), the presidents of the international prisoner committees of Auschwitz, Bergen-Belsen, Buchenwald, Dachau, Flossenbürg, Mittelbau-Dora, Neuengamme, Ravensbrück, and Sachsenhausen presented a joint statement to the president of the German Bundestag. The "bequest" of concentration camp survivors, as they called the declaration, included not only the memories of the terrible years of their imprisonment, but also their often bitter experiences with Europe's memory of the unparalleled crimes of the Nazi regime. From the point of view of the survivors, the statement specifies the future tasks and requirements of a European culture of remembrance:

> But Europe also has its task: instead of asserting our ideals for democracy, peace, tolerance, self-determination, and human rights, history is too often used to sow discord between human beings, groups, and peoples. We object to the comparative assignment of blame, to the creation of hierarchies in the experiences of suffering, of competition between victims, and the confusion of historical phases. For this reason, we endorse the words of the former President of the European Parliament, Simone Veil, when she addressed the German Parliament in 2004 and appealed for the transmission of memory: "Europe should recognize and stand by its mutual past as a whole, with all the bright and dark sides; every member state should know about its mistakes and failures, and acknowledge they are at peace with their past, so that they can be at peace with their neighbors."[11]

Günter Morsch was director of the Brandenburg Memorials Foundation and head of the Sachsenhausen Memorial and Museum until 2018. He studied modern history, psychology, and philosophy at the Technische Universität and Freie Universität in Berlin. In 1988, he was awarded his doctorate with the dissertation "Arbeit und Brot. Studies on the Situation, Mood, Attitude, and Behavior of the German Workforce, 1933–1936/37." He worked as a research assistant on various large historical exhibition projects. In January 1993, he began his work as director of the Sachsenhausen Memorial and Museum. In 1997, he was assigned the duties of the director of the Brandenburg Memorials Foundation, which includes institutions in Ravensbrück, Brandenburg/Havel, and Potsdam-Leistikovstrasse in addition to Sachsenhausen. Since 1993, he has worked as a lecturer at the Otto Suhr Institute of Freie Universität Berlin, and in 2001, was appointed honorary professor. His publications focus on the history of the Nazi regime, the history of the SBZ/GDR, the industrial and social history of the nineteenth century, the history of the Weimar Republic, Jewish history, memorials, the Sachsenhausen memorial, the history of the concentration camp system, and the politics and culture of remembrance in Europe. Morsch has served on numerous museum and memorial committees, including the Board of Trustees of the Memorial to the Murdered Jews of Europe Foundation.

Notes

This essay has already been published as "Geschichte als Waffe" in the Blätter für deutsche und internationale Politik 5 (2010), 109–121. It has been revised and supplemented with references for this publication. The "Charter" proposed at the end of the essay was discussed and accepted by the memorial and museum working group of the Task Force for International Cooperation on Holocaust Education, Remembrance and Research in Jerusalem in June 2010 and at the general meeting of IC-MEMO in October 2010.

1. The declaration was published in various places. Since the list of signatories did not always remain the same, please refer to the website of the Foundation for the Study of Communist Dictatorship in East Germany, www.23August1939.de; cf. also my comment in the Jüdische Allgemeine (Morsch 2009, 1).

2. European Parliament Resolution of 2 April 2009 on European Conscience and Totalitarianism, P6_TA-PROV(2009)0213, accessed 7 December 2017, www.europarl.europa.eu/sides/getDoc.do?pubRef=-//EP//TEXT+TA+P6-TA-2009-0213+0+DOC+XML+V0//DE. Cf. also the motion relating to this: European Parliament, Plenary session document of 30 March 2009, European Parliament Resolution on European Conscience and Totalitarianism, accessed 7 December 2017, RC\778929EN.doc, www.europarl.europa.eu/sides/getDoc.do?pubRef=-//EP//NONSGML+MOTION+P6-RC-2009-0165+0+DOC+PDF+V0//DE. According to the undated press release from the European Parliament, the resolution was adopted with 553 votes in favor, forty-four against, and thirty-three abstentions. This was preceded by a public hearing on 18 March 2009 (European Conscience and Crimes of Totalitarian Communism: 20 Years After), convened by Alexander Vondra, deputy prime minister of European affairs, and Milena Micenová, permanent representative of the Czech Republic to the EU.

3. European Parliament Resolution of 2 April 2009 on European Conscience and Totalitarianism, point 10.

4. Ibid., point K.

5. Ibid., point 13.

6. Resolution on European and International Protection for Nazi Concentration Camps as Historical Monuments of 11 February 1993 in Official Journal of the European Communities 15 (March 1993), no. C 72/118.

7. Ibid., 1.

8. See Judt 2006.

9. European Parliament Resolution of 2 April 2009 on European Conscience and Totalitarianism, P6_TA-PROV(2009)0213, accessed 7 December 2017, www.europarl.europa.eu/sides/getDoc.do?pubRef=-//EP//TEXT+TA+P6-TA-2009-0213+0+DOC+XML+V0//DE.

10. European Parliament Resolution of 2 April 2009 on European Conscience and Totalitarianism, point 10.

11. The "Bequest" has been published many times and can also be found on the websites of most concentration camp memorial sites. The text is printed, e.g., in the magazine *Gegen Vergessen. Für Demokratie*, May 2004, 14–19, here 18.

References

Assmann, Alaida. 2006. *Der lange Schatten der Vergangenheit. Erinnerungskultur und Geschichtspolitik.* Munich.
Beattie, Andrew H. 2007. "Learning from the Germans? History and Memory in German and European Projects of Integration." *Portal Journal of Multidisciplinary International Studies* 4, no. 2: 1–22.
Cornelißen, Christoph. 2003. "Was heißt Erinnerungskulture? Begriff – Methoden – Perspektiven." *Geschichte in Wissenschaft und Unterricht* 54: 548–563.
Davies, Norman. 2000. *Im Herzen Europas. Geschichte Polens.* Munich.
Judt, Tony. 2006. *Die Geschichte Europas seit dem Zweiten Weltkrieg.* Bonn.
Kalniete, Sandra. 2008. "Eine gemeinsame Geschichtserzählung für Europa?" In *Vergangenheit in der Gegenwart. Vom Umgang mit Diktaturerfahrungen in Ost- und Westeuropa*, edited by T. Großbölting and D. Hoffman, 131–139. Göttingen.
Kertész, Imre. 2007. "Europas bedrückende Erbschaft." *Aus Politik und Zeitgeschichte*, nos. 1–2: 3–6.
Kittel, Manfred, and Horst Möller. 2006. "Die 'Benes-Dekrete' und die Vertreibung der Deutschen." *Vierteljahreshefte für Zeitgeschichte* 54, no. 4: 541–582.
Koselleck, Reinhart. 2002. "Formen und Traditionen des negativen Gedächtnisses." In *Verbrechen erinnern. Die Auseinandersetzung mit Holocaust und Völkermord*, edited by Volkhard Knigge, 21–32. Munich.
Larat, Fabrice. 2008. "Aufarbeitung der Vergangenheit und Zivilisierung Europas." In *"Schmerzliche Erfahrungen der Vergangenheit" und der Prozess der Konstitutionalisierung Europas*, edited by Joerges Christian, Matthias Mahlmann, and Ulrich K. Preuß, 48–62. Wiesbaden.
Leggewie, Claus. 2009. "Schlachtfeld Europa. Transnationale Erinnerung und europäische Identität." *Blätter für deutsche und internationale Politik* 54, no. 2: 81–94.
Morsch, Günter. 2009. "Schlachtfeld EU. Wie der Jahrestag des Hitler-Stalin-Pakts für einen erinnerungspolitischen Deutungskampf missbraucht wird." *Jüdische Allgemeine* 34 (20 August 2009): 1.
———. 2010. "Geschichte als Waffe." *Blätter für deutsche und internationale Politik*, no. 5: 109–121.
Rousso, Henri. 2004. "Das Dilemma eines Europäischen Gedächtnisses." *Zeithistorische Forschungen* 3: 363–375.
———. 2007. "Vers une mondialisation de la mémoire." *Vingtième Siècle. Revue d'histoire* 94: 3–10.

Snyder, Timothy. 2008. "Diktaturen in Osteuropa: Regionalgeschichte oder europäisches Erbe?" In *Vergangenheit in der Gegenwart*, edited by T. Großbölting and D. Hofmann, 33–42. Göttingen.

Verbeeck, Georgi. 2008. "Erinnerungspolitik in Belgien." *Aus Politik und Zeitgeschichte*, no. 8: 25–31.

Wajda, Andrzej, dir. 2007. *Katyń*. Film in Polish. Produced by Akson Studio, TVP, Polski Instytut Sztuki Filmowej, and Telekomunikacja Polska.

Welzer, Harald, ed. 2007. *Der Krieg der Erinnerung. Holocaust, Kollaboration und Widerstand im europäischen Gedächtnis*. Frankfurt a. M.

Widmaier, Benedikt, and Peter Zorn, eds. 2016. *Brauchen wir den Beutelsbacher Konsens? Eine Debatte der politischen Bildung*. Bonn.

Chapter 16

Analogies and Imbalances

The Effects of Memorial Site Policies on Dealing with
Places from the GDR Past on NS Reappraisal

Carola S. Rudnick

The following pages explore how the politics of remembrance of the German Democratic Republic (GDR) have affected the treatment of the National Socialist (NS) era. It traces important milestones in the handling of the GDR, as well as possible directions for the overall German landscape of remembrance. Since it is hardly possible to examine scientific, judicial, cultural, and political reconditioning initiatives and accompanying debates in the scope of a single chapter, I will attempt to examine the correlation between reappraisals of the GDR and NS by looking closely at memorial site policies. This essay includes the following theses:

First, in 1989/1990, researchers and politicians underestimated how the coming reappraisal of the Soviet Occupation Zone (German: Sowjetische Besatzungszone, SBZ) and the GDR would have a fundamental impact on the ways that contemporary history was dealt with. This meant not only an end to GDR antifascism but also a belated rethinking of the culture of remembrance in the old Federal Republic. The spirit of antifascism pervaded memorial sites of the former GDR, generating massive political pressures to act. It is a prank of history that East German initiatives for dealing with SBZ/GDR crimes achieved something that the ambitious West German civic, peace, and historical initiatives of the late 1970s and

1980s, as well as internationally organized Holocaust victims groups, failed to achieve for decades: a memorial policy firmly anchored in federal politics in the form of promoting and safeguarding a pluralistic, civic, and human rights–oriented memorial landscape. This memorial policy was "invented" less by the historians' guild and more by governmental action and symbolic power, which is described in the first part of this chapter.

Second, at the same time and in concert with governmental action, the end of the GDR refocused contemporary historical analysis and prompted a reassessment of the layers of the German past and the international dimensions of crimes committed. Thus, NS research and NS remembrance lost its de facto "singularity." Since the victims of Stalinism were also to be given a place in the collective memory, the victims of Nazi terror were "joined" by the victims of Stalinist terror. Victims of concentration camps and forced labor were joined by victims of the Gulag, even if in the collective memory, industrial mass extermination continued to represent an incomparable breach of civilization. When the Wall fell, paradigms of memory also crumbled. How was that possible? How was memorial policy "invented?" What interpretations of contemporary history were advanced? This chapter attempts to answer these questions.[1]

The Smoldering Fire and New Foundation Myths

After the demise of the GDR, historical reappraisal by the upper echelons of the political establishment did not even resemble something like a smoldering fire. With the exceptions of the dismantling of the monuments and symbols of socialism, the renaming of streets, and the rapid demolition of the Berlin Wall, the introduction of October 3 as the Day of German Unity, the abolition of GDR Remembrance Days, and the extensive dismissal of GDR historians immediately before and after the GDR's accession, political elites, especially West Germans, showed little interest in history. At first, there was no political awareness on behalf of the government of a need to comprehensively reappraise the dictatorial past. Like the immediate postwar period, politicians did not want to touch this political "hot potato." The prevailing view was that after the end of the Cold War, any policy with a history that had been nourished by the Cold War could be shelved for the long term. With its superficial treatment of public space, the dismantling of the GDR regime by the federal government seems to have ended by 1992 (Eckert 1996: 215–216). In the spirit of the conservative government, this short-lived "eradication of socialist historical symbols" was accompanied by a search for new founding myths, such as "German unity." Thus 17 June 1953 was reinterpreted as a harbinger of 9 November 1989 (Wolfrum 1999: 356). The reform movements of autumn 1989 were declared a popular "vote by feet" with the goal of "German unity,"[2] while lively myths about the glorious citizens' movement and opposition groups circulated (Pollack 1995: 34–35). This first wave of historico-political activities and historical interpretations, which lasted until 1992, corresponded with the legitimized government's desire for the fastest possible integration of East Germans into the new republic while removing all references to the GDR past and historical images.

Less harmonious was the process of historical reappraisal at the grassroots level. In 1990, for example, victims of the SBZ and the GDR, who had been forced to remain silent until 1989, experienced a conflagration of re-education and remembrance, supported by various civic movements and victims associations. Yet due to a lack of financial security, the fixation on state terror, state security, and Stalinist crimes, and everyday problems facing citizens of the new federal states, this fire threatened to go out by 1992 at the latest (Boll 1999: 24–25). "What took place in phases, one after the other after 1945 when dealing with the National Socialist past . . . all took place simultaneously and with great emotional intensity," which for Wielenga (1994: 1064), justified "symptoms of fatigue."

Initially, the governing parties became politically involved only when and where totalitarian theory could be revived. Thus, as a reaction, so to speak, against tendencies toward trivialization (*Ostalgia* or "nostalgia for the East"), and in accordance with the fixation on GDR state security and the apparatus of rule, the vacuum for coming to terms with the past was filled by conservative scholars and politicians who sought to determine the course of historiography by forcing comparisons between dictatorships and founding a research institute for that purpose (the Hannah Arendt Institute for Totalitarianism Research). As early as April 1991, the Saxon State Parliament decided in favor of the founding of an Institute for Research on the Resistance against Dictatorship and Tyranny from 1918 to 1990 in Saxony. The federal government supported this development; the creation of an institute seemed to be enough to deal with the situation. But this sparked discussion and provoked considerable criticism. Institutional analogies to the NS dictatorship and continuities between NS and the SBZ/GDR had been prematurely constructed, or brought to the fore, and declared the vanguard of contemporary historical research. Left-wing scholars, and, in particular, NS victim representatives, rejected the totalitarian model as a strategy that trivialized, leveled, and relativized, and insisted that not only in Saxony but also in future debates, NS and the SBZ/GDR should be dealt with as fundamentally different, separate entities (Wallbaum 1991; Leyrer 1992). Despite this opposition, the Institute began its work in 1992 as the first academic institution for systematic research on the GDR dictatorship (Bäumel 1992).

The establishment of the new institute was therefore tantamount to a scandal, since the major memorials and numerous citizens' initiatives founded between autumn 1989 and the accession in 1990 to deal with wide-ranging areas of the GDR's past were under existential threat. It became necessary to fundamentally clarify not only the existing landscape of memorial sites but also how to deal with new SBZ/GDR-related crime sites. These included places where special camps[3] operated after 1945, former prisons, places of German division, and former centers of power.

A Readjustment of the Politics of Memory and History

To counteract an "offside trap," on the one hand, and leveling tendencies toward NS, on the other, a readjustment of the politics of memory and history became necessary. Because of uncertainty surrounding the future of the GDR's major memorials and the urgent need to revise their contents—but also because of chronic underfunding of NS memorials in West Germany and the existential threat to many smaller reappraisal initiatives—at first only a few individuals pleaded for the development of criteria for federal funding. Both old and new states seemed financially overburdened by this task. These individuals were concerned with federal funding for memorials in the five new federal states but also with equipping memorials in the old federal states. They aimed for an all-German solution from the federal government in the form of comprehensive participation at memorial sites in Germany. As early as September 1991, the Social Democratic Party of Germany (SPD) submitted a preliminary motion for the uniform federal regulation of former memorial sites of the GDR, calling on the federal government to submit a concept for its participation at memorial sites.[4] With the introduction of a second, more comprehensive, motion in August 1992, the SPD parliamentary group extended its demand for a federal solution to the memorial site situation to the territory of the entire Federal Republic, including NS memorial sites in West Germany. At the same time, the SPD demanded that the equation of the NS and GDR dictatorships be prohibited because of their differences and sought to overcome the instrumentalization of memorial sites. Their demand: "The crimes of National Socialism must not be relativized by the crimes of Stalinism, nor the crimes of Stalinism trivialized by reference to the crimes of National Socialism." These were not merely words;[5] the motion recommended, for example, promoting places where politically persecuted people experienced consecutive injustices.[6]

Conservative-liberal government factions rejected federal participation at memorial sites, citing the competence of states and municipalities. Initially, the federal government saw its duty fulfilled with the establishment of a central memorial to the memory of all victims of war and tyranny in the Neue Wache (New Guardhouse) in Berlin. The Kultusministerkonferenz (Conference of the Ministers of Education) and the Bundesministerium des Innern (Federal Ministry of the Interior) agreed with black-yellow government factions.[7] They supported the construction of memorials for the victims of Stalinism and commemoration of the division of Germany without exception and according to the capabilities of the federal states.[8] The expansion of federal participation was rejected as "not scientifically justified."[9] The German Historical Museum, appearing as an expert, proposed at least a case-by-case examination for memorials at Buchenwald, Sachsenhausen, Bergen-Belsen, Ravensbrück, Neuengamme, Mittelbau-Dora, and Bernburg, and of places of national importance in Berlin and its surroundings in Brandenburg.[10]

The *Gesamtkonzeption zur Beteiligung des Bundes an Gedenkstätten in der Bundesrepublik Deutschland* (Overall concept for the participation of the federal state in memorial sites in the Federal Republic of Germany), presented by the Federal Ministry of the Interior on 5 May 1992, formulated the principles for federal participation at memorial sites.[11] But following the example of the Deutsches Historisches Museum (German Historical Museum), which argued for examining sites on a case-by-case basis, the principles were limited to ten years. The promotion of memorial sites would remain an interim solution. On 24 March 1993, the Budget Committee approved this compromise with the proviso that financial participation by the federal government would remain limited to the new federal states.[12] Although the CDU/FDP (Christian Democratic Union of Germany / Free Democratic Party) government also adopted the eligibility principles and the criteria of the SPD initiative without restrictions,[13] it did not accept their demand that West German memorials of national importance should also be included. NS memorials on the territory of the old Federal Republic thus had to hope for municipal support and state funding until further notice.

In the meantime, tough negotiations regarding East German places of remembrance and Berlin institutions were taking place, and decisions were being made with the help of experts. This, however, affected only the former Buchenwald and Sachsenhausen memorial sites and the Berlin NS memorials Haus der Wannseekonferenz (the villa where the Wannsee Conference took place), the Topography of Terror, and the German Resistance Memorial Center in Bendlerblock. The last two memorials received federal institutional funding in June 1993,[14] alongside the

Memorial to the Murdered Jews of Europe, the Brandenburg Memorials Foundation, and the Mittelbau-Dora Memorial in November 1993.[15] In the field of SBZ/GDR reappraisal, the memorials Berlin-Hohenschönhausen, Bautzen, and Mödlareuth were promised institutional funding as well as the Torgau Memorial project funds, provided that Saxony and Berlin submitted concepts and financed them on behalf of the state. In addition, it was recommended that the federal government bear all construction costs for the Berlin Wall Memorial. Only subsidies for a memorial in Marienborn and a memorial in Waldheim were rejected. The same applied to the NS Euthanasia Memorial in Bernburg. Due to the focus on East Germany, the internationally renowned West German memorials Neuengamme and Bergen-Belsen did not figure in the discussions.[16] The government did not want these NS memorials to be promoted by the federal government. Its conservative historical policy was to ensure that only German victims— soldiers, bombing casualties, resistance fighters, and SS officers—were remembered at a central location in Berlin. The federal government's "overall concept for memorial sites in the Federal Republic of Germany" was still a long way from a uniform, nationwide regulation.

The "Anti-Totalitarian Consensus"

In the course of the work carried out by the Enquete Commissions, which were established by the German Bundestag between 1992 and 1998, this situation changed. In 1992–1994, the Enquete Commission for the Reappraisal of History and Consequences of the SED Dictatorship in Germany revealed that engagement with the SBZ/GDR dictatorship could not take place without references to the NS dictatorship. Social Democratic and left-wing lobbyists and experts were primarily concerned with demarcating the two German dictatorships and drawing sharp distinctions between Stalinism, present-day socialism, and National Socialism, while deputies and experts for the governing parties spoke of "the two socialist sides of the same coin"—that is, the proximity and similarities between both totalitarian systems. Occasionally, they even portrayed the GDR as the more totalitarian dictatorship, thus relativizing the crimes of National Socialism. Examples included equating the special camps of the Soviet zone with NS concentration camps, the Stasi with the Gestapo, and the Socialist Unity Party of Germany (SED)[17] with the National Socialist German Workers' Party (NSDAP). The discussions temporarily amalgamated communism and National Socialism (Faulenbach 1997: 83; Elm 1997a: 208–210; Elm 1997b: 55–56). Representatives of the SPD and the Party of Democratic Socialism (PDS), who adhered to the singularity of NS crimes and appealed to the world-historical ambitions of the NS regime, argued against this view. Experts on the left and close to the SPD attempted to counteract the interpretation of the GDR through the lens of totalitarianism by drawing on differentiated perspectives and analyses (Rudnick 2011: 48–63).

In the end, the Commission concluded across party lines that unilateral support for memorials to the victims of the SBZ/GDR dictatorship would leave a bitter taste for the international community and undermine the idea that a united Germany had rid itself of its NS past and its sources. At the same time, even long-serving antifascists had to admit that the reappraisal of the NS dictatorship was no longer "singular" but that, in addition to NS memorials, new ones commemorating Stalinist or communist crimes now also had a right to exist. The "anti-totalitarian consensus" reached at the end of the first Enquete Commission turned the "singularity" of the "brown" NS to "red." But it also helped end opposition to the promotion of decentralized West German NS memorials.

In particular, the second commission, the Enquete Commission on Overcoming the Consequences of the SED Dictatorship in the Process of German Unity, changed the memorial landscape and established an unprecedented pan-German memorial policy. The second commission's main objective was to develop regulations for the continuation of SBZ/GDR historical reappraisal. Beyond a doubt, this was to include safeguarding the "culture of remembrance" in the form of concrete recommendations for action to promote memorial sites. Guidelines that were to be drawn up for dealing with the GDR past could not ignore the way the NS culture of remembrance was dealt with but had to remain valid for the NS past as well. It was therefore necessary to find solutions for an equal remembrance of different crimes without suggesting a "ranking" of crimes. It was also necessary to prevent an equivalence between victim groups, which was strongly rejected, especially by Holocaust victims.

Since 1992, the sensitive issue of the equal remembrance of victims of successive injustices has caused bitter disputes between various groups and their lobbies. Two groups of special camp victims demanded belated recognition for their suffering. These were people imprisoned by the Soviet occupying power on suspicion of National Socialist involvement after the end of the war and in the context of denazification, or were former special camp prisoners who, beginning in 1946 and on suspicion of anti-Soviet activities, were stuck in special camps and collected the severest of sentences from the Soviet Military Tribunal (SMT). They were confronted by victims of the NS regime, who opposed the equation of suffering before and after 1945 and the softening of the concept of victim by equating deceased SS men, NSDAP group leaders, and Hitler Youth train drivers with the millions of victims of the Holocaust, NS persecution, and the German war of annihilation. The magazine *Konkret* commented, rather cynically, "According to the will of the local CDU, Buchenwald is to become a 'memorial site for all victims of human dictatorships' and thus the Jewish Muselmann [an outdated term for 'Muslim,' used here to mean 'outsider'] is to become a victim like the SS-Sturmbannführer [officer], who watered him with ice water and left him standing in the cold" (Anton 1991: 45–46).

Although today this conflict remains unresolved, the results of the memorial policy— listed in the final report titled *All-German Forms of Remembrance of the Two German Dictatorships*—no longer bore the signatures of the conservatives and liberals of the early 1990s (Deutscher Bundestag 1999: 587–588).

The Germans' commitment to inalienable and inviolable human rights as the basis of every human community was declared the core of the anti-totalitarian consensus and democratic culture of remembrance in Germany. Furthermore, the fundamental tasks of memorial sites, expectations, and prerequisites for federal funding—following the SPD recommendations of 1992—were further developed. It was agreed that the history of the dictatorships should be presented in their respective contexts, i.e. through decentralized exhibition sections and separate individual exhibitions, in order to counteract the equation of the NS regime and the GDR/SBZ with a mixture of victim groups. The final report also stated that pluralistic rather than uniform images of history should be conveyed, that there should be no hierarchization of victim groups, and that contemporary witnesses should be included wherever possible. The Enquete Commission also associated the "democratic culture of remembrance" with the claim that collective remembrance was a task for society as a whole, supported by civic commitment, by the respective state and ultimately also by the federal government. The federal government was therefore given the unique task of consolidating and further developing the heterogeneity, plurality, and decentralization of remembrance throughout Germany (Deutscher Bundestag 1999: 614–615).

The Desiderata of Memorial Policy

The results of the SBZ/GDR Reconciliation Commission were a novelty for German domestic politics and gave birth to memorial policy. The recommendations for all German forms of remembrance formed the foundation for the federal government's subsequent memorial site concept. These were incorporated without changes into the Federal Memorial Site Concept, which was implemented by the red-green federal government[18] (Deutscher Bundestag 1999: 631–632).

On 27 July 1999, the federal government presented the draft law on the Federation's participation at memorial sites of national importance.[19] In addition to a financial increase of almost 50 percent and the removal of the deadline for federal funding, the federal government's memorial concept was associated above all with the paradigm shift in remembrance and history policy that was prepared by the Enquete Commission. For the first time, a panel of experts reviewing the facts became the basis for federal endorsement. In other words, funding no longer depended on political negotiations, but rather on a specialist vote—in addition to the distinctive character of the historical site and its significance. "In this sense, the Federal Government will respect the independence of memorial sites from political directives," stated the memorial site concept.[20] In addition, federal funding was extended to the old federal states so that, for the first time, the Neuengamme concentration camp memorial site and the Bergen-Belsen memorial site also had opportunities to apply for federal funding.

This applied to other NS institutions, at least regarding project funds—subject, of course, to the budgets of the Federation and the states as well as favorable expert opinion. This has proved highly significant in several ways. First, there is no federal foundation for NS memorials comparable to the Foundation for the Reapparaisal of the SED Dictatorship for the SBZ/GDR Memorials, which has existed since 1998, and through which NS memorials might apply for project grants per project. The previously one-sided supply of SBZ/GDR memorial sites in the new federal states and Berlin from the Stiftung zur Aufarbeitung der SED-Diktatur (Foundation for the Reapparaisal of the SED Dictatorship) and the federal government's memorial site funding of 1994 was at least partially abolished with the memorial site concept of 1999. Still, to date, there has been no foundation to deal with the NS dictatorship, which would make it possible for smaller initiatives to carry out projects involving commemoration, exchange programs, exhibitions, and theater, and could promote archival and other academic research. The Stiftung Erinnerung Verantwortung Zukunft (Foundation for Remembrance, Responsibility, and the Future) offers only marginal compensation through a narrowly formulated foundation mission statement.

The nationwide memorial conference, representing more than 264 full-time and honorary memorials, spoke out in December 2016 at its conference in Cologne in favor of an urgent readjustment of federal funding. "In the course of a further development of the federal government's memorial site concept, which was last modified in 2008, a structure is to be created which . . . permits support for processing initiatives, research and educational projects, as is the case with the Federal Foundation for the Processing of the SED Dictatorship," reads an open letter dated 5 May 2017.

The establishment of the Research Network on the Topic of SED Injustice, endowed with thirty million euros, for which the budget committee created prerequisites in November 2016, has meanwhile added to the imbalance between the NS and GDR processing of the Open Letter, and has prompted the authors of the Open Letter to demand that alongside the Foundation for the Reapparaisal of the SED Dictatorship and the incipient Research Network, comparable funding is also needed in the field of NS memory.[21]

Second, the federal government's memorial concept placed NS remembrance culture in West Germany—which had grown over the decades and was supported solely by civic commitment—on equal footing with the young SBZ/GDR remembrance culture in East Germany, in terms of funding and through indirect "late recognition." The sign was clear "with regard to the principle of equal status of memorial work in the East and the West."[22] Siegfried Vergin (SPD) and Knut Nevermann (SPD) interpreted this development as a success for the SPD, since it appeared that many of its 1992 demands had been implemented (Vergin 2001: 94). The federal government's memorial site concept of 2008 also tied into this "success," even though the GDR's reappraisal of memorial sites performed better than the NS memorial site landscape in terms of new institutional federal funding since at least 2008 (Rudnick 2011: 99–100). While GDR memorials sprouted from the ground like mushrooms, NS memorials hardly managed to preserve their structure, with dramatic consequences for conservation. At various concentration camp memorial sites, barracks and foundations crumbled.

Third, the "singularity of the NS reappraisal" ended with this process and the principle of equal status; the crimes of communism were upgraded to equally relevant objects of reappraisal. At times, the commitment to meeting a backlog in demand in the field of communism reappraisal and GDR dictatorship led to the omnipresence of SBZ/GDR projects and topics in the field of research and education, especially in Berlin. It would be desirable here not only to reduce the gap between the center and the periphery, between East and West Germany, but above all to increase the commitment to no longer putting the events of the past in competition with one another.

Concluding Remarks

Since the federal government's memorial site concept in 2008, the essential outcome of the second Enquete Commission (Overcoming the Consequences of the SED Dictatorship in the Process of German Unity) was unusual and unexpected: the development of a "model" for the East German federal states that was finally also transferred to the West German states. Disputes in the federal parliament over the East German reappraisal landscape and the remembrance of the SBZ and GDR after 1990 inevitably led to new regulations for all memorial sites and processing initiatives, and finally to the federal memorial site concept, from which individual NS memorial sites in West Germany profited, despite existing imbalances (Morsch 2001; 26).

Only through the processing of the SBZ and GDR in two inquiry commissions in the German Bundestag and state support for contemporary historical initiatives and formerly central memorial sites in the new federal states was the support of concentration camp memorial sites as a whole possible. NS memorial sites in the old federal states also finally benefited from state support by the Federation. It can be argued that a paradigm shift and a functional change in the politics of history and remembrance occurred, as well as the beginning of a comprehensive memorial policy as part of the government's symbolic policy after 1990. The political crisis of the legitimation of memorials in Germany seems to have been overcome, even if historico-political lines of conflict persist. This is illustrated by the impressive demand for a foundation or research association for NS memorials to compare to the Stiftung Aufarbeitung der SED-Diktatur (the Federal Foundation for the Reappraisal of the SED Dictatorship) and the Forschungsverbund zum Thema SED-Staat (Research Association of the SED State). The Hannah Arendt Institute for Totalitarianism Research will not and should not fill this gap.

Carola S. Rudnick, born in 1976, studied cultural studies at the University of Lüneburg. From 2005 to 2009, she was a graduate fellow at the Friedrich-Ebert-Stiftung. From 2009–2011, she headed the Pedagogical Center of the Bergen-Belsen Memorial. In 2011, she completed her doctorate in history with the dissertation "The GDR in German Historical Politics after 1989." Since 2011, she has freelanced at Leuphana University Lüneburg and elsewhere, and from 2012–2015, she was head of the EU project Respecting Diversity, Strengthening Participation: Lüneburg Inclusion Training. Since 2015, she has been the scientific and pedagogical director of the Euthanasia Memorial site in Lüneburg. She has numerous publications, most recently "Links between 'Euthanasia' Murders and Holocaust Crimes: Opportunities and Possibilities of Bilateral Engagement with Nazi 'Racial Hygiene' and Perpetrators of 'Aktion T4'" in *Im Schatten von Auschwitz. Zeitbilder Schriftenreihe der Bundeszentrale für politische Bildung*, edited by Martin Langebach and Hanna Liever (Bonn, 2017), 465–479; and *Still, stumpf, beschäftigt mit Kartoffelschälen, verlegt—Frauen als Opfer der "Aktion T4"* (Husum, 2019).

Notes

1. The author refers to her research between 2006 and 2009 (Rudnick 2011).

2. Interpretations of the GDR in retrospect ignore that German unity was originally *not* the goal of GDR reform demands in autumn 1989, but only a consequence of failed internal reforms (Ash 1999: 5; Spreen 2001: 720).

3. Immediately after the surrender of Germany, people who were considered opponents of Soviet policy were interned in special camps on the territory of the Soviet Occupation Zone (SBZ). Special camps were what the Soviet authorities called internment camps. Some of these special camps were located on the territory of previous concentration camps (Buchenwald, Sachsenhausen). The internees were all labeled fascists. However, not all of the internees were convinced Nazis. There were also quite a few democrats among the prisoners. See a detailed explanation later on in this text.

4. Ministry of the Interior of Saxony-Anhalt, Note dated 6 October 1992, Holdings: 11331–10, vol. 1.

5. Printed matter (Drs.) 12/3179 of 21 August 1992, Parliamentary archive of the German Bundestag.

6. Ibid.

7. That is, government factions from the Christian Democratic Union of Germany (CDU, or "black") and the Free Democratic Party (FDP, or "yellow").

8. Kultusministerkonferenz (KMK), Recommendation of 9 October 1992, Archiv Stiftung zur Aufarbeitung der SED-Diktatur (StAufarb), Holdings: Enquete Commission (13th parliamentary term), SED 65.

9. Federal Ministry of the Interior, "Overall Concept for the Participation of the Federal Government in Memorial Sites in the Federal Republic of Germany," Status: 2 May 1992, 2, Ministry of the Interior of Saxony-Anhalt, 11331-10. Vol. 1.

10. Deutsches Historisches Museum, Statement, (n.d.), Ministry of the Interior of Saxony-Anhalt, 11331–10, Vol. 1.

11. Since then, criteria have included, for example, the need for the nation as a whole to be of outstanding importance, standing for an exemplary complex of persecution, the existence of foreign policy references, research and documentation, and a favorable expert opinion.

12. Drs. 13/8486 of 5 September 1997, Parliamentary Archives of the German Bundestag.

13. Drs. 12/6111 of 10 November 1993, 2–3, 5, Parliamentary Archive of the Berlin House of Representatives.

14. Federal Ministry of the Interior, Results note of 9 November 1993, 2, Ministry of the Interior of Saxony-Anhalt, 11331-10, Vol. 1.

15. Ibid.

16. Ibid., 3–5.

17. The SED, or Sozialistischen Einheitspartei Deutschlands, was the governing political party of the GDR.

18. A red-green government is made up of factions from the Social Democratic Party of Germany (SPD, or "red"), and the Greens.

19. Drs. 14/1569 of 27 July 1999, 4, Parliamentary Archives of the German Bundestag.

20. Ibid., 4; German Bundestag, Report of the Federal Government on the Participation of the Federation in Memorial Sites in the Federal Republic of Germany, 27 July 1999, 6.

21. Cf. Arbeitsgemeinschaft der KZ-Gedenkstätten der Bundesrepublik Deutschland/Forum der Landesarbeitsgemeinschaften der Gedenkstätten, Erinnerungsorte und -initiativen in Deutschland, "Strengthening the Culture of Remembrance and Historical-Political Education—Memorials in the Places of NS Terror Demand Greater Efforts to Come to Terms with and Mediate the Situation and Put an End to Imbalances," open letter from 5 May 2017, copy in possession of the author.

22. See Drs. 14/1569 of 27 July 1999, 4, Parliamentary Archives of the German Bundestag.

References

Anton, Karl. 1991. "Ein Mischgebiet." *Konkret*, no. 9: 45–46.
Ash, Timothy Garton. 1999. "Zehn Jahre danach." *Transit. Europäische Revue* 18: 5-6.
Bäumel, Matthias. 1992. "Diktaturen erzeugen seit jeher Anpassung und Widerstand." *Dresdner Neueste Nachrichten*, 19 March 1992, n.p.
Boll, Friedhelm. 1999. "Thesen zur Wahrnehmung der politischen Repression in der SBZ/DDR seit der Wende." In *Politische Repression in der SBZ/DDR und ihre Wahrnehmung in der Bundesrepublik*, edited by Friedhelm Boll, Beatrix Bouvier, and Patrik von zur Mühlen, 24–25. Bonn.
Deutscher Bundestag, ed. 1999. *Materialien der Enquete-Kommission "Überwindung der Folgen der SED-Diktatur im Prozess der deutschen Einheit."* Baden-Baden.
Eckert, Reiner. 1996. "Straßenumbenennungen. Revolutionsforderung oder Ausdruck westlicher Kolonisierung." In *Von der Wiederkehr des Sozialismus. Die andere Seite der Wiedervereinigung*, edited by Christian Striefler and Wolfgang Templin, 215–216. Frankfurt a. M.
Elm, Ludwig. 1997a. "'Zwei Diktaturen'—'Zwei totalitäre Regimes'? Die Enquete-Kommissionen des deutschen Bundestages und der konservative Geschichtsrevisionismus der neunziger Jahre." In *Die selbstbewusste Nation und ihr Geschichtsbild. Geschichtslegenden der Neuen Rechten—Faschismus/Holocaust/ Wehrmacht*, edited by Johannes Klotz and Ulrich Schneider, 208–209. Cologne.

———. 1997b. "DDR und 'Drittes Reich' im Vergleich. Kritische Anmerkungen zur Instrumentalisierung des Totalitarismustheorems." In *NS-Vergangenheit, Antisemitismus und Nationalismus in Deutschland. Beiträge zur politischen Kultur der Bundesrepublik und zur politischen Bildung*, edited by Christoph Butterwegge, 55–56. Baden-Baden.

Faulenbach, Bernd. 1997. "Das SED-System in vergleichender Perspektive und die Bedeutung seiner Aufarbeitung." In *Getrennte Vergangenheit, gemeinsame Zukunft*, edited by Ingrun Drechsler, Bernd Faulenbach, and Martin Gutzeit, 83-84. Munich.

Leyrer, Katja. 1992. "Nicht unsere Sache." *Konkret*, no. 12: n.p.

Morsch, Günter. 2001. "Die Bedeutung kleinerer Gedenkstätten für die Erinnerungskultur in der Bundesrepublik Deutschland." In *Das Gedächtnis des Landes. Engagement von BürgerInnen für eine Kultur des Erinnerns*, edited by Detlev Gause and Heino Schomaker, 14-26. Hamburg.

Pollack, Detlef. 1995. "Was ist aus den Bürgerbewegungen und Oppositionsgruppen der DDR geworden?" *Aus Politik und Zeitgeschichte*, nos. 40–41: 34–35.

Rudnick, Carola S. 2011. *Die andere Hälfte der Erinnerung. Die DDR in der deutschen Geschichtspolitik nach 1989*. Bielefeld.

Spreen, Dirk. 2001. "Schamkultur und Bußgemeinschaft. Die deutsche Erinnerungskultur ist nicht zeitgemäß." *Frankfurter Hefte* 12: 720–721.

Vergin, Siegfried. 2001. "Wende durch die 'Wende.'" *Gedenkstättenrundbrief* (edited by Stiftung Topographie des Terrors), no. 100: 94.

Wallbaum, Klaus. 1991. "Wissenschaftler streiten über die Erforschung der SED-Diktatur." *Hannoversche Allgemeine Zeitung*, 30 September 1991, n.p.

Wielenga, Frieso. 1994. "Schatten der deutschen Geschichte." *Deutschland Archiv* 10: 1064.

Wolfrum, Edgar. 1999. *Geschichtspolitik in der Bundesrepublik Deutschland. Der Weg zur bundesrepublikanischen Erinnerung 1948-1990*. Darmstadt.

Chapter 17

From the Ideological Repudiation of Culpability to Ethnocentric Propaganda

Anetta Kahane

In recent years, debates on the reception of the German Democratic Republic's history have become increasingly polarized. There is an obvious parallel here to present-day discussions surrounding German identity. Following the successes of PEGIDA (Patriotic Europeans Against the Islamization of the Occident) and the AfD (Alternative for Germany), with their ethno-centric agendas, conflicts in mainstream German society that were hitherto ignored or repressed—for example, how to deal with right-wing extremism, antisemitism, and racism—are emerging with increasing clarity. This has also altered our perspective on the GDR's history. With increasing frequency, the historical narrative of the GDR is being misused to underpin particular political agendas.

Yet in almost every reference to the GDR in current political debates, one thing is missing: the fact that it, too, was a product of the war, the Shoah, and postwar history. That the GDR would not have existed without Auschwitz—and that without the war of extermination unleashed by the Germans, Europe would have looked different and the world could have been saved from sixty million deaths—seems to have lost its perceived relevance. As a reference point, the crimes of the Germans have vanished from these disputes, to such an extent that invoking ethnicity is gradually becoming the norm (Bergmann, Erb, and Lichtblau 1995).

In the current political controversies, references to the GDR are diverse. Positive and negative perspectives from different political positions exhibit marked contradictions. Politicians in every ideological camp, however, assess the GDR in terms of its external features, not its origins story. These references, both positive and negative, ignore the Holocaust and the war as significant influences for the GDR, almost without exception. Focusing on how to classify the GDR based on these views means losing sight of some important aspects. Clinging to the question of communism and anticommunism in today's reception of the GDR fails to offer an adequate perspective on the German drama, to which the GDR also belonged, and still does when it comes to its legacies.

Blind spots and neglected perspectives on the GDR and the consequences of its history have disparate dimensions. Some of these dimensions will be highlighted below.

Globalization

Well beyond twenty-five years after reunification, when the GDR was subsumed in the Federal Republic of Germany, a crisis has emerged in many Western democracies. It is expressed in terms such as "national identity," "corruption," "incompetent elites," "immigrant overload," and "insecurity." Right-wing parties have gained political stature or are already shaping government policy. The achievements of modern-day liberalism are not only being questioned but also described as an inherent evil of present-day society. Today, open society, with its freedoms and individual rights, is disparaged and held responsible for the decline of the West (Herzinger and Stein 1995).

There are many reasons for these developments, including the consequences of globalization, which has profoundly destabilized the self-image of white industrialized nations in Europe and the United States. The globalized economy means growth outside the white West, and thus competition in the labor market and at educational institutions, research institutes, and sites for innovation and the technology industry.

All this also means more movement, more tourism, more global transfer of work and skilled labor, more job-seekers' migration, and more possible destinations. Meanwhile, more people are fleeing their homelands, which has increased the number of refugees around the world, on account of much more than conflict. On the contrary: in proportion to the total population, there have never been so few conflicts and wars. That people are fleeing their homelands is due not least to the fact that they can. These diverse factors may be only very indirectly perceptible in Germany's everyday life. But what is palpable since the refugee crisis—a symbol of worldwide change—is the pressure of migration, which is perceived as a danger.

All this has led to a growing sense of insecurity in once-privileged countries. The effects of these uncertainties are particularly pronounced in places that have had little experience with immigration. This applies in particular to the countries of the former Eastern bloc.

A Transformational Society

The societies of former socialist countries have had another obstacle to overcome on the path to globalization. They lack the traditions, and thus some of the key social structures, of Western democracies. Following the fall of the Berlin Wall, it was at first only economic conditions that were brought into line with the West—that is, a free-market economy supplanted a planned economy. This meant upheaval for society. A democratic infrastructure based on the rule of law and a fully functional civil service took time to develop (Lauth and Liebert 1999). This was also the case for other forms of infrastructure, such as the public sector, which included roads, schools, health care, and much more. Enormous tasks had to be mastered in a compressed time frame, since there was not much available on which to build.

Living conditions and everyday circumstances changed with unprecedented speed, but civil society had almost no chance to evolve. The structures required for democracy and the rule of law, when they began to function, were imposed from above. These could not simply develop from historical context, and the process did not involve quotidian experience. Within a few years, a new political reality emerged that was not able to build on people's experiences, nor was it integrated into a translational or mediatory narrative that could have rendered this revolution comprehensible. This upheaval within a very short period might have, with international assistance and the support of the European Union, been completed more or less successfully, but societal reality was unable to keep up.

The term "civil society" became established in the post-reunification era as a kind of synonym to the word "opposition." All movements directed against socialist, authoritarian, and undemocratic forms of governance were described in the West as "civil society." Within the oppositions of various socialist countries, however, were disparate ideological camps (Pollack and Wielgohs 2004). Some were merely opposed to communist rule, seeking to replace it with a different but equally authoritarian regime. Others advocated for a democratic society, which, though admittedly nationalist in character, was designed to ensure its citizens various freedoms. Still others called for an open society, in which affiliation was determined not by ethnic criteria, but by constitutional rights that were to apply without restriction to minorities as well.

Placing these three groups under the umbrella term "civil society" has blurred significant differences and led to the still-prevalent misunderstanding that opposition to the socialist system was a value in itself. This has contributed to a sense of surprise when it comes to how some former protagonists of the civil rights movement now actively promote authoritarian and racist positions. Today, the mantle of "civil rights activist" covers everyone against the regime, whether they were democrats, racists, antisemites, or died-in-the-wool nationalists. Opposition to the regime is not in itself an indicator of democratic content. This confusion and misinterpretation applies to all nations of the former Eastern bloc.

Eastern Europe and the Holocaust

That the GDR, or the five new federal states of Germany, formed part of the societies of Eastern Europe that were affected by this transformation is undisputed. The term "transformational society," however, was only seldom used for the eastern states of Germany after reunification. The fact that the GDR simply ceased to exist transferred all the elements of the transformational society into the realm of the personal or psychological, or simply led to repression and denial. The site where the problems of the transitional society could have been described and addressed was lost.

Whereas the countries of Eastern Europe stood alone, each having to cope with its own history (Petersen and Salzborn 2010) and its own transformation—which was widely viewed as a difficult process—the GDR was absorbed into the Federal Republic, which handled restructuring procedures, the transfer of legislation, and the expectation that all living conditions would be raised to Western standards (Heydemann and Vodička 2017). Wherever this did not succeed, the response was moralizing and political instead of encouraging of grassroots development and self-reliance. The process of a structural new beginning was sometimes rendered more difficult, or even toxic, by the fact that large numbers of West Germans supplanted their East German counterparts, particularly in middle-management positions, and with moralistic, politically charged gestures.

But this is only one part of the structure that impeded the reception of the GDR's history. The other part is the approach to German history and the consequences of World War II and the Holocaust. Here, the GDR differed from other Eastern European countries in that it was perceived as part of the country that brought war and devastation to Europe. The fraternal nations of socialism regarded the GDR with ambivalence, since it was precisely the wartime generation that constructed postwar society. This, too, is why the GDR repressed and ideologized this history, more than societies that had been victims of the Germans.

After all, it was the Germans who committed massacres in Eastern nations, laid waste to entire regions, and destroyed existential conditions for millions of people. The response to the murderous excesses of National Socialism and its expansionist war of extermination was the character of the Soviet Union after the war, the existence of the GDR, and the enlargement of the socialist bloc in Eastern Europe. From the Soviet perspective, this response, in the form of the postwar order, was rigorous and dictatorial. The establishment of a dictatorship was understandable after murderous, ethnically driven policies left twenty-seven million people dead.

That the GDR was relatively well liked in Eastern Europe in the postwar period can be regarded as an impressive achievement. This was, admittedly, based on ideological subterfuge. To be counted among the victims, the GDR as a state and a people had to repudiate and repress the past much more profoundly than other socialist countries. Beyond a doubt, the populations of these countries were victims of German crimes. But what was not discussed in the GDR and other socialist countries—not before or after the fall of the Berlin Wall—was antisemitism and hatred of minorities. Places where there has been discussion on the population's involvement in murdering the Jews have now assumed ethnically nationalist and authoritarian features. The discussion is now being prevented by social pressure and even legislation.

Unification, Nationalism, and Reappraisal

The fact that the promises and expectations of salvation expressed by both sides with the unification of the GDR and the FRG were imbued with nationalist undertones (without too many reservations) contributed in substantial ways to this process of repression. The West accepted and encouraged the East Germans' need to feel themselves as "genuine" Germans. But it ignored, indeed denied, that West Germany had long since become an immigration society. The experiences of everyday life clashed with perceptions of Helmut Kohl's policies, in which the very question of whether Germany was an immigration country was vehemently rejected.

Following reunification, many East Germans felt the need to embrace their national identity. The West-East gradient transmuted this need into a pathology that was soon reflected in an authoritarian attitude toward non-Germans. The West, with its denial of immigration and resurgence of nationalism as a part of German identity, bore its share of culpability. The implications of this development were neither immediately nor vigorously repudiated, which opened the doors to every kind of racism (Jander and Kahane 2020: 11–36).

Questions about the reappraisal of National Socialism after reunification must be seen in this context. It was after unification that a reconceptualizing of memorial sites in the east of Germany began. This was not based on memorialization work in a local context, local debates concerning memorialization culture in the GDR, or regional or familial memories of National Socialism. On the contrary, these were glossed over.

Instead, what emerged was a need for relativization, by drawing a partial or complete equivalence between National Socialism and Stalinism and between National Socialism and the GDR or the Soviet Union. For East Germans, the narrative of victimization was thus extrapolated without any engagement with reappraisals of National Socialism. This reluctance was visible wherever attempts at reappraisal were made. Since these attempts were relatively rare, an exculpatory narrative emerged, almost unnoticed, that relativized the "two German dictatorships," both believed to have been nearly overcome. This replaced the process of reappraising National Socialism, and not only in the east of the country.

This shift in focus in debates on reappraisal laid the foundations for mainstream theories of extremism that subsequently impaired the acknowledgment and assessment of the neo-Nazi movement in the east of the country. Who in the West could have been expected to insist on a reappraisal of National Socialism in the five new states of eastern Germany? The policy of "spiritual-moral transformation" under Helmut Kohl saw no need for this at all.

In the former GDR, opinions were split into two camps. On the one hand, the hardline antifascists of the GDR defended their viewpoint as the legitimate heritage of an authentic policy of opposing capitalism as the root cause of fascism. On the other hand, there were those for whom the GDR's antifascist position had always appeared as a necessary and purely symbolic evil that had to be accepted in exchange for a life without feelings of guilt.

With the collapse of the GDR, the will to address antifascism collapsed as well. The West German Left was essentially absent from this debate, since up until the fall of the Berlin Wall it had approved of the GDR's authoritarian and nationalist character, thereby forfeiting legitimacy. An East German Left that was truly committed to this issue was nowhere to be seen.

Ideological Repudiation of Culpability

In the GDR, the repudiation of culpability and the relativization of victims' narratives were the result of analyzing society and history as a manifestation of class struggle—in which there are rulers and the oppressed, ownership of the means of production and exploitation, and seducers and the seduced. The class struggle between capitalists and workers and between capital and labor determined everything. These mutual antagonisms formed the principal contradiction behind all conflicts. In addition, there were also ancillary contradictions, construed as a distraction from the main contradiction. These included racism and antisemitism, which could flourish only on capitalist soil, since both sought to divide the working class to hinder it from carrying out its historic mission. Thus both were placed in the inventory of capitalist machinations against the rights of workers and peasants.

Dimitroff's (1974: 58) definition of fascism as a "terrorist dictatorship of the most reactionary, chauvinist, and imperialist elements of finance capital" has up until now determined or relativized the debate in left-wing circles on German culpability for National Socialism and the Holocaust. Until today, the Left's narrative has depicted the German working class as victims of the war. The guilty parties opposing them were capitalist financiers—reactionary, chauvinist, and imperialist. This repudiation of culpability abetted the "little man" (German: *Kleiner Mann*) who could repress and justify his own part in the crimes.

In the battle between East and West in the Cold War, the East could point to its moral superiority over West Germany, where, after 1945, many leading Nazis occupied important positions in postwar politics. Whether this moral weapon in the Cold War really interested the "little man" in East Germany is moot. What is certain, is that for the population, the identity of the GDR can be traced back to the failure to recognize any obligation to confront personal culpability to collectively lead a conflict-free life as an ethnic entity. Irrespective of whether this "little man" served state and party with conviction or was against them, the tacit agreement between the two sides functioned with only a few exceptions (Lepsius 1993: 229–248).

The party's leadership was comprised of individuals who were imprisoned or had chosen exile in the Soviet Union during the Nazi era because of their membership in the German Communist Party. The party's middle and lower echelons included far fewer people with a comparable biography. Comrades from the resistance and exile who had kept their faith in the party despite the mistrust they encountered as emigrants from the West found themselves in the second echelon of party or governmental posts, or headed various artistic and cultural institutions. They had little influence overall. The proportion of former resistance fighters among functionaries was relatively high, but the vast majority were normal Germans who had supported National Socialism just like their counterparts in the West. This is an important precondition for comprehending the present-day response to the GDR. The ideology of class struggle had a relativizing effect, and ethnic national pride continued to exist in the GDR as a defense mechanism.

The Taboo Regarding the Jews

Some keys are needed to comprehend Germany's postwar history. One is the antithetical ties that bound the two parts of Germany. The FRG and the GDR exhibited marked affinities in terms of social and practical policymaking. As the partners of two hostile blocs, they were admittedly embedded in these opposed alliances—that is, the FRG affiliated with the West, and the GDR with the Soviet Union, but as two competing parts of the same perpetrator nation they shared the joint history of the Holocaust.

One key to understanding the present-day situation is to realize that this shared history as perpetrators is being largely ignored. In retrospective assessments of the GDR, both the Shoah and World War II are not seen as part of the narrative that resulted in the GDR (Kahane 2010). Here, the taboo continues with similar potency to its functioning in the GDR. This is why it is important to describe the GDR in terms of how it dealt with National Socialism. When we take a closer look, the GDR was far from having overcome National Socialism to the extent that was officially claimed. So an analysis of antisemitism in the GDR and concomitant historical culpability is needed. In this context, the relationship of the GDR to the Jews living there is of symbolic significance (Radvan and Troschke 2012).

There were about three thousand Jews living in the GDR, among which around three hundred were organized in congregations and religiously active. Most of the others, as communists in exile, had fought in the resistance and survived in camps or as illegals. When they settled in the GDR, they hoped for a life free from threats, wishing nothing more sincerely than to rebuild their country for the better, at least in the east of Germany.[1] Their ideology fostered the illusion that the society of the perpetrators could really transform itself into a society of socialist brothers. This turned out to be an illusion, indeed, which was demonstrated by their subsequent treatment.

In the late 1940s, a wave of Stalinist persecution began against communist Jews. Later, too, Jewish comrades were suspect as far as the party was concerned. They were put under surveillance, suspected of espionage, or branded as Zionists. These Jews, by contrast, had done everything they could to fit in with the society around them and to remain invisible as Jews. In the GDR's view, the Shoah had not been directed against Jews, but against resistance fighters. People from many countries were murdered in the camps; the role of their Jewish identity was ignored in the narrative. After all, Jewishness was merely a religious attribute, and like all religions was reactionary. A Jewish identity was completely taboo (Herf 1997).

The absence of Jews and Jewish life and death can be explained by more than ideological factors. This taboo enabled the Germans of the GDR to avoid having anything to do with the culpability of the perpetrators. No Jews meant no individual guilt. Besides the exculpation—by which fascism was equated with imperialism, the working class represented merely the seduced victims, and the fascists were just Hitler and the SS—in a way, it was also the Jews' fault. The personal dimension, that Jews were also neighbors, vanished from the collective memory with this taboo.

Jews in the GDR entered something like a deal. They renounced any mention of their Jewishness or were extremely reticent about it. In return, they received from the state a certain deceptive security against antisemitic attacks. Rendering Jewishness invisible was not completely successful. The GDR's society fulfilled its part of the bargain: it tolerated the Jews, even in party functions, provided that it was not reminded of its culpability.

For the people of the GDR, this was much easier than it was for the Jews who had to renounce remembrance, solidarity, mourning, memories, and public atonement, let alone compensation. In the tensions inherent between an antifascism whose purpose was exculpation, and a population whose antisemitism was unspoken but also unassailed, the Jews in the GDR endured. The fact that their history is so little known and has remained unexamined is one of the reasons why in the east of Germany today, antisemitism and racism exist in a particularly virulent and unapologetic form.

This verdict is not altered by occasional attempts to address the Holocaust more directly in art and literature. Wherever the extermination of the Jews was not embedded in the ideological image of German workers as the primary victims of capitalist warmongering interests, and of German communists who fought against these, art had no easy task. The few artists who succeeded exerted hardly any influence over the historical self-image of the people of the GDR as victims. Against this exculpatory narrative, works intending to depict racist antisemitism in Germany had no chance.

Summary

On the one hand, the GDR is self-transfigured in memory, depending on who is praising it for what. It continues to be defended from the left-wing of the political spectrum, which describes its policies as progressive. This praise applies to its domestic policies—with its childcare centers for everyone, equal rights for women, state-subsidized housing, full employment, and much more—and to foreign policy, in which the GDR adopted an anti-imperialist position alongside the Soviet Union, supporting oppressed peoples and national liberation movements.

There is also obstinate denial that this transfiguration includes a refusal to address National Socialism, particularly the GDR's own involvement in it. Similarly, the GDR's support for states and movements that aimed to extirpate Israel is also denied. Efforts to encourage future generations to approach this kind of critical engagement with the GDR and its policies already seem excluded from the somewhat blinkered vision of most left-wing protagonists.

But this transfiguratory view of the GDR is not just espoused by the Left. Ethnocentric populist right-wingers also have fond memories of the GDR. There, the ethnic communality was still intact, people helped one another, there were hardly any foreigners, close contact with these outsiders were not desired, national identity and traditional customs were cultivated, and, apart from a general profession of commitment to antifascism, there were no other personal inconveniences due to one's membership in the Nazi Party or other Nazi organizations.

A not-inconsiderable proportion of PEGIDA demonstrators and AfD voters want precisely this GDR without immigrants or democracy to be restored. No efforts at all can be expected from them to compensate for the GDR's shortfalls in dealing with National Socialism. On the contrary, reappraisal of this kind is ridiculed as nurturing a "cult of guilt."

Yet alongside this transfiguration from Right and Left, the GDR is condemned in political debate. This condemnation mostly follows the pattern dictated by the Cold War. In this interpretation, the communists and their polity outside the rule of law was a mirror image of National Socialism. Here, the GDR is regarded as the "second German dictatorship," which, following the first—the Nazi era—was established in the east by "the Russians" in opposition to the freedom of the West and its democracy.

This approach has proved important for engaging with National Socialism in the west of reunited Germany. But in the five new states of eastern Germany, such an approach does not affect the sense of self-victimization communicated to many Germans qua antifascism. On the contrary, it is reinforced. It offers yet another justification for refusing to engage with guilt and liability.

In these new circumstances, it is possible to pose not only as victims of the Nazis but also as victims of their opponents, the communists.

Following the collapse of the GDR, forces in civil society that in the transformational process toward a Western-style democracy began to address the GDR's shortfalls in reappraising National Socialism were never very powerful, though their efforts should be recognized. Their basic assumption, however, is correct. Without further efforts to engage in an overdue reappraisal of National Socialism, democracy will not take root in the five new states of eastern Germany (Kahane 2004, 2006). Without recognizing the crimes and assuming liability for them, the Federal Republic of Germany will never become a full-fledged democracy.

For the time being, it appears that increasing success—and not only in the east of reunited Germany—rewards those who are able to embrace, almost unreservedly, the assertion that the German working class under Hitler fell victim to fascism, imperialism, and capitalist financiers. Today they interpret this proposition in terms of ethnic affiliation, capitalism, the free market economy, and democracy. Shadowy, international forces and refugees are allegedly responsible for Germany's decline. Concentrated efforts by politicians and civil society are needed to banish racist, ethnically tainted, antisemitic extremism. The debate on how the GDR dealt with the heritage of National Socialism belongs to these efforts.

Anetta Kahane, born in 1954 in East Berlin, is a German journalist and author. She holds a degree in Latin American Studies and has worked as a translator. In 1990, she was the first commissioner for foreigners of the East Berlin Magistrate, and after reunification she helped establish the Regional Office for Foreigners (RAA) in Berlin and advocated intercultural education at schools in the new federal states. In late 1998, she cofounded the Amadeu Antonio Foundation, where she has been full-time chairperson since 2003. From 1974 to 1982, she was forced to work as an unofficial collaborator with GDR State Security. She ended this forced cooperation in 1982 because she no longer wanted to support racist practices of GDR functionaries. Since this collaboration became publicly known in 2002, right-wing extremists and right-wing populists have targeted her in campaigns against her and the foundation. In 1991, she was awarded the Theodor Heuss Medal, alongside Joachim Gauck, Christian Führer, David Gill, Ulrike Poppe, and Jens Reich. In 2002, she was awarded the Moses Mendelssohn Prize of the State of Berlin. For several years, she has worked as a columnist for *Berliner Zeitung* and has written for *Zeit, Tageszeitung, Stern, Tagesspiegel*, and other publications. She is the author of the book *Ich sehe was, was du nicht siehst* (I see what you don't see) (Berlin 2004).

Note

1. See my chapter "The Effects of a Taboo: Jews and Antisemitism in the GDR" in this volume.

References

Bergmann, Werner, Rainer Erb, and Albert Lichtblau, eds. 1995. *Schwieriges Erbe. Der Umgang mit Nationalsozialismus und Antisemitismus in Österreich, der DDR und der Bundesrepublik Deutschland*. Frankfurt.
Dimitroff, Georgi. 1974. "Arbeiterklasse gegen Faschismus" (1935)." In *Texte zur Faschismusdiskussion I*, edited by Reinhard Kühnel, 57–75. Reinbek.
Herf, Jeffrey. 1997. *Divided Memory: The Nazi Past in the Two Germanys*. Cambridge, MA.
Herzinger, Richard, and Hannes Stein. 1995. *Endzeit-Propheten oder Die Offensive der Antiwestler*. Reinbek.
Heydemann, Günther and Karel Vodička, eds. 2017. *From Eastern Bloc to European Union: Comparative Processes of Transformation since 1990*. Oxford.
Jander, Martin, and Anetta Kahane, eds. 2020. *Gesichter der Antimoderne. Gefährdungen demokratischer Kultur in der Bundesrepublik Deutschland*. Baden-Baden.
Kahane, Anetta. 2004. *Stärken. Entwickeln. Fördern: Handeln für Demokratie ist Handeln gegen Rechtsextremismus*. Berlin.
———, ed. 2006. *Reflektieren. Erkennen. Verändern: Was tun gegen gruppenbezogene Menschenfeindlichkeit?* Berlin.
———, ed. 2010. *Geteilte Erinnerung? Zum Umgang mit Nationalsozialismus in Ost und West*. Berlin.
———. 2020. "Das Unbehagen am Jüdischen und die Antimoderne." In *Gesichter der Antimoderne. Gefährdungen demokratischer Kultur in der Bundesrepublik Deutschland*, edited by Martin Jander and Anetta Kahane, 37–64. Baden-Baden.
Lauth, Hans Joachim, and Ulrike Libert, eds. 1999. *Im Schatten demokratischer Legitimität: Informelle Institutionen Und Politische Partizipation Im Interkulturellen Demokratievergleich*. Opladen.
Lepsius, Mario Rainer. 1993. *Demokratie in Deutschland*. Göttingen.
Petersen, Hans-Christian, and Samuel Salzborn, eds. 2010. *Antisemitism in Eastern Europe. History and Present in Comparison*. Frankfurt am Main.
Pollack, Detlef, and Jan Wielgohs, eds. 2004. *Dissent and Opposition in Communist Eastern Europe: Origins of Civil Society and Democratic Transition*. Farnham.
Radvan, Heike, and Hagen Troschke, eds. 2012. *Germany after 1945: A Society Confronts Antisemitism, Racism and Neo-Nazism*. Berlin.

Chapter 18

The Book and the Audience

Comments on the Reception of
Undeclared Wars with Israel in Germany

Jeffrey Herf

When my *Undeclared Wars with Israel* was published in 2016 by Cambridge University Press, it was well received by scholars and found a modest public audience (Herf 2016). With the publication of the German translation, *Unerklärte Kriege gegen Israel* in fall 2019 by Wallstein Verlag, it struck a nerve with the audience most familiar with the history it seeks to record and interpret (Herf 2019). The pattern of a work by a Jewish historian working outside Germany whose work addresses Jewish questions less examined within Germany is a familiar pattern. It is one of the consequences of the destruction of German Jewry during the Holocaust and is a regular aspect of the international community of scholars that works on the history of Nazi Germany and the Holocaust. Now, it has become an aspect of the community of scholars who work on Jewish questions in German history since World War II and the Holocaust as well. These comments are preliminary thoughts about the connection between this book and this audience.

In April and July 1990, representatives in the Volkskammer, the first freely elected parliament in Eastern Germany since the early 1930s, passed two remarkable resolutions. The first, in April, expressed regret over the antagonism of the German Democratic Republic (GDR; in German, DDR) to the state of Israel. The second, in July, rejected the United Nations resolution of 1975 that described Zionism as a form of racism (Herf 1997: 364–365). Both passed with overwhelming majorities and with support from prominent figures who had participated in the German revolution of 1989, most prominently Konrad Weiss, but also the future *Bundespräsident* of the Fedral Republic of Germany (FRG), Joachim Gauck. The rejection of the GDR's antagonism to Israel became a defining moment of the German revolution and peaceful unification of 1989–1990, one that associated the return of liberal democracy in Eastern Germany with a determination to reject the anti-Israeli policies of the entire history of the East German dictatorship. The letter and spirit of those two resolutions were at one with the general spirit of those years across the post-Soviet bloc. In unified Germany, political leaders and scholars promised to face the realities of the Communist dictatorship more effectively than their predecessors had done regarding the realities of the Nazi regime in either West or East Germany in the 1950s.

In accord with this spirit, the Bundestag held extensive hearings that led to publication of the multivolume Enquete Commission reports. These volumes, however, contained very little about the issues raised by the Volkskammer resolutions. An entire office, the Federal Commissioner for the Records of the State Security Service of the former German Democratic Republic, was established to preserve and make the "Stasi" files accessible. All of the most sensitive records of the East German regime, in addition to the Stasi files needed to write the history of East German policy toward Israel, among them those of the Politburo, Ministry of Defense, and the Foreign Ministry, became available, some by the mid-1990s and others in the first decade of this century. Several research institutes with a focus on the history of East Germany with varying political perspectives were established. A large body of historical scholarship emerged that revealed the inner workings of the East German dictatorship in both domestic and foreign policy, its instruments of repression, and its international relations as well. Yet the publications of these institutions did not focus much effort on the GDR's antagonism to Israel and the antisemitic tones that accompanied it.

In 1992, the late Sigrid Meuschel published *Legitimation und Parteiherrschaft in der DDR*. This brilliant and bold work examined the antisemitism that exploded in the "anticosmopolitan" purges that reached a peak in East Berlin in 1952. Meuschel (1992) provided a sound foundation for further work, including my own in *Divided Memory*, on the domestic and foreign policy implications of the repression of sympathy for Zionism and Israel that had previously been Soviet and Communist policy in 1947 and 1948. In 1993, essays by Mario Keßler (1993: 149–151) and

Olaf Groehler (1993: 129–131) in a volume edited by Jürgen Kocka (1993) addressed the issue of the purges and their consequences. Kessler, in his 1995 work, *Die SED und die Juden — zwischen Repression und Toleranz*, examined the impact of the purges on Jews in the Socialist Unity Party. In 1997, Angelika Timm (1997) documented the GDR's public hostility its role in East German foreign policy strategy in *Hammer, Zirkel und Davidstern: Das Zerstörte Verhàltnis der DDR zu Zionismus und Staat Israel*. In 1998, Ullstein Verlag published *Geteilte Erinnerung: Die NS Vergangenheit im geteilten Deutschland*, a German translation of *Divided Memory* (Herf 1998). Yet much remained to be done.

In 2004, Anetta Kahane, the founder of the Antonio Amadeu Stiftung in Berlin, published *Ich sehe was, was du nicht siehst: Meine deutschen Geschichten* (I see what you don't see: My German stories). Kahane discussed her parents' involvement in the German Communist Party before 1945, and in the SED after 1948. The book traces her disenchantment with the GDR, in particular regarding issues of antisemitism and Israel (Kahane 2004). In 2007, Kahane and others at the Antonio Amadeu Stiftung brought the issue of antisemitism in the GDR further to public attention in a traveling exhibit titled *Das hat's bei uns nicht gegeben: Antisemitismus in der DDR*. In 2010, the foundation published the material in the exhibit in book form (Kahane, Radvan, and Leo 2010). The exhibit received considerable attention in the German press and media. It drew extensively on published scholarship and the expert advice of a number of scholars at various universities and institutions.[1] It also received strong support from a remarkable array of government, media, archival, and media institutions including the Federal Ministry for Family, Seniors, Women and Youth; the Foundation for the Reappraisal of the SED Dictatorship; the Fritz Bauer Institute; the Freudenberg Foundation; the German Broadcasting Federal Archives in Koblenz and Berlin; the Federal Commissioner for the Records of the State Security Service of the Former German Democratic Republic; the German Historical Museum; the Berlin State Archives; the Berlin-Brandenburg Broadcasting Company, and the newspaper *Neues Deutschland*.[2] The Volkskammer spirit of spring and summer 1990 was evident in this impressive array of support.

In my view, *Das hat's bei uns nicht gegeben* represented a welcome application of the tradition of coming to terms with the past (*Aufarbeitung der Vergangenheit*) that began in the 1950s in West Germany, though this time it applied truth-seeking to the second German dictatorship. It did so without suggesting that the SED regime was identical to Nazi Germany or that its antagonism to Israel was comparable to the Holocaust. It did, however, not shy away from drawing attention to the entry of antisemitic themes in the GDR's ideology and policies toward Israel. That it was done by a foundation devoted as well to addressing issues of racism toward immigrants and people of color was also welcome. When I decided to write a successor work to *Divided Memory*, one that would explore the consequences of anti-Zionist propaganda for the foreign and military policy of the GDR, I understood that, in part as a result of these previous efforts, there was an audience among scholars and a general public for historical scholarship about these issues.

By 2011, when I began work on what became *Undeclared Wars with Israel: East Germany and the West German Far Left, 1967–1989*, the crucial archives of the GDR were available for scholars to examine. I was pleased to learn that Lutz Maeke, a student of Herman Wentker, director of the Institut für Zeitgeschichte (Institute for Contemporary History) in Berlin was writing a doctoral dissertation about the relationship between the SED and the PLO. In 2017, De Gruyter Oldenbourg published Maeke's (2017) DDR und PLO: Die Palästinapolitik des SED Staates. It is a careful, important and extensive examination of the interaction between the East German regime and the PLO, one that will be part of the ongoing scholarly and public discussion of these issues. The publication of *Undeclared Wars with Israel: East Germany and the West German Far Left, 1967–1989* in 2016 hit a nerve with German historians and intellectuals, such as Richard Herzinger. Writing in *Die Welt*, he appreciated it as a scholarly work that plunged deeply into the archives to reveal both the operational details of the GDR's antagonism to Israel, and that addressed the historical importance of a post-Holocaust German government that was assisting others in attacking the Jewish state with force of arms.[3]

This previous scholarship and public discussion, within and outside the universities, created a climate in Germany ready to welcome the German edition. In the fall of 2019, Wallstein Verlag published Unerklaerte Kriege gegen Israel: Die DDR und die westdeutsche radikale Linke, 1967–1989, the German translation of Undeclared Wars with Israel. The densely researched and heavily footnoted work received favorable and well-informed reviews in the leading daily newspapers in Germany.[4] The book "crossed over" to an interested and intellectual engaged public beyond fellow scholars. Invitations to lecture to the public about it came from the Bundestiftung zur Aufarbeitung der SED Diktatur, several local chapters of the Deutsch-Israelische Gesellschschaft, and the Antonio Amadeu Stiftung. Due to the efforts of many people in Germany and of some of us engaged outsiders, what began with the Volkskammer resolutions of 1990 has grown now into a significant scholarly and public *Aufarbeitung der Vergangenheit* of the Jewish question in its various dimensions in the history of the Communist regime in East Germany.

The Holocaust itself and the destruction of German Jewry has had a profound impact on the writing of German history in Germany. The small numbers of Jewish scholars living and working in Germany has meant that those of us working abroad, especially in the United States and Israel, have been important for bringing Jewish questions to the fore within the historical profession in Germany. It is perfectly understandable that in the past and today, sometimes Jewish questions are asked with greater urgency by those of us working outside Germany. Yet we Jewish scholars working abroad know that we have had, and have, excellent colleagues in the German universities and in German public life. We know that when books lack an audience, they remain voices in the wilderness. The fact that *Unerklärte Kriege gegen Israel* has touched a nerve with German readers is due both to the quality of the work itself as well as with the readiness of a German readership to welcome its findings and interpretations. That the work has found its audience was not only the result of the efforts of its author, but also of the hard and good work of many others as well. As a result, the chances are good that the issues raised in the Volkskammer in spring and summer 1990 will continue to be the subject of an informed and engaged scholarly and public discussion.

Jeffrey Herf, born in 1947, is an American historian and Distinguished University Professor at the University of Maryland, College Park, where he is a professor of modern European and German history. Herf graduated with honors in history from the University of Wisconsin-Madison in 1969 and received a PhD in sociology from Brandeis University in 1981. He taught at Harvard University and Ohio University before joining the faculty of the University of Maryland in 2000. His publications include *Reactionary Modernism: Technology, Culture and Politics in Weimar and the Third Reich* (Cambridge University Press, 1984); *War by Other Means: Soviet Power, West German Resistance and the Battle of the Euromissiles* (The Free Press, 1991); *Divided Memory: The Nazi Past in the Two Germanys* (Harvard University Press, 1997), in German, *Zweierlei Erinnerung: Die NS Vergangenheit im Geteilten Deutschland* (Ullstein/Propylaen Verlag, 1998); *The Jewish Enemy: Nazi Propaganda during World War II and the Holocaust* (Harvard University Press, 2006); *Nazi Propaganda for the Arab World* (Yale University Press, 2009); and *Undeclared Wars with Israel: East Germany and the West German Far Left, 1967–1989* (Cambridge University Press, 2016), in German, *Unerklaerte Kriege gegen Israel: Die DDR und die westdeutsche Linke, 1967–1989* (Wallstein Verlag, 2019). He is currently working on a book titled *Israel's Moment: Support and Opposition in the United States and Europe, 1945–1949*.

Notes

1. The scholarly advisor council (Wissenschaftliche Beirat) included Dr. Lothar Mertens (Ruhr Universität Bochum), Dr. Peter Fischer (Zentralrat der Juden in Deutschland), Dr. Thomas Haury (Universität Freiburg), Dr. Hermann Simon (Centrum Judaicum, Berlin), and Dr. Andreas Zick (TU Dresden).

2. Das Bundesministeriums für Familie, Senioren, Frauen und Jugend; die Stiftung zur Aufarbeitung der SED-Diktatur; das Fritz Bauer Institut; Die Freudenberg Stiftung; die Stiftung Deutsches Rundfunkarchiv Bundesarchiv in Koblenz und Berlin; die Bundesbeauftragte für die Unterlagen des Staatssicherheitsdienstes der ehemaligen Deutschen Demokratischen Republik; das Deutsches Historisches Museum; das Landesarchiv Berlin; der Rundfunk Berlin-Brandenburg; and *Neues Deutschland*.

3. See, for example, Richard Herzinger, "Der unerklärte Krieg der DDR gegen Israel," *Die Welt*, 11 July 2016.

4. See the following: Martin Jander, "Jeffrey Herf über 'Holocaust Inversion' in der Deutschen Außen- und Innenpolitik," *Bell Tower News, Netz für Digitale Zivilgesellschaft*, 16 December 2019; Marko Martin, "Eine ungemütliche Lektüre," *Deutschlandfunk Kultur—Buchkritik*, 9 December 2019; Rainer Hermann, "Besorgniserregendes Kapital deutscher Geschichte," *Frankfurter Allgemeine Zeitung*, 14 October 2019; Anja Reich and Jeffrey Herf über radikale Linke, "Unerklärte Kriege gegen Israel," *Frankfurter Rundschau*, 20 January 2020; Elvira Grözinger, "Unerklärte Kriege gegen Israel: Das neue Buch über das Verhältnis der DDR und der westdeutschen radikalen Linken zum jüdischen Staat," *Jüdische Rundschau: Unabhängige Monatszeitung*, January 2020; Ludger Heid, "Arafats Komplizen," *Süddeutsche Zeitung*, 14 January 2020; Christine Brink, "Der Brand im jüdischen Altersheim," *Der Tagesspiegel*, 10 December 2012; and Stephan Grigat, "Feindliche Allianzen," *Die Tageszeitung*, 21 December 2019.

References

Groehler, Olaf. 1993. "Integration und Ausgrenzung von NS-Opfern: zur Anerkennungs- und Entschädigungsdebatte in der Sowjetischen Besatzungszone Deutschlands 1954 bis 1949." In *Historische DDR-Forschung—Aufsätze und Studien*, edited by Jürgen Kocka, 105–127. Berlin.

Herf, Jeffrey. 1997. *Divided Memory: The Nazi Past in the Two Germanys*. Cambridge, MA.

———. 1998. *Geteilte Erinnerung: Die NS Vergangenheit im geteilten Deutschland*. Berlin.

———. 2016. *Undeclared Wars with Israel: East Germany and the West German Far Left, 1967–1989*. New York.

———. 2019. *Unerklärte Kriege gegen Israel: Die DDR und die westdeutsche radikale Linke, 1967–1989*. Göttingen.

Kahane, Anetta, 2004. *Ich sehe was, was du nicht siehst: Meine deutschen Geschichten*. Berlin.

Kahane, Anetta, Heike Radvan, and Anette Leo. 2010. *Das hat's bei uns nicht gegeben—Antisemitismus in der DDR*. Berlin.

Keßler, Mario. 1993. "Zwischen Repression und Toleranz. Die SED-Politik und die Juden (1949–1967)." In *Historische DDR-Forschung — Aufsätze und Studien*, edited by Jürgen Kocka, 185–197. Berlin.
——. 1996. *Die SED und die Juden — zwischen Repression und Toleranz*. Berlin.
Kocka, Jürgen, ed. 1993. *Historische DDR-Forschung — Aufsätze und Studien*. Berlin.
Maeke, Lutz. 2017. *DDR und PLO: Die Palästinapolitik des SED Staates*. Berlin.
Meuschel, Sigrid. 1992. *Legitimation und Parteiherrschaft in der DDR*. Frankfurt a. M.
Timm, Angelika. 1997. *Hammer, Zirkel und Davidstern: Das Zerstörte Verhältnis der DDR zu Zionismus und Staat Israel*. Bonn.

Chapter 19

Another Past That Lives On

My Trying Journey from Contemporary Witness to Contemporary Historian

Patrice G. Poutrus

I would like to begin by noting that this type of public self-reflection is unusual for me. As a (contemporary) historian, I am used to having contemporary witnesses meet my work with suspicion. They never feel adequately represented and know exactly why; in contrast to the (contemporary) historian, they were actually there. Despite its openness to dialogue, contemporary history often produces unsatisfying compromises as a source of conflict and asymmetry. Now I find myself in the role of those who usually sit across from me. Consequently, I feel the need to point out that what I write here constitutes highly personal statements about my past and Germany's recent past. In this autobiographical approach, I try to explain how I went from being a loyal defender of the "first workers' and peasants' state on German soil" to becoming a contemporary historian who eventually confronted issues such as migration, xenophobia, and racism in the German Democratic Republic (GDR).

My Life in the GDR: A Bitter Lesson

Up until 1989, the GDR was the crux of my life. I was born there and grew up near the Berlin Wall. I went to school in East Berlin, where I received my first vocational training, identified with the socialist state, was a proud Thälmann-Pioneer (the GDR's version of Scouts), and received my *Jugendweihe*, the GDR's secular equivalent to first communion. At eighteen, I became a member of the Socialist Unity Party of Germany (Sozialistische Einheitspartei Deutschlands / SED) and served in its army, the NVA, as an officer for three years. During my military service, my high school sweetheart and I started a family. We soon became the parents of two sons and were granted an apartment by the benevolent state. My wife, a student at Humboldt University, became a teacher. I became a functionary of the state youth organization Freie Deutsche Jugend (FDJ), first at my training center and then in the Berlin district office of the centralized GDR youth organization. Until the mid-1980s, my life seemed to be picture perfect, at least from the perspective of the SED propaganda machine.

Things were more complex, however. Since I was a child I lived right next to the Berlin Wall, but as I grew older it began to irritate me. As true of almost all Berlin families, some of our relatives lived in West Berlin. These nice people were allowed to come and visit us every once in a while, yet we could never visit them. That just didn't conform to my image of the historical and moral superiority of the "first workers' and peasants' state on German soil." On top of that, in contrast to the East German youth radio station DT64, better, newer, and more rebellious rock music was almost always broadcast on the West Berlin radio stations Sender Freies Berlin (Free Berlin Station) and the RIAS (Radio in the American Sector), which we could easily tune into from our side of the Wall. And so the Wall became more and more an expression of shortcomings and constriction. Other former GDR citizens could surely provide more impressive examples; for me, these were the first cracks in the facade of the SED state that caused me to become dissatisfied. And by the time I had been conscripted for military service, the notion began growing in me that an improved, reformed, and ultimately more democratic GDR would no longer need such a threatening border.

Only a few of my friends shared this hope. Some simply wanted a career and didn't trust me because any change to the system would have reduced their chances of success. Others no longer believed in real change and looked for ways to leave as quickly as possible. But even these friends distrusted me because for them I was, after all, a representative of the system. Yet all my efforts to bring about change in the GDR ended in a deceptive limbo between trying to prevent "the worst" and trying to remain as reputable as possible in an East German society riddled with mistrust. As to whether I was successful in this respect, I cannot say. To this day, I am not completely sure to what extent the consequences of my actions as a young functionary (*Kader*) of the SED state were harmless, and the more I learn, the more I have doubts.

The year 1989 was a great disappointment for me. Between rigged local elections and the open approval of the Tiananmen Square Massacre, it became obvious that none of the long overdue changes in the GDR were going to be possible with its existing leaders. Amid rising emigration and mass protests, it became clear to me that there would be no reformed socialism. The long-sought-after and surprising opening of the border on 9 November 1989 revealed that the SED regime had lost any credibility as a sovereign state. The head of the SED state could no longer govern, and the people did not want to continue to be governed as before. In the communist theory of revolution, this was the very definition of a revolutionary situation. I did not see any of this coming, and, frankly, I did not want any of it to happen either. And so, at the end of 1989, I was quite disappointed. I was disappointed with communism, with the GDR (as a purported alternative to West Germany), and, above all, with myself. I didn't belong to the winning side of history as I had been taught at school, in the military, and in the SED. This was a bitter lesson that took time for me to accept. At some point in the early 1990s, I left the SED, which had already changed its name several times.

The History of the *Goldbroilers*

I returned to work at my old vocational training center. Like thousands of other East Berliners, I would probably soon lose this job. But before that happened, at the age of twenty-nine, I began studying history and social sciences at Humboldt University in East Berlin (HUB), an opportunity I had been denied several times in the GDR. But now the admissions restrictions had been lifted. And it was only then that I discovered what I had not known or learned in the GDR. I was lacking skills in classical and modern languages, and my knowledge of capitalism (which I once vehemently rejected), understandings of civil democracy, and the history of communism proved rudimentary. Finally, I noticed that my German differed from that of West Berlin and West German students, who, along with the new professors of HUB, set the tone. This period in which my shortcomings came to light was also a time of constant debate between students and professors. We argued with old East German professors about their past and the poor conditions of the present; we argued with new West German professors about our past in the GDR and how they could be so sure what was best for HUB and East Germany; and, finally, we argued among ourselves about what kind of life we had lived in the GDR and what that meant now.

In these debates, I got the impression that judgments about the GDR as a totalitarian dictatorship were based on superficial knowledge (Meuschel 1992). I often found myself using the phrase, "It wasn't that simple!" I directed this not only at skeptical West German professors and their assistants but also at students who wanted to put the GDR behind them and move on. I was not done with my past and believed—like a typical historical witness—that it would be easier to reach a better, ostensibly fairer understanding of the SED state and East German society through the experiences of my biography. I decided that not only would I study history, I would also write it (down). I was not interested in the political rehabilitation of the SED state, nor was I interested in categorical condemnations. Rather, I wanted to grasp the links between communist dictatorship and everyday life (Lepsius 1994: 17–19) and how these help us understand East German society today.

After completing my first university studies—a challenging attempt at the postwar history of Berlin University (Poutrus 1999a: 101–103)—I chose a topic in the area of consumer development in the GDR: the history of the *Goldbroilers*.[1] To my great surprise, this landed me a position as a doctoral candidate in the newly founded Center for Contemporary Historical Research (Zentrum für Zeithistorische Forschungen) in Potsdam. The upswing in research at the time was certainly helpful (Lindenberger 2015: 100–102). But in contrast to growing "exposure" and "unmasking" research (Mitter and Wolle 1993), I wanted to demonstrate what eating and satisfying one's hunger meant to East Germans and how this became possible within the framework of the planned economy. Despite my assumptions, my prescholarly experiences eating *Goldbroilers* in a *Goldbroiler* bar on Alexanderplatz (Poutrus 1996: 138–140) proved to be of little (if any) use. As I sifted through endless files in the National Archive and in the archives of the East German federal states, my experiences seemed useless. They simply failed to illumine the anything-but-straightforward decision-making and planning structures of the SED state when it came to food production and their relationship to consumer habits and popular expectations of economic welfare in the GDR (Poutrus 1999b: 391–393).

What I learned during my studies was by no means suitable for writing a simple (hi)story of a pleasant life behind the Wall. Rather, I explored political voluntarism, mismanagement, scarcity, and daily life in East Germany, which was rather tiring (Ciesla and Poutrus 1999: 143–145). It was about improvisation, ingenuity, and the self-will (*Eigensinn*) of GDR citizens (Poutrus 1999c: 235–237) but also nepotism, distrust, and arbitrariness (Poutrus 200: 275–277). At the beginning of my studies, I had already associated these "phenomena" with the collapse of the GDR, and now I had to admit to myself that they had permeated relations in the "first workers' and peasants' state" decades before the end. As I was busy trying to tie together the loose ends of the convoluted storylines of my research into a book, a new "blame debate" broke out in the German public in which the history of the GDR was once again the focus.

Arguing about "Being Strange" in the GDR

Here I am referring to fierce public disputes about the causes of an unparalleled wave of xenophobic violence that shook East Germany in the summer of 2000. This presented an opportunity for Jan C. Behrends, Dennis Kuck, and me to publish a working paper pointing to the (contemporary) historical significance of these events in East Germany. From our perspective, xenophobia and economic crisis in East Germany resulted from specific conditions in the GDR. At the time, sociohistorical research on this subject was still in its early stages (Siegler 1991; Waibel 1996). Initially, the political system of the GDR was the focus, while research on socially marginalized groups in the socialist dictatorship was consciously or unconsciously neglected (Weber 1998: 249–251).

We tried to explain the historical conditions for how "strangers" were dealt with and perceived in the former GDR. We took into account the historical mentality of the East German population, as well as the historical, social, and economic conditions of state socialism, but our focus was the living conditions of "strangers." Our main arguments were as follows:

- The walled-in SED dictatorship's fundamental lack of legitimization led to a deep rift between a large part of the population and the state. The presence of foreigners in the walled-in GDR was not a matter of course, but rather closely linked to the interests of the SED. Thus, it can be assumed that the presence of "strangers" was always perceived as a symbol of socialist rule.

- Unlike in the Federal Republic, a public devaluation of National Socialist ideologies never took place in the GDR. In the collective consciousness, the German nation remained the reference point for the regime and the population. Therefore, the socialist nation tended to be imagined as a closed community whose resources should not be available to "strangers" ("class enemies" or "foreigners").

- The SED's stage-managed friendship rituals contrasted with the population's many different experiences with "strangers." Because conflicts between Germans and "strangers" were taboo, no culture of conflict—but also no culture of tolerance—could develop. In fact, the SED tried to limit the possibilities for contact with "strangers" by "quartering" them (Poutrus, Behrends, and Kuck 2000: 15–17).

Our aim was to bring a historical perspective to discussions of the origins of xenophobia in the new federal states, which were almost entirely traced back to the hardships of the economic transformation process. At the same time, we recognized that historical explanations of xenophobia in East Germany—that is, turning to the conditions and facts of the past—could not entirely explain the phenomenon. Although we did not discard the economic and mentality-related upheavals of system transformation, we believed that in the GDR, the ambivalent social status of "strangers" and the ways the ruling SED party dealt with them were highly significant. In our analysis, pre-existing social tensions were catalyzed after 1989/90 (Poutrus, Behrends, and Kuck 2001: 184–186).

Debates on the roots of xenophobic violence in the East became deeply polarized. The history of the GDR was used as an excuse for political shortcomings after 1990,[2] or the difficulties of the transformation were held up as the source of growing right-wing extremism.[3] But we were of the opinion that if authors from the former GDR were going to argue that the particularities of East Germans needed to be recognized in public debate, then these discussions should also include a critical look at the dark sides alongside what was currently virulent. We found it problematic that in the new federal states, the fixation on the state and the importance of "social equality" in the GDR was considered a value and piece of heritage to be preserved and passed onto united Germany. As we saw it, the problem was about both social burdens and the construction of norms. The flipside of the "equality" that was granted and organized by the state is still felt today in the new federal states as a lack of social capital in civil society, which compromises the social standing of "strangers" in East German society and has hindered their integration after 1989. We saw an urgent need to dispel the illusion, passed down from the GDR and then continually nourished, that only the state was capable of solving social conflicts "from above." In pointing to the historical roots of these expectations, however, we did not in any way seek to absolve the new perpetrators—or the society that stood back and watched their crimes—of accountability (Behrends, Lindenberger, and Poutrus 2003: 9–21).

At the heart of our reflections were questions related to constructions of "self" and "other," the limits of the "self" (*Eigenem* and *Fremden*) and the consequences of these constructs in the GDR's dictatorial society. Using these constructs, right-wing ideologies and mindsets could be preserved, and racist violence legitimized. Xenophobia, however, encompasses more than right-wing extremism and racist violence. Intercultural encounters that result from transnational migration represent a fundamental challenge in all modern societies. For this reason, we initially focused on how foreigners were dealt with in the GDR. Who exactly was categorized as a "stranger" and perceived that way in the GDR was not only based on racist ideas, however. The image of the "class enemy," for example, was not a racist construction but a flexible mechanism of exclusion. Vociferous anti-Americanism and widespread hostility toward West Germans showed that the boundaries of the "imagined community" in the GDR were fluid. Otherness also played an essential role between sociocultural groups, including between the functionary elite of the SED state and GDR citizens (Behrends and Poutrus 2005: 155–157).

As we began to verify the assertions of our working paper, rudimentary research on how "strangers" were dealt with and perceived in the GDR emerged as a central problem. In 1998 (two years before our working paper), the conference "Precarious Living Circumstances: Discipline and Normalization Pressures in the GDR Working Society" took place in Brühl. There, Almuth Berger, commissioner of foreigners' affairs of the Federal State of Brandenburg, proposed that living conditions and social conventions should be studied as a separate, independent project when it came to dealing with foreigners in the GDR. After some preliminary considerations by the research group on Governance and Self Will at the Leibniz Center for Contemporary Historical Research, and the conference "Strangers and Being a Stranger in the GDR" in December 2001, a new group by the same name was formed at the Center in 2001. Two smaller research projects were financed through foundation funds. Their results have been published widely (Müller and Poutrus 2005; Priemel 2011).

Yet, for me, the scholarly, historical, and historical-political discussion by no means ended with the conclusion of this project, even though my research interests shifted from the history of the GDR and the history of communism to migration history in general, and specifically to the history of political asylum (Poutrus 2016a: 853–854).

Coming Home to a Strange Country

Coming to terms with the regime structures and rule of the SED state as well as my own past continued to be part of my work. It led me to topics that, as a student, I held as sacrosanct proof of the historical uniqueness of the socialist GDR experiment. After the end of Nazi rule, communists returning to Germany from exile were deemed the true leaders of the future SED state and the personification of its new antifascist beginnings (Möller 2010: 96–98; Kessler 2002). By examining how these small but prominent groups were dealt with in pre- and early GDR history, one can account for how social relations in the GDR were later influenced by the amalgamation of persistent xenophobic attitudes in the (East) German population and the burden of the Stalinist regime that was installed in the Soviet occupation zone.

Even before the planned return of exiled communists, the Soviet military administration, the Moscow party leadership of the Soviet Communist Party, and exiled leaders of the German Communist Party (KPD) granted their unconditional trust only to those KPD members who had gone into exile in Moscow and survived various cleansings and the "Great Terror" (Müller 2001). At best, German communists from other, especially Western, capitalist countries of exile were considered additional personnel for the construction of socialism.[4]

Many German communists, who for the most part were politically experienced, wanted to return to their former homeland as soon as possible. In the immediate postwar period, this desire came up against a collapsed postwar society, as well as emerging conflicts of interest between the Allies. The United States in particular showed little interest in facilitating the return of communist emigrants. Interestingly, the Soviet military administration in Germany (SMAD) was also initially hesitant. Only when it became evident that there was a shortage of trustworthy political personnel for the new administration did the SMAD ease the granting of entry permits. This ended the early phase of communist returnees (*Remigranten*) in which the return of individual emigrants from the West was difficult but possible. From then on, the Berlin KPD leadership took control (Scholz 2000).

There was no right to return for German communists who had emigrated. Before their arrival, those who wanted to go back to Germany were required to present an application that was to include their CV, proof of professional qualifications, and an internal recommendation from the party. If their political trustworthiness was verified after their arrival, returnees were often housed in isolation until the local party leadership arrived at a decision. Furthermore, pro-Soviet or pro-socialist emigrants who had not belonged to the KPD were met with considerable distrust from both Soviet occupation authorities and Communist Party leaders. Noncommunist Jewish or Social Democratic emigrants from the West were allowed to return only as an exception, or temporarily.

After receiving permission to enter the country, returnees were repeatedly subjected to reviews of their political trustworthiness at their assigned worksites. Part of this process was formal recognition as a "victim of fascism" (*Opfer des Faschismus* / OdF), which was tied to a specific interpretation of the National Socialist regime. The conferral of OdF status also required pledging unconditional allegiance to the KPD and later the SED. Only when this was established could Western emigrants receive numerous benefits for OdFs, alongside former communist prison camp prisoners or former members of the communist underground during the National Socialist regime (Hölscher 2002). They became privileged "strangers" in a scarcity-dominated GDR society. Yet advancing to prominent positions in the new power apparatus was by no means a certainty (Foitzig 2002: 93–95).

Similar to Communist Party functionaries from the so-called Sudeten areas (Sudetengebiete),[5] many returnees from the West found themselves entangled in diverse lines of conflict. Outsiders and authorities often viewed them as pesky competition. It was especially autochthonous party authorities who thwarted the eagerness of communist returnees. For locals outside the KPD/SED, "foreign comrades" embodied the unpopular Soviet occupying power. As a result, both groups, feeling provoked by "strangers" or "outsiders" because of the latter's OdF status and resulting self-confidence, reacted defensively and with hostility (van Hoorn 2003: 133–135).

Yet the return of German communists from emigration to the West belongs to narratives that, to this day, are supposed to support the image of a fundamentally antifascist GDR. The continuous political threat to the status of Western returnees in the SED state remains overlooked (Schleiermacher 2009: 79–81). With the radicalization of the communist regime in Eastern Europe from 1948 onward, they were automatically suspected to have been influenced by the "class enemy" while in exile. The resulting accusations against often Jewish returnees ran the gamut from social decadence to spying for Israel and the United States. Furthermore, anti-West, anti-American propaganda openly criticized Western culture and used antisemitic arguments that could have been taken from the "Ideas of 1914" tradition or the arsenal of National Socialist propaganda (Jarausch 2005: 34–36).

After Stalin's death in 1953, this wave of hostilities ended and most returnees from the West experienced rehabilitation. Only in rare cases could they go back to their former positions, however. Their time in the West continued to fuel suspicions that they were unreliable (Leo 2004: 9–11). Under these circumstances, communist returnees were faced with the same alternatives that all GDR citizens had in this period: comply with the demands of the Communist Party leadership; give up and withdraw into an inner emigration; or, like hundreds of thousands of other East Germans, leave the SED state for the West (Hartewig 2000).

With the end of Stalin's long rule over the Soviet Union and subsequent "thaw" that began to take effect there, those considered German citizens or "ethnic Germans" were given a chance to enter the GDR (Baberowski 2000: 617–619; Kępińska and Stola 2004; Matthews 1993). According to researchers, around 180 German emigrants survived the "Great Terror" in the Soviet Union and returned to the Soviet occupation zone—that is, the GDR. This was, however, subject to certain conditions. The only destination the Soviet administration granted permission for was the Soviet Occupation Zone (German: Sowjetische Besatzungszone, SBZ). There, the KPD/SED leadership required them to sign a declaration of confidentiality and allegiance, according to which they were not to make their imprisonment and experiences in concentration camps in the USSR public (Stark 1998: 282–284). Both requirements of return would later become obligatory for all former Gulag prisoners.

But the first emigrants released from Soviet imprisonment in the mid-1950s could no longer obtain the political and social status of "victims of fascism" that applied to those who had returned to the SBZ immediately after the end of the war. Most of these returnees had been severely marked, physically and mentally, by often more than fifteen years of detention in prison camps. For two decades, they were politically, socially, and culturally estranged from (East) German society. In the 1950s, they were considered potential informants who could reveal the actions of GDR party and state leaders who had not only survived the "Great Terror" in Soviet exile but also had been part of the communist movement (Müller 2001). So as not to jeopardize the public image of Wilhelm Pieck and Secretary General Walter Ulbricht in particular, the personnel department of the SED's lead authority, the Central Committee, oversaw social inclusion as well as political control of late returnees from the Soviet Union to the GDR. This was carried out with the involvement of several government agencies, the mass organization responsible for allocating social welfare benefits, and, last but not least, the Ministry for State Security (Ministeriums für Staatssicherheit / MfS or Stasi). The returnees were allocated temporary financial aid, food ration cards, apartments, and jobs. In Berlin, a settlement ban ensured that no colonies of former Gulag prisoners could develop (Stark 1999: 209).

The inclusion process entailed efforts to achieve internal rehabilitation within the party and recognition of former Gulag prisoners as victims of National Socialist persecution (*Vereingung der Verfolgte des Naziregimes* / VVN). In practice, both were half-hearted steps in making amends for Stalinist wrongdoing. In the end, those who suffered persecution and the resulting party sanctions and exclusion were simply erased from personal records. At the same time, pensions for victims of National Socialism were especially important in ensuring a basic livelihood for those who were not able to start anew in East German society (*Arbeitsgesellschaft*) due to their long imprisonment and miserable detention conditions. This recognition also meant that late returnees from the Soviet Union became part of the healthcare system that the SED leadership borrowed from its exile in Moscow. Former Gulag prisoners who had returned to the GDR, however, only received this privilege in exchange for their silence about the tyranny they experienced under Stalinist persecution and in Soviet prison camps (Erler 2001: 1734).

Conclusion

Both the victims of Stalinism who returned from the Soviet Union and returnees from the West had to prove their loyalty to the SED state by strictly conforming to everyday life in the GDR. These threatening expectations did not just apply to the treatment of Communist Party members whose deviant paths aroused the paranoid suspicions of political nonconformity in the SED state, however. This pattern could also be found in the institutional handling of German and foreign groups of migrants. In their own self-image and in perceptions of them by the SED state and the East German population, they were characterized by ambiguity, which turned them into a marginal group in a largely homogenized and closed community of East Germans. The inevitable consequences were conflicts in which these strangers found themselves in an institutionally dependent and thus weaker and ultimately vulnerable position (Poutrus 2016b: 967–969).

The treatment of "strangers" in state socialism has now emerged as an independent field in international research on the GDR and communism (Dennis and LaPorte 2011; Rabenschlag 2014; Slobodian 2015). Yet the social circumstances that were the starting point for our research on "Strangers and Being a Stranger in the GDR" seem to have developed more slowly than knowledge about it. For a while, I myself was considered an expert on xenophobia in the GDR and East Germany, which led to numerous invitations to give talks in Saxony and Brandenburg. It was then that I arrived at the disconcerting realization that there is a blatant discrepancy between contemporary historical knowledge on the subject and public debate. When it comes to xenophobia and racist violence in East Germany, only the SED regime is blamed, or the challenging period of social transformation is invoked. This trivializes the problem and frees GDR history from both. Former representatives of the SED and leaders of state and federal politics prefer to avoid heavy debates on breaks and continuities between past and present. In such debates, I was sometimes criticized for pointing to demonstrable continuities and accused of arguing like a "know-it-all Westerner" (*Besser-Wessi*). If these experiences have shown me something, then it is that there is no causal relationship between the scholarly work of contemporary historians and public debates about the past. At the same time, pointed debates about xenophobia and racism in East Germany have made the places of my own East German past increasingly strange to me.

Patrice G. Poutrus, born in 1961 in East Berlin, is a historian and migration researcher. He is currently a research assistant at the University of Erfurt. He received his doctorate in 2001 from the European University Viadrina, Frankfurt/Oder, and subsequently conducted research at the German Historical Institute in Washington, DC; the Center for Contemporary Historical Research in Potsdam; the Simon Wiesenthal Institute for Holocaust Studies in Vienna; and the Institute for Contemporary History at the University of Vienna. He is a member of the DFG research network Grundlagen der Flüchtlingsforschung. His book *Umkämpftes Asyl. Vom Nachkriegsdeutschland bis in die Gegenwart* was published in spring 2019.

Notes

1. *Broiler* (from the American English word "broiler," from the verb "to broil," meaning "to roast or grill") is a specialized term used in Germany to designate a "fattened chicken." The word is also a common regional term for roast chicken, especially in the territory of the former GDR, where it is recorded in the *Lexicon for the Hotel and Restaurant Industry*, 1972 (*Lexikon für das Gaststätten und Hotelwesen*). The term *Goldbroiler* was also used for advertising purposes. From this context came the vernacular terms *Silberbroiler* ("silver broiler") or *Bronzebroiler* ("bronze broiler"), which have a similar meaning to *Gummiadler* ("rubber eagle"), all of which refer to a chicken of low-quality that is tough to chew or has little meat.

2. That is how the shortened version of our working paper tended to be treated in more conservative daily papers, such as *Die Welt*, 15 August 2000, and *Berliner Morgenpost*, 15 August 2000.

3. Such as Thomas Ahbe's controversial response to our position paper in the weekly magazine *Der Freitag*. Thomas Ahbe, "Wilde Zucht der Muttermale." *Der Freitag*, 18 August 2000, 5.

4. The KPD leadership exiled in Moscow estimated that six hundred party members lived in the Soviet Union. Another three hundred so-called *polit. Emigranten* (political emigrants) were thought to have lived in Britain, and three hundred in Sweden. It was assumed that approximately three hundred potential communist officials had found refuge in the United States, Mexico, Switzerland, France, Belgium, the Netherlands, and Norway. In the literature on communist "returnees" (*Remigranten*) after World War II, the actual number of KPD members

who wanted to return home is believed to be higher. However, those who did not pursue further political ambitions were not of any interest to the KPD leadership in Moscow and thus could not expect any material or institutional support (Schleiermacher 2009: 79–81).

5. Areas in Czechoslovakia where ethnic Germans made up the majority of the population until their expulsion in 1945.

References

Baberowski, Jörg. 2000. "'Entweder für den Sozialismus oder nach Archangel'sk!' Stalinismus als Feldzug gegen das Fremde." *Osteuropa. Zeitschrift für Gegenwartsfragen* 50: 617–637.

Behrends, Jan C., Thomas Lindenberger, and Patrice G. Poutrus. 2003. *Fremde und Fremd-Sein in der DDR. Berlin. Zu historischen Ursachen der Fremdenfeindlichkeit in Ostdeutschland*. Berlin.

———. 2005. "Xenophobia in the Former GDR: Explorations and Explanation from a Historical Perspective." In *Nationalisms Across the Globe: An Overview of Nationalisms in State-Endowed and Stateless Nations*, vol. 1: *Europe*, edited by Wojciech Burszta, Tomasz Dominik Kamusella, and Sebastian Wojciechowski, 155–170. Poznan.

Ciesla, Burghard, and Patrice G. Poutrus. 1999. "Food Supply in a Planned Economy: SED Nutrition Policy between Crisis Response and Popular Needs." In *Dictatorship as Experience: Towards a Socio-Cultural History of the GDR*, edited by Konrad H. Jarausch, 143–162. New York.

Dennis, Mike, and Norman LaPorte. 2011. *State and Minorities in Communist East Germany*. New York.

Erler, Peter. 2001. "'Mich haben die persönlichen Erlebnisse nicht zum nörgelnden Kleinbürger gemacht.' Deutsche GULag-Häftlinge in der DDR." In *Vielstimmiges Schweigen. Neue Studien zum DDR-Antifaschismus*, edited by Annette Leo and Peter Reif-Spirek, 173–196. Berlin.

Foitzik, Jan. 2002. "Remigranten in der Medienpolitik der sowjetischen Besatzungsmacht." In *Zwischen den Stühlen? Remigranten und Remigration in der Medienöffentlichkeit der Nachkriegszeit*, edited by Claus-Dieter Krohn and Axel Schildt, 93–113. Hamburg.

Hartewig, Katrin. 2000. *Zurückgekehrt. Die Geschichte der jüdischen Kommunisten in der DDR*. Cologne.

Hölscher, Christoph. 2002. *NS-Verfolgte im "antifaschistischen Staat." Vereinnahmung und Ausgrenzung in der ostdeutschen Wiedergutmachung (1945–1989)*. Berlin.

Jarausch, Konrad H. 2005. "Missverständnis Amerika. Antiamerikanismus als Projektion." In *Antiamerikanismus im 20. Jahrhundert. Studien zu Ost- und Westeuropa*, edited by Jan C. Behrends, Árpád von Klimó, and Patrice G. Poutrus, 34–49. Bonn.

Kępińska, Ewa, and Dariusz Stola. 2004. "Migration Politics and Policy in Poland." In *Migration in the New Europe: East-West Revisited*, edited by Agata Gorny and Paolo Ruspini, 159–176. Basingstoke.

Kessler, Mario. 2002. *Exil und Nach-Exil. Vertriebene Intellektuelle im 20. Jahrhundert*. Hamburg.

Leo, Annette. 2004. "Die 'Verschwörung der Weißen Kittel.' Antisemitismus in der Sowjetunion und in Osteuropa." In *Ereignisse und Auswirkungen: Das Jahr 1953*, edited by Jan Foitzek, Werner Künzel, Anette Leo, and Martina Weyrauch, 9–22. Potsdam.

Lepsius, Rainer M. 1994. "Die Institutionenordnung als Rahmenbedingung der DDR." In *Sozialgeschichte der DDR*, edited by Hartmut Kaelble and Jürgen Kocka, 17–29. Stuttgart.

Lindenberger, Thomas. 2015. "Ist die DDR ausgeforscht? Unsere Zeitgeschichte zwischen nationalem Boom und Globalisierung." In *Potsdamer Almanach des Zentrums für Zeithistorische Forschung ZeitRäume*, edited by Martin Sabrow, 100–116. Potsdam.

Matthews, Mervyn. 1993. *The Passport Society: Controlling Movement in Russia and the USSR*. Boulder.

Meuschel, Sigrid. 1992. *Legitimation und Parteiherrschaft: Zum Paradox von Stabilität und Revolution in der DDR 1945–1989*. Frankfurt a. M.

Mitter, Armin, and Stefan Wolle. 1993. *Untergang auf Raten. Unbekannte Kapitel der DDR- Geschichte*. Munich.

Möller, Horst. 2010. "Die Emigration aus dem nationalsozialistischen Deutschland—Ursachen, Phasen und Formen." In *Mitteilungen der Gemeinsamen Kommission für die Erforschung der jüngeren Geschichte der deutsch-russischen Beziehungen*, edited by Horst Möller and Alexandr O. Tschubarjan, 96–104. Munich.

Müller, Christian Th., and Patrice G. Poutrus, eds. 2005. *Ankunft—Alltag—Ausreise. Migration und interkulturelle Begegnungen in der DDR-Gesellschaft*. Cologne.

Müller, Reinhard. 2001. *Menschenfalle Moskau. Exil und stalinistische Verfolgung*. Hamburg.

Poutrus, Patrice G. 1996. "Kurzer Abriß der Geschichte des Goldbroilers." In *Wunderwirtschaft. DDR-Konsumkultur in den 60er Jahren*, edited by NGBK, 138–143. Cologne.

———. 1999a. "Vor der Spaltung kam der Klassenkampf. Die Berliner Universität nach dem Zweiten Weltkrieg." In *Sterben für Berlin? Die Berliner Krisen 1948–1958*, edited by Burghard Ciesla, Michael Lemke, and Thomas Lindenberger, 101–131. Berlin.

———. 1999b. "Lebensmittelversorgung, Versorgungskrise und die Entscheidung für den 'Goldbroiler.' Problemlagen und Problemlösungen der Agrar- und Konsumpolitik in der DDR 1958–1965." *Archiv für Sozialgeschichte* 39: 391–421.

———. 1999c. "'. . . Mit Politik kann ich keine Hühner aufzieh'n.' Das Kombinat Industrielle Mast und die Lebenserinnerungen der Frau Knut." In *Herrschaft und Eigen-Sinn in der Diktatur. Studien zur Gesellschaftsgeschichte der DDR*, edited by Thomas Lindenberger, 235–265. Cologne.

———. 2001. "Industrieproduktion auf dem Lande? Das Model KIM." In *Der Schein der Stabilität. DDR-Betriebsalltag in der Ära Honecker*, edited by Renate Hürtgen and Thomas Reichel, 275–293. Berlin.

———. 2016a. "Zuflucht im Nachkriegsdeutschland. Politik und Praxis der Flüchtlingsaufnahme in Bundesrepublik und DDR von den späten 1940er Jahren bis zur Grundgesetzänderung im vereinten Deutschland von 1993." In *Handbuch Staat und Migration vom 17. Jahrhundert bis zur Gegenwart*, edited by Jochen Oltmer, 853–893. Berlin.

———. 2016b. "Migranten in der 'Geschlossenen Gesellschaft.' Remigranten, Übersiedler, ausländische Studierende, Arbeitsmigranten in der DDR." In

Handbuch Staat und Migration vom 17. Jahrhundert bis zur Gegenwart, edited by Jochen Oltmer, 967–995. Berlin.
Poutrus, Patrice G., Jan C. Behrends, and Dennis Kuck. 2000. "Historische Ursachen der Fremdenfeindlichkeit in den neuen Bundesländern." *Aus Politik und Zeitgeschichte. Beilage zur Wochenzeitschrift 'Das Parlament'* B39: 15–21.
———. 2001. "Fremd-Sein in der staatsozialistischen Diktatur. Zu historischen Ursachen von Fremdenfeindlichkeit und rassistischer Gewalt in den Neuen Bundesländern." In *Afrikabilder. Studien zu Rassismus in Deutschland*, edited by Susan Arndt, 184–204. Münster.
Priemel, Kim Christian, ed. 2011. *Transit / Transfer. Politik und Praxis der Einwanderung in die DDR 1945–1990*. Berlin.
Rabenschlag, Ann-Judith. 2014. *Völkerfreundschaft nach Bedarf: ausländische Arbeitskräfte in der Wahrnehmung von Staat und Bevölkerung der DDR*. Stockholm.
Schleiermacher, Sabine. 2009. "Rückkehr der Emigranten. Ihr Einfluss auf die Gestaltung des Gesundheitswesens in der SBZ/DDR." In *Medizin, Wissenschaft und Technik in der SBZ und DDR. Organisationsformen, Inhalte, Realitäten*, edited by Sabine Schleiermacher, 79–94. Husum.
Scholz, Michael F. 2000. *Skandinavische Erfahrungen erwünscht? Nachexil und Remigration. Die ehemaligen KPD-Emigranten in Skandinavien und ihr weiteres Schicksal in der SBZ/DDR*. Stuttgart.
Siegler, Bernd. 1991. *Auferstanden aus Ruinen. Rechtsextremismus in der DDR*. Berlin.
Slobodian, Quinn, ed. 2015. *Comrades of Color. East Germany in the Cold War World*. New York and Oxford.
Stark, Meinhard. 1998. "'Traten keine Probleme auf . . . .' Zur Rückkehr deutscher Exilanten aus der UdSSR." In *Heimkehr 1948. Geschichte und Schicksale deutscher Kriegsgefangener*, edited by Annette Kaminsky, 282–298. Munich.
———. 1999. "Ich muß sagen, wie es war." *Deutsche Frauen des GULag*. Berlin.
van Hoorn, Heike. 2003. "Zwischen allen Stühlen. Die schwierige Stellung sudetendeutscher Antifa-Umsiedler in den ersten Jahren der SBZ/DDR." In *Fremde und Fremd-Sein in der DDR. Zu den historischen Ursachen der Fremdenfeindlichkeit in Ostdeutschland*, edited by Jan C. Behrends, Thomas Lindenberger, and Patrice G. Poutrus, 133–152. Berlin.
Waibel, Harry. 1996. *Rechtsextremismus in der DDR bis 1989*. Cologne.
Weber, Hermann. 1998. "Zum Stand der Forschung über die DDR-Geschichte." *Deutschland Archiv* 31: 249–257.

Chapter 20

Nonconformity in a German Postwar Society

Questions for GDR and Transformation Studies

Raiko Hannemann

Current right-wing extremism and the conspicuously high number of nonvoters in what came to be called Neue Bundesländer (new states) are often[1] justified by *zweifacher Diktaturerfahrung* (the twofold experience of dictatorship) and the absence of a democratic civil society, mostly by disregarding the transformation process that has taken place since 1990. These developments have given rise to questions about the image of the German Democratic Republic (GDR), reality, and notions of domination and resistance in the East. On the occasion of a discussion in which I participated as a democracy researcher in Berlin/Marzahn-Hellersdorf in November 2017, one participant pointed out that historical processes, such as the October Revolution, shape people over generations. The October Revolution may not have had such a formative effect in Russia or Germany as the National Socialist war of extermination, and yet the psychological dimensions of the latter have been neglected. Addressing these shows how the complex experiences of the post-Nazi GDR and transformation period must be taken into account when assessing the development of East German democracy.[2]

Understanding what motivates people in the GDR and today's new federal states to act in conformity or nonconformity in quotidian, real-life situations requires taking a look at the overall picture. Classical GDR opposition research, which forces resistance into the rigid corset of totalitarianism theory, does not take into account the entire constellation of events and interactions. Often ideologically motivated, totalitarianism theory compresses historical realities into a simple, ahistorical dualism between dictatorship and opposition. Deciding how to deal with domination in the GDR is historically relevant when confronting questions such as these:

1. What does opposition mean in a German state where rulers consistently understood the founding of the state as diametrically opposed to National Socialism and its prehistory?

2. What have experiences of nonconformism in the GDR meant for the transformation of society after 1990? What do these experiences mean for democracy in East Germany today? Did and does every act of resistance or rebellion belong to a democratic tradition?

3. What effects have decades-long experiences of agency and powerlessness had on people's understandings of democracy in East Germany?

4. What is the relationship between the Nazi past, the history of the GDR, and the history of transformation when it comes to motivations for or against democracy?

While this short text cannot provide fully satisfactory answers to these questions, it can demonstrate their virulence. In this essay, I will formulate my doubts regarding familiar interpretations, engaging with some of the deficits of opposition research. In doing so, I call for a different view of nonconformity before and after 1990. Presenting new perspectives, my theses are intended to counter a discourse on the East German "incapacity for democracy" that has been shaped by historical scholarship.

Criticism of Current GDR Opposition Research

A paradigm shift in GDR research took place in 1989/90. The involuntary "handover of the baton" from old GDR political science research (conducted in West Germany) to more historically oriented "new" GDR research was not just an institutional and personal caesura. The return and ideological dominance of the doctrine of the 1950s—totalitarianism theory—in the old Federal Republic of Germany became a heavy burden. This also applied to opposition research, which since then has forced every episode of resistance into the theoretical template of totalitarianism, promoting ideologically motivated idealizations, dehistorizations, and personifications of historical contexts. The resulting iconization and heroization of resistance figures corresponds to a culture of memory that is oriented to state politics. The ahistorical concept of resistance that follows the simple dictum of freedom versus totalitarianism constructs an ideal type of "a small group of dissidents" who "opposed the party and the state for political and moral reasons" (Port 2010: 23). This leaves little room for differentiation and alternative approaches. Reinforced by analogies to anti-Nazi resistance research, it also makes it possible to equate resistance against the "brown" with that against the "red dictatorship." Furthermore, it has undertones of historical revisionism, which certainly occur in (traditional) German historiography as well (Hannemann 2014b).

In the early 1990s, the aggressive cutting off of important strands of "old" GDR research by new actors (Hüttmann 2008: 313) offered new insights. Peter Christian Ludz's (1968) study of the SED party elite (conducted at the end of the 1960s), for example, still offered important directions for research on nonconformism. The one-dimensional theory of totalitarianism led to a narrow view of society and its vertical lines of conflict. This explains the overwhelming focus on sources produced by GDR security organs such as the Stasi and Grenz-Regime (border patrol). The result was that the population's heterogeneity and historicity and the complex dynamics of conflict situations and "horizontal" conflict constellations (Port 2010: 345) were lost. Sociological or sociopsychological approaches received little attention. To complicate matters, trends in the social sciences, including the re-biologization of psychology (Galliker 2016) and the condemnation of sociopsychological approaches, created analytical voids where anthopologisms or mythical-ontical concepts such as "memory" and "national myth" penetrated (Weilnböck 2007: 35–36).

A lack of critical reflection on the biographical influences of historical actors posed another problem. Instead, biographical information was often regarded as an "authentic" approach to historical truth. Adopting a critical perspective, I call this an *unreflected auto-oral history*.

The GDR as a German Postwar Society

Here we arrive at the obvious: the GDR was a German postwar society. Motivations for nonconformism in the GDR, which were complex, should be of great interest for the historiographical evaluation of resistance but also should be situated in a diachronic context. This becomes clear when looking at 17 June 1953.

The date 17 June 1953 is still one of the most sacrosanct sites of memory in totalitarianism theory. In Germany, the traditional view of 17 June

(Neubert 2013) as an iconic moment of democratic resistance[3] and as "the first failed freedom movement in the GDR that nevertheless ha[d] an impact,"[4] has mostly remained the same, even in current publications by the Federal Agency for Civic Education.[5]

Eight years after the defeat of the "German Reich," people of all ages and classes, some armed with stones, moved to the former center of Nazi rule, Wilhelmstraße in Berlin (Nachama 2012). Until 1945, this street, which housed all central governmental institutions, was regarded as synonymous with German power and government (Demps 2010). After 1945, some government and Nazi party buildings were used on a provisional basis by the Soviet Military Administration (SMAD) and GDR governments. The Neue Reichskanzlei (New Reich Chancellery), however, was demolished as a preventive measure, since it was feared to be a Nazi gathering site and symbol of "national resistance." Between 1945 and 1948, all Allied military administrations were reasonably concerned about the possibility of resistance actions.[6] Not only Goebbels's announcement of guerrilla resistance by the so-called Werwolf but also the fanatical warfare of the SS and Wehrmacht, as well as the Volkssturm until total defeat, worried the Allies. There was no reason to trust the German population. And indeed, in 1948, there was resistance against the rule of the occupying military administrations, triggered by decisions on economic policy (Roesler 2008: 47–49).

Concentrated in the industrial centers of Stuttgart, Nuremberg, and Munich, 1.3 million people in Bavaria and around one million in Baden-Württemberg participated in general strikes, culminating in what came to be called the Stuttgart Incidents on 28 October 1948. The riots in Stuttgart were extremely violent, which their trade union initiators had not intended, and were defeated by police and US military (Roesler 2008: 52–53). These "incidents," which according to reports by the US administration were escalated in some cases by "apparently systematically distributed groups of youths" (Roesler 2008: 54), prompted General Lucius Clay to impose a curfew for days. I interpret these developments as one of many resistance events against the Allies that were cross-zonal. In light of these events, the sizable Allied military presence, including in Berlin, was a message to the population that the monopoly on the use of force was in Allied hands.

A few years later, in June 1953, thousands of angry demonstrators moved toward the buildings of Herrmann Göring's former Reichsluftfahrtsministerium (Reich Aviation Ministry / RLM) and Joseph Goebbels's Propaganda Ministry. Both locations were provisionally used by the GDR Volkskammer (People's Chamber) and Ministerrat (Council of Ministers).

The spatial and temporal dimensions of these events call for contextualization: Who moved along Leipziger Straße with the aim of reaching Wilhelmstraße? What tradition did the uprising's violent forms fit into? What slogans were shouted by the protesters? What political claims did they make (and not only in Berlin)? What did the temporal proximity to the German war of extermination mean, given that an entire society was involved in a "total war?"[7] To what extent did decades of discourses—antisemitic, racist, social-chauvinist, race-theoretical, anti-Bolshevist, etc.—shape views of the resistance against the SED and Soviet occupiers? What symbolic meanings of Wilhelmstraße, as a German site of memory, were reconstructed for the demonstrators? Did the angry demonstrators read it as the "occupied national government center of Germany?"

These questions illustrate how previous developments led to particular motives and tendencies. These motivations cannot be derived retrospectively by using the rigid model of "democratic anti-totalitarianism" abstracted from history. It is astonishing that conventional research hardly relates the proximity of 17 June 1953 to the Nazi era, or the resistance against occupation authorities in the 1940s to 17 June. Totalitarianism interpretations, on the other hand, extract the constantly changing political system of the GDR, which was still under construction in 1953, from its historical context and compare it to other abstractions. Events that are far apart in time, such as June 17, the Prague Spring, and the Solidarność movement, are set in relation to one another, rather than to the closer Nazi past. If, on the other hand, GDR society is understood as a German postwar society, profoundly different insights might emerge.[8] As complex as the causes, motivations, and occasions for the uprising on 17 June 1953 may have been, they cannot be located exclusively in the ahistorical dualism of "resistance against a dictatorship."

Totalitarianism theory–orientated opposition research even manages, curiously, to subsume the nonconformist GDR punk subculture of the 1980s under the same category as adolescents in the 1950s who opposed the "SED dictatorship," for example, in the Kampfgruppe gegen Unmenschlichkeit (Fight Group against Inhumanity)—youths who were socialized under the Nazis (Heitzer 2015). This research, meanwhile, fails to probe historical continuities in opposition phenomena, such as the desecration of Jewish cemeteries by neo-Nazi youth in the 1980s. Youth resistance against GDR authorities extends other historical lines of development than the nonconformity of the punk or hip-hop/skater scene.

In "classical" opposition research, however, neo-Nazism in the GDR is not understood as oppositional behavior. It is caused, following these approaches, by the "totalitarian socialist system." In his standard work on the history of opposition, Erhart Neubert only mentions neo-Nazism once. It appears as a spontaneous and almost apolitical phenomenon, resembling a phase like puberty (Neubert 1998: 355). Today, this view persists in research on right-wing extremism in East Germany (Michelsen, Przybilla-Voß, and Lümann 2017).

Right-wing extremist resistance against the SED government before 1990 and against the Grundgesetz (Basic Law) and the west-German liberal constitutional order after the entry of the GDR into the Federal Republic in 1990 have similar political, sociopsychological, and historical sources. Anyone who ascribes the motivations of these actions against the authorities to only the "totalitarianism" of the GDR singles out SED rule as responsible for obedience to the authorities. They also locate the source of anti-authoritarian thinking in the opposition Protestant church, for example, while failing to recognize that the other two post-Nazi societies have confronted neo-Nazism. GDR society—like the Federal Republic of Germany (FRG) and Austria—was more strongly influenced by the aftermath of German history than by Soviet communism, which, according to the oppositional GDR philosopher Rudolf Bahro, could only be incorporated into the GDR in a "Germanized" way (Bahro 1977: 17).

Discomfort and Conflict in a Scientifically and Technically Administered Industrial Society

Understanding the GDR as a late-industrial class society opens up additional perspectives on nonconformism and its motivations. The systemic logic of these societies implies striving for total integration of all human labor into the production process, the efficiency of which is to be increased through scientific and technological innovation. Incorporation into the social totality follows through mechanisms of state control, while the mitigation of strong social differences and the levelling influence of the culture industry on mentalities have a stabilizing effect. The technical-bureaucratic orientation of administration, the state, economy, health, education, leisure activities, etc. depicts *one* aspect of the GDR system of rule that shaped consciousness and mentalities in this way. Here, too, mechanisms of modern consciousness formation were at work: labor ideology, nation, law, discipline, purity, order, petty bourgeois family ideas, and other modern fetishes. They are central elements of a "necessarily false consciousness" (Adorno 1975: 190) that was handed down long before 1945. State propaganda had to take such dispositions of consciousness into account to become "effective" at all.[9]

The adaptation of the individual to the state and production, which the West German author Rüdiger Thomas (1975) described as "calculated emancipation" (in accordance with the modernist Zeitgeist of the Federal Republic of Germany), was evident in the government's standard for school: the polytechnic secondary school (politechnische Oberschule / POS). But it was also performed in technical-scientific courses at universities and other academic institutions, in the organization and planning of leisure by the state, in enterprise, and in the presence of state medicine at schools and factories. It was evident in the welfare state integration of the working and nonmanual working classes and in the macroeconomic focus on consumption, especially beginning in the 1970s (Steiner 2007: 165–167).

Those who refused to accept modernity's integration stood in contradiction to this socialization process. In the GDR, the so-called "work shy," "strollers," or conscientious objectors suffered repression and/or marginalization. State welfare for the working population and simultaneous social discrimination directed at non-working employees, such as the aging poor (Geißler 2011: 222–223), underline the GDR's modern character.[10]

Social mobility was to integrate the population, which was also burdened by the Nazi past, into the postwar order.[11] Until the 1970s, it integrated large sections of the population. The denazification of the education and science system—but also administration, industry, and agriculture—enabled many young people to rise from once underprivileged positions. Their rapid education in the so-called *Arbeiter- und Bauernfakultäten* (workers' and farmers' faculties), for example, and the subsequent creation of *Kombinate* (industrial multi-production units) fueled enormous social mobility (Solga 1995: 210). As was the case for the FRG until the 1960s, the GDR also displayed an *Aufbau* (reconstruction) myth of busy creation and production. Since the 1970s, the cultural industry strengthened the entertainment sector (sports, music, and film) and created a national GDR narrative to paper over class distinctions with new forms of identity.[12]

It is often disregarded that since 17 June 1953, conflict appeasement evolved into a stabilizing factor for the ruling system. From the perspective of totalitarianism theory, concepts such as "negotiation" or even "compromise" in a dictatorship may seem strange. But the relatively strong position of workers in company decisions in the production sphere also contributed to stabilization (Solga 1995). While the role of state force should not be underestimated, it is often overemphasized in conventional research. Constant complaints about labor standards, wages, supply shortages, and inadequate housing, or refusals to join the party, occupied the ruling apparatus—as did persecuting "spies," "saboteurs," "revisionists," and "republic refugees." Andrew Port (2010: 149–150) aptly characterizes the GDR as a *Meckergesellschaft* (complaining society).

The dynamics of appeasement and social mobility, however, suddenly turned into social stagnation at the end of the 1970s. The former *Aufbaugeneration* that profited from opportunities for mobility in the 1950s and 1960s was now an established elite that blocked the social mobility of subsequent generations. The GDR changed rapidly from a "society of ascenders" to one of "the establishment," causing alienation and leading many young people to leave, which filled the state leadership with fear (Solga 1995: 207–209). Youth subcultures became the site for nonconformity; the rulers mostly reacted repressively and ignored the subcultures' lack of any particular social agenda.

The effects of GDR modernism were contradictory. Education for discipline, work ethic, tidiness, and, since the 1970s, modular prefabricated housing units with standardized furnishings are viewed in the context of a general history of precarity in modern society, like the emancipatory potential of modern living and working in the GDR. Certain disciplinary mechanisms that operate in an economically liberal society, such as the permanent threat of social decline, ceased to exist in the GDR.

The traditional social structure that was dissolved by social mobility and the social improvements that began at the end of the 1960s, including the housing construction program, ensured the stabilization of the GDR. Yet the emerging culture industry did not always successfully strive for the standardization of thought. In literature, for example, the archetype of the worker (Engler 2010: 171–173) was to be deeply imprinted by the framework of the "Bitterfelder Weg," the general integration of the worker's habitus into the national culture (such as literature). But at the same time, this intensified characteristically modern tensions between functional elites, employees, clerks, and the working class, voiced as annoyance with "party bosses" and "apparatchiks."

Social Psychology and Remembrance Work

It is remarkable that the psycho-historical repression processes that Alexander and Margarete Mitscherlich (1967) described in the FRG were never examined for the GDR. Such an analysis could reveal new insights into the workings of this repression in society.

As is well known, in 1967, the Mitscherlichs interpreted the industrious efforts of postwar Germans to rebuild the country as a collective repression. This process of diligent amnesia was backed up by the Western Allies, who increasingly gave up their program of *Aufarbeitung* of the recent Nazi past. After 1945, according to Mitscherlichs, the collective loss of the libidinously occupied (super)father figure, the "Führer," should have led to mass and potentially liberating melancholy; it could have urged people to reflect on society and change. But the myths of *Trümmerfrauen* (industrious women in ruins) and the so-called *Wirtschaftswunder* (the West German economic miracle) hampered this potentially liberating process. The continuation of anti-communist ideology and practice, as well as the propagation of a "national liberation struggle of the German brothers and sisters in the East," only strengthened the status quo (Mitscherlich 1987: 13–14). On familiar, almost unchanged ideological paths, it was possible to continue as if nothing had happened. A large part of the elite remained the backbone of society. Old hierarchical structures of classes and power often persisted. Until the 1970s, there was hardly any basis for the often invoked feelings of guilt among Germans.

But according to Margarete Mitscherlich (1987), it was only by digesting feelings of guilt toward the father figure of "the Führer," that the basic preconditions for (genuine) feelings of guilt toward the victims of National Socialism would appear. In a busy Biedermeier, and alongside the national persecution of communists, feelings of failure were suppressed. In the 1980s, Mitscherlich (1987: 23) summarized that "Jews" were no longer proclaimed targets for aggression, while "the Bolshevist," as a concept of the enemy, continued to resonate. The Mitscherlichs (1967; and Mitscherlich 1987), like Erich Fromm and Theodor W. Adorno, assumed from the perspective of depth psychology that the German population was still dominated by authoritarianism. Similar questions are obvious for the postwar society of the GDR. Furthermore, it must be asked how postwar Germans in the GDR dealt with their experiences of war, violence, disinhibition, and trauma in the face of their socialization, which presumably shaped their hardened and authoritarian personality structures and made them incapable of happiness.[13]

There have been attempts to create a "psychogram" of the East Germans. Hans-Joachim Maaz (1992), for example, searched for the first time in 1990 for the causes of socially generated discomfort, which were located in at least parts of the GDR population. He indeed touched on mechanisms of psychological mutilation through rule, repression, education, and social pressures, which—typical for late modern industrial societies—caused privation, repression, and false sublimation, as well as an "emotional blockage." Maaz's conclusions are debatable, especially since he attributes the failure of democratic movements in the GDR before the opening of the Wall to "repulsion against any hierarchy" (Maaz 1992: 115). Yet the "leaderless, unstructured group" (Maaz 1992: 115) of GDR citizens of 1989—most of whom were not willing to leave the country, but, in need of democratization, were inclined toward the "leaderless, unstructured group"—is precisely an indication of the "democratic potential" of East

Germans (the second and third generations). It is also an indication of a longing for criticism of power and hierarchy, for utopia and happiness, which has not been attributed to the "red" Prussians.[14]

A decade later, Wolfgang Engler (2000) examined the "East German psyche." He characterized "the East Germans" as shaped by a particular GDR modernism. While the pressures of late industrial societies caused psychological damage, social dynamics and state welfare—forced by an intensified policy of social security under Erich Honecker's leadership—could generate new states of consciousness. Less fear of existence and an imposed lack of interest in state politics made people more eager to experiment in life (Engler 2000: 61). These modernization processes stabilized the GDR on a psychological level. Paradoxically, they were also able to build the foundations for a mental—but not necessarily democratically motivated—withdrawal from the GDR. But important questions have not yet been asked:

1. On the basis of Mitscherlich's (1987) theses, questions must be asked about individual motives for conformism or nonconformism in the GDR.

2. Furthermore, the effects of authoritarian education, not only in state institutions but also in families must be examined. What painful experiences of the war and postwar period became socially relevant?

3. According to depth psychological approaches, psychological dispositions anchored in the unconscious are transmitted from generation to generation (in a deformed way) (Moré 2013). What does this mean for constituents of the GDR—and GDR studies? What are the generational and family backgrounds?

Classical opposition research, which is stuck heroizing and personifying its material and speaks out in favor of a publicly ritualized "culture of memory," is too strongly charged to allow for new reflections on GDR society and its transformation. In academia, too, the "preservation of memory" seems to be more important than *remembrance* work. Weinböck has pointed to the small increase in knowledge of such memory ontologies on the one hand, and their counterproductivity for reducing personal suffering on the other. *Memory* preservation that is morally transfigured by discourse not only prevents enlightenment but also implies aggression and resentment because it repels it (Weinböck 2007: 36). The self-image that has been preserved statically, and not without psychological investment, is defended against uncontrollable, dynamic *remembrance*. A history of nonconformism should therefore be an open process of working and understanding. This does not only help victims of state persecution in alleviating their suffering.

East German Experiences of GDR Society, the Transformation of GDR Society, and Democracy in East Germany

Today, public complaints about East Germans and their supposedly underdeveloped civil society can be heard often in public discourse. This alleged "defect," according to the discussion, can be traced to the socialization of East Germans in a dictatorship enabled by obedient followers, against which only a few dissidents resisted. Compared to West Germans, East Germans are said to have a lot of catching up to do in democracy and in dealing with the Nazi "past." The Federal Republic, or its image of itself as "the world champion" in dealing with the Nazi past and as a model for democracy, offers the blueprint. As much as "Ossis" (East Germans) serve as a projection screen for the negative construction of "the Other," this accusation causes bitterness in the "new federal states," where people are extremely diverse. Socially and politically, this bitterness can hardly be overestimated.

The picture of everyday life in the GDR, "the perfect world of dictatorship" (Stefan Wolle), must be drawn in more complex ways than what GDR research, shaped by totalitarianism theory, usually does. It can hardly be denied that there were special forms of civic life in the GDR that contributed to political upheaval in 1989. Admittedly, such an understanding of opposition and nonconformism goes far beyond what is usually represented in German memorial culture at memorial sites and in the media landscape of the FRG, where concessions are made for only a relatively small group of "dissidents" and "civil rights activists." Alongside numerous attempts by some actors within the SED or in mass organizations to achieve reform — even radical changes via circumscribed paths and actions — there were daily, widespread forms of civil engagement and nonconformism beyond political organizations and dissident groups and beyond elitist circles in science, art, culture, and politics. But their motives did not always have to be democratic. (Opposing a communist regime is not democratic per se.)

Today, evaluations of civil society engagements in the GDR are often made ex post facto and extrinsically by using the classical political division between the private and public spheres. Social and societal — that is, political—action, for example, in the GDR's unofficial barter economy, sexuality and gender roles, and neighborhood cooperation and solidarity in various cultural (youth) subcultures and company brigades generally fall off the radar of civil society and scientific terminology that is modeled on West German reality (Hannemann 2019b).

Since the 1970s, social policy has been associated with massive public housing construction that brought new forms of housing and, unlike in Western democracies, did not create socially segregated prefabricated suburbs for the socially disadvantaged. Instead, it offered people new and unconventional possibilities and lifestyles. The prefabricated housing complex fueled aspirations to an entirely new life.[15] The effects were contradictory. On the one hand, job guarantees and housing in strictly modern prefabricated housing complexes (Wolle 1999: 187) strengthened state loyalty and political control (Hannemann 2019a; Rubin 2016). On the other hand, it was precisely these conditions that led to the disappearance of the existential fear of unemployment and social decline; these residential environments produced new neighborliness (Engler 2000: 61). As long as the public rituals of SED rule were respected, for example, in political celebrations such as the First of May or the Tag der Republik, one could rediscover "the political" within the "private niche."[16] In these unofficial niches grew the potential for social change.

In 1989, departure and rupture came at the same time. Despite these East German experiences of engagement and conflict management, democracy and protest, how did civil society structures collapse? And how did the above-mentioned skepticism toward democracy emerge? GDR-specific traditions of civil society and engagement were shattered by negative experiences with the new and unfamiliar political, cultural, and socioeconomic system of the FRG. Furthermore, the social order of the Federal Republic—its legal, security, and social order—especially in the early 1990s, was in many ways, not fully established in East Germany. In the early transformation phase, collective experiences with spaces that were at times free of law, where the state's monopoly on the use of force could not be implemented against right-wing extremists in certain city districts, for example, left lasting impressions on collective memory. The sometimes opaque and even illegal process of deindustrializing the former East German state economy also conveyed feelings of powerlessness in a climate of lawlessness (Hannemann 2019a; Wendel 1995; Böick 2018).

Simultaneously, many East Germans, who had just experienced unprecedented self-efficacy through democratic engagement, found themselves at the mercy of socioeconomic and political processes over which they had no influence. In many respects, the new states within the Federal Republic's legal, economic, social, and cultural order became "special zones," even in later years when it came to wages, labor laws, pension regulations, and more.

The extent to which East German experiences of nonconformity and resistance had an effect on the transformation period since 1990 has been poorly researched.[17] Problems of democratic development in East Germany, however, are still attributed, more than twenty-nine years after the fall of the Berlin Wall, to the dictatorial character of the GDR, while the Nazi past of Germany as a whole is obscured.

Alongside the self-initiated democratic awakening, experiences of powerlessness amid "external" historical and social forces, enormous biographical disruptions, the millionfold decay of life plans and "forms of interaction" (Lorenzer 1973)[18] in families and social life, and the invalidation of knowledge—for example, on linguistic-symbolic forms of societal behavior—have been poorly researched in every respect. Curiously, traditional academic GDR opposition research has played a part in disconnecting these collective experiences of subjectivity. Paradoxically, it has at the same time avoided and blocked a reappraisal of East German postwar society as a post-Führer and post-violence society.

Raiko Hannemann, born in 1980 in Cottbus, is a historian, philosopher, and political scientist at the Alice Salomon Hochschule Berlin, where he is engaged in the research project "Democratic Attitudes in a Commune: The Example of Marzahn-Hellersdorf." Supervised by Hartmut Rosa, he is a doctoral student in sociology at the Friedrich Schiller University in Jena and is writing a dissertation titled "World Relations and Democracy in East Germany: Alienation and Resonance in the East Berlin District Marzahn-Hellersdorf since the 1980s." In his 2014 book, *Die unerträgliche Leichtigkeit des Vorurteils* (The unbearable lightness of prejudice), he critically examined contemporary antisemitism research and the politics of history using the example of Götz Aly. He assisted Helga Grebing in a publication on Fritz Sternberg, a Zionist and socialist. He has published on the GDR, East Germany's social and political transformation after 1989, the East German Cityoen, social inequality, antisemitism, right-wing extremism, and democracy research.

Notes

Since the 1990s, the East Berlin district Marzahn-Hellersdorf has become synonymous with a "problem district" in the media (Hieronymus and Dušan 2014). After an invitation by members of Bündnis 90/Die Grünen to discuss the relationship of the population of the (East) Berlin city district Marzahn-Hellersdorf to democracy, I assumed the role of democracy researcher (Hannemann 2016, 2017, 2018, 2019a, 2019b).

1. This was the case in a study commissioned by the Federal Government (Michelsen, Przybilla-Voß, and Lümann 2017: 33–35).
2. I presented similar theses in 2013 (Hannemann 2014a, 81–83).
3. This includes the interpretation of 17 June 1953 as a proletarian strike in the tradition of the left-wing workers' movement. Today, this interpretation persists.
4. These words were used by the *Bundeszentrale für politische Bildung* (Federal Agency for Civic Education) to advertise a book published in 2013 on 17 June (Kowalczuk 2013).
5. Questionable attempts in the 2000s to establish 17 June as the "positive founding legend of the new Federal Republic" in addition to Auschwitz as the "negative founding legend of the Federal Republic" cannot be dealt with here (Eisenfeld, Kowalczuk, and Neubert 2004).
6. Before 8 May 1945, there was no mass resistance against the Nazi order (strikes, weapon resignations, etc.) (Morsch 1988: 649–651).
7. That practices of warfare could be reactivated was demonstrated in front of the former RLM. Demonstrators jumped on Soviet tanks and, as they had learned, broke down antennas to interfere with radio communications (Schultze 2014: 28). Similar phenomena occurred during a spontaneous revolt in 1951 in Saalfeld, Thuringia. During an early morning brawl on 16 August 1951 near a police station, a group of spectators quickly turned into an aggressive crowd. Some were arrested, causing an angry mob to storm the police station. Police officers were injured (Port 2010: 66–68). On the one hand, the mob demanded higher wages and better working and living conditions. On the other, general tensions that had been accumulating were unleashed. Meanwhile, anonymous and angry letters reached local authorities, insulting police officers as "Russian henchmen," and Soviet liberators as "scourges of humanity" (Port 2010: 83–85). These letters linked social, anti-Bolshevik, and liberation-nationalist demands. In form and content, these resistance events (as in Stuttgart) were not in the tradition of the labor movement but recalled the archaic violence of late medieval peasant uprisings (Port 2010: 34, 84).
8. This was recently shown by Gerd Kühling (2016: 253–255), who looked at June 17 from the perspective of survivors of the Nazi terror regime, who perceived the uprising as a nationalist, antisemitic wave of rage and who were reminded of the pogrom of 1938. Viewed from the history of generations, temporal dynamics were also at work. A review of the anthology *Die GDR aus Generationengeschichtlicher Perspektive. Eine Inventur* (Schüle, Ahbe, and Gries 2005), however, makes the crucial point that even in the history of generations, too few diachronic and synchronous lines of development that reached deep into the GDR are taken into account. Dietrich (2006) wanted "more references to historical experiences and research on the generations of the Empire, the Weimar Republic, and the Third Reich . . . who continued to live and work in the GDR."
9. Propagandists must be able to assess the effect on the "masses," while the masses must "cooperate" in the propagation of enemy images (Gries and Satju-

kow 2004: 845–847). The "blind" interaction between sender and receiver results in an uncontrollable propaganda effect.

10. The modernization of the GDR, a class society "in itself" (Solga 1995), also had liberating effects. Productivity pressure and the almost complete integration of women into the production process, despite the double burden and family inequality, led to the transformation of the social role of women through economic independence.

11. Whether, as frequently stated in scholarly publications and journalism, the GDR's antifascism, which cleared the entire population of guilt for Nazi crimes, was the most important offer of integration to the population, is questionable. This thesis is based on the assumption of widespread awareness of guilt among the population. This is doubtful.

12. Ironically, for many East Germans it was the post-reunification period that evoked the GDR identity of "Ossis" on a massive scale.

13. It is, of course, far from my intention to twist the relationship between victim and perpetrator. On the contrary, it is a matter of understanding these postwar people in the GDR, regardless of their political systems. Here, suffering and trauma are analytical categories, not moral ones.

14. Maaz's (2015) commendable effort to draw a psychogram unfortunately ignores the historical dimension of psychological phenomena that the Mitscherlichs analyzed for West Germany. This also is evident in his benevolent remarks on the right-wing movement "Pegida," which emerged in 2014 in the East German city of Dresden.

15. The East Berlin district of Marzahn-Hellersdorf played a central role as a showcase settlement (Rubin 2016: 7–8).

16. West German journalist and politician Günther Gaus (1983) called the GDR society a "Nischengesellschaft," or "niche society."

17. Even if transformation research has made great progress in the area of theoretical exploration, for example. The work of the Commission for the Study of Social and Political Change in the New Federal States (KSPW) between 1992 and 1996, or research by the Sonderforschungsbereich 580 of the Deutsche Forschungsgemeinschaft (DFG) conducted between 2001 and 2011/12 (Best and Holtmann 2012) should be emphasized.

18. Alfred Lorenzer's historical-critical psychoanalysis could open up completely new fields of research.

References

Adorno, Theodor. 1975. *Negative Dialektik*. Frankfurt a. M.
Bahro, Rudolf. 1977. *Eine Dokumentation*. Frankfurt a. M.
Best, Heinrich, and Everhard Holtmann, eds. 2012. *Aufbruch der entsicherten Gesellschaft. Deutschland nach der Wiedervereinigung*. Frankfurt a. M.
Demps, Laurenz. 2010. *Berlin-Wilhelmstraße. Eine Topographie preußisch-deutscher Macht*. Berlin.
Dietrich, Gerd. 2006. "Review: Annegret Schüle, Thomas Ahbe, and Rainer Gries, eds. *Die DDR aus generationengeschichtlicher Perspektive. Eine Inventur*." H-Soz-

u-Kult, 28 August 2006. Accessed 27 January 2018, http://hsozkult.geschichte.hu-berlin.de/rezensionen/2006-3-141.

Eisenfeld, Bernd, Ilko-Sascha Kowalczuk, and Ehrhart Neubert. 2004. *Die verdrängte Revolution. Der Platz des 17. Juni 1953 in der deutschen Geschichte*. Bremen.

Engler, Wolfgang. 2000. *Die Ostdeutschen. Kunde von einem verlorenen Land*. 2nd ed. Berlin.

———. 2010. "Der Arbeiter." In *Erinnerungsorte der DDR*, edited by Martin Sabrow, 171–182. Bonn.

Gaus, Günter. 1983. *Wo Deutschland liegt*. Hamburg

Galliker, Mark. 2016. *Ist die Psychologie eine Wissenschaft? Ihre Krisen und Kontroversen von den Anfängen bis zur Gegenwart*. Heidelberg.

Geißler, Rainer. 2011. *Die Sozialstruktur Deutschlands. Zur gesellschaftlichen Entwicklung mit einer Bilanz zur Vereinigung*. 6th ed. Wiesbaden.

Gries, Rainer, and Silke Satjukow. 2004. "Seid wachsam! Feindbilder in sozialistischen Gesellschaften." *Deutschland Archiv* 37, no. 5: 845–854.

Hannemann, Raiko. 2014a. "DDR-Oppositionsforschung und Erinnerungsprozesse. Konflikte in und mit einer deutschen Nachkriegsgesellschaft." In *Geschichte im Dialog."DDR-Zeitzeugen" in Geschichtskultur und Bildungspraxis*, edited by Christian Ernst, 81-96. Schwalbach/Ts.

———. 2014b. *Die unerträgliche Leichtigkeit des Vorurteils. Zu einer Funktionalisierung des historischen Antisemitismus im gegenwärtigen Geschichtsdiskurs*. Berlin.

———. 2016. *Demokratieentwicklung am Ort der Vielfalt Marzahn-Hellersdorf. Jahresbericht 2015*. Berlin. Accessed 29 May 2017, https://www.berlin.de/ba-marzahn-hellersdorf/politik-und-verwaltung/beauftragte/integration/artikel.217980.php.

———. 2017. "Demokratie, Demokratieverhalten und -verhältnis/ Maßnahmen für demokratieaffine und demokratiedistanzierte Gruppen." In *Demokratienähe und -distanz. Zwischenbericht mit Empfehlungen an die Politik*, edited by Raiko Hannemann, *Stefan* Komoß, Andrea Metzner, Paula Moldenhauer, and Heinz Stapf-Finé, 33–77. Berlin. https://www.ash-berlin.eu/fileadmin/Daten/_user Home/158_stapf-fineh/Zwischenbericht.pdf.

———. 2018. "Nonkonformität in einer deutschen Nachkriegsgesellschaft. Fragen an die DDR- und die Transformationsforschung." In *Nach Auschwitz: Schwieriges Erbe DDR*, edited by Anetta Kahane, 292–309. Frankfurt a. M.

———. 2019a. "Demokratieverhältnis zwischen lebensgeschichtlicher Erfahrung und (bezirklichen) Beteiligungsbedingungen. Forschungsbericht zur qualitativen Erhebung." In *Demokratienähe und -distanz. Das Forschungsprojekt Demokratieferne Einstellungen in einer Kommune*, edited by Heinz Stapf-Finé, 117–186. Berlin.

———. 2019b. "Der ostdeutsche Citoyen. Beobachtungen zu Tiefstrukturen der Demokratieentwicklung in Marzahn-Hellersdorf. Generationen, Erfahrungen, Erkenntnisschranken." *Sozialer Fortschritt* 68, nos. 8–9: 701–730.

Hauser, Richard, Wolfgang Glatzer, Stefan Hradil, Gerhard Kleinhenz, Thomas Olk, and Eckart Pankoke. 1996. *Ungleichheit und Sozialpolitik* (Bericht 2 der Kommission zur Erforschung des sozialen und politischen Wandels in den neuen Bundesländern). Opladen.

Heitzer, Enrico. 2015. *Die Kampfgruppe gegen Unmenschlichkeit (KgU). Widerstand und Spionage im Kalten Krieg 1948–1959*. Vienna.

Hieronymus, Andreas, and Dušan Ugrina. 2014. *Europe's White Working-Class Communities*, edited by Open Society Foundations. Berlin.

Hübner, Peter. 1995. *Konsens, Konflikt und Kompromiss. Soziale Arbeiterinteressen und Sozialpolitik in der SBZ/DDR, 1945–1970.* Berlin.
Hüttmann, Jens. 2008. *DDR-Geschichte und ihre Forscher. Akteure und Konjunkturen der bundesdeutschen DDR-Forschung.* Berlin.
Kowalczuk, Ilko-Sascha. 2013. *17. Juni 1953. Geschichte eines Aufstands.* Accessed 27 January 2018, http://www.bpb.de/shop/buecher/schriftenreihe/162853/17-juni-1953.
Kühling, Gerd. 2016. *Erinnerung an nationalsozialistische Verbrechen in Berlin. Verfolgte des Dritten Reiches und geschichtspolitisches Engagement im Kalten Krieg, 1945–1979.* Berlin.
Lorenzer, Alfred. 1973. *Über den Gegenstand der Psychoanalyse oder: Sprache und Interaktion.* Frankfurt a. M.
Ludz, Peter Christian. 1968. *Parteielite im Wandel. Funktionsaufbau, Sozialstruktur und Ideologie der SED-Führung. Eine empirisch-systematische Untersuchung.* 2nd ed. Cologne.
Maaz, Hans-Joachim. 1992. *Der Gefühlsstau. Ein Psychogramm der DDR. 1990.* Munich.
———. 2015. "Pegida auf der Couch: Eine konservative APO?" *Deutschlandfunk,* 23 January 2015. Accessed 12 December 2017, http://www.deutschlandfunkkultur.de/hans-joachim-maaz-pegida-auf-der-couch-eine-konservative-apo.1008.de.html?dram:article_id=309503.
Michelsen, Danny, Marika Przybilla-Voß, and Michael Lümann. 2017. *Ursachen und Hintergründe für Rechtsextremismus, Fremdenfeindlichkeit und fremdenfeindlich motivierte Übergriffe in Ostdeutschland sowie die Ballung in einzelnen ostdeutschen Regionen.* Accessed 3 August 2017, http://www.beauftragte-neuelaender.de/BNL/Redaktion/DE/Downloads/Publikationen/studie-rechtsextremismus-in-ostdeutschland.pdf?__blob=publicationFile&v=6.
Mitscherlich, Alexander, and Margarete Mitscherlich. 1967. *Die Unfähigkeit zu trauern.* 19th ed. Munich.
Mitscherlich, Margarete. 1987. "Trauerfähigkeit der Deutschen—Illusion oder Hoffnung?" In *Erinnerungsarbeit. Zur Psychoanalyse der Unfähigkeit zu trauern,* edited by Magarete Mitscherlich, 13–35. Frankfurt a. M.
Moller, Sabine. 2010. "Erinnerung und Gedächtnis." Version 1.0. *Docupedia-Zeitgeschichte,* 12 April 2010. Accessed 2 March 2013, https://docupedia.de/images/d/d7/Erinnerung_und_Ged%C3%A4chtnis.pdf.
Moré, Angela. 2013. "Die unbewusste Weitergabe von Traumata und Schuldverstrickungen an nachfolgende Generationen." *Journal für Psychologie* 21, no. 2. Accessed 12 December 2017, https://www.journal-fuer psychologie.de/index.php/jfp/article/view/268/310.
Morsch, Günter. 1988. "Streik im 'Dritten Reich.'" *Vierteljahreshefte für Zeitgeschichte* 36, no. 4: 649–689.
Nachama, Andreas, ed. 2012. *Die Wilhelmstraße 1933–1945—Aufstieg und Untergang des NS-Regierungsviertels. Stiftung Topographie des Terrors.* Berlin.
Neubert, Ehrhart. 1998. *Geschichte der Opposition in der DDR.* 2nd revised and expanded edition. Berlin.
———. 2013. "Geschichtspolitische Aspekte des 17. Juni." *Deutschland Archiv,* 28 June 2013. Accessed 27 January 2018, http://www.bpb.de/164144.
Port, Andrew I. 2010. *Die rätselhafte Stabilität der DDR. Arbeit und Alltag im sozialistischen Deutschland.* Bonn.
Roesler, Jörg. 2008. *Die Wiederaufbaulüge der Bundesrepublik. Oder: Wie die Neoliberalen ihre "Argumente" produzieren.* Texte/Rosa-Luxemburg-Stiftung 43. Berlin.

Rubin, Eli. 2016. *Amnesiopolis: Modernity, Space, and Memory in East Germany.* Oxford.
Solga, Heike. 1995. *Auf dem Weg in eine klassenlose Gesellschaft? Klassenlagen und Mobilität zwischen Generationen in der DDR.* Berlin.
Schultze, Sven. 2014. *17. Juni 1953: "Die Hennigsdorfer kommen!"* Edited by the City of Hennigsdorf. Hennigsdorf.
Schüle, Annegret, Thomas Ahbe, and Rainer Gries, eds. 2005. *Die DDR aus generationen-geschichtlicher Perspektive. Eine Inventur.* Leipzig.
Steiner, André. 2007. *Von Plan zu Plan. Eine Wirtschaftsgeschichte der DDR.* Bonn.
Weilnböck, Harald. 2007. "Trauma Must Remain Unavailable to Memory: Trauma Ontology and Other Misuses of Trauma Concepts in Spiritual Science Excursions." *Mittelweg* 36, no. 16: 2–64.
Wendel, Kay. 1995. "Die Treuhandanstalt und die Deindustrialisierung Ostdeutschlands." In *Kolonialisierung der DDR. Kritische Analysen und Alternativen des Einigungsprozesses,* edited by Wolfgang Dümcke and Fritz Vilmar, 142–153. Münster.
Wolle, Stefan. 1999. *Die heile Welt der Diktatur. Alltag und Herrschaft in der DDR, 1971–1989.* 2nd revised ed. Bonn.

Chapter 21

Monumental Problems

Freedom and Unity Come to Berlin

Daniela Blei

On 13 April 2011, Bernd Neumann, Germany's minister of culture and a member of Angela Merkel's ruling center-right party, made an announcement. After two rounds of competition that garnered 532 proposals from around the world, officials had approved a design for a new memorial in Berlin. The Monument to Freedom and Unity (Freiheits- und Einheitsdenkmal) was to commemorate the peaceful revolution that brought down the Berlin Wall in 1989 and ushered in national reunification in 1990, serving as "a positive reminder of the successful events of recent German history."[1] Neumann hailed the project for its inspiring, self-empowering message. The winning design, called *Citizens in Motion*, was the work of Johannes Milla, an architect in Stuttgart, and Sasha Waltz, the star choreographer based in Berlin. An expression of collective experience, their fifty-meter-long steel structure resembled a giant bowl that would seesaw when visitors climbed in, requiring a group of at least twenty to get it moving. Emblazoned on the memorial's asphalt bed would be the slogans of the 1989 revolution: "We are the people" and "We are one people." The date for the unveiling was set: 9 November 2014, when Germans were to celebrate the twenty-fifth anniversary of the Wall's demise.

Today, more than eight years after Neumann's message, and eleven years after the project was first authorized by a parliamentary vote, Berlin's Schlossplatz, where the monument is slated for construction, stands empty. While the project and its planners have been mired in bureaucratic and budgetary red tape, a series of unexpected challenges have arisen: how to handle a colony of rare bats roosting underground; what to do with imperial-era mosaics discovered in the damp cellar vaults on the site; and how to weatherproof the memorial's surfaces and make it wheelchair-accessible.[2] Estimated costs have escalated from the initial ten million Euro price tag by more than 50 percent, and Sasha Waltz has withdrawn from the project, citing irreconcilable differences over proposed revisions to the design. Writing in 2015, Niklas Maak, an editor and critic at the *Frankfurter Allgemeine Zeitung*, called on Berlin to abandon a "foreseeable disaster" that would satisfy only its planners, a pair of skaters, and perhaps the Federal Association of German Fruit Bowl Manufacturers.[3] More recently, Ulf Porschardt, editor-in-chief at *Die Welt*, decried the seesaw design as "the banalization of the revolution . . . reminiscent of the handicraft exhibition section of church fairs." But German lawmakers, having made it through a regulatory morass, are committed to realizing the project.

"Citizens in Motion"

What lies behind this Monument to Freedom and Unity, its origins and intentions? This question is now more relevant than ever, following the June 2017 decision to greenlight the on-again, off-again project to bring freedom and unity to Berlin. In April 2016, the Bundestag's budgetary committee postponed construction indefinitely, blaming spiraling costs. "It's better to end it now, instead of having a never-ending saga," explained Eva Högl, a senior member of the Social Democratic Party (SPD), reflecting the lack of enthusiasm—on behalf of parliament and the public—to see freedom and unity translated into an enormous modernist seesaw in central Berlin.

But in early 2017, lawmakers changed their tune. Officials believed "the time was ripe" for a unity monument, a formal gesture that would serve as "a clear commitment to recognizing the power of East German citizens," declared Martin Dörmann, SPD spokesman on culture and media.[4] His CDU counterpart, Marco Wanderwitz, spoke defiantly: "The Einheitsdenkmal can't and won't fail because of financing. We intent to build."[5] The goal to arrive at a decision before October's general election was achieved on 1 June, following a late-night parliamentary session that included heated exchanges between supporters of the monument—conservatives, Greens, and the SPD—and opponents in the Left Party. Shortly after midnight, the votes were cast, and lawmakers overwhelmingly approved, The Einheitsdenkmal had a new estimated completion date: 9 November 2019, the thirtieth anniversary of the fall of the Berlin Wall.

"*Wipp wipp hurra!*" announced Berlin's *Tagesspiegel*, not without sarcasm, the following morning.[6]

In a city crowded with historical landmarks, where the politics and aesthetics of remembrance have shaped the built environment, the tradition is for new memorials to set off minor civil wars. Berlin, the stage for the drama of German history, is where historians, artists, political leaders, and the public have negotiated which narratives of the past should prevail in the present. It took seventeen years of wrenching debate before the Memorial to the Murdered Jews of Europe opened to visitors in 2005. The cemetery-like structure, solemn but nonrepresentational, has been faulted for appearing too vague, leaving the memorial's message open to interpretation. For the Central Council of Jews in Germany and others, the abstract design by the American architect Peter Eisenman elides the historical specificity of the Holocaust. The passive voice of its title poses a semantic problem for critics: murdered by whom? Some, objecting to the exclusion of Nazism's non-Jewish victims from Germany's most important commemorative project, proposed new monuments to homosexuals, Sinti, and Roma (Till 2005: 65). The bitter back-and-forth, which flared years before shovels hit the dirt, showed how controversies over memorials become part of the building process. Memory is collective, but far from monolithic.

An Absence of Controversy

Remarkably, the Monument to Freedom and Unity—an imposing structure that will take up residence in central Berlin—hasn't generated much controversy, or even attracted the attention of scholars or the general public, aside from a few reports in the media about construction delays and officials squabbling over the design. "When I discuss the monument during lectures on German memory politics," said Cornelia Siebeck, an expert on memory and Berlin's representative spaces at Ruhr-University Bochum, in an interview, "most people haven't even heard of it, and hardly anyone has preoccupied themselves with the initiators' ideological intentions." While presented as a "citizens' initiative," a grassroots effort to celebrate the "people power" that brought down a detested regime, the monument is anything but that. It is the work of a coterie of politicians and public intellectuals who have lobbied, strategically and effectively, to win parliamentary approval. Memorial practices in Germany have long been democratized and decentralized. The Monument to Freedom and Unity, however, tells a different story.

The project's genesis lies with four men prominent in the political and cultural arenas, which distinguishes it from initiatives "from below" by artists and activists commemorating Germany's Nazi and GDR pasts. Memorials like Berlin's *Orte des Erinnerns*, by Renata Stih and Frieder Schnock (1993) and Gunther Demnig's immensely successful *Stolpersteine* (ongoing since 1992), show the extent to which nonstate actors have shaped a memory culture that belongs not only to institutions and officially sanctioned public spaces but also to the lived experience of the city. The Einheitsdenkmal is the opposite, explains Siebeck (interview). It is a traditional, centralized monument, in the sense that it concentrates memory in one spot, but even more noteworthy is that it originated with four men—not exactly a broad political consensus. Rather than seeking to build public support for their project, explains Siebeck (interview), its planners dedicated themselves "to convincing influential politicians and later parliament to adopt the project and integrate it into representative German memory politics."

Backing from the Federal Foundation for the Reappraisal of the SED Dictatorship helped persuade lawmakers. The organization, created in 1998 by the Bundestag to shape the public memory of the German Democratic Republic and address the legacies of state socialism, supports research and the commemorative politics of "dictatorship in the twentieth century." Charged with distributing government funds to grassroots organizations, such as the Union of Organizations for the Victims of Communist Dictatorship (UOKG), the foundation has become a powerful memory agenda-setter in the Federal Republic. Victims' groups under its aegis have "regularly challenged the established memory consensus," writes Jenny Wüstenberg (2001: 65), a scholar of German commemorative politics, "sometimes by competing directly with victims of Nazism for (what they regard as limited amounts of) recognition and resources."

Founding Myths

The Monument to Freedom and Unity was conceived in 1998—when East and West Germany still seemed worlds apart—by Florian Mausbach, an urban planner and the president of the German Federal Office for Building and Regional Planning. Mausbach soon found allies: Günther Nooke, a former civil rights and democracy activist in the GDR; Lothar de Mazière, the last prime minister of the bygone republic; and Jürgen Engert, a well-known journalist. Their proposal, rejected by Parliament in 2000, was revised and finally endorsed in November 2007 on the eighteenth anniversary of the fall of the Wall.

While serving as the Federal Republic's human rights representative, Nooke advocated for the project, seeing an opportunity to establish a new "founding myth" for a newly reunited Germany. The memory of the Holocaust and the Federal Republic's "exemplary treatment of Nazi crimes" were "insufficient" as a basis for a "strong national identity," argued Nooke (2006: 111). He was not opposed to constructing memorials to "the victims of crimes committed by the state," he explained, but collective memory should not be so limited. "The positive events of recent German history" were somehow suppressed in the nation's collective psyche, and the Einheitsdenkmal would provide a "necessary counterbalance." When citizens valued "the positive sides of German history," a national void would be filled (Nooke 2006: 117). The Monument to Freedom and Unity, like the collective experience it referred to, would transcend historical divisions and the roiling antagonisms of memory politics. Berlin's giant seesaw would be a place of pilgrimage for everyone: left and right, former citizens of East and West, and the country's young and old.

Aufhebung

The 2007 decision to break ground barely made headlines. The plan, according to the official proposal, was to honor "all movements for freedom and unity in German history," from the revolutions of 1848 to 1989 (Mausbach 2009: 33). What did this mean? Mausbach (2009: 33) drew a "direct line" from the nineteenth century to the twentieth, describing a long democratic tradition: "What failed in the revolution of 1848 became a European event after 1989: victory for liberal, democratic, national movements." Was this an attempt to create a new master narrative of German history? Mausbach has described Berlin's official memoryscape as "too negative" and missing a "positive counterpoint" (quoted in Meyer and Haarmann 2011). But the first competition to select a design, failing to produce a winner, confirmed that no architect could transform the sweep of 1848 to 1989 into a coherent public monument. Nooke helped reformulate the proposal, suggesting that a monument focused on 1989/90 could bring about a paradigm shift in German memory politics.

Mausbach's 2008 booklet, *On the Meaning and Location of a National Freedom and Unity Monument*, is a testament to the planners' ambitions to change Berlin's memorial terrain, not simply add to it. Invoking the Hegelian notion of *Aufhebung*, an esoteric concept that suggests the synthesis, or mediation, of opposites, Mausbach describes the Monument to Freedom and Unity as "sublating" the negative aspects of German history. His argument is that the monument will shift collective memory away from a dark chapter and closer to a "more positive" view of German history. "This is not a historical, but actually a metaphysical narrative," says Siebeck (interview). "There have always been good and evil struggling against each other, but ultimately, good has triumphed." In Mausbach's formulation, 1989/90 figures as the final destination in German history; the triumphant finish, or telos, in a century-and-a-half-long march to national freedom and unity. In the final passages of Mausbach's treatise, he imagines a stroll from Berlin's Bundestag to the Monument to Freedom and Unity at Schlossplatz. "It becomes evident," says Siebeck (interview), "that the idea is to 'complete' the national memoryscape by 'closing' it with a monument that embodies the happy ending of German history, thereby transcending the 'negative' parts."

Officially, the monument that lawmakers approved in June 2017 is a tribute to the events of 1989/90, but Mausbach continues to invoke the longer arc of German history. "It is precisely this memorial site," he explained in April 2017, defending the location at Schlossplatz from Left Party detractors led by Klaus Lederer, Berlin's culture secretary, "that not only reminds us of the democratic movement for freedom and unity," but also of 1848, "the culmination of the liberal revolution at St. Paul's Church," and 1918, when "the Workers' and Socialists' Councils met in the Marstall."[7] Seen in the context of his own comments, the monument is about more than marking 1989/90 as the "high point" of German history. Like Edgar Wolfrum's (1999) analysis of 1968 as a "revolutionary myth," Mausbach's 1989 is a caesura containing contradictory impulses. On the one hand, his idea is to celebrate the peaceful revolution that took place twenty-eight years ago as a point of rupture with a terrible, anti-democratic past. On the other, Mausbach makes a case for continuity: 1989 was analogous to 1848 and even 1918. In this narrative, it is the people that shaped modern German history, not the state or the consolidation of representative democracy, a plodding process to be sure. The slogans of 1989—"We are the people" and "We are one people"—underscore this message.

Fading into Irrelevance

Now awaiting construction, the Monument to Freedom and Unity will stand just one mile from the Memorial to the Murdered Jews of Europe, allowing locals and tourists to read it as a counterweight to Holocaust commemoration. Its location at Schlossplatz, once the site of a grandiose memorial to Kaiser Wilhelm I, razed in 1950 by GDR officials, who repurposed the site as a socialist parade ground called Marx-Engels Square, prompts more questions than answers. "Why Schlossplatz?" asked Franziska Eichstädt-Bohlig, a Green Party politician and building expert in 2008, addressing Mausbach at one of the few public meetings held to discuss the project. "Who sees a connection between Schlossplatz and the revolution of 1989? No one!"

Unlike Berlin's Alexanderplatz, the square played no part in the 1989 demonstrations that precipitated the fall of the Wall. Politicians in Leipzig have argued that it makes more sense for a tribute to the popular protests that led to the end of the GDR to be built in their city, East Germany's second largest. Wolfgang Tiefensee, former SPD mayor of Leipzig, remarked that "the peaceful revolution of 1989 took place throughout the entire GDR, and it is only right that it be remembered in other places" (quoted in Anderson 2010: 253). But plans for a commemorative project in Leipzig, where tens of thousands of citizens first took to the streets, putting pressure on the regime and forcing the resignations of its leaders, have stalled. As lawmakers deliberated on the floor of the Bundestag before the June 2017 vote, some claimed that Berlin's initiative would give Leipzig the push it needed to break ground on the city's Wilhelm-Leuschner Platz.

But perhaps even more noteworthy than the proposed Monument to Freedom and Unity is the silence that has surrounded it. "Twenty years ago, it would have been impossible to realize a so-called positive national monument," says Siebeck (interview), "without encountering strong resistance on the part of leftist and leftist liberal intellectuals, who always reacted with great sensitivity to any attempt to normalize German history." Since the 1980s, what Eric Langenbacher (2003: 46) has called the "Holocaust-centered memory regime" has governed Berlin's landscape, and by extension, the nation's. Monika Grütters, Angela Merkel's culture minister, described the June 2017 decision to go forward with construction as a turning point: "The memorial is a sign that we have not only grown from the depths of our history, but we also appreciate the high points."[8]

Is the Nazi past sufficiently institutionalized? Is it now visibly and successfully integrated into Berlin's and, by extension, Germany's, official self-image? German conservatives used to speak of "healing" and "redeeming" a vanquished nation from the burdens of history. That discourse, while extant in some corners, has been banished from conventional politics. "One can say that leftist and leftist-liberal intellectuals have simply lost their classical target," concludes Siebeck (interview). "It is hardly possible anymore to claim that the memory of the Nazi past is 'suppressed' or warded off by mainstream society and politics."

If that is the case, then is the Monument to Freedom and Unity such a bad idea? While its initiators can be accused of updating old efforts by conservatives to diminish the Nazi past, by undertaking the more sophisticated approach of "sublating" it, does it even matter if reminders of the Holocaust appear at every turn in central Berlin? Political scientist Jeffrey Anderson (2010: 237) has written that the "characteristic zeal with which the Berlin city government permitted the Berlin Wall to be dismantled, piece by piece, over the course of the 1990s almost certainly contributed to the perceived need to erect (anew) a structure to commemorate its dismantling." But only four men shared this perceived need for an Einheitsdenkmal, and their plans unfolded without significant debate or even disseminating knowledge of the project. Political and cultural elites usually clash over representations of the German past, and the broader public consumes these debates and their outcomes in the context of education or tourism. But until recently, even elites were not talking about the project.

Following the June 2017 decision to build, more Berliners have become aware of the monument. A public opinion poll published two days before the Bundestag's June 2017 decision to move forward with Mausbach's monument asked Berliners to choose between *Citizens in Motion* and the reconstruction of the Kaiser Wilhelm colonnades, part of a larger plan to resurrect the nineteenth-century City Palace.[9] Of the survey's respondents, 43 percent opted for the imperial-era colonnades, while 35 percent expressed "no opinion." Only 16 percent supported the Einheitsdenkmal, and 6 percent said the site should be left alone, without any changes, old or new. The irony of realizing a monument to the people is that not many people want it, despite its self-celebratory message. Where citizens have voiced indifference, critics have shown hostility, denouncing the design as tacky—a gimmick that turns history into a game. Berlin's Akademie der Künste hosted a discussion in October 2017 where plans for the entire site, from the reconstructed "fake castle" to the "infantile swing," were subjected to harsh criticism.[10]

Like all monuments, the Einheitsdenkmal will come to have a life of its own apart from the intentions of its creators. Its success will depend on the broader political and cultural context, and visitors will relate to it in different ways. "Neither the monument nor its meaning is really everlasting," writes James Young (1999). Will freedom and unity, appearing in material form, change Berlin's famous memoryscape? The monument, offering more myth than historical understanding, and even reminiscent of the GDR's pseudo-Hegelian determinism, might undermine its own message. Any commemorative structure, as scholars from Pierre Nora (1989) to Andreas Huyssen (2003) have noted, can displace rather preserve public memory, by signaling to society that there is no longer an obligation to remember; its memory-work is already done.

More pressing, perhaps, is that the men behind the Monument to Freedom and Unity did not anticipate the dramatic developments that began in 2015, when approximately one million refugees from Syria and other countries in turmoil arrived in Germany. How the monument's message— a Francis Fukuyama–like ending to German history—will be received in a society that has experienced what some have called a second Wende, bringing far-reaching political and economic restructuring, remains a mystery. The rise of the Alternative für Deutschland (AfD), the xenophobic far-right party now in parliament, has tested the rhetoric of inner unity. For the Left Party, the successor to the Partei des Demokratischen Sozialismus (PDS) and East Germany's communist Socialist Unity Party (SED), *Citizens in Motion* represents little more than a monument to defeat. Despite efforts by the monument's initiators to foster a common view of the German past, unity has proved elusive.

Underlying the Einheitsdenkmal is the sanguine assumption that German history has reached its happy ending. Many questions remain about the feasibility of the design, a moving, interactive, fifty-meter-long structure. Once the technical hurdles are cleared, the appointed architects, Milla & Partner, will break ground. When all is said and done, the Monument to Freedom and Unity might fade into irrelevance, unable to commemorate anything but itself. If so, it will quite unintentionally serve as an enduring reminder that German history is far from over and unity is hardly complete.

Daniela Blei holds a doctorate in modern European history from Stanford University. She taught European history and humanities at Reed College in Portland, Oregon, and at the University of California, Berkeley as an Andrew W. Mellon Postdoctoral Fellow. She works as an editor of scholarly books in San Francisco, where she lives with her family. Her essays and reporting have appeared in the *Atlantic, Smithsonian, New York Magazine, Foreign Policy*, and elsewhere. Originally from Chicago, Daniela Blei visited Berlin for the first time as a college student in the 1990s. She has been observing the city's culture of remembrance ever since.

Notes

A brief version of this chapter was published in Marginalia Review of Books (Blei 2016).

1. Presse-und Informationsamt der Bundesregierung, "Pressemitteilung: Kulturstaatsminister Bernd Neumann: Freiheits- und Einheitsdenkmal wird nach Entwurf von *Milla und Partner mit Sasha Waltz* realisiert," Bundesamt für Bauwesen und Raumordnung, 13 April 2011, accessed on 20 October 2017, https://www.bbr.bund.de/BBR/DE/Bauprojekte/Berlin/Kultur/FED/pmbkm.pdf?__blob=publicationFile&v=1.

2. "Berliner Einheitsdenkmal kommt später," *Der Tagesspiegel*, 28 May 2015, accessed 20 October 2017, http://www.tagesspiegel.de/kultur/verzoegerungen-im-bau-berliner-einheitsdenkmal-kommt-spaeter/11839458.html.

3. Niklas Maak, "Die Wippe auf der Kippe," *Frankfurter Allegemeine Zeitung*, 24 August 2015, accessed 20 October 2017, http://www.faz.net/aktuell/feuilleton/kunst/berliner-einheitsdenkmal-die-wippe-auf-der-kippe-13762323-p2.html.

4. "Einheitsdenkmal in Berlin soll doch gebaut werden," *Deutsche Welle*, 14 February 2017, accessed 25 October 2017, http://www.dw.com/de/einheitsdenkmal-in-berlin-soll-doch-gebaut-werden/a-37548691.

5. "Bundestag mit klarer Mehrheit für Einheitsdenkmal," *Frankfurter Allgemeine Zeitung*, 2 June 2017, accessed 25 October 2017, http://www.faz.net/aktuell/feuilleton/debatten/bundestag-stimmt-mit-mehrheit-fuer-einheitsdenkmal-in-berlin-15043614.html.

6. "Grünes Licht für Einheitsdenkmal: Wipp wipp hurra!," *Der Tagesspiegel*, 2 June 2017, accessed 10 September 2020, https://www.tagesspiegel.de/kultur/gruenes-licht-fuers-einheitsdenkmal-wipp-wipp-hurra/19888736.html.

7. "Florian Mausbach, Kultursenaror Lederer und die 'Vielschichtigkeit der Ereignisse von 1989,'" *Der Tagesspiegel*, 14 April 2017, accessed 24 October 2017, http://www.tagesspiegel.de/berlin/gastkommentar-kultursenator-lederer-und-die-vielschichtigkeit-der-ereignisse-von-1989/19665648.html.

8. "Frieheits- und Einheitsdenkmal. Stimmen zum Kenkmal," Deutsche Gesellschaft e.V., accessed 23 October 2017, http://www.freiheits-und-einheitsdenkmal.de/das-denkmal/stimmen-zum-denkmal.html.

9. "Bundestag entscheidet am Donnerstag erneut," *Der Tagesspiegel*, 29 May 2017, accessed on 25 October 2017, http://www.tagesspiegel.de/kultur/das-berliner-einheitsdenkmal-bundestag-entscheidet-am-donnerstag-erneut/19865494.html.

10. "Hey Wippe, hey Schlossattrappe: Niemand hier mag euch!" *Berliner Morgenpost*, 19 October 2017, accessed on 27 October 2017, https://www.morgenpost.de/kultur/article212283021/Hey-Wippe-hey-Schlossattrappe-Niemand-hier-mag-euch.html.

References

Anderson, Jeffery J. 2010. "The Federal Republic at Twenty: Of Blind Spots and Peripheral Visions." In *From the Bonn to the Berlin Republic: Germany at the Twentieth Anniversary of Unification*, edited by Jeffrey Anderson and Eric Langenbacher, 253–250. New York.

Blei, Daniela. 2016. "Monumental Problems: Freedom and Unity Come to Berlin." *Marginalia Review of Books*, 28 January 2016. Accessed 20 November 2017, http://marginalia.lareviewofbooks.org/monumental-problems-freedom-and-unity-come-to-berlin-daniela-blei/.

Huyssen, Andreas. 2003. *Present Pasts: Urban Palimpsests and the Politics of Forgetting*. Stanford.

Langenbacher, Eric. 2003. "Changing Memory Regimes in Contemporary Germany?" *German Politics & Society* 21, no. 2: 46–68.

Mausbach, Florian. 2008. *Über die Bedeutung und Lage eines nationalen Freiheits- und Einheitsdenkmals*. Berlin.

Mausbach, Florian. 2009. "Initiative Denkmal Deutsche Einheit. Berlin, 13 May 1998." In *Der Weg zum Denkmal für Freiheit und Einheit*, edited by Andreas H. Apelt, 33–35. Schwalbach/Ts.

Meyer, Robert, and Lutz Haarmann. 2011. "Das Freiheits- und Einheitsdenkmal. Die geschichtspolitische Verortung in der Ideengeschichte der Bundesrepulblik." *Deutschlandarchiv 9/2011 der Bundeszentrale für politische Bildung*, 13 September 2011. Accessed on 23 October 2017, www.bpb.de/geschichte/zeitgeschichte/deutschlandarchiv/53296/freiheits-und-einheitsdenkmal?p=all.

Nooke, Günther. 2006. "Ein Denkmal für die Einheit in Freiheit? Formen der Auseinandersetzung mit der DDR." In *Woran erinnern? Der Kommunismus in der deutschen Erinnerungskultur*, edited by Peter März and Hans-Joachim van Veen, 111–122. Cologne.

Nora, Pierre. 1989. "Between Memory and History: Les Lieux de Mémoire." *Representations*, no. 26 (Spring): 7–24.

Thaa, Lotte. 2015. "Sei Freiheit, Sei Einheit, Sei Berlin: Das Berliner Freiheits- und Einheitsdenkmal als geschichtspolitische Inszenierung." *WerkstattGeschichte* 65: 79–102.

Till, Karen E. 2005. *The New Berlin: Memory, Politics, Place*. Minneapolis.

Wolfrum, Edgar. 1999. *Geschichtspolitik in der Bundesrepublik Deutschland*. Darmstadt.

Wüstenberg, Jenny. 2001. "Transforming Berlin's Memory: Non-State Actors and GDR Memorial Politics." In *Remembering the German Democratic Republic: Divided Memory in a United Germany*, edited by David Clarke and Ute Wölfel, 65–76. London.

Young, James E. 1999. "Memory and Counter-Memory: The End of the Monument in Germany." *Harvard Design Magazine*, no. 9: 1–10.

———. 2002. "Germany's Holocaust Memorial Problem—and Mine." *The Public Historian* 24, no. 4: 65–80.

Index

Academy of Sciences (AdW), 26, 29
Action Atonement Sign (Aktion Sühnezeichen), 192–193, 196
Aktives Museum, Fascism and Resistance in Berlin, 42, 53
Adenauer, Konrad, 7, 74–84
AHAWAH, 209–210
Al Assad, Hafez, 118, 123, 124
Alice Salomon University, 11
Alternative for Germany (AfD), 5, 247, 256, 307
Amadeu Antonio Foundation, 6, 10, 12, 261, 262
Amado, Jorge, 29
Anderson, Jeffrey, 305
Antifascism: historical myth, 91–95, 181, 182; ideology of GDR, 7, 184, 199, 209, 233; political concept, 3, 34, 38, 116, 133, 255–256
Antigypsyism, 175–184
Anti-Hitler Coalition, 67
Anti-totalitarianism, 7, 97, 216–230, 238–240, 285
Anti-Zionism, 115–133, 196
Arafat, Yassir, 125–127
Arndt, Siegfried Theodor, 197
Aufbau publishing company, 27
Auschwitz, concentration camp, 11, 30, 148, 177, 181, 194, 222, 247; memorial and museum, 48, 193, 229; discourse, 140, 221; reception, 147; trial, 78
Ayad, Abu, 128–130

Bad Elster, 62
Bahro, Rudolf, 286
Bauer, Fritz, 74, 78–79
Behrens, Fritz, 28
Behrends, Jan C., 270
Benser, Günter, 96
Bergen-Belsen, concentration camp, 180, 183; memorial and museum, 229, 237, 238, 241, 243

Berger, Almuth, 272
Berger, Gabriel, 66
Bergmann, Werner, 4
Berlin, 41–53, 166, 209–215, 284, 285
Berlin Congress Hall, 50
Berliner Zeitung, 46, 47, 49
Bevers, Jürgen, 79
Biddiscombe, Perry, 67
Biermann, Wolf, 194–195
"Bitterfelder Weg," 288
Black September, 126
Bloch, Ernst, 83
Blue S, 59
Bonhoeffer, Dietrich, 195
Bourdieu, Pierre, 107
Bräutigam, Otto, 44
Brecht, Bertolt, 19, 20, 23, 25; theater, 194
Breitscheid, Rudolf, 46
Brezhnev, Leonid, 120, 121
Buchenwald, concentration camp, 93, 181, 222; museum and memorial, 167, 181, 229, 237, 240
Buchenwald Soviet special camp, 217
Bunge, Hans, 26

Center for Research on Antisemitism (ZfA), 30
Central Intelligence Agency (CIA), 65
Christian Democratic Union of Germany (CDU), 237, 300
Civil society, 249–250
Committee for German Unity (ADE), 42, 43, 45
Committee of Anti-Fascist Resistance Fighters (KdAW), 48
Confessing Church (Bekennende Kirche), 195
Criminal law code (Strafgesetzbuch), 164–165

Dachau, concentration camp, 179, 222; memorial and museum, 180, 222, 229

Index

Danyel, Jürgen, 41
Davies, Norman, 221
de Mazière, Lothar, 302
Demnig, Gunter, 302
Democratic Resistance Movement of Germany, 62
Dirks, Christian, 79

Ecumenical Assembly for Justice, Peace, and the Integrity of Creation, 195
Eichmann, Adolf, 36, 77
Eichstädt-Bohlig, Franziska, 304
Eisenfeld, Peter, 66
Eisenman, Peter, 300
Eisler, Gerhart, 94
Engert, Jürgen, 302
Engler, Wolfgang, 290
Enquete Commissions on the SED Dictatorship, 238–241, 243, 260
Erb, Rainer, 4
Escape and expulsion memorial, 225
Eschwege, Helmut, 4, 9, 197–198
Euthanasia Memorial, Lüneburg, 10

Fascism, 32, 64, 82, 138, 139, 144, 199, 252; analytical concept, 3; Dimitrov definition, 90–95, 253; universalization of, 194, 195
Fechner, Max, 165
Federal Commissioner for the Records of the State Security Service of the former GDR, 260–261
Federal Criminal Police Office (BKA), 82
Federal Intelligence Service (BND), 68, 77–78, 82, 103
Fighting Group against Inhumanity (KgU), 57, 62–63, 66, 285
Foundation for the Reappraisal of the SED Dictatorship, 241, 243, 261, 302
Foundation for Remembrance, Responsibility, and the Future (EVZ), 241
Free Democratic Party (FDP), 237
Freedom and Unity monument, 11, 299–307
Free German Youth (FDJ), 153, 155, 267
Freund, Walter, 26–27
Führer, Christian, 14
Fukuyama, Francis, 306
Fulbrook, Mary, 64
Fürstenwalde, 59

Galinski, Heinz, 51
Gauck, Joachim, 14, 39, 257, 260
Gehlen Organization, 77
General German News Service (ADN), 34
Genin, Salomea, 199
German Communist Party (KPD), 48, 82, 93, 272–275
German Freedom Movement (DFG), 63
German-Soviet Non-Aggression Pact, 91, 216, 223
Gieseke, Jens, 68, 101, 103
Gill, David, 14
Gilsenbach, Reimar, 182
Globke, Hans, 7, 36–37, 44, 45, 46, 49, 74–84, 94, 179
Goebbels, Joseph, 61, 284
Gorbachev, Michail, 198
Göring, Hermann, 61, 284
Greußen Boys, 62
Groehler, Olaf, 261
Grotewohl, Otto, 178
Grütters, Monika, 305

Hahm, Lotte, 165
Hannah Arendt Institute for Totalitarianism Research, 235–236, 243
Hanstein, Ewald, 177–178
Haury, Thomas, 193
Havemann, Robert, 194, 195
Herbstritt, Georg, 101
Herf, Jeffrey, 4, 41, 139, 146, 191, 193
Heym, Stefan, 199
Himmler, Heinrich, 46, 63, 67
Hitler, Adolf, 43, 44, 94, 195, 196, 212, 255, 257; civil servants of, 76, 82; "Heil Hitler," 61, 62, 66; Hitler's generals, 83; Hitler's Germany, 77; Hitler's judges, 179; ideas of, 20; seduction by, 6, 33; seizure of power by, 21, 90
Hitler Youth (HJ), 61, 63, 103, 210, 240
Hoffmann, Heinz, 120, 123–125
Holocaust Remembrance Day, 220
Homosexual Interest Group Berlin (HIB), 166
Honecker, Erich, 33, 37–38, 95, 116, 120, 125–127, 152–153, 156–157, 290
Honigmann, Barbara, 199
House Committee on Un-American Activities, 20
Huchel, Peter, 21
Humboldt University, 268

Index

Independent Commission of Historians for the History of the Federal Intelligence Service, 65
International Committee of Memorial Sites in Remembrance of the Victims of Public Crimes (IC-MEMO), 226–227
Investigation Committee of Free Lawyers (UfJ), 65–66, 68

Janka, Walter, 27, 198
Jewish Cultural Society (Jüdischer Kulturverein), 199

Kahane, Anetta, 6, 10, 12, 199–200, 261
Kahane, Max, 36
Kalniete, Sandra, 218
Kant, Immanuel, 211
Kantorowicz, Alfred, 20–23, 25–28
Karway, Rudolf, 180
Katyń, 221, 224
Kaul, Karl, 77
Kenawi, Samirah, 168
Keßler, Mario, 260
Kisch, Egon Erwin, 23
Klemperer, Victor, 37
Kloski, Daniel, 79
Kohl, Helmut, 251
Konrad, Weiß, 191
Korn, Salomon, 5
Koselleck, Reinhart, 228
Kreyssik, Lothar, 196
Kuck, Dennis, 4, 270
Kuckhoff, Greta, 26
Kuczynski, Jürgen, 21–30
Kunzelmann, Dieter, 133
Khrushchev, Nikita, 25

Langenbacher, Erik, 305
Lauenburger, Erna, 182
Lepsius, Mario Reiner, 193
Linse, Walter, 65
League of German Writers (SDA), 19
Leggewie, Claus, 220
Leibniz Center for Contemporary History Research in Potsdam (ZZF), 7, 13–14, 69, 98, 269, 272
Leide, Henry, 78, 104
Leipzig, 151, 153, 166, 196
Leipzig Central Institute for Youth Research, 68
Leo, Anette, 212

Leo, Gerhard, 30
Lesbian, gay, bisexual, transgender, and intersex community (LGBTI), 163–171
Leuschner, Wilhelm, 46
Lichtblau, Albert, 4
Loginski, Dagobert, 30
London Agreement and Charter, 8 August 1945, 80
Lübke, Heinrich, 94
Lukács, Georg, 27
Luther, Martin, 198

Maaz, Hans Joachim, 289
Maeke, Lutz, 262
Maier, Charles S., 67
Mausbach, Florian, 302–304
Memorial to the Murdered Jews of Europe, 300, 304
Merkel, Angela, 299, 305
Merker, Paul, 24, 116, 198
Meuschel, Sigrid, 260
Mielke, Erich, 128, 130, 151, 154
Milla, Johannes, 299
Ministry of State Security (MfS), 7, 66, 79, 100–112, 116, 128–131, 235, 275; district offices, 156; impeded by, 164; lexicon of, 150; reports to the, 26; Rosenholz files, 107–111; surveillance by, 29, 167, 168; youth analysis reports, 154
Mitscherlich, Magarete, 288–290
Mlynar, Zdenek, 4
Museum of German History (MfDG), 42, 46, 49, 237, 261
Mussolini, Benito, 90

Nasser, Gamal Abdul, 118
National Democratic Party of the FRG (NPD), 66
National Democratic Party of GDR (NDPD), 67
National Socialist German Workers Party (NSDAP), 76, 83, 238, 240
Nazi Elite School (NAPOLA), 63
Neubert, Erhart, 57, 65–66, 285
Neues Deutschland (ND), 9, 61, 176, 212, 261; on Sinti and Roma, 178–181; various articles or reports in, 36, 43, 45, 46, 80, 123, 127, 151, 153
Neumann, Bernd, 299
New Reich Chancellery (Neue Reichskanzlei), 284

Index

Nooke, Günther, 302–303
Nora, Pierre, 218, 306
Norden, Albert, 21, 45, 48, 118
Nuremberg Laws, 75, 80

Oberländer, Theodor, 45–46, 49, 78
Overall concept for the participation of the federal state in memorial sites in the Federal Republic of Germany, 237, 241
Oz, Amos, 212

Palestine Liberation Organization (PLO), 125–133, 198
Patriotic Europeans Against the Islamization of the Occident (PEGIDA), 5, 247, 256
People's Chamber (Volkskammer), 191–192, 259–260, 261, 284
Peters, Jürgen, 22
Plötzensee memorial, 43
Pößneck, 8, 151, 154–157
Poliakov, Léon, 44
Port, Andrew, 287
Poppe, Ulrike, 14
Popular Front for the Liberation of Palestine (PFLP), 131–132
Poutrus, Patrice G., 4

Rajk, László, 24
Ravensbrück Memorial, 9, 167–168, 181, 229, 237
Red Army Faction (RAF), 128
Reich, Jens, 14
Reinhard, Kati R., 165
Revolt of June 17, 1953, 283–287
Revolutionary Cells (RZ), 128
Round Table, 200
Runge, Irene, 199
Rupp, Rainer, 106
Rüter, Frederic, 83

Sachsenhausen, concentration camp, 49, 212, 222; international prisoner committee of, 229; memorial and museum, 6, 10, 69, 168, 181, 237
Sachsenhausen Soviet special camp, 62, 217
Schenk, Claus Philipp Maria (Graf von Stauffenberg), 46
Schirdewan, Karl, 28
Schmidt, Helmut, 181

Schnock, Frieder, 302
Schoenberner, Gerhard, 42, 48–49
Schutzstaffel (SS), 63, 222, 240, 255, 284
Seghers, Anna, 20–25, 27, 29
Shamir, Yitzak, 197
Sholem, Gershon, 34
Siebeck, Cornelia, 301, 304–305
Sinti and Roma, 9, 82, 175–184, 192
Social Democratic Party of FRG (SPD), 236–237, 300, 305
Social Democratic Party of GDR (SDP), 197
Socialist German Student Organization (SDS), 123, 193
Socialist Unity Party (SED), 22, 24, 176, 178, 238, 267–269, 274, 307; Central Committee (ZK), 152; control commission (ZPKK), 24; district office Pößneck, 154–156; Politbüro, 118
Soviet Gulag system, 221–223, 234, 275
Soviet military administration in Germany (SMAD), 273, 284
Soviet military tribunal (SMT), 61–62, 239
Stalin, Josef, 37
Steinitz, Inge, 26
Steinitz, Ruth, 21
Steinitz, Wolfgang, 5, 19–30
Stern, Jeanne, 21–23
Stern, Kurt, 21–23
Stih, Renata, 302
Stoph, Willi, 118
Strecker, Reinhard, 42
Stuttgart Incidents (28 October 1948), 284
Suckut, Siegfried, 66–67
Sumnal, Romano, 183
Supreme Court of GDR (OG), 27, 74, 79, 81
Supreme Court of Israel, 77

Task Force for International Cooperation and Holocaust Education (IHRA), 220
Telegraf, 45
Thälmann, Ernst, 93
Thomas, Rüdiger, 286
Timm, Angelika, 121, 262
Tlass, Mustafa, 124
Totalitarianism, 64, 97, 103, 220–230, 269, 281–283, 285–287, 291; analytical model, 239; European Parliament Resolution of 2 April 2009 on European Conscience and Totalitarianism, 216, 217, 221, 224; language, 37; paradigm, 10–11
Track 17 Memorial, 51–52

Index

Ulbricht, Walter, 27–28, 37, 116, 118–119, 120, 151–152, 165
Union of German Youth (BDJ), 65, 68
Union of Organizations for the Victims of Communist Dictatorship (UOKG), 302

Victims of fascism, 36, 163, 166, 167, 209; memorial day, 43, 61, 62; monuments, 66, 125; status, 275; Union of (VVN), 43, 62, 177–178

Waibel, Harry, 65–66
Wajda, Andrzej, 224
Waltz, Sasha, 299–300
Wander, Fred, 138–149
Wannsee Conference Memorial and Educational Site, 6, 42, 75, 237
Wasungen, Josef, 176

Wegener, Bettina, 95
Welzer, Harald, 224
Wierling, Dorothee, 64, 157
Weinke, Annette, 78
Weiskopf, Grete, 181
Weiß, Konrad, 192, 260
Wilkomirski, Binyamin, 146
Winzer, Otto, 116, 118, 121–123, 126
Wolf, Christa, 8, 88, 138–149, 199
Wollweber, Ernst, 28
Wroblewsky, Vincent von, 199
Wulf, Joseph, 44
Wunderlich, Rudolf, 48
Wurzen, 176

Zaisser, Wilhelm, 165
Zionism, 3, 35, 115–134, 147, 196, 260–261
Zuckermann, Leo, 116

www.ingramcontent.com/pod-product-compliance
Lightning Source LLC
Chambersburg PA
CBHW071333080526
44587CB00017B/2823